November 12–17, 2011
San Diego, CA, USA

Association for Computing Machinery

Advancing Computing as a Science & Profession

SIGUCCS'11

Proceedings of the 2011 ACM on SIGUCCS Annual Fall Conference

Sponsored by:

ACM SIGWEB

In cooperation with:

ACM SIGDOC

Supported by:

Google, Adobe, Hewlett-Packard, and Xerox

Association for
Computing Machinery

Advancing Computing as a Science & Profession

The Association for Computing Machinery
2 Penn Plaza, Suite 701
New York, New York 10121-0701

ISBN: 978-1-4503-1381-0

Additional copies may be ordered prepaid from:

ACM Order Department
PO Box 30777
New York, NY 10087-0777, USA

Phone: 1-800-342-6626 (USA and Canada)
+1-212-626-0500 (Global)
Fax: +1-212-944-1318
E-mail: acmhelp@acm.org
Hours of Operation: 8:30 am – 4:30 pm ET

ACM Order Number: 459111

Printed in the USA

Conference Chair's Message

Welcome to the 39th annual ACM SIGUCCS Conference in sunny San Diego, California! This year's theme One Team…One Mission has so many special meanings to this organization as well as to the many colleges and universities world-wide represented here this week.

"One Team" is a great new vision for SIGUCCS…to have both of our conferences in one location at one time of year is a bold venture. Hopefully as the week unfolds, the possibilities of "One Mission" will come into focus as well. Just as the vision of a pilot becomes expanded, almost limitless, as they break through the cloud dome, so is my hope for each of you…that your opportunities for sharing and learning, for helping and growing, are limitless. I hope your vision of the future is a little brighter as you reenter your home "airspace", taking with you the resources, relationships, innovative ideas and energy from your friends, colleagues and speakers.

Maybe you were able to take advantage of the change in scheduling and attend both conferences or possibly enjoy some team-building time with your colleagues. Or maybe you didn't change a thing. Either way, I'm thankful you are here. You are an important part of the SIGUCCS Team. Whether you are a veteran attendee or this is your maiden flight, I'm certain you will find something or someone to inspire you.

As with any endeavor, there are many who dedicate hundreds of hours to a common goal – a successful conference. Volunteers are the "mission critical" component. To the 2011 Conference Committee, you have my sincerest appreciation for your hard work, tireless patience and devotion to each and every detail of this week. You are, simply, awesome! To all who have volunteered their time and effort, SIGUCCS can't and won't happen without you. To the SIGUCCS Board of Directors and appointees, many thanks for your support that allowed a committee to learn and grow.

I am particularly grateful to the authors of the 2011 SIGUCCS Conference. I believe the papers to be particularly inspiring this year and look forward to attending as many sessions as possible and sharing the wise words of authors worldwide.

Now…have you made your way to the spectacular oceanfront just waiting for you to come sink your toes into the sand? Have you stood outside under a gorgeous blanket of stars WITHOUT A PARKA and planned which rooftop restaurant or club will be the spot for old and new friends to gather? Between the receptions and the Gala Event at Wavehouse at Mission Beach, world class sites to see and a spectacular program for you to attend…how could it be anything except MISSION ACCOMPLISHED?!?

Elizabeth Wagnon
SIGUCCS 2011 Conference Chair

Service and Support Chairs' Welcome

Welcome to the 39th annual, SIGUCCS 2011 Conference in San Diego, California. It is truly a challenging/exciting time to be in Information Technology as many of us are asked to look at existing processes, past projects and think about things we were told could never happen. San Diego, a diverse city inspired by religious missionaries, demonstrative of the power of technological innovations (Qualcomm and others) and the inspiration of multiple military branches, provides a great setting for the first combined ACM SIGUCCS conference. San Diego brings together different cultures and a history of progress, providing inspiration and guidance as IT communities look to find better ways to work together. As one technology team, from the Chief Information Officer to the front line Help Desk representative, SIGUCCS attendees should find invigoration in the similarities the city and our careers provide. We feel this year's Service and Support program will give attendees some of the same diversity found in San Diego, with the mission of sharing ideas, works in progress, failures and successes so you can make your IT organization better for you and the customers you serve.

We invite you to enjoy the paper presentations, panels, posters and Discuss IT sessions provided to you by the authors and Service & Support Program committee (readers, track chairs). We were one team with a mission to cultivate a spread of revelations, technical advances, and managerial opportunities, despite any obstacles that may have gotten in our way. For those who were unable to attend the Management Symposium part of the conference this year, please take the opportunity during the evening reception and crossover day to share ideas, look for targeted opportunities, and enjoy the creative spark that these two conferences provide to their respective demographics. Our keynote speakers will not only bridge the gap between the conferences, but provide you with the communications tools needed to assist you and your organization on the road to successful. As we all know, great ideas can be lost when you return to the office. Before you depart back to work, please take the time to create an action plan for each of the ideas you want to move forward with when you return. And after you return to your office, please share what you've learned and thank your bosses for letting you take part in this conference. SIGUCCS is unique in providing professional development through learning, collaboration, networking, situations which engage a vision from your bosses/their boss's perspective, while bringing home ideas which aid your department in this every changing world of Information Technology.

Parrish Nnambi
SIGUCCS 2011
Service and Support Program Co-Chair

Chris Wiesemann
SIGUCCS 2011
Service and Support Program Co-Chair

Table of Contents

SIGUCCS 2011 Conference Organization ix

SIGUCCS 2011 Sponsor & Supporters xii

Session 1: Tuesday November 15, 1:30PM

- **Developing Service Assessment Metrics** 1
  Nik Chaphalkar, Brian Stawowy, Sara Freidank, Javier Fernandez, Ian Mukherjee
  (Michigan Technological University)
- **Unifying the ITS Department Through Ticketing** 7
  Loraine Graves, Mark Zocher *(University of San Diego)*
- **Divide & Conquer** 11
  Kathy M. Lyons, Ryan T. Sharpe *(University of Illinois at Urbana-Champaign)*
- **User State Migration Tool: Migrating to Windows 7 with Ease and Efficiency** 15
  Nicholas Jannini, Bryce Harper *(Massachusetts Institute of Technology)*

Session 2: Tuesday November 15, 2:30PM

- **The Mission – Teaming with Microsoft and Adobe for Licensing** 21
  Michael Cooper *(West Virginia University)*
- **Information and Communication Technology Infrastructure and Management for Collaboration with Regional Universities and Colleges** 25
  Takashi Yamanoue *(Kagoshima University)*, Robert J. Fouser *(Seoul National University)*,
  Tomohito Wada *(National Institute of Fitness and Sports in Kanoya)*, Masayasu Hidaka *(Kagoshima University)*,
  Yusei Suzuki *(Shigakukan University)*, Masaharu Terada *(Kagoshima University)*,
  Akira Takenoshita *(Kagoshima Immaculate Heart University)*,
  Yutoku Beppu *(National Institute of Fitness and Sports in Kanoya)*,
  Yoko Nedachi *(Kagoshima Immaculate Heart University)*,
  Koji Yukawa *(International University of Kagoshima)*, Holmes Rodriguez *(Universidad de Antioquia)*,
  Katsuyuki Suenaga *(Kagoshima Immaculate Heart College)*, Yuichi Yamanaka *(Kagoshima University)*,
  Toshihiko Okamura *(Kagoshima Prefectural College)*, Anne Elizabeth Brasier *(Kagoshima University)*,
  Hiroyuki Seto *(Kagoshima Women's Junior College)*,
  Kazuhide Dogome *(Kagoshima National College of Technology)*,
  Takeshi Yamada *(Daiichi Institute of Technology)*, Noritaka Oto *(International University of Kagoshima)*,
  Masakazu Ito, Munetomo Nedachi *(Kagoshima University)*
- **Enhanced Student Technology Support with Cross-Platform Mobile Apps** 31
  Bobby Siegfried *(Lehigh University)*

Session 3: Tuesday November 15, 4:00PM

- **Leveraging Both Quantitative and Qualitative Data Sources to Improve IT Help Desk Support Services** 35
  Kenneth Janz, Dean Feller *(Winona State University)*
- **Maintaining Creative Integrity While Implementing Successful University Branding** 43
  Christopher Donald *(North Carolina State University)*
- **Revitalize and Re-brand Your IT Image** 45
  Thom Mattauch, Hannah Pettit *(Virginia Commonwealth University)*
- **Managing iOS Mobile Devices** 49
  Kristen Dietiker *(University of Washington)*

Session 4: Wednesday November 16, 8:30AM

- **Charting a New Course from Blackboard to Sakai** 53
  Beth Rugg *(Ithaca College)*

- **The Circle of Internal Communication** 61
  Jean Tagliamonte, Chad Fust *(Vassar College)*
- **This Isn't Your Father's Computer Lab: Computer Labs Redefined** 65
  Dan R. Herrick *(Colorado State University)*
- **Trusted Computing Architectures for a Mobile IT Infrastructure** 73
  Vijay Anand *(Southeast Missouri State University)*, Jafar Saniie, Erdal Oruklu *(Illinois Institute of Technology)*

Session 5: Wednesday November 16, 9:45AM

- **Can You Hear Me Now? Communicating to the Campus Community** 79
  Laurie Fox, Andy Camidge, Kirk Anne *(State University of New York, Geneseo)*
- **Successful Implementation of an Active Learning Laboratory in Computer Science** 83
  Hossein Hakimzadeh, Raman Adaikkalavan, Robert Batzinger *(Indiana University, South Bend)*
- **IT Collaboration Across Institutions** 87
  R. Mark Koan *(Phoenix College)*
- **Orchestrating an Institution-Wide Transition to Google Calendar** 95
  Stephen G. Lewis, Stacey Kimmel-Smith *(Lehigh University)*

Session 6: Wednesday November 16, 11:15AM

- **UR Mobile: There's an App for That** 103
  Melisa Tanger-Brown *(University of Rochester)*
- **The Awkward Hallway: Getting Inside an Applicant's Head** 107
  Nathan Carpenter, Ryan C. Tucker *(University of Illinois at Urbana-Champaign)*
- **The Windows 7 Build Key: Redesigning and Automating Image Deployment** 111
  John B. Tyndall *(The Pennsylvania State University)*
- **Session Poster 7: Wednesday November 16, 1:30PM** ....
  Session Chair: Elizabeth Rugg *(Ithaca College)*
- **Read, Write, and Present for ACM SIGUCCS Conferences** 119
  Trevor Murphy *(Williams College)*
- **Superstar Student Staff Teams** 123
  Karen McRitchie *(Grinnell College)*
- **The Mission: Delivering Technology Information to Those Who Need It Most** 129
  Jace Laakso *(University of Montana)*
- **A Comparison of the Usage and Experience of a File Sharing System with Different Operation Policies** 131
  Naomi Fujimura, Zen'ichi Hirayama *(Kyushu University)*
- **The Cultivation of a Help Desk Dashboard** 135
  Shereese Thomas, Adam Perkins *(Wayne State University)*
- **What's Growing on Your Keyboards?** 141
  Jason Wagner *(University of Rochester)*
- **We've Been Over This Before! Tracking the Lifecycles of Scheduled Events** 143
  Nathan Carpenter, Ryan C. Tucker *(University of Illinois at Urbana-Champaign)*
- **Which Web Solution Is Best for You? A Decision Tree** 145
  Debbie Durant *(University of Delaware)*
- **Physical Security and Data Projectors** 147
  Nason Simpson *(Pima County Community College)*
- **Sun Ray Self-Help Guide** 149
  Dan R. Herrick *(Colorado State University)*
- **A Space Just for YOU: Specialized Learning Centers** 153
  Laurie Sutch *(University of Michigan)*

- **Raising the Bar – Cell Phones the GGC Way** 157
  Susan M. Kerr *(Georgia Gwinnett College)*
- **InnovatEDU a Collaboration to Reduce Higher Ed Security Risk** 161
  George F. Claffey Jr. *(Charter Oak State College)*, Harry J. Regan *(ETC Support)*

Session 8: Wednesday November 16, 3:00PM

- **Windows 7 – Trials and Tribulations** 165
  David Dean *(Lewis & Clark College)*
- **Investigating and Implementing Mobility** 171
  Fred Morris, Chris Higgins *(University of Maryland, College Park)*
- **Ubiquitous Computing** 175
  Matthew West *(Lewis & Clark College)*

Session 9: Wednesday November 16, 4:15PM

- **Team Mission: Solutions for Managing Software** 183
  Gordana Brouilette *(University of Alberta)*, Cynthia Dooling *(Pima Community College)*, Cheryl Stahler *(Bloomsburg University)*, Cindy Stewart *(University of Alberta)*, Janice Tulloss *(University of North Carolina, Greensboro)*
- **Utilizing Educational Lean to Enhance the Information Technology Project Intake Process** 189
  Robin Honken, Kenneth Janz *(Winona State University)*
- **Leading from the Middle** 195
  Melisa Tanger-Brown *(University of Rochester)*
- **CourseCast – A New Angle on Course Capture Technology** 199
  William C. Klein *(Valparaiso University School of Law)*

Session 10: Thursday November 17, 8:30AM

- **UMConnect One Year Later: Promoting Live@Edu Services** 203
  Kathy Garramone *(The University of Montana)*
- **Moodle Integration of an Automated Account Enabling System and a User Status Collection System** 207
  Hideo Masuda, Kazuyoshi Murata, Yuki Shirakawa, Yu Shibuya, Yasuaki Kuroe *(Kyoto Institute of Technology)*
- **Homework and Hangovers: The Joys of Empowering a Student Staff** 211
  Thom Mattauch, Hannah Pettit *(Virginia Commonwealth University)*
- **Bringing Students and Faculty Together Through Mobile Devices** 215
  Allison Czapracki, Cyd Burrows *(University of San Diego)*

Session 11: Thursday November 17, 9:40AM

- **Enriching Scholarship: Sustaining Effective Campus Collaborations** 219
  Laurie A. Sutch *(University of Michigan)*
- **Student Employees: Hire 'em, Mold 'em, Keep 'em** 223
  Dana Peiffer *(University of Northern Iowa)*
- **Visualizing User Activity in Open E-Learning Contexts: Challenges and Techniques for Operational Management** 229
  Owen G. McGrath *(University of California, Berkeley)*

Author Index 235

SIGUCCS 2011 Conference Organization

Conference Chair: Elizabeth Wagnon *(Texas A&M University)*

Management Symposium Program Co-Chairs: John Bucher *(Oberlin College)*
Terry Wolff *(University of Southern California)*

Service & Support Program Co-Chairs: Parrish Nnambi *(University of California, San Diego)*
Chris Wiesemann *(University of Oregon)*

Treasurer: Mat Felthousen *(University of Rochester)*

SIGUCCS Board Liaison Outgoing: Kelly Wainwright *(Lewis and Clark College)*

SIGUCCS Board Liaison Incoming: Parrish Nnambi *(University of California, San Diego)*

Audio-Visual Coordinator: Mat Felthousen *(University of Rochester)*

Birds-of-a-Feather (BOF) Chair: Cyd Burrows *(University of San Diego)*

Communication Awards Chair: Greg Hanek *(Indiana University)*

Communication Awards Team: Allison Oslund *(Texas A&M University)*
Francesco de Leo *(American University)*
Charles A. Walker *(North Carolina State University)*
Denise Brown *(Indiana University-Purdue University Indianapolis)*
Keith Allison *(New York University)*
Stacey Kimmel-Smith *(Lehigh University)*
Matt Smith *(Valparaiso University)*
Chet Cook *(West Virginia University)*
Daphne Siefert-Herron *(Indiana University)*
Charles Rondot *(Indiana University)*
Vern Yoneyama *(University of Pennsylvania)*

Conference Registration/Help Desk: Melissa Bauer *(Baldwin-Wallace College)*

Evaluations Chair: Cynthia Dooling *(Pima College)*

Local Arrangements Chair: Herman Tidmore *(Point Loma Nazarene University)*

New-Comers Orientation Coordinator: Laurie Fox *(SUNY-Geneseo)*

Newsletter Editor: Allison Czapracki *(University of San Diego)*

Photography Coordinator: Karl Owens *(University of Oregon)*

Photographers: Mat Felthousen *(University of Rochester)*
Rick McDonald *(South Dakota School of Mines & Technology)*
Parrish Nnambi *(University of California, San Diego)*
Hank Pletscher *(Saginaw Valley State University)*
Terry Wolff *(University of Southern California)*

Poster Chair: Beth Rugg *(Ithaca College)*

Publicity Co-Chairs: Karen McRitchie *(Grinnell College)*
Gail Rankin *(Salem State College)*

Management Symposium Publications: Richard Nelson *(The Citadel)*

Service & Support Conference Publications: Kayla Stephenson *(Sam Houston State University)*

Management Symposium Session Chair Coordinator: Jennifer Stewart *(The Pennsylvania State University)*

Service & Support Session Chair Coordinator: Leila Shahbender *(Princeton University)*

Social Networking Chair: Greg Deitz *(Texas A&M University)*

Vendor Chair: Gail Farally-Semerad *(Widener University)*

Volunteer Chair Nancy Bauer *(Ross University School of Medicine)*

Webmaster: Jim Yucha *(Virginia Commonwealth University)*

Workshop Chair: Karen McRitchie *(Grinnell College)*

Management Symposium Program Assistants: Rob Patterson *(Molloy College)*
Cynthia Dooling *(Pima College)*
Tim Foley *(Lehigh University)*
Richard Nelson *(The Citadel)*

Service and Support Track Chairs: Nancy Bauer *(Ross University School of Medicine)*
Gordana Brouilette *(University of Alberta)*
Laurie Fox *(SUNY Geneseo)*
Patti Mitch *(University of Wisconsin - Platteville)*
Evelyne Roach *(Princeton University)*
Beth Rugg *(Ithaca College)*
Cindy Stewart *(University of Alberta)*

Program Committee Reviewers:

Lisa Barnett *(New York University)*
Allisa Becker *(University of California, San Diego)*
Miranda Carney-Morris *(Lewis and Clark College)*
Richard Coffey *(University of Washington)*
Cynthia Dooling *(Pima Community College)*
Kathy Fletcher *(West Virginia University)*
Kathy Gregory
Bob Haring-Smith *(West Virginia University)*
Kenneth Janz *(Winona State University)*
Derek Kaser *(Saint Vincent College)*
James Lewis *(University of Oregon)*
Teresa McCarver *(University of Mississippi)*
Diana McKinney *(Purdue University)*
Johnathon A. Mohr *(Philadelphia University)*
Trevor Murphy *(Williams College)*
Maureen Novozinsky *(Princeton University)*
Rob Pettigrew *(University of Michigan)*
Darin Phelps *(New York University)*
Gail Rankin *(Salem State University)*
Carol Rhodes *(Indiana University Bloomington)*
Angi Ruble *(Webster University)*
Jennifer Scales *(Haverford College)*
Frank Sirianni *(Fordham University)*
Kate Sprague *(Webster University)*
Christine Vucinich *(Duke University)*

SIGUCCS 2011 Sponsor & Supporters

Sponsor:

Platinum Supporters:

Gold Supporter:

Silver Supporters:

Bronze Supporters:

Developing Service Assessment Metrics

Nik Chaphalkar
Service Systems Engineering
Michigan Tech University
Houghton, MI 49931
nschapha@mtu.edu

Brian Stawowy
Service Systems Engineering
Michigan Tech University
Houghton, MI 49931
bdstawow@mtu.edu

Sara Freidank
Service Systems Engineering
Michigan Tech University
Houghton, MI 49931
sjstewar@mtu.edu

Javier Fernandez
Support – Co-Director
Engineering Information Technology
Michigan Tech University
Houghton, MI 49931
906-487-2901
jfernand@mtu.edu

Amlan Mukherjee
Associate Professor
Service Systems Engineering
Michigan Tech University
Houghton, MI 49931
906-487-1952
amlan@mtu.edu

ABSTRACT
Developing performance metrics for assessing the efficiency of services is a growing need within organizations. The Engineering Information Technology (EIT) Department at Michigan Technological University (MTU) is a service-based organization. The User Services branch of EIT responds to a wide range IT service requests from users and attempts to resolve them with as little delay as possible. This paper presents a methodology to develop a metric that can be used to establish the level of service for MTU EIT. The current service delivery was assessed using a two pronged approach: by statistically characterizing the service times using historical service request records, and by accounting for both the service providers' and users' perception of the current service delivery using a structured survey. Using this analysis, and the idea of a service being a shared platform for co-creation of value, between service provider and customer, a trade-off based model was developed to identify the level of service that EIT can deliver given its resource constraints. A Senior Design project team in the Service Systems Engineering program conducted the work in this paper.

Categories and Subject Descriptors
H.1.2.

General Terms
Management, Measurement, Performance, Design, Human Factors

Keywords
User services, co-creation of value, performance metrics, level of service.

1. INTRODUCTION
The goal of this paper is to develop a methodology for information technology (IT) departments to support and enhance the delivery of their user services. The objective is to develop metrics to assess the level of services that IT departments can promise in service agreements. Specifically, the study considered customer satisfaction with respect to the time to response and resolution of their complaints, within the context of resources available to the service provider. The proposed methodology is based in trade-off approaches that aim to find expected service times that a provider can feasibly promise to satisfy customers, given the constraints of available resources.

It is very important for IT service departments to establish such service metrics because they can be used to communicate to customers the level of service an IT department can feasibly promise to deliver given budgetary and human resource constraints. It also helps customers recognize what they can expect of their services. Clients contracting with IT service delivery departments and/or organizations can use these metrics to form the basis of service agreements.

The study presented in this paper was conducted by the Service Systems Engineering Senior Design Team, in collaboration with the User Services department of Engineering Information Technology (EIT), at Michigan Technological University. Therefore this study has a dual purpose. On the one hand it supported EIT's efforts at continuously improving its user services. On the other hand it also served an educational goal for three Service Systems Engineering students (first three authors) by providing the opportunity to examine a real world service system, and address the challenges of modeling data from an imperfect real world system. The students were advised by the Director of User Services at EIT and a faculty member in the Service Systems Engineering Department, (the forth and fifth authors respectively) at Michigan Technological University.

The work described in this paper is directly related to and a departure from recent advances in user service delivery methods and frameworks in the literature. The common idea that governs such frameworks is the need to improve user satisfaction [1] using quantifiable approaches [2]. Typically, these ideas have been applied to develop a service-oriented approach to providing user support for Management Information Systems [3], with an emphasis on collaborative service delivery through strategic customer-provider alignments [4].

2. BACKGROUND

Engineering Information Technology (EIT) provides user and computer support services to students, staff, faculty, and research groups within the College of Engineering and the School of Technology at Michigan Tech. At the time when this study was conducted EIT combined three support organizations: Central Engineering Computing Network (CECN), East Engineering Computing Network (EECN), and West Engineering Computing Network (WECN). Some of their services provided are user support, desktop support, application support, printing services, hardware replacement, and large format printing. Service providers – EIT employees - spend the day performing a variety of tasks, with a portion of their time spent on addressing service requests.

In the user support service scenario, users are faculty, staff and students in the College of Engineering. When they encounter problems with their computer systems they submit a service request by email, which in turn automatically generates a user ticket. Users have varying levels of computer expertise and needs. As a result, service requests cover a wide range, including server and database configuration issues to email client setup needs. At creation all tickets are treated equally irrespective of urgency, and placed in a queue. The ticket remains in queue until a service provider is available and can resolve the issue at hand. At times the service provider may not be able to complete the request the first time they attend to it, for example, when they need to wait for a software upgrade, or if they need more information about the problem from the user. Once the issue is resolved, the service provider contacts the user and lets them know that their request has been resolved.

From the user's perspective, the time to resolution of a service request spans from the time they initiate their request email to the time when they are informed of its resolution. Typically, in this scenario, users are satisfied with the earliest resolution of their issues, while providers are constantly struggling to resolve as many requests as time and resources permit. In the absence of an established minimum expected resolution time, it can become difficult for users and providers to assess the cost and value of the service being provided.

Based on the idea of co-creation of value for both the customer and the provider, EIT aims to balance the value of the service provided to the customer and the cost to the provider. Therefore, the minimum level of service they expect to provide maximizes the value to the customer, while minimizing the cost to the provider given the constraints of human and budgetary resources. This presents an optimization problem that's often difficult to formulate, because of the difficulty in accurately evaluating service cost and value provided to customer. Even if the problem can be formulated, it is often over constrained with no optimal solutions. Therefore, the proposed method employs the use of service heuristics and consideration of trade-offs, with the aim of establishing a service system that co-creates value for the service provider and the customer.

Currently, EIT is contractually bound to their customers through Service Level Agreements, though there are no metrics to measure the levels at which the services are being delivered levels. This paper proposes a method to develop a Trade-Off Analysis to help EIT assess and monitor service delivery, and examine their existing level of service.

The method developed in this paper consists of the following steps:

1. Characterize the service from the service provider, i.e. EIT's point of view.
2. Characterize the service from the user's point of view.
3. Develop a service metric considering user dissatisfaction and service load.

Each of these is described in detail in the following sections.

3. SERVICE CHARACTERIZATION

This section describes the life cycle of a service request, and characterizes it using a statistical analysis of historical service request records. A service request is generally described as a request or issue about a computer related problem. Service requests enter the system as "tickets" via email, phone, or walk-ins by the user. If the request is sent in by email, the ticket is automatically generated; otherwise the service provider manually enters the ticket into the database. From the perspective of the service provider, three time stamps mark the life cycle of a service request. They are the time at which the ticket is *created* or entered into the database, the *started time* or time when a service provider starts working on resolving the issue, and the *resolved time* or the time when the request is completed and the issue is resolved. Figure 1 provides a schematic of this life cycle. Based on records of these time stamps, the following wait times can be computed.

Total time in system is the difference between the *created time* and *resolved time*. It is the total time that a service request spends in the system. *Service time* is the time difference between the started time stamp and the resolved time stamp. It is the total time taken by the service provider in resolving the service request. The difference between the total time in the system and the service time is the *wait time* or the time a request has to spend waiting in the system. In addition, the time difference between the created times and resolved times of any two consecutive service requests – referred to as the inter-arrival and inter-departure times, respectively are also calculated to determine the rate at which requests are entering and leaving the system.

From the user's perspective, wait time is considered to be different than the calculated wait time. The user sees the wait time as the total time that the service request is in the system. The user does not see the wait time and service time as two different times, as does the service provider.

3.1 Analysis

In order to characterize the life cycle of a typical service request, historical records of service request time stamps maintained by EIT were analyzed. The data available for analysis spanned service requests made between 2002 and 2009 and included around 50,000 records. There was a lot of variability in the data with peaks in service requests noticeably around sensitive IT events on campus. This included times when users were introduced to new email clients, when there were major server overhauls, web-site conversions and when EIT was re-organized.

Data around these events were excluded and a smaller subset of data spanning from fall 2006 through spring 2007 was considered for analysis. In addition, only the requests from the WECN support queue were used as it had maintained better organizational records than EECN or CECN. Finally, the records considered in the data sets included only tickets that had been resolved.

A statistical analysis of the different time intervals led to the following observations:

1. All service times were exponentially distributed with an average service time of about 6 day. (Kolmogorov-Smirnov Test, p value < 0.01)
2. All inter-arrival times were also exponentially distributed

Both these observations can be used to justify that the requests arrive to the system as a Poisson process. In addition, the service times being exponentially distributed also indicates that at steady state the system can be treated as a Markovian system.

4. SERVICE SURVEY

To determine the requirements and priorities for better service, the service provider and user perception of the system needed to be defined. One service provider survey and two user surveys were distributed and the results from each were analyzed. The purpose of these surveys was to model user satisfaction in the system. This was needed in order to start developing service metrics.

The service provider survey was distributed to all the EIT employees. This survey helped to classify the service provider perspective of the system. Six employees completed the survey, and the results provided a brief insight into the service provider perspective of the system. General information was collected about: hours worked per day, time spent on customer service, number of requests handled during that time, average completion time for a service request, and how many providers were engaged at any given time. Service providers also provided information on how they prioritized service requests, their own definition of customer service, and their perception of what users expected from EIT.

The initial user survey was distributed through email. It was sent to all of the users of EIT, including undergraduate students, graduate students, staff, faculty, and researchers within the College of Engineering. This survey helped understand the user's perspective of the system. More than 350 users completed the survey, and the results provided an insight into the users' perspective of the system. General information was collected about: how often the users need help from EIT, what they use it for, and how EIT is contacted. Users also rated how critical their need for help is, how long it takes to resolve an issue, how often their request is completed correctly the first time, how satisfied they are with the current system, and what services they expect to get from EIT.

A follow-up user survey was distributed in some of the student labs, both undergraduate and graduate, after it was determined that more information was needed about wait times and issue criticality. Twenty nine users completed this survey, and the results provided additional insight into user expectations related to wait times and how critical IT issues are. Users rated what they feel is an acceptable time to wait for help with IT issues, and how critical the issues are to them.

4.1 Analysis

The difference in perceptions of the system is an important concept to grasp because the different perceptions clearly impact the system. EIT's perception affects the required level of service, and the level of service based on EIT's understanding of user perception.

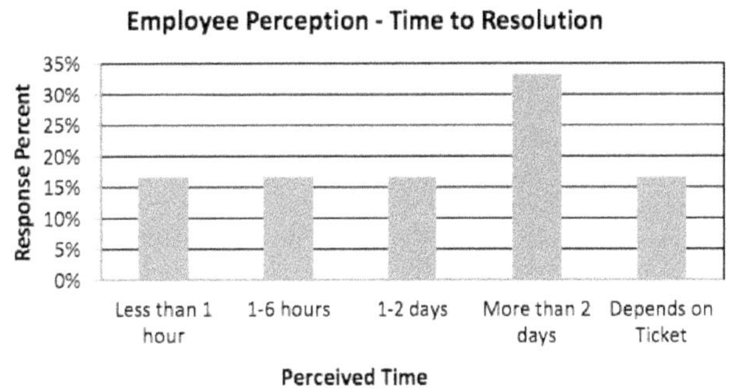

Figure 1. Employee Perception of Time to Resolution

The outcome of the surveys illustrated that from the service provider's perspective the majority of the service requests are completed within a day (Figure 1), even though the average is skewed due to long service times on a portion of the service requests. Perceived time to resolution for the user increases as the wait time goes past the eight-hour workday (Figure 2). Depending on what the complexity of the service request is, the average user feels that they wait less than one day for a service request to be completed.

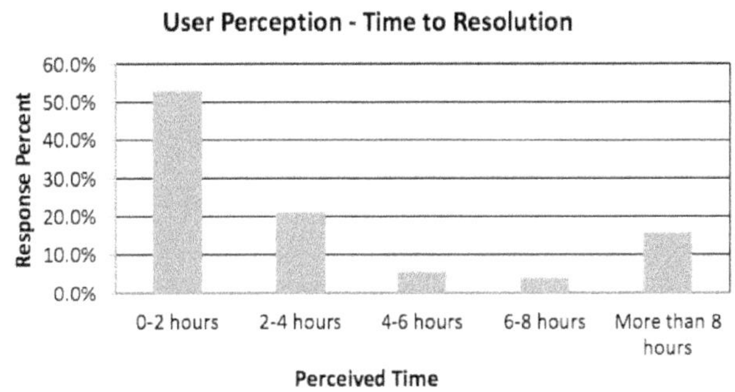

Figure 2. User Perception of Time to Resolution

In addition, users were asked to rate the criticality of their requested service (Figure 3). On average users surveyed indicated that their need for help was not very critical.

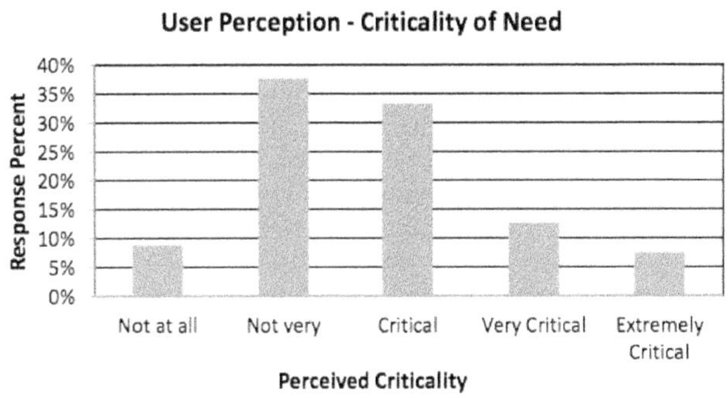

Figure 3. User Perception of Criticality

Users were also asked to rate how satisfied they are with the current system. On average users surveyed indicated that they were satisfied with EIT, but the results were difficult to correlate with perceived criticality (Figure 4).

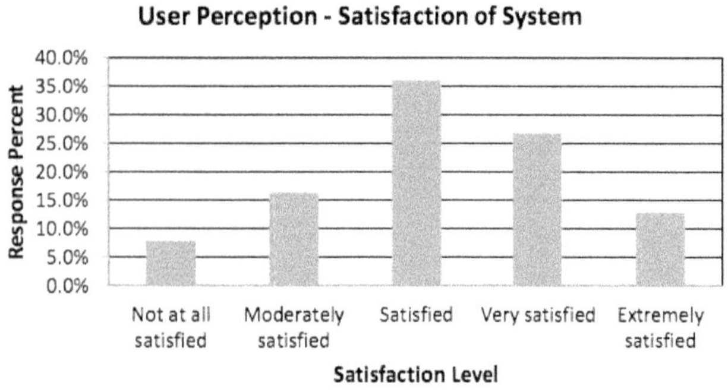

Figure 4. User Perception of Satisfaction

A follow-up survey was conducted to address the need to relate the user satisfaction to the varying service levels. Users were required to rate times that they were willing to wait to resolution given the criticality of the service request.

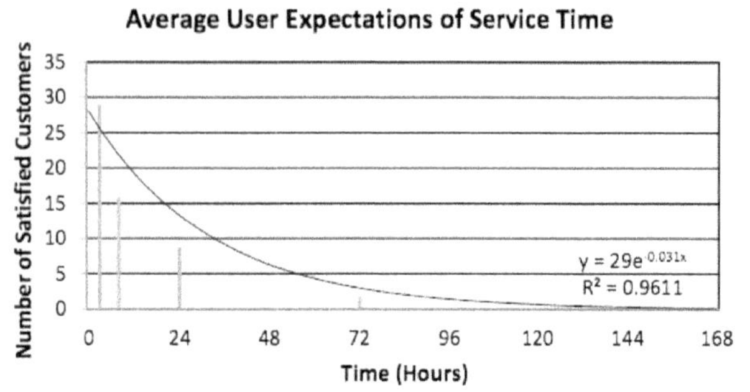

Figure 5. User Expectation of Service Times

Figure 5 illustrates the wait times as indicated by a percentage of the customers. This is a close approximation for a curve representing customer satisfaction. As the "willingness to wait" period translates to the period of time within which the customer is satisfied if their service request is completed.

The model fitting the curve is expressed as follows:

$$N = N_0 e^{-kt} \tag{1}$$

Where N = Number of Satisfied Users

N_0 = Number of Total Users at Time Zero

t = Time in days that service is delayed = Time in System

k = Decay Constant

The idea supporting the model is that when the delay in the system in 0, i.e. service is delivered to the customer immediately, then the percentage of customers satisfied, (N/N_0) is 100%. As the value of t or the time taken to deliver service increases, the percentage of satisfied customers decays exponentially with constant k. The model was identified from the survey data with N_0 = 29 (number of surveyed respondents) and an exponential decay fit with the largest R^2 value was chosen. This provided the satisfaction curve as follows:

$$N = 29\, e^{-0.031\, t} \tag{2}$$

It is important to note that the value of the exponent ($e^{-0.031\, t}$) provides the percentage of satisfied customers (N/29).

Therefore the percentage of unsatisfied customers is presented by the dissatisfaction curve as:

$$D(t) = 1 - e^{-0.031\, t} \tag{3}$$

This leads to the development of a dissatisfaction curve – an arguably more useful tool as dissatisfaction directly correlates to loss in revenue to the customer or cost incurred by the customer. This curve is illustrated in Figure 6.

5. METRIC DEFINITION

The next step involves the definition of parameters based on an understanding of resource usage by EIT. Parameters of interest are the amount of resources which EIT uses to perform the support service and how EIT utilizes its resources, the length of time service requests take to complete, the number of services requests in the system, the value of the service as perceived by the user. The first step is to establish the fraction of the annual budget that is allocated for user support services. This is presented as a fraction of the total time that is spent by personnel in user support services during any given period and is presented as follows:

$$B_f = B.(T_s/T_T) \tag{4}$$

Where B_f = fractional budget

B = Annual budget

T_s = Service provider time working on support services during a period

T_T = Total value of service provider time during a period

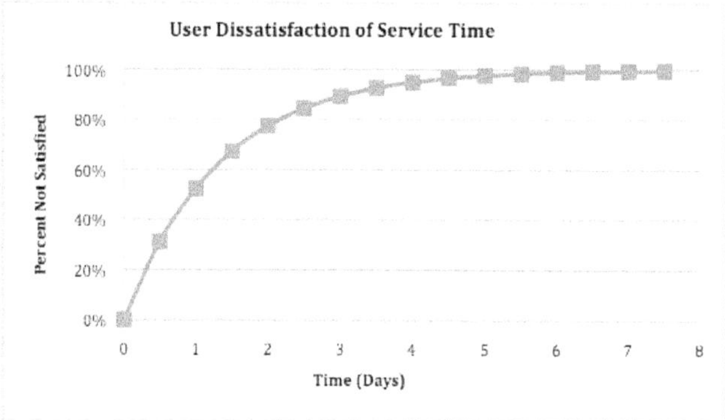

Figure 6. User Dissatisfaction Curve

The next relationship to be represented is the cost to the service provider in resolving a request. The underlying assumption is that the cost to providing service to the provider is directly proportional to the promptness of the response. Hence, the shorter the response time, the more expensive the cost to the provider and higher the value to the user. Therefore as the time to response increases, the cost to the service provider decreases. Of course, the ability to promptly provide service is directly related to the number of service providers or employees available to service requests (assuming that all employees provide the same quality of service). Hence, higher the number of available employees, shorter the response time, and higher the cost to EIT.

This notion is characterized as the portion of budget allocated for support per employee per day measured over time spent completing a service request and presented as follows:

$$C_{SP} = B_f / [E.t] \qquad (5)$$

C_{SP} = Cost to service provider per day for delaying service

B_f = Fractional budget

E = Number of employees

t= Number of days until completed service

The user cost can be computed based on a product of user dissatisfaction with the service and the number of unattended service requests in the system ("incomplete tickets in the support queue") at the point in time of analysis.

Similarly the user's costs due to delays in a service request being completed are calculated as follows:

$$C_U = R.C_{du}.Pr(t).t.D(t) \qquad (6)$$

Where, C_U = Cost to user per day for waiting to receive service

R= Average number of service requests in system

C_{du} = Cost to user per day for service

$Pr(t)$ = Probability that a service request will be in the system at time t

t = Number of days until service is completed

$D(t)$ = Percentage of users dissatisfied from survey data at time t

The quantity C_{du} is derived from fees that users pay per semester for service, expressed as a daily cost. R, the average number of service requests in the system was calculated using a time average of the queue length calculated from the historical records. $Pr(t)$ is calculated from the probability density function of service requests calculated from the data as illustrated in Figure 7.

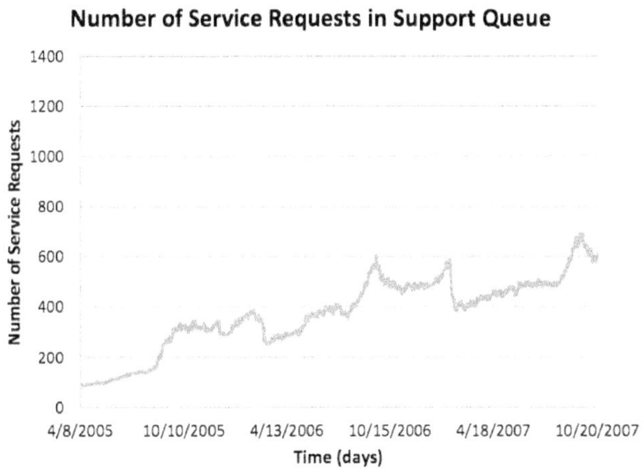

Figure 7. Service Request Support Queue

The length of time each service request stays in the system, from the time it enters as "created" to the time it leaves as "resolved", is characterized by Weibull distribution.

5.1 Trade-off Assessment

The fundamental trade-off that defines the service delivery problem at hand is, given the number of service providers (employees) available to EIT, what is the most *feasible level of service* that can be promised, while minimizing the cost to the service provider (C_{SP}), and the cost to the user (C_U). These two functions are both costs per day ($/day) and are functions of the number of days to service completion t. Therefore, the level of service is defined as the maximum number of days that EIT feasibly expects to resolve a service request. This corresponds to the number of days at which $C_U = C_{SP}$.

Figure 8, illustrates a joint plot of these two functions against the number days to service completion. C_{SP} is plotted for 15, 25, 35 and 45 employees (E). The value of B_f for EIT was calculated using employee production rates. These numbers are proprietary to EIT. The function C_U was plotted using the observed service queue data.

The plot illustrates that as the number of employees increases, the expected number of days to service completion decreases. In other words, if staffed at 45 employees, EIT could promise to service requests within 3 days and with 15 employees approximately within 5 days. This provides a template for a metric that EIT can use to define its expected level of service given its available resources.

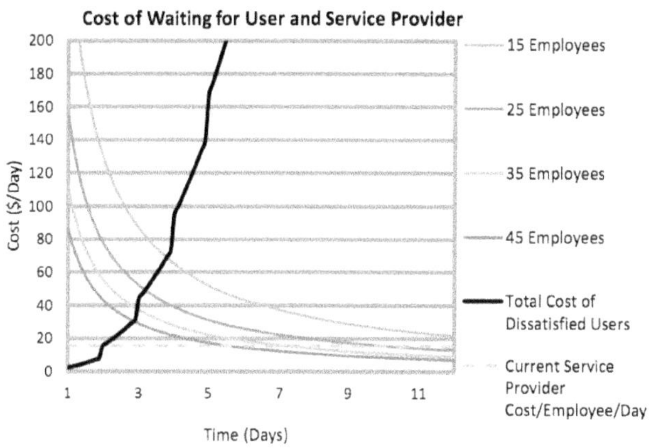

Figure 8. Plot of C_U and C_{SP} (varying E)

The plot in Figure 8, assumes uniform load in the request queue as was derived from the service records, and does not account for any variability in the loads. In order to illustrate the sensitivity of the cost to the user (C_U) a plot was made of C_{SP} and C_U for 25 employees, and varying the average number of requests in the system (R) between 100 and 350 requests. This is illustrated in Figure 9.

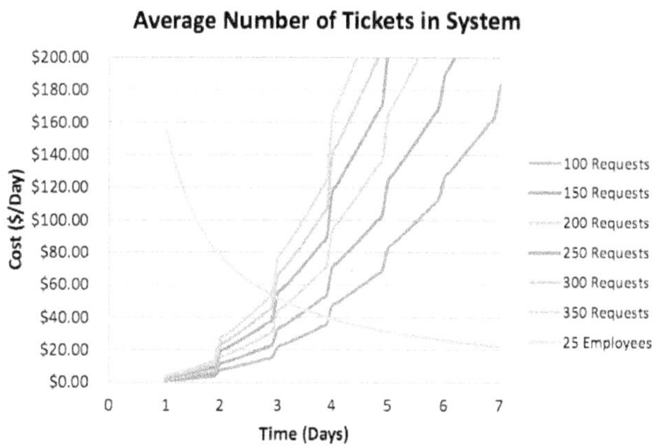

Figure 9. Plot of C_U and C_{SP} (varying R, E=25)

Figure 9, illustrates that at 25 employees, and given the average request load between 100 and 350, EIT can at best provide a service time of 3 days. For the lower load scenarios, at a lower cost, it can afford up to 4 days.

6. CONCLUSION

In conclusion, the method described in this paper provides a first step towards the development of a metric for monitoring IT user services. The method is motivated by the growing need among user services to develop quantifiable metrics that can be used to support service level agreements between service providers and customers. The method described has its theoretical underpinning in the idea of shared co-creation of value for the customer and the service provider in the delivery of the service.

The proposed method develops a metric specifically for EIT at MTU. In this case, the metric presents the expected number of days to resolution of user service requests. The paper describes a method based in balancing cost to user and to the provider to establish the expected level of service that EIT can promise, given resource constraints. While the method itself is robust, the approaches taken to estimating model parameters are based on assumptions, e.g. all service requests have been treated as equal and all employees have been treated as equally capable of assessing all requests. These assumptions will require further investigation and fine-tuning in future work.

7. ACKNOWLEDGMENTS

Our thanks to all employees at Engineering IT, at MTU.

8. REFERENCES

[1] Kettinger, W.J., and Lee, C. C. 2007. Perceived Service Quality and User Satisfaction with the Information Services Function. *Decision Sciences*. 25, 5-6, 737-766. DOI=10.1111/j.1540-5915.1994.tb01868.x

[2] Ives, B., Olson, M.H., and Baroudi, J. J. 1983. The measurement of User Information Satisfaction. *Magazine, Communications of the ACM,* 26 (10). DOI=10.1145/358413.358430

[3] Leitheiser, R.L. and Wetherbe, J.C. 1986. Service Support Levels: An Organized Approach to End-User Computing. *MIS Quarterly,* 10(4), 337-349.

[4] Luftman, J., Brown, C.V., and Balaji, S. 2011. Customer-Provider Strategic Alignment: A Maturity Model. In *Service System Implementation* in series, *Service Science: Research and Innovation in the Service Economy, Ed.* Demirkan, H., Spohrer, J.C., and Krishna, V., Springer US. 145-163. DOI=10.1007/978-1-4419-7904-9_9

Unifying the ITS Department Through Ticketing

Loraine Graves
Help Desk Manager
5998 Alcala Park UC 117
San Diego, CA 92110
(619) 260-5978
lgraves@sandiego.ediu

Mark Zocher
Student Tech Services Mgr
5998 Alcala Park UC 117
San Diego, CA 92110
(619) 260-6805
mzocher@sandiego.edu

ABSTRACT

In 2008, the University of San Diego's ITS department tracked the work they did in over a dozen different ticketing projects. Learn how we unified our ticketing system and ultimately unified our problem solving and change management process. Learn how we gathered input and buy-in along the way, the headaches we felt and the tasks we had to juggle. Two years later, how is the unification working? Have we seen changes in ITS because of this process?

Categories and Subject Descriptors

H.5.2 [**User Interfaces**]: Evaluation/Methodology

General Terms

Documentation

Keywords

Ticketing System, Unification, Grassroots

1. INTRODUCTION

In August of 2008 ITS went from 8 separate ticketing instances representing the 8 different divisions within ITS into 1 unified issue tracking workspace by using a product known as Footprints.

The process of getting to this 1 system was a slow, step by step process because in a university setting census is the process that works when change is needed.

Some background is needed to understand the whole process that got us where we are today. In November of 2003, Desktop Support and the Help Desk were the only departments tracking their work, aside from the student help desk which had a home grown spreadsheet system that they used to track the student issues. By the Spring of 2005 senior management wanted to begin working toward a system where all of the work ITS was accomplishing could be tracked . Up until that time the Faculty /Staff Help Desk had an onsite server application with 5 user licenses. Overpriced licenses and a lack of access to the application to update tickets was frustrating to all who used the ticketing software. In a very short time the ticketing system was used only by the Help Desk coordinator and the part-time Help Desk staff to track their work.

SIGUCCS'11, November 12–17, 2011, San Diego, California, USA.

In the Fall of 2006 the CIO decided that ITS needed to find a web based software that could be hosted to beginning tracking all of the ITS departments work. With representatives from each of the divisions within ITS, we settled on our current issue tracking system. However, even with the consensus of the representatives from each area of ITS, getting each area to adopt the practice of tracking their work was a difficult one. Since the Help Desk had already been tracking their work it was determined by senior management that we would be the team to help the other divisions embrace the practice of using the new issue tracking system. To do this the management of each division determined what they needed, wanted, and desired and each was different from the next. We built a project instance for each division to give them what they want so each division would begin to track their work. We made an agreement with each manager that if we spent the time to create their individual project that they would commit to having their staff use it.

By 2008 we had a new CIO. After looking at the 8 projects and the information being collected it was determined that we needed to work to move all 8 project into one unified project.

2. Unification

The task of combining the processes of 8 different areas felt quite daunting to the team. Each group wanted different information, used different statuses, and tracked different stats. Not only that, but the rift between the projects reflected the rift of communication the group had with the help desk. The help desk team did not know what information to collect for specific problems, and our technical support partners would get infuriated when we had missed a critical piece of information. Solutions to common problems were not documented, but were treated as tribal knowledge between the technicians. The help desk team started by identifying and gathering key players behind each group (either a manager or an influencer who had our ear) to serve on our committee.

2.1 The Processes

Before diving into the ticketing system itself, the group focused on the process. Our first goal was to identify how we handle customer problems in ITS, and ultimately how we should best handle them. We recognized that our customer base was too used to contacting friends in ITS when a problem surfaced, and the group would waste more time trying to break that habit than we would solving problems the customer had. So the first deliverable from the team was the Support Swim Chart.

A swim chart is a diagram tool where different groups (customer, first tier, management, etc) that handle a problem are given a horizontal lane, similar to a swimming pool lane. Then, arrows and diamonds represent the workflow of a support call, whether it came through our ACD system, in person with a desktop technician, or direct to a manager. Using a template from BlueprintAudits.com, we worked to determine this process first. Then, the team documented basic handoffs between teams, technology to facilitate support, and detailed information we wanted to get from all customers. We also determined some basic tasks that the help desk would take on no matter what, including contacting the customer to confirm resolution if the person who solved the problem (say an email administrator) was too busy or not comfortable contacting customers. Within the first few weeks of the project, the managers were already able to go back to their teams and gather by-in for the project - this helped cement support for later deliverables.

2.2 Data Collection

Once the process was in place, we started looking at the data we were collecting. What was critical for every ticket to have? While each group wanted to require very specific information for each ticket, limitations with our ticketing system meant a field was required for every ticket or was optional for every ticket. To keep ticketing simple, the team decided to only require a category, a detail, and the basic customer information. The category, detail, and occurrence fields would be the way we'd report statistics on the number of problems for different areas, so making these fields easy to navigate was critical.

To determine the best category/detail for every system we support, the team started by brainstorming all the services that we received phone calls on or wanted to collect statistics on. Each system (say Blackboard) was written on a separate index card. We based our high level categories from a template by BlueprintAudits.com, and included categories such as "Accounts & Passwords" or "Classroom Technologies". During one of our regular team meetings, we posted the categories around the room, gave each team member some system/service names, and let them loose. Our resulting list of categories and systems was not only thorough, it was already vetted by the managers and key players!

2.3 Change Management

Our unification of Change Management came differently. Only a small group of ITS was using change management, and the process they created was quite simple. We were able to easily incorporate process into unified project, and only needed to gather buy-in from a few of the managers.

With our fields, change management, and requirements in mind, we created a test project for the team to see. Not only did we show the test project to the people in the unification project, we showed it to teams and agents across ITS. We tried to remain transparent about the design, letting all our stakeholders know of the changes, why they were being made, and how it would impact them (for the better, we hoped). The test project also allowed us to determine the best way to migrate the data from 8 separate projects to one.

Once the changes were solidified by the team and ITS was onboard, we created a production environment with all our changes. For a few days between summer and fall semesters, we used the systems in tandem - to our users, it was just one more project to have to worry about. We helped groups cut down the number of open tickets, then moved projects one by one into the unified ticketing system. Within a week, all old projects were closed off, and the unification was complete.

Subsequent Pages

3. Aftermath

Since the unification of our ticketing system in Fall 2008, the ITS Help Desk has seen some major benefits. Over 65,000 tickets were created in 2.5 years, and the amount of duplicated content has decreased dramatically. A unified project allowed us to unify our customer ticket portal, allowing customers to see the status of tickets for ALL ITS problems, not just the tickets they submitted through the help desk. Other areas of ITS have seen the benefits of an automatic ticketing system and have gotten on board the last two years. In Spring 2011, we moved the Telecommunications group away from printing email work requests and into our ticketing system for tracking.

The unification has even allowed us to start unifying our internal support knowledge base with our technical support teams teams. We created a template for Level 1 Scripts (L1S), which are documents created for each supported system on campus. Each L1S tells our support team who's responsible for the system, what troubleshooting to try over the phone, and what information we need to collect before we escalate the ticket. What we once did with separate projects and ticket templates we now do with a standard document and training. This allows us to change the troubleshooting we do or information we gather easily, without having to change our ticketing system template each time. With this information, we were less reliant on "tribal knowledge" and were able to bring an off site after hours support team up to speed easier. Not only did we unify our internal documentation, but our public documentation as well. Our public knowledge base is slowly growing, seeing ~1500 views a month.

While we have seen benefits from the unification, the progress has been slow at times. While the initial project was directed by the CIO, support for the project and the initiative has really been from the help desk itself. We find that a chunk of our time is now spent serving as "Footprints Cheerleaders", encouraging groups to ticket their work and to provide feedback on the service. Over the last two years, we have tried to add extra features to improve adoption, including custom escalations and dashboard tools to make work easier. Our job as cheerleaders also includes celebrating our milestones of tickets across ITS, letting the team know how much work they have done together. We have discovered that teams who are more active in our ticketing system (suggesting changes, actively updating their tickets) have proven to be stronger allies in the department.

The process of unifying our ticketing system has not unified our ITS processes as much as we had hoped. Since we've not seen policy from "on high" about all tickets and changes going though our ticketing system, we see different levels of support across ITS. At least one director came up with their own way to track change management, leaving the help desk unaware of many changes that have taken place. Other areas of ITS still maintain separate email addresses for customers to request help, which are not turned into tickets unless a message is forwarded to us (which assumes someone from their team was around to forward it). When we meet with groups who use "alternatives" to our ticketing or change management, the groups seem blissfully unaware that a unified solution exists. Even with our cheering, not everyone in the stands can hear us.

4. CONCLUSION

As we've discovered in the years after our unification, the goal is always a moving target, and we have to adjust accordingly. To get every employee in ITS using the issue tracking system to track their work without having support from "on high" is difficult, but still doable. Here are a few of the initiatives the ITS Help Desk is taking on to help promote our unified project:

- Providing weekly and monthly reports for each division and ITS as a whole to the senior management, helping show the value of one ticketing system
- Posting statistics and information on the ITS web site to be more transparent to the university community
- Ongoing pruning and care
    - Want to have a yearly 'spruce-up' program to gather input from ITS to add options and fix nagging problems
    - Reminder trainings each summer to break bad habits
- Working to build relationships over summer with unorthodox methods, to help bring them back to interacting with the help desk regularly (food!)

Divide & Conquer

Kathy M. Lyons
University of Illinois at Urbana-Champaign
1304 W. Springfield Ave.
Urbana, IL61801
1-217-265-0892
kmsimpso@illinois.edu

Ryan T. Sharpe
University of Illinois at Urbana-Champaign
1304 W. Springfield Ave.
Urbana, IL61801
1-217-265-0754
rtsharpe@illinois.edu

ABSTRACT

"Work smarter not harder", "Do more with less". These are phrases we all hear on a daily basis as we face difficult budgets. The CITES Help Desk at the University of Illinois took the opportunity to redesign itself to create efficiencies, provide better services without increasing the budget, and begin creating career paths for its IT professionals. To support new services, more services, more groups, and larger audiences we focused on two major areas. The Help Desk full time staff is now broken into two groups: student management & project support.

This presentation will focus not just on why, but what in regards to this move. The Student Management Team has helped refine the hiring, training and disciplining of the ever evolving student consultant. The Project support team now has direct involvement in the rollout of new services including Unified Communications which will replace our entire email and phone infrastructure and services. With a clear understanding of each group's responsibilities, the Help Desk has seen improved morale, better communication, and has slowed down the always expanding "duties as assigned" role.

Categories and Subject Descriptors
K.6.1[Management of Computing and Information Systems]: Project and People Management-*Management Techniques*

General Terms
Management, Measurement, Human Factors

Keywords
Student Management, Help Desk, Projects

1. INTRODUCTION
Many organizations and groups have heard the saying "do more with less". It has become a standard in our vocabulary and it seems to roll off of the tongue easily when trying to justify change or financial problems. Our organization is no different. With the downturn of the economy three years ago, we started scaling back resources without turning away customers or projects. Now, we are all faced with burnout, low morale, and employee turnover just to name a few things.

At the CITES Help Desk, we realized that we could only do so much with the resources we had. Although some groups were getting new positions within the organization, the CITES Help Desk was not able to acquire such resources. Therefore, it was apparent that we had to take a look at what our priorities were and the capacity of the current staff so we could make changes and refocus our resources to better suit the group and the organization.

2. OUR ENVIRONMENT
The CITES Help Desk is the primary provider of computer support at University of Illinois at Urbana Champaign. Our support is campus wide as we assist over eighty thousand students, faculty, staff, and retirees. The Help Desk employs 9 full time professionals and around 50 part-time student workers. At any given time we usually have five to eight workers on shift helping clients over the phone, by email, face-to-face, and through instant messaging. Last year we were contacted fill in times for assistance with a variety of issues, from resetting passwords to help with networking.

3. PROBLEMS WE WERE FACING
At a time when most companies, states, and organizations are cutting millions from their budgets, the University of Illinois is no different. In 2009, a committee was created to address the financial challenges facing the University. This committee looked for ways to establish efficiencies and reduce duplication across the university. They specifically targeted information technology. As a result, the IT organizations across the three campuses of the university system were to reduce IT spending by $15 million.

CITES looked at this problem head on and decided to retire old email and phone services, consolidate data server rooms, and develop a green initiative. The major task at hand for the moment is to retire the old email and phone systems although other initiatives are being implemented as well.

In a matter of 18 months campus will be outsourcing all student email to Google or MS Live (the student will get the choice between the two services or to have both, although email can only be forwarded to one); move all faculty, staff, graduate students, and retirees to a campus exchange service; and move all phone numbers from Centrex to Microsoft Lync. All of these changes roll into our Unified Communications project, which is scheduled to be complete June 30, 2012.

4. CHANGES FOR CITES HELP DESK
With so many changes coming, we realized that it was imperative to focus our efforts on training tier one support to handle the influx of calls, developing stronger customer service standards, changing the support structure to begin supporting the phone services, and restructuring staff to focus on Unified

Communications. The first phase of the project was to outsource all student email to Google and MS Live starting April 2010. Every student was given a choice as to whether they wanted to use Google or MS Live for their email. They also had a third option of forwarding all mail off to a third party of their choosing. Many of our higher education peers have outsourced student email although most schools do not give students 3 options to choose from. From conversations with our peers, we estimated a 75-100% increase in help desk tickets.

	No. of tickets	% change
April 2009	4959	
April 2010	4389	-11.5%
April 2011	6181	41%

Table 1

As you can see in Table 1, in 2010 we saw a decline in our ticket numbers from the year before. We had a six-month trend of ticket numbers decreasing due to other service changes that were implemented prior to our Unified Communications initiative. Therefore, the influx of tickets for the student outsourcing wouldn't be as big of an impact. By 2011, we realized that the 75-100% influx was heavily inflated; however, we have seen our business increase around 40% over the year before due to student outsourcing.

Phase two of the Unified Communications project is developing our current Microsoft Exchange service as an enterprise email service. Our campus has used the Microsoft Exchange service for many years, but it has been a small boutique service. Now, it will be the email service used by all faculty, staff, graduate students, and retirees. In order to roll out this service, the current Microsoft Exchange service had to be upgraded from version 2007 to 2010 and the infrastructure had to be built to handle the increased load and accounts. Once the infrastructure was built, all 2007 accounts must be migrated to the new service and new customers will be transitioned to Microsoft Exchange. As part of this second phase of Unified Communications the CITES Help Desk took on a more dominant support role for the exchange email service. With the previous boutique service, we were able to do most support within the service management group. As of March 2, 2011, the CITES Help Desk provides all intake and tier one support for the enterprise service. The second phase of Unified Communications is expected to be complete on November 30, 2011.

	No. of tickets	%change
March 2010	3994	
March 2011	5306	33%
April 2010	4389	
April 2011	6181	41%
May 2010	3949	
May 2011	5398	37%

Table 2

As illustrated in Table 2, we are seeing an average of 37% increase in our tickets due to the move to Microsoft Exchange. Our business is increasing but our staff levels are staying the same.

Phase 3 of this project is to move all Centrex based phone lines to Microsoft Lync. The pilot phase started in April 2011, although most changes will not begin until August 2011. As we move to the new Lync phone system, the CITES Help Desk is also taking on the role as "one stop shop" for IT support. With this brand new service, we can only anticipate the increased volume in business. With the Unified Communications project, and other smaller projects, filling our time we needed to find a way to create efficiencies within the help desk.

5. SOLUTION: DIVIDE & CONQUER

The Unified Communications initiative is currently broken down into more than 51 projects. In the early stages of the initiative, the Help Desk Manager and the Exchange specialist were attending many of the project meetings. That quickly became overwhelming and unmanageable. We needed to focus on two major areas in the Help Desk 1)providing the best tier one support possible, especially through migration of email and provisioning of the new phone services and 2)representing the Help Desk and customers in the multitude of projects for the Unified Communications initiative. As a result, two teams were created from the full-time staff: the UC project team and the student management team. Both teams are made up of 4 full-time Help Desk staff .

The project team is assigned to the 51+ Unified Communications projects. They meet regularly to keep each other aligned, develop knowledge base articles regarding the initiative, and provide general information and training to the rest of the staff. These staff members were given these primary responsibilities in place of managing students on a daily basis, which was also part of their day to day job responsibilities..

The student management team focuses on developing on-going and new training for student consultants, quality control reviews, hiring, mentoring, and discipline of students, and daily management of students. This team does very little project work for Unified Communications, however, they work on projects for other initiatives taking place during the same time frame.

6. CLOSER LOOK AT Student Management Team

The focus of the remainder of this paper will be on the Student Management Team as I am a member of the group and can speak to its usefulness. I will discuss how our group handles the hiring, training, reviewing, disciplining, and rewarding of our student consultants. As anyone working with students in higher education knows, turnover is generally high in this field whether it be through graduation, other opportunities becoming available, or simply workers wanting to focus primarily on their studies. Having a system in place can remove the uncertainty of how to get new workers from point A to point B. The only real challenge that remains is making sure you hire the right students ☺.

7. INTERVIEWS & TRAINING

Our interview process consists of three parts: a technology portion, a CITES lighting round portion, and a question & answer session. The technology portion revolves around on campus services provided by CITES and whether or not they can either complete the task (i.e. configuring a desktop client for email) or at least locate the documentation stating how to do so. This gives us a gauge on their troubleshooting ability or if they know how to use the internet effectively aside from Facebook. The lightning round assesses their ability to identify which services we support on campus. This information is located on our main webpage and lets us know if they have done their research , or if they have an idea of who maintains what. We point out that although we don't support "everything" on campus; we are considered a "one stop shop" and need to know where to direct clients. The final portion is a the typical "getting to know you" part. Our aim is to determine if customer service comes naturally to them or if they will need to be molded to our model of consultant. We make it very clear this job isn't just about answering phones and email, but also very heavy on face to face interaction.

Once the consultants are hired, obviously the next step is training. It is almost guaranteed that all the students hired consider themselves IT problem solvers, but doing so in a Help Desk environment can be a daunting task. There are tools to learn, rules to follow, powers to respect. As opposed to throwing them to wolves and enticing them to quit within 48 hours, we break training into a two dayevent. The first day covers the basics of being a Help Desk consultant, from common scenarios, general questions to ask, and how to use our ticketing system. We present them with example tickets and let them work together on how to solve them. Both days end with job shadowing with seasoned consultants who provide a "learn by watching/doing" which, according to feedback, is the most useful part of the training. The veteran consultant also goes over the tools available to them, which is helpful as the new consultant can watch them being used in real-time as opposed to seeing it in a PowerPoint slide in our classroom. As the amount of information fed to them grows, we ask them to break off and start looking at cases in our queue, plus make themselves available through our On-line support chat service. We allow one week before we require them to be on the phones. It's always a pleasant surprise to see who tackles that first.

8. CASE REVIEWS

Although we like to think our consultants are flawless and do everything the right way, supervisors know this is extremely unlikely. Case reviews are essential to building the best employee possible, (generally student workers don't think they are doing anything wrong unless they are told). Before the creation of the Student Management Team, timely case reviews were hard to come by. Each supervisor had their own list of students with varying hours and was allowed free reign on how to handle reviews. We were lacking standard expectations, communications, , and documentation on what was discussed or if a case review had even been done. This method wasn't fair to other supervisors who wanted to see every consultant get better, and it wasn't fair to the consultant when it came time for raises, promotions, or examples of good/bad work.

One of our first tasks when the SMT was created was to reform the case review system. We decided we would break the forty consultants into four groups. Each month the groups would be rotated amongst our team so that each review period would be with a new supervisor giving input on that group. We created a wiki page where we document when cases were reviewed, when we met face to face with the student (no more communication through email), were they meeting their case to call ratio and knowledge base linking, and focused goals for the next review period. This made it easy for the next supervisor to know what to discuss and look for when it was their turn to work with the consultants. There were also sections to list example cases, compliments and complaints, and even feedback from the student workers themselves. These details made it apparent who was improving, and more importantly who wasn't. Raise reviews and promotions were no longer decided by memory and "sure I like him". The feedback we gathered eventually led to monthly "all consultant" staff meetings to cover issues we noticed that were affecting workers across the board, plus discuss IT changes across campus.

9. DISCIPLINE & TRACKING

Another area that the fulltime staff members struggled with was student discipline and tracking malfeasances. There was a constant struggle from how to share noticeable problems with a consultant among the other full-timers to "how many times do we let people be late?". There was disagreement on whether to put someone on probation or cut ties completely and terminate employment. With nine full timer staff members with varying shifts in the Help Desk, consistency was non-existent. When a student worker would be penalized for missing a shift by one supervisor, we would find out later that consultant emailed a different supervisor for the reason. Other times what bothered one supervisor wasn't deemed a problem by another supervisor. If we couldn't agree on what was expected, how would the consultant know what is right and wrong? Aside from the case review reform, the Student Management Team's other main goal was to create a clear, manageable way to deal with these inconsistencies. The first step was to rewrite the CITES Help Desk Standard Operating Procedure handbook. Originally weighing in at 42 pages, there was no way a student worker would be able to follow (or care) what was in that document. We set out trimming the fat , stopped implying behavior and procedures and followed the "say what you mean" ideology. No longer were sections about dress code three paragraphs long. We mapped out absences, covering shifts, what constitutes being late, behavior expectations and also created a new email alias for consultants that would distribute to every supervisor.

The most important thing that came out of the SOP was the creation of our point system. We followed a model similar to one presented by Lisa Effing at Ithaca. Our model maps out 10 possible violations, from being tardy to excessive printing.

Each point would be either ½ a point or a full one. The goal is to stay under five. Five points would result in a face-to-face conversation with the SMT and the Help Desk Manager. At that point, the SMT and Help Desk Manager would vote to either put the student on probation or terminate. The points are tracked on our internal webpage, where supervisors on shift use a dropdown menu to add points, list reasons, or edit violations. The consultants (who use the IWP every shift) can see their points updated in real-time and why they were assigned. The workers also sign a form acknowledging they have read the SOP and also understand the discipline form. The point system has drawn a clear line in the sand for consultants and efforts have noticeably increased to follow procedure. The consultants are also aware that having a low point total is necessary for being eligible for promotions, which aside from a raise also, allows them to work at outreach events and get assigned a spot in the laptop room (a little cushier environment). At the end of each semester we reset the points to zero (unless there have been some serious grievances) giving the students a clean slate for the next semester.

Unexcused Absence: 1 pt	Unprofessional attitude and/or behavior: 2 pts
Arriving Late: ½ pt	cell phone in the HD: 1 pt
Leave Early : 1 pt	Leave messy work area: 1 pt
No Nametag: ½ pt	Poor work ethic** : 1 pt
Improper Use of Equip: 1 pt	Excessive Printing: ½ pt
Improper Attire: ½ pt	Gaming/Movies at work: ½ pt
Foul Language: 1 pt	Other (TBD): TBD pt

10. WHERE'S THE FUN?

While a lot of the SMT's attention was focused on behavior and job expectations, we understand that it is just as important to make the Help Desk as much fun as it is serious. Let's be realistic: being responsible for coming up with solutions to other people's problems everyday can be exhausting, especially for a student with a full course load. We agreed that the Help Desk has to be a place where it is OK to make a mistake, and rewards are plenty. Before our group was created, the supervisors did a good job of coming up with fun events that provided a change in the day-to-day grind of the Help Desk. The only problem is that there was no schedule and nothing official. If a full time staff member just happened to bring in donuts or pizza, the only students who benefited were the ones on that particular shift. So we set out to make yearly events in the Help Desk, some new and some old, that consultants would know are for them.

We started with Student Appreciation Week that is observed nationally. We would provide a different type of food every day that week, with menus, and the supervisors doing the cooking and serving. Grilled cheese goes a long way to making student workers feel loved. There is our annual "Souper Bowl" day in February in which each supervisors brings in a unique soup for the consultants, and also Cinco De Hat day in May where everyone is treated to Mexican cuisine (so long as they wear a hat of course). We also have an Iron Chef competition where a required ingredient is voted on by the consultants and the supervisors each have to present a dish. Their dish is then voted on by the student workers. An important goal is doing a better job of recognizing our seniors, as they are usually the ones that contribute the most to our organization. They get the opportunity to give parting words of wisdom and future plans at the last consultant staff meeting. We offer drawn portraits on their last day by one of our artistic co-workers and we are especially proud of our Battle on the Links Challenge where we put the Full-timers versus the seniors in a game of Putt-Putt. Bragging rights, pictures and a nice trophy are on the line in that event.

We invite students to submit ideas for naming of new Help Desk tools, plus created a Fantasy Football/Baseball league for people to participate in. Costume contests and door decorating competitions take place around Halloween and Christmas. We have a light-hearted "end of year" trophy ceremony to recognize workers for their efforts. Some of the categories include "most likely to drop a call", "infected the most Help Desk machines", "longest phone call", and "case of the year". We name the awards after past consultants and urge them to aim for a lifetime achievement award in a category so they too can get a trophy named after them. Trophies (purchased at a local dollar store) include unique statuettes such as a lion head, an elephant, and a hula girl. With all these events happening yearly now, there is a feeling of Help Desk holidays that consultants look forward to. Student feedback always mentions at least one of the above events as a highlight of working for us.

11. CONCLUSION

Since the division to Project Management Team and the Student Management team, tasks are clearly assigned and the uncertainty of "what needs to be done or what meetings do I need to go to" have all but been removed. Supervisors are updated at weekly meetings with relevant information from the project team and vice versa. With the boundaries in place, decisions are reached relatively quickly in a environment where this is a necessity. The supervisors benefit, as well as the consultants that offer their services to our department. "Duties as assigned" now falls on only one side of the group and no longer carries the same dark mantra as it did in the past. With a renewed sense of purpose and obligation we approach the looming changes at our university with confidence.

12. ACKNOWLEDGMENTS

Our thanks to the CITES Help Desk and all of its workers.

User State Migration Tool: Migrating to Windows 7 with Ease and Efficiency

Nicholas Jannini
Sloan Technology Services
Massachusetts Institute of Technology
Cambridge, MA 02144
617-253-2708
njannini@mit.edu

Bryce Harper
Sloan Technology Services
Massachusetts Institute of Technology
Cambridge, MA 02144
617-253-4486
sharper@mit.edu

ABSTRACT
As early adopters of Windows 7 here at MIT's Sloan School of Management we were spending a lot of time on data migration. The greater the number of machines that we deployed with Windows 7, the more envy and desire arose throughout the community. Being a high-touch department and catering to such desires, as well as the rise in Windows XP malware infections, we found that too much of our time was being siphoned away by the tedious art of moving data manually. We needed a solution.

Since User State Migration Tool 4.0 (USMT) is a free and highly customizable tool we decided it was the best route. We will review how and why we implemented USMT, first looking into some of the general terminology that is used and then the specifics of our execution. This includes: the reasoning behind our storage method, our batch scripts, what [data types] we include and exclude, and how we were able to automate the entire process of capturing the data and putting it back down onto a new device. We will also discuss the time and energy saved by not only the technician but also the user.

Categories and Subject Descriptors
The ACM Computing Classification Scheme: http://www.acm.org/class/1998/

General Terms
Performance, Reliability, Experimentation, Security, Human Factors, Standardization.

Keywords
USMT, Migration, Microsoft, Batch, Automation.

1. INTRODUCTION

1.1 MIT
Massachusetts Institute of Technology (MIT) is a private research university located in Cambridge, MA focusing largely on science and engineering. Comprised of 1,017 faculty[1] and 10,556 students[2], it is unusual in that the graduate population exceeds 60% of the student base. MIT is a decentralized institute which includes six schools and colleges as well as myriad departments, labs, and research centers.

SIGUCCS'11, November 12–17, 2011, San Diego, California, USA.

1.2 MIT Sloan
One of MIT's schools, Sloan School of Management, is currently ranked 2nd and 3rd by U.S. News & World Report in U.S. Undergraduate[3] and U.S. MBA[4] rankings, respectively. Sloan is most widely known for its MBA program although they issue bachelor's, master's, and doctoral degrees across 10 different programs.

Sloan Technology Services (STS) supports the Sloan community which is made up of 1600 students and 400 full-time faculty and staff. The scope of support includes 900 faculty and staff machines as well as one laptop per student (student owned). In a department of 24 there is a team of six technicians, a couple transient student and temp workers, and a manager that is charged with the high-touch all-encompassing support that Sloan is trying to achieve.

2. Original Deployment Process
In an environment where the mean number of computers per faculty member is over three and the individual departments have control over when they purchase new computers, it has always been critical for STS to have a well-groomed deployment process.

For many years we have followed the same model:

Machine gets shipped to user → Pick up → Start "setup sheet" → Image new machine → Manually capture old data → Manually transfer captured data → Configure → Finalize process in user's office.

2.1 Setup Sheets
The paper-based setup sheet was the mainstay for our setup process. It would capture the computer information including user info, model, serial number, and the IP address that is created/requested by the technician as MIT uses a Class A static IP address system.

The second objective of the setup sheet was that it was used as one large check list. It would step the technician through the image process, configuration, and data transfer process in fine resolution. This was important as the department had ever-changing image builds that came with their own obstacles as well as recurring consistency issues. These consistency issues involved the technicians either not being on the same wave-length or not thoroughly completing all of the steps agreed upon by the team.

2.2 Data Migration

Data migration consisted of copying large amounts of personal and work data from the expiring or problematic computer to an external hard drive. Once this was done everything was then, theoretically, copied from the external drive back to the same location on the new machine.

2.3 Opportunity for Change

While the manual data migration procedure worked for many years, it had some flaws. Among the problems identified with this process were:

- Tedious processes
- Missing data and inconsistency of transfers
- Excessive data transfer time
- Security of user data

With all of these different negative factors we saw room for improvement and thus started the quest for a different, more automated, solution.

3. User State Migration Tool 4.0

3.1 What is USMT?

Windows User State Migration Tool (USMT) 4.0 is a scriptable command-line tool that provides a highly-customizable user-profile migration experience for IT professionals. USMT includes two components, ScanState and LoadState, and a set of modifiable .xml files: MigApp.xml, MigUser.xml, and MigDocs.xml. In addition, you can create custom .xml files to support your migration needs. You can also create a Config.xml file to specify files or settings to exclude from the migration.[1] USMT is part of the Windows Automated Installation Kit (AIK); a set of tools and documentation that support the configuration and the deployment of Windows operating systems.[5]

3.2 Obtaining USMT:

The AIK toolkit is available to download from Microsoft at no charge.[6][7] Once the AIK ISO file has been downloaded, burnt to disk, and installed on your machine you can access the USMT tools at the following location:

```
C:\Program Files\Windows AIK\Tools\USMT\
```

The Windows AIK also includes other tools that may be useful like WinPE and ImageX; the USMT files can be used within the AIK directory or parsed out. After the files have been extracted from the .iso, they can be used directly from the command line or via various scripting languages.

3.3 Introduction to USMT

USMT consists of two major executable files, ScanState and LoadState. These files are used to capture the data from the source machine and push it back down to a new machine. They can also be used to do an in-place upgrade: moving the data off, putting down a new image, then migrating the user data back. A basic use would look something like this:

```
scanstate <StorePath> /v:13 /l:<logFilePath>
```

- Call the ScanState component
- Specify a storage path for user data (local or on a server)
- Set verbosity level
- Specify a storage path for the log file

The LoadState component would be used in a similar manner. You can also run a test scan with the script below to show a preview of the data to be captured.

```
scanstate /genmigxml:<filepath.xml>
```

3.4 Customization of USMT

In addition to ScanState and LoadState, there are three .xml files to help specify what data will be captured. Custom .xml files can also be created using the /genconfig switch with ScanState for a more granular approach. The newly created file can be edited to exclude certain data.

- MigApps.xml – Migrates Application settings
- MigDocs.xml – Migrates user files and profile settings
- MigUser.xml – Migrates user files and profile settings

These .xml files are called alongside the two main components. The .xml files can be used together or alone, depending on what data you would like to capture. One exception: the MigDocs.xml and MigUser.xml should not be used together because it can duplicate data during transfer.

```
scanstate <StorePath> /v:13 /l:<logFilePath>
/i:MigApps.xml /i:MigUser.xml
```

Various other switches are available via the command line. Visit the Microsoft USMT User Guide for more information.

http://technet.microsoft.com/en-us/library/dd560801(WS.10).aspx

4. Proof of Concept Phase

We wanted to first verify that this tool would work in our environment so we started the pilot phase. Since we were unsure how different features would work we started off with a minimalistic approach.

4.1 Initial Execution

Testing began by running the ScanState and LoadState files directly from the command line. We quickly moved them to a set of batch scripts called scan.bat and load.bat. These files allowed for repeated tests and experimentation. We ran several testing phases against sample data on source and destination machines. Each standard .xml was used to find the combination that made the most sense for our environment.

Portable hard drives were used in our first iteration of USMT. This was similar to how the technicians in STS were already performing data migrations. A technician could simply connect a USB hard drive that contained the batch files which would then save all of the data to the aforementioned external drive. They could then repeat the process to migrate the data from the drive to the new machine.

4.2 Scripting

The final proof of concept scripts used ScanState, LoadState, MigApps.xml, MigUser.xml, with a few additional switches. The scan.bat script did the following:

- Set a user variable for the drive letter of the portable device
- Copied the scripts and supporting files to the local machine
- Created a new directory based on the system computer name
- Ran ScanState and .xml files
  - The /nocompress switch disables compression of the captured data
  - The /o switch would allow data to be overwritten if it already existed in the migration store. This was primarily used for testing
  - The /vsc swtich allows for the migration of locked or "in-use" files
  - The /ue switch was used to exclude our local administrator from migration
- Prompted the user that the process had finished

The load.bat script was very similar. It also used the included .xml files above along with various user interface requests. It did the following:

- Set a user variable for the drive letter of the portable device
- Queried the user to enter the computer name of the source machine
- Copied the scripts and supporting files to the local machine
- Ran LoadState and .xml files
  - The /lac switch specifies that is a non-domain account to be migrated does not exist, it will be created
  - The /lae switch enables all migrated users
  - An extra custom .xml was called (exclude.xml) that excluded information from the c:/drivers and c:/I386 directories from being migrated

4.3 Difficulties

The main issue with utilizing USB hard drives was the "updateability". Since we were making frequent changes to the scan.bat and load.bat scripts it became a tedious process to then update the technician's drives each and every time.

Depending on the environment, one potential flaw with using USB hard drives for storage is the security risk. Portable hard drives are, by definition, portable and thus have a high risk of being lost or stolen. Since these drives contain personal data which could include sensitive or confidential information, it was in our best interest to find an improved solution. Another issue with USB drives occurs because they are swapped from computer to computer increasing the risk of data contamination which includes viruses and other malicious or accidental modification.

USMT does provide a method of encryption, however since our scripts and data storage resided together we saw this as unnecessary. More information about USMT encryption can be found at the link below:

http://technet.microsoft.com/en-us/library/dd560781(WS.10).aspx#BKMK_StorageOptions

5. Implementation Phase

We were quite happy with the results from our first phase, having verified that USMT successfully met our needs. It proved to us that it was essential to devise an approach that didn't require carrying around portable drives; it was also clear that we didn't want to primarily use USB flash drives as a means to run the scripts, due to the challenges of keeping those scripts up to date. However, in certain circumstances, USB hard drives and USB flash drives are valued methods for utilizing USMT.

5.1 Network Storage

The natural progression for our USMT initiative was to move our scripts and data storage off to a server since our main points of discontent resided around local storage.

Another question that arose around this time was how to manage the data. We changed from portable drives to network storage to circumvent the access of user data but this left us collecting excessive amounts of data. We devised a system that took several variables into account:

- Average size of each users
- How long we should keep user data
- Max # of system rebuilds at a given time

Once we identified each of these points we could then submit a request to the network team for server space. This also led us to decide how frequently we should purge data from this network location. We concluded to do so on the first of every month.

$$\begin{aligned} &\mathit{Total\ Server\ Space\ needed} \\ &\qquad = \mathit{Average\ size\ of\ data} \\ &\qquad \times \mathit{Max\ \#\ of\ systems} \end{aligned}$$

5.2 Scripting

The scripts to enable network storage of migration data were practically identical to those used for local storage. The main difference was the specification of network storage. This new network storage location was created on our EMC SAN and access was given only to STS technicians.

We did create two new supplemental scripts at this stage. Up to this point we had no need for 64-bit migration. We were primarily moving data from WinXP to Win7 but using the x86 OS versions on both machines. The new scripts were identical, only changing the directory of the supporting files being copied to the local machine for ScanState and LoadState. Both sets of supporting files are located in the USMT folder of the AIK install.

x86 :

```
\\ServerShare\USMT\x86\scanstate
%dletter%:\USMT\Capture\%computername%
```

x64:

```
\\ServerShare\USMT\amd64\scanstate
%dletter%:\USMT\Capture\%computername%
```

6. Production

During the course of our implementation stage we had already seen a huge benefit from time savings alone. The technicians were spending an average of 90 minutes per deploy/redeploy solely on data migration. This process requires constant attention and one can easily miss single files or even large swathes of data. USMT asks for very little user intervention, which allows the technician to focus on computer personalization or other tasks altogether. In turn, the smaller amount of time that the technician needed with either the new or older computer, the less downtime the user experienced.

6.1 Automation

We found that running USMT on the source machine "over night" (at the end of the day) was the most efficient way to maximize productivity and it also had the least amount of impact on the client. This spawned the idea to have an even further automated solution; starting the ScanState as well as the LoadState at the same time and thus being able to "set it and forget it".

6.2 Scripting

The major change in our production scripts was the implementation of the LoadState automation. This was accomplished by starting both scripts simultaneously: scan.bat on the source machine and load.bat on the new machine. We then used the load.bat script to monitor the log file created by the ScanState process. We periodically searched the file for a specific line indicating that the process had completed. Once that line was found, the script would continue on just as it would in our implementation phase.

Another change was the addition of error checking. We added a check to see if the computer name that was provided by the technician actually existed on the server. Since we are primarily running this script after hours, this new check would prevent a possible error later on that would prevent the migration. If needed, it would then ask the technician to re-enter the computer name if it is not found. The new automated load.bat did the following:

- Set a user variable for the ScanState check
- Queried the user for the computer name of the source machine
- Checked to make sure that directory exists
- Copied the scripts and supporting files to the local machine
- Checked to see if the ScanState process had finished
    - If not, it waits and checks again
    - If so, it proceeds with the usual LoadState script
- Ran LoadState and .xml files
    - The /lac switch specifies that is a non-domain account to be migrated does not exist, it will be created
    - The /lae switch enables all migrated users
    - An extra custom .xml was called (exclude.xml) that excluded information from the c:/drivers and c:/I386 directories from being migrated

```
@ECHO OFF
REM Setting variable to check if scanstate has finished
set finished=no

REM Get computer name from Scanned machine and set as
variable
ECHO.
set /p comp_name="Enter Computer Name of captured machine
and press Enter: "
ECHO.

:foldercheck
REM Check to see if that folder exists on the server
if not exist \\SeverShare\USMT\Capture\%comp_name% (goto
resetvar) else (goto copy)

:resetvar
REM Allow the user to re-enter folder name
ECHO That Computer name does not exsist.
ECHO.
set /p comp_name="Enter Computer Name of captured machine
and press Enter: "
@ECHO OFF
goto foldercheck

:copy
REM Copy server files to a local folder
ECHO Copy files to local directory c:\usmt
xcopy \\ServerShare\USMT\x86\*.* /e /v /y /i C:\USMT\x86
xcopy \\ServerShare\USMT\sleep\*.* /e /v /y /i
C:\Windows\System32
REM Change to local directory
ECHO Changing to local directory c:\usmt
Cd c:\usmt\x86\

:top
REM Check to see if scanstate is finished.  if yes begin
loadstate, if no wait and check again.
if %finished% ==no (goto look) else (goto load)

:look
REM look for success line in scanstate log.  If found
reset variable, if not wait and retry.
ECHO Looking for confirmation that Scanstate has ended
findstr /C:"MIGACTIVITY_SUCCESS"
\\ServerShare\USMT\Logs\%comp_name%scan.log
if %errorlevel% ==0 (set finished=yes) else (ECHO
Scanstate is not complete)
if %finished% ==no (set var=5) else (goto load)
sleep 10 /quiet
goto wait

:load
ECHO Running Loadstate
REM Run Loadstate and pull capture file from the server
created from Scanstate
REM Pull file from server based on computer name given by
user
REM Save log of Loadstate to server
ECHO Begin Loadstate Migration for %comp_name%
c:\usmt\x86\loadstate
\\ServerShare\USMT\Capture\%comp_name%
/l:\\ServerShare\USMT\Logs\%comp_name%load.log /c /lac
/lae /config:config.xml /i:exclude.xml /i:migapp.xml
/i:migdocs.xml /v:13
REM Wait for user to see that the process finished
successfully
pause

:wait
REM Display 5 minute countdown to user while waiting for
recheck
REM clear screen to remove extra lines after multiple
tries.
cls
ECHO %var% minutes remiaing before recheck....
if %var% ==0 (goto top) else (sleep 60 /quiet)
set /A var-=1
goto wait

:EOF
```

6.3 Script Maintenance

At this stage we have a total of six scripts that are in production:

- x86 Scan and Load
- x64 Scan and Load
- x86 and x64 Automated Load

Since we are deploying mostly 64-bit operating systems and the large majority of retiring computers are 32-bit, we must keep all 6 scripts up-to-date. Since they are all housed on the network share it is quite easy to make any changes necessary.

6.4 Packaged Data - MIG File

We have set the Scan process to store the captured data in a self-contained compressed file. This seems easier to manage than the unpackaged raw data structure that we had previously produced using the /nocompress switch. This method also gives some illusion or deterrent from looking at user data because it's not readily accessible. USMT provides the MIG Recovery tool, which is very straightforward and allows you to take the packaged .MIG file and unpack it to any location you need without running the full LoadState command.

6.5 Logs

Another helpful USMT component is the creation of the log files. USMT automatically creates a scan and load log for each machine. This is helpful when researching any issues that arise. We find it useful to save all log files as a sort of inventory of past deploys. These can, of course, can be purged at anytime if they're not wanted.

7. Conclusion and Future

To conclude, USMT has been a great tool and resource for our department. We are able to provide a quicker and more precise migration for our users. Since USMT also captures customizations such as Outlook settings and profile desktop pictures, the user is getting a much more consistent experience and therefore can be more productive out of the gate. The technicians are also a great deal more productive as less time is spent with manual processes.

The automated/overnight stage was our most recent endeavor which has seemed to pay off dividends. In the foreseeable future our USMT project could coincide more with another departmental undertaking. Sloan, as also seen across the industry, is relying more heavily on virtual machines. Our next steps with USMT will involve manipulating our current methods into the use of migrating desktops to virtual machines/thin clients.

8. REFERENCES

[1] MIT Facts 2011: Faculty and Staff. Retrieved June 1, 2011, from http://web.mit.edu/facts/faculty.html

[2] MIT Facts 2011: Enrollment 2010-2011. Retrieved June 1, 2011, from http://web.mit.edu/facts/enrollment.html

[3] Best Undergraduate Business Programs. U.S. News & World Report. 2010. Retrieved June 1, 2011, from http://colleges.usnews.rankingsandreviews.com/best-colleges/rankings/business-overall

[4] Best Business Schools. U.S. News & World Report. 2011. Retrieved June 1, 2011, from http://en.wikipedia.org/wiki/U.S._News_%26_World_Report

[5] Microsoft TechNet. (2009). User State Migration Tool 4.0 User's Guide. Introduction to USMT 4.0. Retrieved May 25, 2011, from http://technet.microsoft.com/en-us/library/dd560801(WS.10).aspx

[6] Microsoft TechNet. Windows Automated Installation Kit (Windows AIK) User's Guide. Retrieved May 25, 2011, from http://technet.microsoft.com/en-us/library/cc749528(WS.10).aspx

[7] The Windows Automated Installation Kit (AIK) for Windows 7. http://www.microsoft.com/downloads/en/details.aspx?FamilyID=696dd665-9f76-4177-a811-39c26d3b3b34&displaylang=en

The Mission – Teaming with Microsoft and Adobe for Licensing

Michael Cooper
West Virginia University
P.O. Box 6357
Morgantown, WV 26506
(304) 293-0777
mhcooper@mail.wvu.edu

ABSTRACT

If you are involved in software licensing and distribution, you will most always deal with two top-tier publishers--Microsoft and Adobe. Students and employees at your school will want to use leading edge technology software from these companies to accomplish their work. It is your task to find the best opportunities for cost savings and delivery methods for the greatest use of these products. Available licensing programs from these publishers can be difficult to understand because of contractual commitments and misunderstood complexities. Licensing criteria for purchasing and distributing is different for each of these publishers. Do you need product support? How do Microsoft and Adobe offerings compare with "open source" products? Are the same products adequate for institutional and student use? What about virtualization and cloud licensing? This calls for teamwork involving you, the publishers, resellers, your institution, and end-users. Let us explore what you need for effective software licensing and distribution of Microsoft and Adobe products and contain costs, establish product use standards, and provide long-term organizational benefits.

Categories and Subject Descriptors

K.6.3 Software Management: Software Selection

General Terms

Management, Economics, Standardization, Legal Aspects.

Keywords

Licensing, Software Distribution, Software Acquisition

1. INTRODUCTION

Microsoft and Adobe are large prolific publishers of software titles that permeate the operating system and productivity suites available on the market today. Almost every institution will find that these publishers will have made inroads into their departments. In some cases these publishers will be the exclusive product being utilized throughout the institution. Microsoft and Adobe have competitors but their products are well developed and deliver a significant set of features. Software publishers are constantly changing their product and licensing procedures. With that in mind, many of the references in this document are subject to change. However, the basic principles should remain the same. It is incumbent upon the user to constantly monitor the publisher's websites for changes. These publishers reserve their right to change any of their licensing terms and conditions by simply posting new terms to their websites. There is no requirement to formally notify end users of these changes. Teaming with these publishers will require you to deal with a wide range of decisions and actions to implement those decisions. The extent and complexity of your implementation is dependent upon a few key factors which may be different for each publisher. These publishers may be willing to offer your institution non-standard terms and conditions. That makes it very important to always maintain a close working relationship with the publisher's representatives. Before you move forward with any licensing decisions, please review the SIGUCCS 2010 paper titled "Charting a Course for Software Licensing and Distribution".[1]

2. Microsoft

Microsoft publishes a wide array of operating systems, applications, and productivity software. Educational institutions have many avenues to explore regarding licensing of Microsoft products. The most prevalent product that most people are aware of is the operating systems for desktops and server platforms. In addition there are many server applications such as Exchange, MS SQL Server, and SharePoint that might be utilized, Additional utilities such as System Management Center for servers and MS Windows Desktop Optimization Pack and many more expand the offerings. Microsoft seems to lean toward unbundling various components. This is good if you only need a certain product. However, be cautioned that those individual components can be costly and it is easy to forget to acquire a component that might be important to your environment.

2.1 Licensing Options

Microsoft products can be licensed in many different ways. The first decision to make is whether to license centrally or license individual copies of products. If the products being licensed are widely used across multiple disciplines then centralized licensing is appropriate. There are multiple options for centralized licensing. Let's look at the options that involve volume purchases and/or commitments for purchasing multiple copies over a period of time.

2.1.1 Microsoft Open Licensing

Open licensing requires an initial purchase of just five licenses of any type. Additional orders can be placed in quantities as low as one unit. Software assurance can be included. The term of the Open license authorization is two years. Licenses are managed through a website called eOPEN.

2.1.2 Microsoft Select Plus Licensing

Select Plus for Academic is the newest transactional program. It is best suited for institutions with 250 or more PCs and is a good compliment for products not covered by a Microsoft Volume Licensing Enrollment for Education Solutions (EES). Select Plus for Academic offers the advantages of a non-expiring agreement, the flexibility to acquire licenses as needed, a single customer ID to streamline account management across multiple affiliates, student licensing through Student Select Plus, and the ability to add value with a full 36 months of Software Assurance. Select Plus for Academic is available through an Authorized Education Large Account Reseller (LAR).

2.1.3 Microsoft Volume Licensing Enrollment for Education Solutions (EES)

With subscription licensing programs, you have the right to run a selection of products, and any upgrades or downgrades of those products, for a designated term. A subset of products including specific application, system, and Client Access License (CAL) products, designated by Microsoft as "desktop platform products," are licensed on an organization-wide basis. For these "desktop platform products" you will place an order for a quantity that is equal to the number of Full-time Equivalent (FTE) employees in your organization once per year. This way even if the number of devices or users grows, you remain fully licensed throughout the designated term, and you only need to report an increase in the number of your FTE employees on your annual order. EES offers the simplicity of licensing desktop platform products organization-wide through an annual count of people instead of PCs/devices and the flexibility to add additional products in any quantity. You may obtain EES subscription licenses one of two ways depending on the size of your organization. Institutions with as few as five (5) Full-time Equivalent (FTE) employees can license through an Authorized Education Reseller (AER) by signing the simplified Open Value Subscription Agreement for Education Solutions, online e-agreement. Larger institutions with a minimum of 1,000 FTE employees may also license through a Large Account Reseller (LAR) by signing the Campus and School Agreement and the Enrollment for Education Solutions.

3. Microsoft Reference Documents

There are many Microsoft documents available that describe in great detail the licensing options. These documents are updated often and the links may change from those listed. These are listed here to provide a beginning point for you to stay abreast of the myriad of options available for licensing Microsoft products.

3.1 Microsoft Document Library

http://www.microsoft.com/licensing/about-licensing/document-library.aspx?filter=Industries: Charity, Education, Government, Health

This is an excellent set of documents that describe the various licensing methods.

3.2 Core CAL (Client Access License) Descriptions

Exchange Enterprise & Standard Cal
http://www.microsoft.com/exchange/en-us/licensing-exchange-server-email.aspx

SharePoint Enterprise & Standard Cal
http://sharepoint.microsoft.com/en-us/buy/Pages/Licensing-Details.aspx
http://sharepoint.microsoft.com/en-us/buy/Pages/Editions-Comparison.aspx

Lync Standard & Enterprise
http://lync.microsoft.com/en-us/HowToBuy/Pages/pricing-licensing.aspx

These documents explain the different features of the various product Cal's.

3.3 CAL Suites

http://www.microsoft.com/calsuites/en/us/products/default.aspx

This document lists the various CALs included in the Core Cal and Enterprise Cal Suites

4. Microsoft Cloud Licensing

Microsoft continues to enhance its licensing options for cloud based applications. Enhancements to the subscription based licensing helps to transition to cloud services at your own pace and move users back and forth between on-premises software and cloud services. You can easily add and adjust new online service users above your contractual commitment. For instance you can purchase a subscription service that is added to your Exchange licensing to allow third party hosting of your Exchange servers in the cloud. Microsoft is introducing new products and services to better accommodate cloud computing simply because of the demand for these services and the ever increasing competition in this marketplace.

5. Microsoft Licensing for Virtualization

Server hardware virtualization uses software to create a Virtual Machine (VM) that emulates a physical computer. This creates a separate OS environment that is logically isolated from the host server. By providing multiple VMs at once, this approach allows several operating systems to run simultaneously on a single physical machine. Rather than paying for many under-utilized server machines, each VM is dedicated to a specific workload. Server virtualization allows those workloads to be consolidated onto a smaller number of more fully-used machines. Microsoft

Virtual Desktop Infrastructure (VDI) is an alternative desktop delivery model that allows users to access secure and centrally-managed desktops running in the datacenter. This is an area that Microsoft has recently made significant improvements. Licensing better defined and suited to meet the needs of an institution that is implementing virtualization.

6. Microsoft Licensing for Students and Employees

Microsoft provides many options for licensing and distributing its software to students and employees. Most of these options are a part of a Select Plus or Enrollment for Education Solutions agreements. There is usually no additional cost for the Select Plus options for students. The Enrollment for Education Solutions for students requires a significant additional cost per FTE student. Work at Home rights and Home Use Rights provide vehicles for distributing Microsoft software to employees.

7. Adobe

Adobe publishes a wide array of applications and creativity suites that are used in a variety of setting in an education institution. From the Acrobat to Creative suites, to the Photoshop family, Adobe publishes just about any kind of software you need to create a document, a drawing, edit a picture, create a DVD, edit video, create a website, create and manage website content, and many more solutions. As with Microsoft Educational institutions have many avenues to explore regarding licensing of Adobe products. These methods follow a similar scheme as with Microsoft but with a more defined path. The methods are simplified into two options: transactional and contractual.

7.1 Adobe Licensing Options

Adobe products can be licensed in many different ways. The first decision again to make is whether to license centrally or license individual copies of products. If the products being licensed are widely used across multiple disciplines then centralized licensing is appropriate. With Adobe There are two options for centralized licensing. Let's look at the options that involve volume purchases and/or commitments for purchasing multiple copies over a period of time.

7.1.1 Adobe Transactional Purchase

This form of licensing involves making a volume purchase of a product on a single purchase. The pricing is based upon the volume associated with this single purchase. Resellers base their pricing upon the Adobe list pricing for specific quantities and their overall volume for Adobe products. This a is a good method for purchasing titles in quantity and then distributing them over time or just making a single volume purchase for a specific implementation. This method of purchase provides a savings over retail and shrink-wrapped education software with one easy purchase. There is no minimum order quantity required. You receive timely notifications of new upgrades with if an Upgrade Plan was purchased. The purchase is made through your local education reseller. Adobe uses a point system to determine your discount level. A calculator for this is located at: http://www.adobe.com/aboutadobe/volumelicense/calculator/avl.html

7.1.2 Adobe Cumulative Licensing Program (CLP) 5 for education

Your institution can enjoy significant saving with Adobe's Cumulative Licensing Program (CLP) version 5, your institution purchases volume software licenses over a two-year membership period. Not only do your software orders provide cumulative savings, but CLP 5 also helps your institution streamline software management with centralized tools to track your Adobe software volume licenses. All qualified orders of any size throughout the two-year membership term earn the same—or a better—discount level. Orders accumulate points, and as your cumulative point total increases, so does your potential savings. With CLP 5, your institution can also extend membership benefits to its affiliates. Member and affiliate purchases contribute toward the overall discount level, offering maximum savings. As a CLP 5 member, you can easily track and manage your software licenses through Adobe's easy-to-use, password-protected Licensing Web Site (LWS). This portal enables you to run reports, track order history, access serial numbers, and download available software from one central location. CLP members are assigned a single CLP 5 agreement number for all orders placed throughout the two-year period so you can easily access a permanent, ongoing record of all your Adobe volume software licenses online. In addition, IT staff and other designated members of your organization can be assigned their own unique login to Adobe's LWS to easily download and then deploy Adobe software to multiple users in various departments and locations across your institution.

7.1.3 Adobe Term Site Licensing Program

The Adobe Term Site License (TSL) offering is available exclusively to higher education CLP members. This program enables members to license selected Adobe education software products throughout the qualified site for a given period of time, or term. The TSL agreement can be initiated at any time during the CLP membership and will become coterminous with the end of the CLP membership period. Proration of the two-year term is available, allowing for a TSL term of 6 to 24 months, depending on when the TSL is initiated during the CLP membership term. Pricing for higher education TSL is based on Full Time Equivalent (FTE) staff, which is calculated based on the number of full- and part-time faculty and staff within the site. With this program you license selected Adobe education software products within a given time frame for an entire site with no need to account for each faculty or staff member's software use. The TSL contributes to your overall CLP education point total. You receive all updates and upgrades to the covered software during the term of the agreement (Upgrade Plan is included in TSL pricing). There is no need to track agreement expiration dates, since TSL will become coterminous with the CLP membership period.

7.1.4 Adobe Student and Teacher Licensing Program

The Adobe Student and Teacher Licensing Program enables your institution with a CLP 5 membership agreement to buy Adobe education products for distribution to their students, faculty, and staff. Distribution of the education products is at the discretion of the school, which may choose to manage the process itself through an Adobe reseller or work with an Adobe authorized reseller to get a website set up where the students can access and purchase the licenses. Under this program, students, faculty, and staff own the Adobe education software licenses and can use the products outside the classroom. Although the education products licensed by the institution become the property of the individual, the total point values accumulated from purchases are credited to the higher education institution's CLP membership total.

8. Adobe Products in a Virtualized Environment

Guest OS installations are considered separate installations and require licensing separate from any licenses installed on standard supported OS environments. If the product is installed on a server all computers that have access to the server must be licensed for the Adobe solution. All usage of the Adobe solution must conform to the End –User License Agreement.

9. Adobe Concurrent Licensing

Unlike Microsoft Adobe offers concurrent licensing. Concurrent licensing allows the institution to use a single license to distribute the software to multiple users as long as only one user is utilizing the software at any given point in time. This requires the use of a key server to ensure that only one copy is in use. Adobe prefers that the SASSAFRAS key server is utilized. (http://www.sassafras.com/licensing.html)

10. Adobe Reference Documents

Adobe Transactional Licensing

http://www.adobe.com/aboutadobe/volumelicensing/tlp/

Adobe Cumulative Licensing

http://www.adobe.com/aboutadobe/volumelicensing/clp/

11. Adobe and Microsoft Licensing at West Virginia University (WVU)

WVU utilizes a combination of Select Plus and ESS for its Microsoft licensing. The ESS is utilized for the Desktop suite which includes MS Office and the desktop OS. The ESS also includes the core CAL suite along with Software Assurance. WVU adds the Visual Studio Suite to the ESS agreement. All other Microsoft products are purchased thru the Microsoft Select Plus agreement. Work at Home rights is used for employees for the OS and Microsoft Office. Students are covered under the Select Plus and order software from a reseller at a significant discount. The Microsoft contracts are administered by a state wide higher education consortium. Adobe products are acquired thru an Adobe CLP agreement. The product is distributed and tracked from a central location. Students and employees utilize the Adobe Student and Teacher option for purchasing Adobe products. This distribution is handled by a reseller.

12. Summary

Centralized software licensing and distribution for Microsoft and Adobe products can be a vehicle for cost savings. It is also a great vehicle to use to increase product usage, drive standardization, and reduce support. The decision to centralize software licensing should not be made without exploring its many factors. Understanding of licensing terms and conditions will be crucial to effectively managing the program. Publishers constantly change their licensing programs and you need to become aware of those changes in a timely fashion. Your client base will demand that new products are made available and you will need to evaluate if these new products are appropriate for centralized licensing. The key factors to weigh are volume and cost savings. The reseller and publisher representatives will become your most sought after consultants. You will be sharpening your business expertise on a daily basis. Ultimately the outcome will be a significant cost savings for your institution and greatly increased availability of software for your employees and students.

13. REFERENCES

[1] Cooper, Michael. 2010. **Charting a Course for Software Licensing and Distribution**. In Proceedings of the 38th annual ACM SIGUCCS conference on User services conference Norfolk, VA, USA, *October 24 - 27, 2010*). SESSION: 8 (Tuesday, 10:30 am), Pages 153-156, Year of Publication: 2010, **ISBN: 978-1-4503-0003-2**, http://doi.acm.org/**10.1145/1878335.1878375**

Information and Communication Technology Infrastructure and Management for Collaboration with Regional Universities and Colleges

Takashi Yamanoue
Kagoshima University
Korimoto, Kagoshima 890-0034, Japan
+81-99-285-7187
yamanoue@cc.kagoshima-u.ac.jp

Masayasu Hidaka
Kagoshima University
hidaka@fish.kagoshima-u.ac.jp

Akira Takenoshita
Kagoshima Immaculate Heart University
k4586491@kadai.jp

Koji Yukawa
International University of Kagoshima
yukawa@ofc.iuk.ac.jp

Yuichi Yamanaka
Kagoshima University
yamanaka@fish.kagoshima-u.ac.jp

Hiroyuki Seto
Kagoshima Women's Junior College
hiset@jkajyo.ac.jp

Noritaka Oto
International University of Kagoshima
n-ooto@ofc.iuk.ac.jp

Robert J. Fouser
Seoul National University
Seoul, Korea
fouser@snu.ac.kr

Yusei Suzuki
Shigakukan University
yousay@shigakukan.ac.jp

Yutoku Beppu
National Institute of Fitness and Sports in Kanoya
beppu@nifs-k.ac.jp

Holmes Rodriguez
Universidad de Antioquia
holmesrodriguez@agronica.udea.edu.co

Toshihiko Okamura
Kagoshima Prefectural College
okamura@biz-kpc.net

Kazuhide Dogome
Kagoshima National College of Technology
dougome@kagoshima-ct.ac.jp

Masakazu Ito
Kagoshima University
showa@sci.kagoshima-u.ac.jp

Tomohito Wada
National Institute of Fitness and Sports in Kanoya
wada@nifs-k.ac.jp

Masaharu Terada
Kagoshima University
t-ict@kuas.kagoshima-u.ac.jp

Yoko Nedachi
Kagoshima Immaculate Heart University
nedachi@jundai.k-junshin.ac.jp

Katsuyuki Suenaga
Kagoshima Immaculate Heart College
sue@juntan.k-junshin.ac.jp

Anne Elizabeth Brasier
Kagoshima University
k9803751@kadai.jp

Takeshi Yamada
Daiichi Institute of Technology
t-yamada@daiichi-koudai.ac.jp

Munetomo Nedachi
Kagoshima University
k7201433@kadai.jp

ABSTRACT

Information and Communication Technology (ICT) infrastructure for collaboration with regional universities and colleges, and management are discussed. The infrastructure consisted of Moodle servers at each institution, Moodle Lite, backup servers, test servers, a Video On Demand (VOD) server, a video meeting system, and other supporting systems. ICT infrastructure was designed and managed by a committee in charge of the collaboration. Members of the committee consisted of fifteen faculty members from each institution in the collaboration. Five technical support staff members were employed for managing the infrastructure.

SIGUCCS'11, November 12–17, 2011, San Diego, California, USA.

Categories and Subject Descriptors

K.3.1 [**Computer uses in Education**]: Collaborative learning – *distance learning, project and people management.*

General Terms

Design, Management, Experimentation

Keywords

ICT Infrastructure, e-learning, Moodle, ubiquitous computing, collaboration

1. INTRODUCTION

The project "Kagoshima is One Campus: Collaboration among Universities and Construction of General Education for Development of Regional Leaders" was selected as part of a program to support projects for strategic university collaborations by the Ministry of Education, Culture, Sports, Science and Technology (MEXT) of Japan in 2008. This project aimed to create an intellectual center for the development of leaders who contribute to regional development with passion, from a "Glocal" perspective, regarding the Kagoshima area as one campus, receiving aid from the regional government and collaborating with universities and colleges in Kagoshima prefecture in Japan. Ten universities and colleges in Kagoshima (member schools) collaborated for three years using ICT infrastructure. The purpose of the collaboration included constructing a new system for general education for 1st and 2nd year students. Seven sub-committees were organized to run this project.

ICT infrastructure was one of the most important means to achieve this goal. The committee for "ICT Utilization," which is one of the seven committees, was in charge of ICT infrastructure. We were members of the committee.

We planned, constructed, and managed ICT infrastructure for collaboration with member schools. The infrastructure consisted of Moodle servers at each institution, Moodle Lite, backup servers, test servers, a VOD server, a video meeting system, and other support systems.

The committee was comprised of fifteen faculty members from each institution that participated in the collaboration. Five technical support staff members were employed for managing the infrastructure. We outsourced the management of Moodle servers.

Since the support period ended, we have continued to manage the ICT infrastructure by ourselves.

2. ICT INFRASTRUCTRE

Figure 1 shows an outline of the ICT Infrastructure of the project. Moodle[7] is the central function of the infrastructure. At least one Moodle server was placed at every university or college. Moodle Lite[4], a Moodle system for mobile phones and devices, was also implemented on each Moodle server. Moodle and Moodle Lite share the same courses. Figure 2 shows a picture of a mobile phone using Moodle Lite. The Application Service Provider (ASP) server is also a Moodle server with Moodle Lite. It was used for sharing common courses with all member schools. This was also used for courses open to the public. The ASP server can be accessed from Moodle at member schools without re-login. It is realized by Moodle network and is a distributed server system. The backup server was used for backing up the course data of Moodle at member schools. A wireless LAN system was placed or enhanced at all member schools in order to use laptop PCs in regular, non-computer-laboratory classrooms.

The VOD server was used for sharing videos of lectures among member schools, while the video meeting system was implemented to conduct project meetings and share lectures among member schools.

Moodle Lite can be used on mobile phones or other mobile devices in regular classrooms without computers. This enables ubiquitous e-learning without PCs. More than that, students can access Moodle outside of the campus during fieldwork projects or while commuting between their home and campus. It can also be used as a clicker, an audience response system, in the classroom.

3. MANAGEMENT AND PROCESS

Figure 3 shows a structure of organizations for the project. Council meetings were held when the project started, ended and when other important events happened. Head office meetings were held about twice a year to decide the basic plan and budget of the project.

Missions of the committee for ICT utilization were as follows:

- Establish environment for using Moodle and system for promoting use of Moodle.
- Construct educational network.
- Lead supporting staff for ICT utilization and management.
- Hold training courses for teaching staff.
- Implement the video meeting system.

3.1 Fiscal year of 2008

Meetings

We had meetings to discuss the following in order to carry out the project.

2008

- October: Choosing the chair and vice chairs, deciding to place savers with same version of OS.
- November: Choosing servers, employing supporting stuff, considering the budget of 2009.
- December: Deciding the specification of servers and ordering servers, installing Moodle, selecting Moodle support company and the video meeting system.

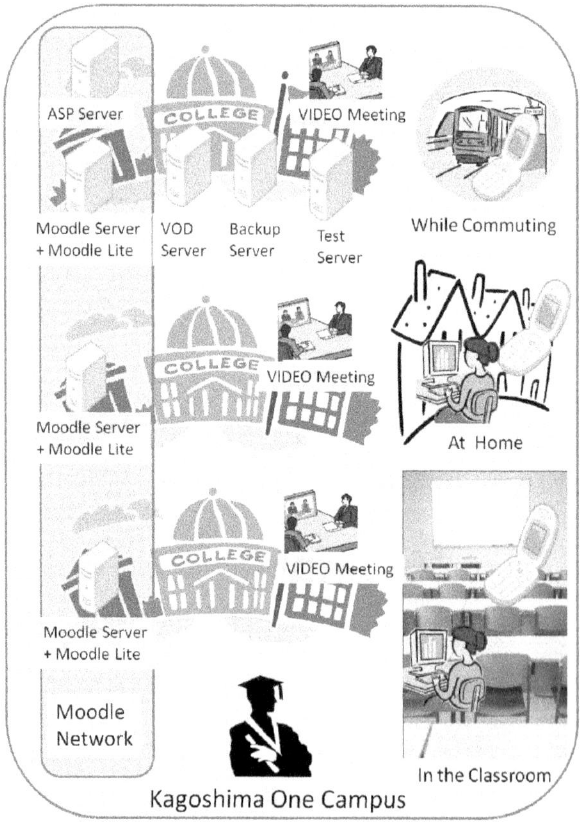

Figure 1. Outline of ICT infrastructure

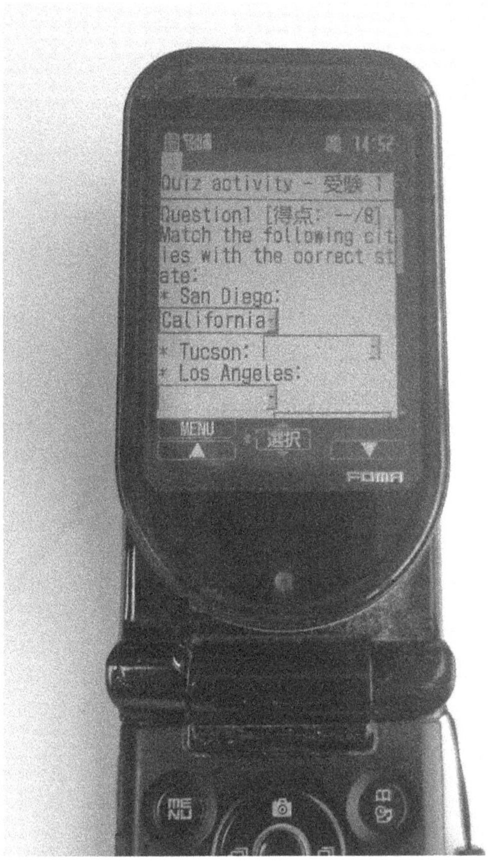

Figure 2. A screen shot of Moodle Lite.

Figure 3. Structure of organizations for the project.

2009

- January: Topics considered included: Moodle supporting company, responsibilities of supporting staff, the budget of 2009.
- February: Topics considered included: the video meeting system, the contract with supporting and management of Moodle, goal of usage of Moodle, surveying students' environment for usage of PCs and mobile phones, support staff, the pamphlet for freshmen, management of Moodle.

Activity

The following activities were carried out by the committee in this fiscal year:

- Installed or enhanced wireless LAN systems in each member school.
- Employed five technical support staff members in charge of the following:
  - Register students in Moodle
  - Make courses in Moodle
  - Help faculties to use Moodle
  - Support training course of Moodle
  - Support to make videos for VOD
  - Support to use the video meeting system
  - Maintain servers
  - Take part in the meetings of the committee as auditors

  The technical support staff members were based within four member schools. However, they had responsibility to look after all other member schools. They had meetings frequently to carry out their work and to share information. The video meeting system was used for conducting meetings after the system was installed.
- Contracted with a Moodle support company who maintain Moodle, add new modules to Moodle and so on.
- Surveyed current ubiquitous computing environments and students' motivation. Figures 4a, 4b, and 4c show the results. About 75% of students responded that having a PC is necessary for study. Almost all students responded that a PC is convenient. However, 1.5% of students responded that they do not need a PC because they have mobile phones or refer to physical bulletin boards. More than 50% of students had their own PC. About 30% of them shared a PC with their family. Nine percent of students had no PC, and 0.1% of students had no mobile phone.
- Installed the video meeting system. This system saved time and money associated with project committee meetings.
- Promoted to use Moodle by holding six training courses at different member schools. Almost all teaching staff participated in the course at one school.

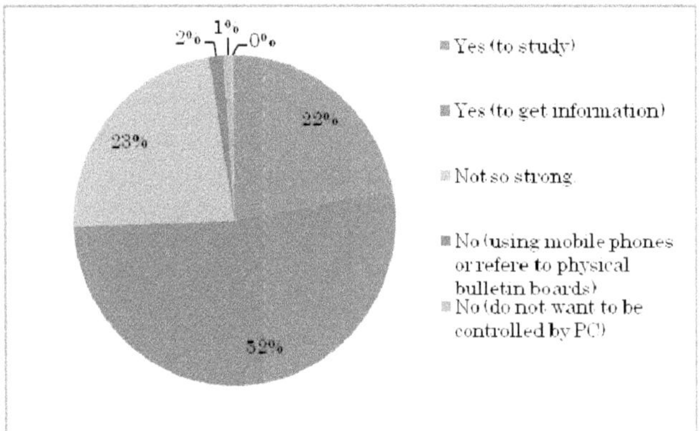

Figure 4a. The survey of ubiquitous computing environments and students' motivation, 2008. "Do you require PC for your studies?" (3126 students total)

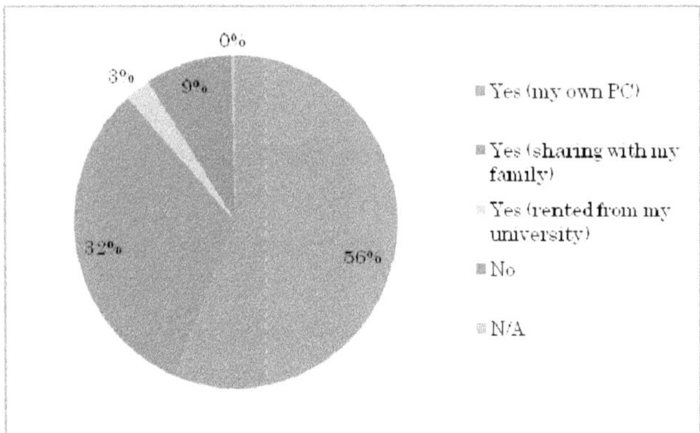

Figure 4b. The survey of ubiquitous computing environments and students' motivation, 2008. "Do you have a PC?" (3106 students total)

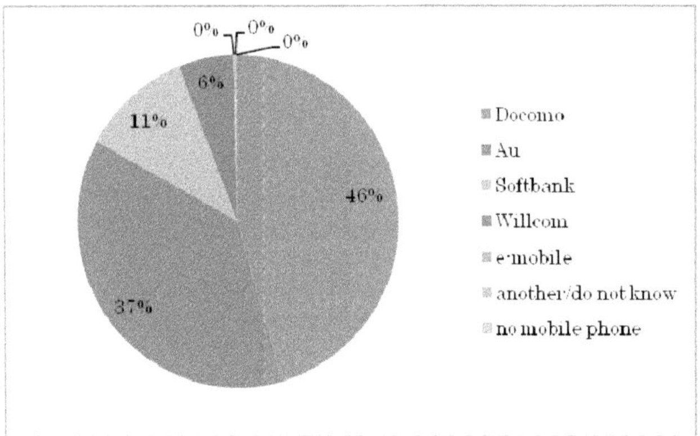

Figure 4c. The survey of ubiquitous computing environments and students' motivation, 2008. "Which is your mobile phone service provider?" (3370 students total)

3.2 Fiscal year of 2009

The following were planned in the fiscal year of 2009:

- Install or enhance wireless LAN system at each member school.
- Prepare learning environment for use of Moodle.
- Hold training courses and establish a help desk for Moodle.
- Support the development of a broad range of lecture content that would enhance ICT literacy of students.
- Periodic maintenance of Moodle; add and correct Moodle modules
- Survey environment of ICT usage twice yearly.
- Research use of Moodle at other universities.

Meetings

The committee met to discuss the following:

2009

- April: Topics included: backup of Moodle servers of member schools, the management of video meeting system, course categories of Moodle, correct order of first and last name for use with Japanese names on Moodle.
- June: Topics included: management of Moodle, considering management of video meeting system, promoting use of the VOD and status of lecture recordings, the current usage trends of Moodle.
- September: Topics included: maintenance of the VOD system, relationship between this committee and other committees, holding an overnight research retreat, confirming the progress of the mission.
- December: Topics included: communication between the board and the committee, confirming the progress of the mission, the next steps, planning to have surveys.

2010

- March: Topics included: Planning the budget of the forthcoming year, confirming the progress of the survey, collaboration with the College Education Committee, for continuation of the project after MEXT support ends.

Activity

- Installed or enhanced wireless LAN systems at schools which could not be installed during the previous fiscal year.
- Moodle could be used at all member schools by September. All general education classes were registered at some member schools. In May 2010 the number of modules registered was 7625 and by February 2011 this number had grown to over 14,000.
- Constructed a test environment for Moodle network.
- Revised Moodle Lite.
- Constructed the VOD server. It was a high availability server using mirroring servers.
- Constructed the test server for test new modules of Moodle.
- Started to operate the ASP server.
- Constructed the backup server for backup contents of Moodle for preventive measures against potential main saver troubles.
- Carried out various tests, such as the test of updated Moodle Lite modules.

- Held a training course for use of the VOD system. A mailing list for the VOD system was also created.
- Held a workshop to use Moodle on December with the committee for FD-SD activity. There were 60 participants. Held training courses of Moodle at all member schools. During the time period, a total 24 courses were held, involving a total of 240 participants.
- Made videos of selected lectures for the video on demand server. Total duration was over one hundred hours. Fifty-five courses for basic scholastic ability and remote education had been made.
- Surveyed general education classes using Moodle at some member schools.
- Maintained Moodle periodically and some Modules were embedded in Moodle. Emergency updates took place four times.
- Surveyed current ubiquitous computing environment and students' needs twice. Moodle was used to carry out a part of this survey.
- Studied usage of Moodle at other universities.
- Corresponded with users and the dealer of the video meeting system when it developed mechanical faults.

3.3 Fiscal year of 2010

Same items, except without the item for wireless LAN, were planned as fiscal year of 2009

Meetings

The committee had meetings to discuss the following:

2010

- June: Confirming the plan for the year, considering the plan after the support.
- October: Considering the plan after the support, making the procedure to use the ASP server, confirming the next steps.
- November: Considering to make the report of the committee, considering to update Moodle Lite, starting to research Moodle 2.0
- December: making the report of the committee.

2011

- February: Considering plans for after the end of MEXT support.

Activity

- Wrote a manual for use and maintenance of Moodle.
- Corrected Moodle Lite. Through this update, the quiz function could be used.
- Carried out tests such as the test of updated Moodle Lite modules.
- Wrote a manual for handing over the administration of Moodle and Moodle server.
- Surveyed general education classes using Moodle at some member schools.
- Maintained Moodle periodically and some Modules were embedded in Moodle. Four emergency updates were also made.
- Surveyed current ubiquitous computing environment and students' motivation twice. Moodle was used to carry out a part of this survey. Almost all students could use e-learning outside of their school, and 99.9% of students had mobile phones. This can be a basis for the use and ongoing improvement of Moodle Lite.
- Corresponded with users and the dealer of the video meeting system when it developed mechanical faults

4. EXPERIENCES

The following positive results and problems were encountered during the project term.

4.1 Positive Results

- There was a school which registered all faculties, students and classes to Moodle from fiscal year of 2009.
- Among its many diverse utilizations, Moodle was used as a learning platform for candidates studying for the national examination for nutritionists. Moodle was also used for courses that help students to prepare for qualification examinations such as the information technology passport examination and the real estate broker exam.
- Some schools had used Moodle for the qualification update course for school teachers. There were many positive comments about the usage of Moodle by students of the course.
- Some schools used Moodle for pre-entrance education and others used Moodle for class evaluations.

4.2 Problems

- The quiz function could be used on the original Moodle Lite. However, it was impossible for us to utilize it until a certain problem was fixed in February 2011.
- When more than 30 students logged into Moodle Lite simultaneously, Moodle Lite could not respond at one school. This issue was not encountered at other schools.
- The Committee for Glocal General Education asked why it seemed that some teachers had not been able to utilize Moodle. The reason of this problem was that policies and procedures of Moodle usage were different among member schools.
- The use of Moodle did not expand so much at certain schools, even though Moodle had been made available at all member schools.
- It was hard to use the VOD system at some schools because the bandwidth of their internet connection was too narrow.
- Meeting with the video meeting system proved to be insufficient for a meaningful exchange of ideas with members.

5. RELATED WORK

"e-Knowledge Consortium Shikoku"[3] and "F-LECCS"[6] are also support projects for strategic university collaborations. They are also collaborations of regional universities and colleges. Their implementation of ICT infrastructure is also similar to ours as Moodle is used in their projects. Our project, "Kagoshima is One Campus," adopted Moodle Lite from the beginning, because one of our schools had developed it while the other projects had not used initially.

The collaboration of helpdesks of Virginia Commonwealth University and James Madison University[1] is an example of fruitful cooperation between universities. Our project also shared knowledge about the use and to maintenance of Moodle and Moodle servers among member schools. This collaboration was possible because basic hardware and software of all member schools are the same in our project.

Wainwright[2] showed how to move to Moodle, and the process to move faculty and students towards accepting Moodle as a part of not only the campus learning environment, but the campus community as a whole. Our use of Moodle is not only for the campus community but the inter-campus community.

Clickers[5] are popular nowadays for collecting feedback from students in university and college classrooms. Clickers are a simple tool to enhance classroom management. However, they regularly require maintenance such as battery replacement. Using Moodle Lite is an effective way to avoid these types of problems.

6. CONCLUDING REMARKS

This project promoted the collaboration of people who are in charge of ICT infrastructure at member schools. We have started a study group which promotes higher education with ICT infrastructure in Kagoshima. We will continue our activity using this group. As a formal organization, "Consortium Kagoshima" has been organized. A part of the project has been taken over by the consortium.

7. ACKNOWLEDGMENTS

A part of this work is supported by the support project for strategic university collaborations by the Ministry of Education, Culture, Sports, Science and Technology (MEXT) of Japan from 2008 to 2010.

8. REFERENCES

[1] Vivian Pair, Debby Boyle. 2005. Internal and external communication and collaboration: building a strong helpdesk environment. Proceedings of the 33rd annual ACM SIGUCCS fall conference. DOI=http://portal.acm.org/citation.cfm?doid=1099435.1099505

[2] Kelly Wainwright 2009. The care and feeding of a Moodle campus. SIGUCCS '09 Proceedings of the 37th annual ACM SIGUCCS fall conference, DOI=http://portal.acm.org/citation.cfm?doid=1629501.1629551

[3] Toshihiro Hayashi, Masanobu Suzuki 2009. Human Resource Development for Promoting Shikoku Region based on Integration of "Knowledge of Shikoku", IPSJ Technical Reports, Vol.2009-IOT-5 No.8

[4] Robert J. Fouser 2010. Using Computer and Mobile Tools To Support u-Learning-Based Self-Study in Teaching Korean in Japan. Proceedings of e-Learning Week 2010: Conference.

[5] Trevor Murphy, Kathy Fletcher, Amy Haston 2010. Supporting clickers on campus and the faculty who use them. Proceedings of the 38th annual fall conference on SIGUCCS. DOI=http://portal.acm.org/citation.cfm?doid=1878335.1878356

[6] Takahiro Kagoya, Toshifumi Sawazaki, Osamu Yamakawa 2011. F-LECCS: Open Platform for Virtual Learning Environments(Institutional Scope), EDUCAUSE Learning Initiative 2011 Annual Meeting, Washington, D.C. or Online February 14-16.

[7] Moodle: http://moodle.org.

Enhanced Student Technology Support with Cross-Platform Mobile Apps

Bobby Siegfried
Lehigh University
Library & Technology Services
bsiegfried@lehigh.edu

ABSTRACT

With smartphones and other web-enabled mobile devices growing quickly in popularity, higher education institutions have the opportunity – and challenge – to leverage this young medium to provide dynamic content regarding services, events, and support documentation, among others. In late 2009, Lehigh University released an iPhone app dubbed "LehighU Live". The mobile device market has changed significantly since then with the addition of the widely-popular Android operating system and others like Blackberry and Windows Phone 7. In spring 2011, the student technology support team revamped their web presence with the goal of also offering support services via students' mobile devices. Our first responsibility was to provide a mobile application that can be used across platforms; however, we also wanted the user experience to feel the same as any other app on a given platform. For example, our app should feel like an Android app if the student is using an Android phone. Our second responsibility was to ensure that we could deliver dynamic content to students quickly regarding services, updates, support tips, and real-time alerts. These two major responsibilities presented significant challenges, not the least of which is that we do not have the resources to develop and/or maintain a separate app for each platform while also managing and pushing out the types of content we needed to get to students quickly. Therefore, we began looking at cross-platform mobile development frameworks such as the Mobile Web Framework (MWF) released by UCLA and other device-agnostic approaches. The challenge quickly became to build a solid, web-based mobile application that could be delivered via an app for individual platforms while at the same time accessible and uasble via mobile web browser for other web-enabled mobile devices.

Categories and Subject Descriptors

D.3.3 [**Programming Languages**]: Language Contructs and Features – *abstract data types, polymorphism, control structures.* This is just an example, please use the correct category and subject descriptors for your submission. The ACM Computing Classification Scheme: http://www.acm.org/class/1998/

General Terms

Management, Measurement, Documentation, Performance, Design, Reliability, Experimentation, Security, Human Factors, Standardization, Theory, Legal Aspects, Verification.

Keywords

Mobile device, tablet, apps, development, student support, communication, documentation, services, web, technology, smartphone, iPhone, iPad, Android, Blackberry, WebOS, iOS, iPod Touch, TouchPad, online, coursework, news, alerts, informed, scalability.

1. CURRENT STATE OF THE MOBILE PLATFORM

1.1 Survey Statistics & Study Data

Whether it is an iPad, Galaxy Tab, Droid Incredible, iPhone, Evo Shift, iPod Touch or a myriad of others, mobile devices have exploded in popularity over a small period of time. Ball State University has been conducting a national survey of college students twice annually since 2005. It comes as no surprise that 99.8% of students own one or more cellphones. However, the more striking statistic is that of those 99.8%, as of June 2010, 49% own smartphones, a significant increase over 38% in October 2009 and 27% in February 2009 (Truong 2010). In a similar study, results show that the percentage as of May 2011 may be in the neighborhood of 58%. In addition to smartphones and other web-enabled cellphones, web-enabled mobile devices such as the iPod Touch, iPad, Motorola XOOM, and other tablet devices are also growing in popularity. Of the percentage of students who already own a laptop, nearly 10% already own an iPad while 70% of those who do not own an iPad report having their eyes on buying one (Kolowich 2011). Still more interesting is the fact that a significant majority of students who do not currently own a smartphone, in fact, own an iPod Touch. According to data gathered in March 2011 from the annual student technology survey administered by the student technology support team at Lehigh University, 52.3% of the 1,200 undergraduate and graduate students surveyed own a web-enabled cellphone. 89% of those students own a Blackberry, iPhone, or Android smartphone. 34% of the 1200 students surveyed owned an iPod Touch and 8% owned an iPad (6%), Android-powered tablet (1%), or other web-enabled tablet (1%) (Eisenhard & Siegfried 2011).

1.2 The case for leveraging the mobile medium

It is easy to get caught up in the novelty of any new or emerging technology – especially in higher education. However, with regard to smartphones and other web-enabled mobile devices, one could argue that we are talking about more than just an emerging technology; rather, we are more likely talking about leveraging a new medium. The mobile medium affords higher-education institutions new opportunities to deliver dynamic content of varying importance to students more efficiently than ever. Lehigh released the *LehighU Live* app for iPhone in late 2009. The app features a university news feed, events calendar, campus map, and campus directory. Since its release, it has already been met with mostly positive feedback from students, staff, and faculty alike. However, with the mobile medium becoming more and more pervasive throughout campus, the university will be able to – and should – provide more important features and functionality beyond simple news feeds and campus maps. For example, in addition to optimizing the library catalog for mobile devices, it could also be possible to reserve or check out materials by generating a barcode from a student's user identification number that can be scanned at the library circulation desk. Furthermore, what if a student's primary laptop becomes infected with a virus and the student cannot access the Internet to request help and does not have a landline phone nearby? Data trends would suggest that a student might first reach for his or her mobile device. It would be extremely helpful if the university could provide a mobile-friendly method of getting technical help. The opportunity to extend this type of service to students is a key functionality the student technology support team at Lehigh focused on when revamping its web presence.

2. PREPARING FOR THE STUDENT SUPPORT MOBILE APP

2.1 Lehigh's Student Technology Support Team

At Lehigh, the student technology support team is known as the WIRED team on campus. WIRED is an acronym for "Worldwide Information Resources in Every Dorm". Over the years, support has expanded far beyond what the name would seem to suggest. The WIRED team provides technical support, troubleshooting, and consulting services for students and their personal computers at Lehigh. From simple wireless setup and assistance with Lehigh online services to virus removal and software reinstallation to hardware repair referrals and everything in between, the WIRED team is the first place for students to find help. In addition to two full-time staff, the WIRED team employs, trains, and manages a team of student consultants that help provide assistance.

2.2 Web revamp and looking toward mobile services

The WIRED team started planning a Web site revamp in spring 2011. In addition to the typical planning that accompanies any Web site overhaul, an additional primary goal was set to design a mobile application through which students could get help, request a service appointment, access popular documentation and services, and important service updates. For example, if a student wants to view WiFi configuration instructions for his laptop running Windows 7, that documentation would be available via the mobile application. If the same student encountered an unusual problem not resolved by following the instructions, he could submit a help request via the same mobile application. If another student wakes up one morning and finds that she cannot send any email, she could view current system alerts via the mobile application.

In order for the mobile application to be successful and prove useful for students, it will need to fulfill two-main responsibilities. First, it will need to function across different platforms and devices, and in a way that is both intuitive and familiar for the user. For example, if the user is using an Android-powered device, then the mobile application should function as if it were any other native Android app. Second, if students are to come to trust or rely on the mobile application for getting help and important information efficiently, then the application must be able to deliver and update dynamic content in real-time without relying on the user to initiate the update.

3. MEETING THE TWO MAIN RESPONSIBILITIES

3.1 Cross-platform, device-agnostic app

Given the mobile device data gathered as a result of the student survey, the only way to reach the maximum number of students is to release an app that performs all essential functions regardless of device or platform. Releasing just an iPhone app would be preferable for iPhone users, but even though the percentage of Blackberry users is steadily declining, they are still the majority of users on campus, with the number of Android-powered phone users making up a percentage just shy of the percentage of iPhone users (Eisenhard & Siegfried 2011). So if an iPhone app is released, then an Android app, Blackberry app, WebOS app, and Windows Phone 7 app versions would also have to be released. However, even if all those versions are available, there is still a significant percentage of students with Web-enabled cellphones that would not be able to benefit from the mobile app.

3.2 Delivering dynamic content and important updates in real-time

While it may be true that most documentation does not change all that often, every IT professional can think of a few instances where certain documentation needs to change fast or new documentation needs to be made available quickly. For example, Lehigh is deploying a new central printing server for fall 2011. This requires new documentation instructing students how to properly map the new printing server. Especially when the students initially move back to campus, there will be updates and small changes that will need to be made to the documentation until the process is fully settled. The WIRED mobile app will need to be able to deliver these updates quickly and accurately and without relying on the user to initiate the update. One of the first questions a student is asked when he or she brings in a laptop with a virus infection is if he or she has updated the computer's virus protection software. More often than not, the user has not installed the updates – even if the updates are set to install automatically. Additionally, the student may cancel the scheduled system scan and forget to restart it. Given these examples, there is a strong argument for taking the user out of the equation when it comes to updating content and even some functionality.

4. DEVELOPMENT CHALLENGES

4.1 Personnel/Organizational resources

Developing versions of the app for all the device and operating system variations is no problem if your university has a dedicated mobile development team. However, at Lehigh (and most likely many other institutions), mobile development is not anyone's primary job responsibility. For example, if one of the mobile developers experiences an unexpected spike in the number of student computers coming to the support desk with virus infections and his primary job responsibility is to first provide support to students, he will need to push development aside and first handle all of the infected student computers. Now assume for a moment, that there is a major content update that needed to get done as soon as possible, or that there was an important system alert that needed to go out. As a result, falling behind with updates seems inevitable. Once the developer is able to return to working on the mobile app, he may only be able to develop for Android initially while he takes whatever time he has left to begin to learn the Apple iOS, Blackberry OS, and perhaps even the Windows Phone 7 OS. Additionally, since the mobile medium is so young, one could assume that new developers are only familiar with one platform, which has the potential to impact the student technology support team's ability to provide equal service to students using other devices.

Giving consideration to these issues, the WIRED program recognized that it is not feasible in the long-term, or the short-term for that matter, to have a developer spend such a large amount of time learning each individual platform before actually getting to work on developing the mobile app. What is most important is that a mobile app be made available as soon as possible to assist students in getting help fast. The real challenge, then, is to ascertain what knowledge and skills the developer(s) already have and what functionality could be created using that skill set.

4.2 Capitalizing on existing knowledge and skills

It was quickly determined that our developer had a solid knowledge and proven track record of Web development. There is a learning curve associated with learning how to optimize a Web-based mobile app for varying devices. However, much of that optimization centers around using CSS effectively to deliver a smooth user-interface that is both intuitive and familiar for a user.

Recently, UCLA released what they call their "Mobile Web Framework", or MWF. The MWF focuses on providing mobile apps that reach the vast majority of users regardless of the device they use by offering as much functionality as possible via a Web-based mobile app. If a developer wanted to take advantage of device-specific hardware (i.e. GPS, camera, accelerometer, etc.), their approach only requires releasing a native app "wrapper" which delivers the same Web-based mobile app, but with added support for device-specific hardware (Davis & Rocchio 2011). The assumption is that it is easier to rely on a developer to build a simple app wrapper for utilizing device specific hardware than it is to build the entire app for each supported platform.

In terms of the functionality the student technology support team wanted to provide for students at Lehigh, all of the features, functionality, and content that was essential from the initial release could be done using a Web-based mobile app. This is particularly advantageous for a few main reasons:

A Web-based mobile app can reach nearly all users who currently own a Web-enabled smartphone or mobile device

Development requires using knowledge and skills already well-known with some additional time spent learning how to create CSS that optimizes the user-interface for a specific device

Content updates and important service updates can be provided in real-time to users without requiring a user-initiated update

Almost any content update can be made by any authorized staff member because he or she need only know how to fill out a web form

Reaching a large user-base will allow the WIRED team to collect usage statistics via tools such as Google Analytics to help guide decisions regarding how to expand the mobile app over the long-term

Since mobile development is no staff member's primary responsibility, this approach will be less costly in terms of time and effort but still successfully provide desired functionality and quality service

4.3 Outlook and Conclusion

There are many different approaches to offering important and useful content and functionality via the mobile medium. As with any other medium, there is a fine line between too much and too little. However, when working with a new medium as young as mobile devices, there is bound to be the need for some trial and error when finding an organization's happy medium. Over time, it may be prudent for universities to create a dedicated mobile development team and hire developers whose primary responsibility will be to develop apps for mobile devices. Should that occur, it may become more feasible and appropriate to offer a separate native app for each device and operating system. On the other hand, if the only functionalities students require can largely be delivered via a Web-based mobile app, then perhaps it is a better use of resources to focus on building solid Web-based mobile apps, releasing an app wrapper only when necessary, and relying on other authorized staff members to deliver important updates. The bottom line really comes down to three major components. Know your users (students, faculty, staff, visitors, etc.), know your development resources and capacity, and take manageable steps, gathering feedback all along the way.

5. ACKNOWLEDGMENTS

6. REFERENCES

[1] Davis, J. & Rocchio, R.A. *Mobile: Letting Go of the Device and Building for Innovation.* Mobile Perspectives: On Devices. Educause Review. March/April 2011. http://www.educause.edu/EDUCAUSE+Review/EDUCAUSEReviewMagazineVolume46/iMobilePerspectivesOndevicesib/226172

[2] [2] Truong, K. *Student Smartphone Use Doubles; Instant Messaging Loses Favor.* Wired Campus: The latest news on tech and education. The Chronicle of Higher Education. 17 June 2010. http://chronicle.com/blogs/wiredcampus/student-smartphone-use-doubles-instant-messaging-loses-favor/24876

[3] [3] Kolowich, S. *Mixed on Media.* Inside Higher Ed. 13 May 2011. http://www.insidehighered.com/news/2011/05/13/new_survey_on_student_technology_preferences

[4] [4] Eisenhard, B. & Siegfried, B. *WIRED Student Survey 2011.* Lehigh University. April 2011.

Leveraging Both Quantitative and Qualitative Data Sources to Improve IT Help Desk Support Services

Kenneth Janz
Winona State University
Somsen Hall 111i
Winona, MN 55987
1-507-457-2299
kjanz@winona.edu

Dean Feller
Winona State University
Somsen Hall 207
Winona, MN 55987
1-507-457-2387
dfeller@winona.edu

ABSTRACT

Information technology organizations in higher education look to customer satisfaction surveys or help desk software tracking data such as number of tickets resolved to measure effectiveness of help desk operations. While that is an excellent starting point to discuss effectiveness is it enough?

A specific case study will be presented and discussed in this paper. Winona State University in 1997 launched its laptop program (now called the e-Warrior: Digital Life and Learning Program), providing every student with a laptop computer to enhance his/her studies. After 14 years, Winona State is still gaining experience with its Digital Life and Learning Program. The program continues to evolve as more faculty and students familiarize themselves with the changing needs of technology for students. Winona State will continue to learn more about the role of our technology program's impact on its students' educational opportunities for years to come.

Using data collected from the e-Warrior Assessment plan information technology user services team improved existing student and faculty annual surveys that result in more specific, valid, and reliable indicators of self-reported academic benefits. Stratified random sampling replaced the current convenience sampling method, improving the ability to generalize. In addition, information will be presented on how the help desk satisfaction survey was used a starting point for follow-up faculty and student focus groups to provide more context to issues of IT student support services. Finally all of these changes fed a broader plan of assessment to evaluate program success.

Categories and Subject Descriptors

K.6.1 [**Project and People Management**]: Management techniques.

General Terms

Management, Measurement, Documentation, Standardization.

Keywords

Help Desk, Higher Education, Information Technology, Quality Improvement, Assessment, Digital Life and Learning.

SIGUCCS'11, November 12–17, 2011, San Diego, California, USA.

1. INTRODUCTION

Higher Education as an enterprise is reaching-out to find leading-edge implementation of information technology to transform the administrative, teaching, research, and service missions of the institution. Information Technology has become an integral part of the academic enterprise.

As information technology taken on a more central role of the institution it is becoming more and more important for information technology service and support units to provide metrics to document performance [1], [2]. But many times these industry metrics are out of step with the assessment techniques used to measure technology use and applications and other applied uses of technology within the organization [3]. Assessing organizational performance (especially information technology) in higher education is vital to continued and evolving accreditation and government accountability efforts [4].

At Winona State University this need for high quality performance data (metrics) for information technology was driven by program and institutional accreditation as well as a request from the Minnesota State College and University Board of Trustees in regards to Winona State University's e-Warrior: Digital Life and Learning Program. However, to meet these requests gaps in information technology assessment strategy emerged requiring a more comprehensive approach. Working with students and faculty, a plan was developed and implemented. The plan has already resulted in improvements to many facets of information technology support. Lessons learned in this process will be presented and discussed.

2. BACKGROUND

Winona State University (mid-sized university located in southeast Minnesota of 9,000 students) IT support is provided by Information Technology Services (ITS) which is organized into four units: User Services, Development and Web Support Services, Infrastructure Services, and Teaching, Learning, and Technology Services. The ITS leadership team consists of the Chief Information Officer and the Directors of User Services, Development and Web Support Services, Infrastructure Service, and Teaching, Learning, and Technology Services.

The e-Warrior: Digital Life and Learning Program provides every student with a laptop computer to enhance his/her studies on the Winona campus. The program has been woven into the fabric of the institution. This program integrates communication and information technology into student's social and learning experience at Winona State University. The program provides students with a powerful set of tools (e.g., a laptop, updated software) and services (e.g., help desk) to support all facets of their academic work and residential life at Winona State. More than just a laptop, the e-Warrior: Digital Life and Learning Program ensures secure, reliable, and supportable technology 24x7.

From November 2009 to April 2010, the e-Warrior: Digital Life and Learning Program Committee, in conjunction with the ITS Leadership Team, completed work on the e-Warrior Digital Life and Learning Program Assessment Plan. After 14 years, Winona State is still gaining experience with the program. As Winona State continues to evolve, the program at its core will always be about enhancing student success. The assessment plan created is the first attempt by the University to holistically examine the program and its impact on the campus. The assessment plan was built around a conceptual model for the program, which was developed a year earlier.

3. CONCEPTUAL MODEL

In December 2008, the *e-Warrior: Digital Life and Learning Program* Committee started to holistically examine the impact of technology in the teaching and learning process. At the core of student success is good teaching, which is supported by Learning goals, Teaching and Learning Activities, and Feedback and Assessments [5]. A visual representation was created to consider the many factors that have influence on and need to be integrated in the overall thinking and design of the program.

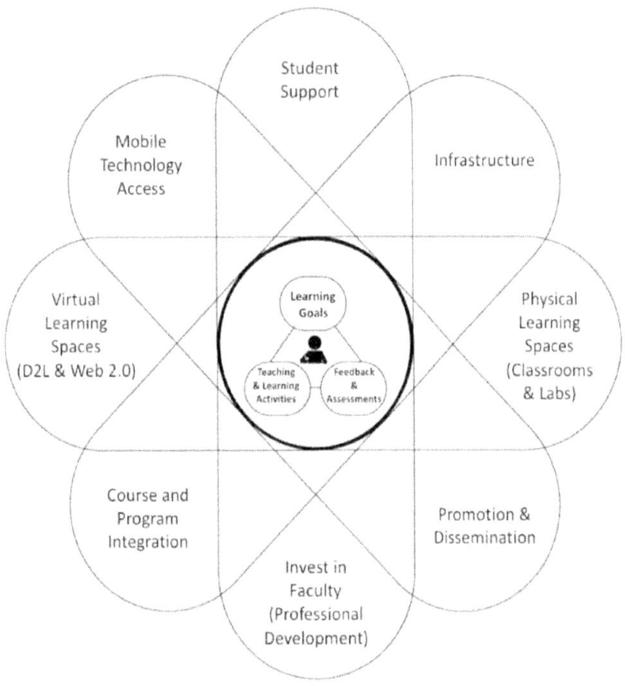

Figure 1. Conceptual Model of the e-Warrior Digital Life and Learning Program.

What does each piece of the conceptual model mean? First, the program commits itself to **invest in faculty** and provide a robust professional development program to inform faculty on the best practices both in the discipline and pedagogy to enhance their thinking on new and future possibilities in classroom instruction. Second, the program encourages **promotion and** dissemination of the findings of the program. Faculty are encouraged to engage in the scholarship of teaching and learning, which involves systematic study of teaching and learning and the public sharing and review of such work through presentations or publications of how the program impacts their instructional environment. Faculty members are encouraged to share findings and contribute to the study of the effectiveness of the *e-Warrior: Digital Life and Learning Program* to build upon current knowledge and to advance the field. The program must take into account the enhancement of the **physical learning spaces** on campus. This includes creating learning spaces that meet the current and future needs of students and faculty. **Mobile technology access** is one of the tools of the program. The equipment (laptop) becomes an important tool, not the center of the project. The student's access and need for mobile technology will always be refined and enhanced. When learning is properly organized and structured, students who use a laptop as an everyday learning tool are better writers, more collaborative and get more involved in their schoolwork [6]. As of spring 2009, Winona State had 100 percent coverage in all academic areas with wireless **infrastructure**. This wireless infrastructure allowed truly anytime, anywhere learning on the campus. The program needs to take into account improved **student support** services with the newly reorganized ITS services. Winona State has greatly enhanced its **virtual learning spaces** and hybrid course design options with the addition of blogs, wikis, podcasts, and journaling.

Finally, the core of program (center of the figure) must focus on matching learning goals with teaching and learning activities, and feedback and assessments. This will be done in this project with TLT working with faculty to foster effective elements of backward course redesign to create significant learning experiences as described by Fink [5]. This conceptual model is further explained in an earlier paper [7].

This conceptual model provides the foundation for the assessment plan. Each area of the conceptual model (i.e. student support) provides a driver for the research questions to be assessed.

4. RESEARCH QUESTIONS

The purpose of the assessment plan was to fill the research gap in knowledge about whether participation in an experience as comprehensive, pervasive, and intensive as the Winona State *e-Warrior: Digital Life and Learning Program* benefits students academically. Given that the program will change over time, this is a process that must be evaluated continuously. All eight research questions are presented, but for purposes of this paper only questions 1 (student support), 4 (promotion and dissemination), and 8 (mobile technology access) will have findings and outcomes reported in this paper.

4.1 Student Support

How are students impacted by their current level of technical support, how do student support services related to technology impact academic success, how does that contribute to our understanding of the use of technology in higher education?

1. Do students have appropriate opportunities for training on software applications?
2. Do students have access to the right applications?
3. Do students have access to online resources for just-in-time support?
4. Are students satisfied with support and resources?
5. Are students developing computer literacy skills that enhance their academic and professional success?
6. How do students use campus technology?
7. Does technology support meet the academic needs of students?
8. Do faculty members think that our level of student support is adequate to meet academic needs?
9. Do students use the support services provided?
10. How does WSU compare to other institutions?

4.2 Infrastructure

Does an adequate infrastructure (wired, wireless, network storage, bandwidth) exist for students and faculty to serve their academic needs, how does infrastructure impact overall student and faculty use of technology, how does that contribute to our understanding of the use of technology in higher education?

1. Are students and faculty satisfied with online storage provided?
2. Are students and faculty satisfied with networking resources provided?
3. Are students and faculty satisfied with the speed and reliability of the WSU network?
4. Can students and faculty do the academic projects they want using the infrastructure available?
5. Do students and faculty leverage the existing technology infrastructure to enhance classroom activities?
6. How does WSU Compare to other institutions?

4.3 Physical Learning Spaces

How does the campus community utilize the technology located in learning spaces, how does the technology located in the learning spaces impact learning in the classroom, how does this contribute to our overall understanding of technology use in higher education?

1. Do physical learning spaces as related to technology meet the needs of faculty and students?
2. Do faculty and students use the technology located in learning spaces?
3. Does the technology work reliably located in learning spaces?
4. Are students and faculty satisfied with learning space services (e.g., emergency help)?
5. How does the learning space enhance or transform instruction?
6. How does WSU compare with other institutions?

4.4 Promotion and Dissemination

How does the University promote the program to new and current students and external audiences, how does the University encourage faculty and staff to disseminate information about the program?

1. Do new and current students and faculty understand details (i.e. policies and procedures) about the e-Warrior: Digital Life and Learning Program?
2. Does the University support scholarship related to one-to-one computing?
3. Does the University provide for an adequate level of marketing for the program to internal and external audiences?
4. Is the program mentioned in the media?
5. Do prospective students know about the program?

4.5 Invest in Faculty (Professional Development)

How does professional development impact faculty members' use of technology, how do professional development opportunities impact student success, how does faculty professional development contribute to our understanding of technology in higher education?

1. How do faculty use technology to facilitate teaching and learning? How do they learn how to do this? Do they rely on support services? In what ways?
2. How are faculty development resources allocated to specific objectives and innovations?
3. What faculty support services are offered?
4. Are faculty members satisfied with ITS support services?
5. Is our investment in faculty development benefitting students – do students see an increase in technology use by faculty and positive changes in instruction related to the effective use of technology by instructors?
6. How does WSU compare with other institutions?

4.6 Course and Program Integration

At what level is technology being integrated into courses and programs, how does this integration impact learning goals in courses, how does course and program integration of technology contribute to our understanding of technology in higher education?

1. Is there departmental and college level integration of technology in a way that's benefitting students?
2. Is technology being integrated into departmental curriculum redesign efforts?
3. Is technology being integrated consistently to achieve programmatic goals?
4. What's the current level of technology integration into the curriculum at the departmental level?
5. How does WSU compare with other institutions in its integration of technology into the curriculum?

4.7 Virtual Learning Spaces (Learning Management System (LMS) & Collaborative software) and Academic Tools

How does the campus community utilize virtual learning spaces and software, how do the virtual learning spaces impact learning on the Web, how does this contribute to our overall understanding of technology use in higher education?

1. Is collaborative software being applied effectively in courses and beyond?
2. How is the current Learning Management System being used? Is it being used effectively?
3. Are our virtual learning spaces and tools meeting the campus teaching and learning needs most effectively?
4. How does our use of these tools compare to other institutions?

4.8 Mobile Technology Access

Does the technology provided by the University meet the academic needs of students, how does the choice of hardware impact a student's use of the technology, how does this contribute to our understanding of technology use in higher education?

1. How are faculty and students using the technology provided?
2. Are faculty and students satisfied with the technology provided?
3. Does the technology meet the academic needs of faculty and students?
4. Is the technology provided usable, reliable? Are there certain features that are more important for academic purposes than others?
5. Is a lease program the best way to achieve our mobile technology access goals?
6. How does our students' use of the technology compare to other institutions?

5. ASSESSMENT TOOLS AND MEASURES

The assessment plan is driven by the program's conceptual design, research questions, and benchmarks and is based on the model described in An Educator's Guide to Evaluating the Use of Technology in Schools and Classrooms [8]. Both formative and summative assessments, incorporating both quantitative and qualitative methodologies and analyses, will be used. The formative assessments will allow for refinement in procedures and design in order to answer the research questions and improve the overall program. The summative assessments or evaluation will provide a comprehensive summary of how the outlined program has been achieved during the course of the evaluation period. Assessment reports will be shared each semester with the e-Warrior: Digital Life and Learning committee, University administration and, annually with the MnSCU Board of Trustees.

Internal evaluators will assess this program. The internal evaluator has been involved in the design of the project. The internal evaluator will coordinate all evaluation activities; develop instruments, interview protocols, and observation rating sheets; assist in the revision of portfolio rubric to include technology; train a graduate student researcher; and provide feedback to the other program stakeholders regarding the status and outcomes of assessment activities and suggestions for modifications based on formative data. The internal evaluator will also assist in the development of and provide expert judgment (i.e., content-related validity checks) with respect to the instruments, interview protocols, and observation rating checklists. They will conduct quality assurance checks of data collection (e.g., interview tapes) and analyses (e.g., statistical analyses, coding of qualitative data) and they will regularly meet with the e-Warrior: Digital Life and Learning committee.

Table 1 describes the measures, type of data each will yield (i.e., quantitative or qualitative), and alignment of each measure to the programs research question. The measures developed during this project are intended to continuously improve the program.

Table 1. Tools used for program assessment related to User Services (Help Desk, etc)

Measure	Description	Research Question	Type of Data	Who
Annual Faculty Technology Survey	Random sample of faculty that complete survey about how faculty members are supported and use technology.	1, 2, 3, 4, 5, 7, and 8.	Quant	Faculty
Annual Student Technology Survey	Yearly survey given to students during assessment day. Covers satisfaction, use, and technical support.	1, 2, 4, 6, 7, and 8	Quant	Students
Alumni Survey	Survey Alumni (Does the technology benefit students)	1, 4, 6, and 8	Quant & Qual	Alumni
ITSM Call Data	Help desk call data.	1, 2, 3, 7, and 8	Quant	Faculty and Students
Quarterly Help Desk Satisfaction Survey	Follow-up survey of help desk clients	1, 3 and 8	Quant & Qual	Faculty and Students
Faculty Focus Group	Structured interview regarding how faculty member integrates technology into classroom and assignments, recommendations regarding technology progress.	1, 2, 3, 4, 5, 6, 7, and 8	Qual	Faculty
Student Focus Group	Structured interview to ascertain level of technology competency, evaluation of faculty's use of technology in courses, and how they (students) integrate technology into assignments, projects, and own use of technology in the classroom.	1, 2, 3, 4, 5, 6, 7, and 8	Qual	Students
Showcase Event Survey	Collection of data related to the laptop selection process.	4 and 8	Quant	Faculty and Students
Educause Core Data	Annual survey done by Educause. Data used to compare WSU to other similar higher education institutions.	1, 2. 3,7 and 8	Quant	External
Lean Process Findings	Focus group data developed through process analysis study.	1, 2, 3, 4, 5, 6, 7, and 8	Qual	Faculty and Students

6. SELECTED OUTCOMES

All of the outcomes presented were changes made as a result of assessments and measures of the *e-Warrior: Digital Life and Learning* assessment plan. The primary emphasis of this paper are changes made related to the areas of student support and infrastructure.

Figure 2. Picture of the front walk-in help desk at Winona State University.

6.1 Overall Program Support

Overall, students report satisfaction with the program. Each year in the spring, Winona State's Institutional Research unit holds an Assessment Day. The Assessment Day Survey includes a section on the *Digital Life and Learning Program*. The survey respondents include students from all Colleges and from multiple years in school. While the number of respondents varies each year, about one-third of the student body is represented. Results indicate consistently high levels of satisfaction with various aspects of the *Digital Life and Learning* program. Satisfaction has increased each of the last four years.

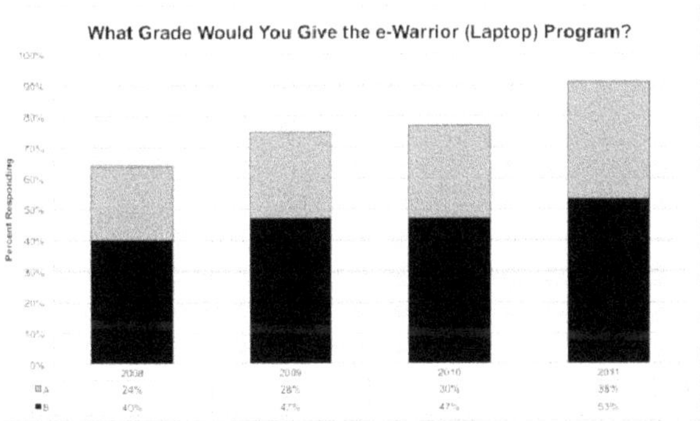

Figure 3. Student satisfaction with the e-Warrior: Digital Life and Learning Program.

6.2 Customer Service and Support

User Services continues to provide high quality customer service. User Services rolled out customer service training for all student workers last year and overall satisfaction with services continues to improve. During FY11, the Technical Support Center (TSC) completed 31,194 support tickets with 12,240 tickets being generated by a call to the call-in help desk and 18,954 tickets being generated by a client visiting the walk-in services of the Center.

Laptop distributions are not included in the above figures. Laptop distribution numbers are as follows:

- Laptop exchanges (current students) in FY10 – 1,146
- Laptop distribution (new students) in FY10 – 1,583

During assessment day activities students reported that 87% who visited or called the TSC gave the Center a grade of "A" or "B". That score has improved by seven percentage points over the last two years. Also of note, in the last year students who gave a grade of an "A" to the TSC increased from 50% to 67%.

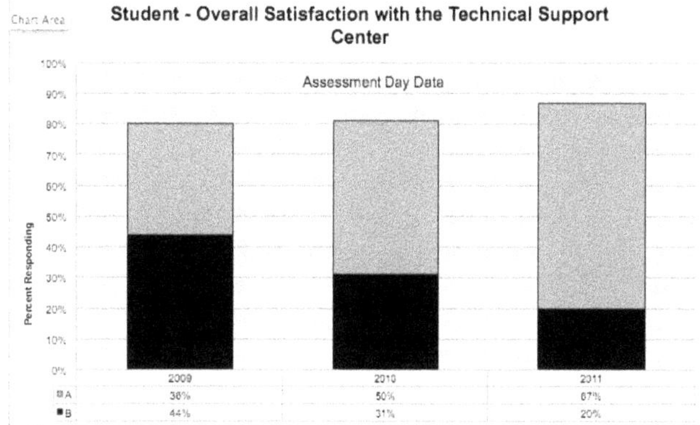

Figure 4. Student satisfaction with Technical Support Center.

Additional validation of improved customer service in the TSC was a 2011 Award Finalist for the Red Carpet Award for Outstanding Service by the Winona Area Chamber of Commerce.

Figure 5. Technical Support Center 2011 Award Finalist – Outstanding Services Award

6.3 Laptop Request For Proposal (RFP)

User Services led the laptop RFP and competitive bid process. The RFP process started in November, 2009 and required a considerable effort from many staff within the TSC area. The comprehensive bid involved a large service and repair component. Based on input from vendor presentations and responses to the RFP, scoring matrix, laptop showcase event surveys, and focus group data the e-Warrior Digital Life and Learning Program Review Committee made two recommendations in regards to laptop model selection. First, the Macintosh laptop selection of the MacBook Pro was made with an 11 – 0 vote. Second, the PC laptop selection of the HP Elitebook 8440p was made with an 8 – 3 vote. Both votes were conducted on February 16, 2010.

6.4 Technical Support Center (TSC) LEAN Redesign

The TSC staff participated in a Lean project to redesign both the processes and physical space for enhanced flow of customer support and inventory management. This Lean project resulted in the redesign of the TSC physical area, which handles processing of 20,000 technical support issues, 4,200 laptop distributions, and 1,200 laptop purchases. This project also looked at the increased security within the area. TSC processes a large number of computer products such as desktop computers, laptop computers, printers, and handheld devices. Additional security locks and security cameras were installed in FY10. Finally, the project assisted the unit in going paperless. Several processes have been transitioned to digital forms. Laptop receipts are now sent to students via email (ie. laptop purchases, laptop returns, laptop exchanges). All registration for laptop distribution sessions are now online. Figure 11 represents the physically redesigned space in the TSC.

Figure 6. Floor Plan of the redesigned Technical Support Center.

6.5 West Campus Technical Support Center

This past fall, User Services implemented a technical support center in Lourdes Hall. This support center was created to provide better access to technical support for students living on West Campus and to provide a quicker response to classroom technology issues on the West Campus. This support center was successfully implemented and the usage grew throughout the year.

6.6 Transition to Information Technology Service Management (ITSM)

The help desk ticket software TSC uses is called ITSM. ITS uses this database to document technical support issues. This database also tracks University technology assets. Transitioning to this new program provides ITS staff with functionality to track technology issues and provide reports to analyze trends. The conversion to this program and subsequent development has streamlined processes in many areas within ITS. Figure 12 is a screenshot of the help desk software ITSM.

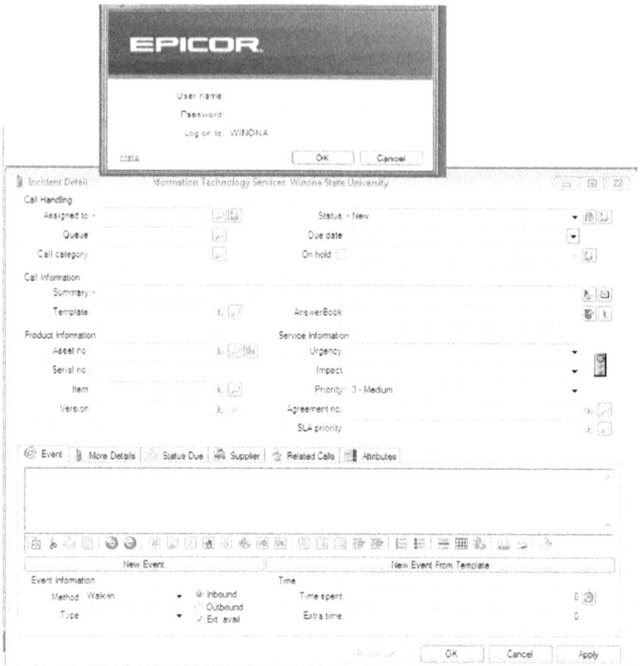

Figure 7. Screenshot of the new help desk system used at the Technology Support Center.

6.7 Combined the Onsite and Phone Support Teams

User Services combined the Onsite and Phone support teams so that they work as one streamlined unit. This has improved call response time and communication between technicians taking phones calls and technicians doing work in the field.

6.8 Better Documentation

Are the policies of the Digital Life and Learning program clearly articulated? Our program is more than just providing a laptop computer. To provide consistent answers to programmatic questions, our Technical Support team used data from our call tracking system to develop a set of commonly asked questions and responses. This information was distributed to students in a variety of ways

6.9 Wireless Enhancement

Surveys in 2009 gave us baseline data regarding how our users were using our wireless network. This data and the increasing wireless usage rates prompted us to focus on improving our infrastructure. A multidisciplinary committee was formed to develop a three-year plan to improve the network infrastructure. Recent surveys show a considerable improvement in the satisfaction of our wireless network.

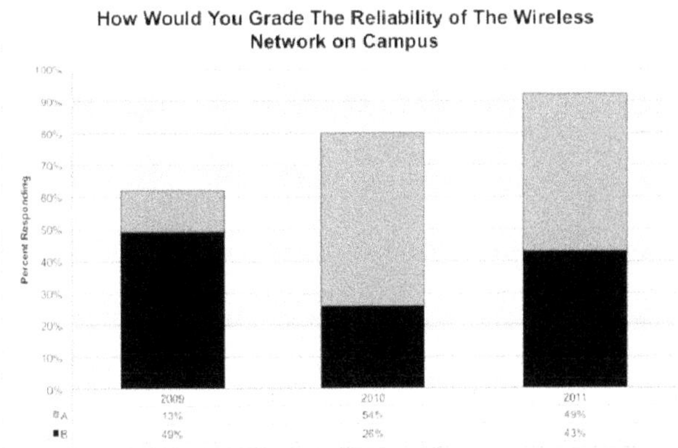

Figure 8. Student satisfaction with the wireless network on campus.

7. CONCLUSION

Students live in a world in which information technology has become truly a ubiquitous part of their lives. Information Technology is playing an increasingly important role in higher education and its influence can be directly observed everyday at Winona State University (WSU). Students are coming to the University with the expectation that technology will be an integral part of their academic and social activities. Information Technology Services (ITS) must support the changing expectations of students.

A key method that WSU and ITS uses to stay on top of these evolving expectations is through a comprehensive assessment process. This assessment plan provides a framework for measuring technology related services and a guide for future technology exploration and implementation at WSU.

This plan will allow the University to better understand the impact of the e-Warrior: Digital Life and Learning Program on faculty and students. This assessment plan will provide a continuous feedback loop for student support, infrastructure, learning spaces, investment in faculty, and technology integration into course and program activities.

ITS continues to provide high quality customer service. During FY10, the Technical Support Center (TSC) in the User Services unit completed 15,702 support tickets. During assessment day activities, students reported that 81% who visited or called the TSC gave the Center a grade of "A" or "B". That score has improved by 10 percentage points over the last two years. Also of note, in the last year students who gave a grade of an "A" to the TSC increased from 44% to 50%.

8. ACKNOWLEDGMENTS

Portions of this paper was originally collected for a report on the status of the Digital Life and Learning program at Winona State University to the MnSCU Board of Trustees written by the authors. The authors would like to thank Ken Graetz, and Patrick Paulson for input and feedback on the original report.

9. REFERENCES

[1] Taylor, S. Foundations of IT Service Management based on ITIL. (2006) Van Haren Publishing.

[2] Steinberg, R. A. Measuring ITIL: Measuring, reporting and modeling the IT Service Metrics that matter most to IT Senior Executives. (2006) Trafford Publishing.

[3] Haertel, G. D. and Means, B. Evaluating Educational Technology. (2003) Teachers College Press: Columbia University.

[4] Miller, B. A. Assessing Organizational Performance in Higher Education (2007) San Francisco, CA: Jossey-Bass.

[5] Fink, L. D. Creating Significant Learning Experiences: An Integrated Approach to Designing College Courses. (2003) San Francisco, CA: Jossey-Bass.

[6] Weaver, B. E., & Nilson, L.B. Laptops in class: What are they good for? What can you do with them? In L. Nilson & B.E. Weaver (Eds.), Enhancing Learning with Laptops in the Classroom, New Directions for Teaching and Learning, 101, (2005), 3-13.

[7] Janz, K., and Graetz, K. Status of a digital life and learning program. Special Interest Group in College and University Computing 2009. (2009), 33-40.

[8] U. S. Department of Education. An educator's guide to evaluating the use of technology in schools and classrooms. Washington, DC: U.S. Department of Education, Office of Educational Research and Improvement. (1998).

Maintaining Creative Integrity While Implementing Successful University Branding

Christopher Donald
Office of Information Technology
NC State University
2620, Hillsborough St, Raleigh, NC
27695
1-919-513-1167
cjdonald@ncsu.edu

ABSTRACT

In this paper, I describe the process the Office of Information Technology (OIT) followed in creating our Computing @ newsletter and other print materials while meeting our university branding requirements. I also describe our methodology for teaching these same processes to members of our faculty, staff, and graduate departments. It is not my intention to provide a word for word example of my presentation. Since the materials I will be referencing are all available online, it seems unnecessary to reproduce them in their entirety here. I will go into each section in greater detail as I speak about our specific experiences in regards to these topics.

Categories and Subject Descriptors

A.0 General Literature

General Terms

Design

Keywords

branding

1. INTRODUCTION

NC State launched a design and editorial brand book in order to unify the look and feel of all official NC State communications. It is available online at http://www.ncsu.edu/brand.

2. Why did NC State institute a Brand Book?

Many of the websites and print materials created in the university are created by non-professional designers. The goal was to give those employees clear guidelines for creating their materials in order to maintain a consistent level of quality across the university.

3. What were the goals of unified university branding?

To standardize logo usage, fonts, colors, editorial style, accessibility, photography, and web design.

4. How has the university promoted the new requirements?

Generally, through high-level web developer meetings. There has been no concerted effort to communicate the branding requirements to the campus.

SIGUCCS'11, November 12–17, 2011, San Diego, California, USA.
ACM 978-1-4503-1023-9/11/11.

How has the university enforced these requirements?

This is the main reason why there has not been a concerted push for branding. There is no effective enforcement. In order to enforce the requirements we would need to give the faculty and staff an alternative to creating the materials themselves. Our Creative Services and University Communications departments are unable to meet that need. Budgets are tight so most departments cannot afford to go outside the University or to pay our internal units.

Another problem is the power of some of the colleges and departments. They can ignore the requirements if they wish.

5. What has the reaction from campus been?

Mixed. Most people are happy to have guidelines but the level of frustration with the brand book is inversely proportionate to the lack of professional training of the designers. The more they know about good design, the more the limitations stand out.

6. What were the unforeseen consequences of the brand book and how could they have been avoided?

One is that departments who can afford to pay for services outside the University do. Because both Creative Services and University Communications are receipts supported, they have to compete with outside design firms. They are historically slow, non-responsive, and expensive. Departments have begun taking their own photographs, using pay photo archives, and increasingly contacting OIT because we don't charge for our services. To avoid this problem, the university could have combined all the design departments, expanded their services, and stopped charging for them. Unified and professional university communications should be standard, not an extra or a luxury. Branding is an investment in the value of our university and should be paid for and managed at an enterprise level.

We also chose a proprietary Adobe font that has a per seat license. It is extremely expensive. We could have avoided this expense simply by having a custom font created for the university, one that we wouldn't need to license. Other universities have done this, especially for logos.

The primary color in the design is extremely difficult to render correctly and is almost guaranteed to display wrong on a monitor. It cannot be used comfortably as either type or a background for type. Just because this is the official school color does not mean we have to use it so much in the design. People should be encouraged to use it but not forced to use too much of it in their designs.

The range of colors we were given was extremely limited. More than half cannot be used with type on them unless we use white type, which is difficult to read. There need to be more colors to give designers some variety and accessibility needs to be a primary deciding factor in choosing them.

7. How has the Office of Information Technology worked as a mediator and role model for the brand book?

We began offering a series of classes on the Adobe Creative Suite but quickly realized that users needed not only training on how to use the software but basic design theory and even project management. Through the classes we were able to educate faculty and staff about the branding requirements and teach them how to start each project by considering those design parameters.

We needed to address their confusion and concern over some of the obvious problems with the branding. At the same time, all the materials coming from our office needed to adhere strictly to the brand book.

We needed to begin offering first classes on buying a digital camera, then classes on digital photography because departments began wanting to handle their own photography. We also began offering photographic services and a library of free campus images for use.

8. Loopholes

Or what I refer to as "working within the parameters of the brand book". These are the things which were not expressly forbidden or addressed in the brand book but which give designers some leeway in addressing their particular departmental needs.

Font Size: Fonts can act as images when used correctly both as positive and negative space. Similarly, changing the font weights, heights, widths, and rendering them on paths can create some powerful visual elements.

Opacity: While specific allowable colors are set, there is no mention of opacity. By using a color at 20 or 30% you can place type on it, making it easy to read and meeting accessibility contrast requirements. You can also gradate the colors or use them to tint photographs.

Photographs: In cases where large blocks of defined colors won't work I like to use photos, sometimes changing their opacity or overlaying them with blocks of color with a high level of transparency.

9. How will the brand book be changing in the future?

The department which created the brand book is currently redesigning the NC State website. In doing so, they have found that the brand book is too restrictive and are rewriting it to reflect the design choices they would like to make for the website.

Revitalize and Re-brand Your IT Image

Thom Mattauch
VCU helpIT Center Manager
901 Park Ave Rm B-30
Richmond, VA 23284
804-827-0532
mattauchtj@vcu.edu

Hannah Pettit
VCU helpIT Center Supervisor
901 Park Ave Rm B-30
Richmond, VA 23284
804-828-4727
pettith@vcu.edu

ABSTRACT

Do you have users who complain about issues that existed years ago, but have now been rectified? Do you provide excellent service but still lack respect from your university community? Maybe it is time you revitalize and re-brand your group. The VCU helpIT Center did just that in an effort to overcome the hurdle of a bad reputation that was set years ago. Before re-branding, they took several steps to bring about change in the service provided by their office. Aggressive metric goals were set and statistics gathered to rejuvenate the group internally. Then, while working with the VCU Technology Services Marketing and Communication Department, the inception of the IT branding took place. Learn what was necessary to bring about the change in people's minds, both internal to the VCU helpIT Center staff and also their external user base. Also see how this effective branding campaign helped raise the respect of the VCU helpIT Center within the university and expanded to a division-wide re-branding of the groups within the VCU Technology Services – User Services Department.

Categories and Subject Descriptors

K.6.1 Project and People Management

General Terms

Management, Measurement, Documentation, Reliability, Experimentation, Standardization.

Keywords

Management, Branding, Customer Satisfaction, Image Improvement.

1. INTRODUCTION

Virginia Commonwealth University is a public university in the commonwealth of Virginia. In the fall of 2010, the University had enrollment of 32,303 Undergraduate and Graduate students. The University also had an estimated 18,657 faculty and staff between the Monroe Park and MCV Campuses. The VCU helpIT Center provides technical support for a user base of over 50,000 Students/Faculty/Staff.

Over the course of history, the VCU helpIT Center evolved from several past iteration of Information Technology Support Centers. Throughout this evolution, there were hurdles and pitfalls along the way. As a result, customer opinion diminished, despite an increase in both quantity and quality of service offerings. Something had to be done and a vision to re-brand the center was developed.

2. It wasn't always the VCU helpIT Center

The VCU helpIT Center is the front line support center for the VCU community. It is part of the Technology Services division at the university. For that matter, the division of Technology Services is new as well. Over five years ago, there were two technology divisions at the university. There was the Academic Technology division (AT) and the Administrative Information Technology division (AIT). A decision was made to centralize the two divisions and out of that came Technology Services. At the time, of the merger, there were two separate help desks. With the merger came the creation of one Technology Services Help Desk. This was the precursor to the VCU helpIT Center

3. Challenges

3.1 Internal Chaos

The internal organization was messy at best. There were two managers over seeing the Help Desk. One was managing the call center, and the other was managing the walk up desk. Both managers were working under their own agendas, which led to confusion. Also, the full time staff was assigned to the call center and the part time employees were assigned to the walk up and call center. This caused confusion in the reporting structure as the part time employees would report up one management change when working the walkup counter and another when they were working the call center.

Also there was disunity between staff based on their classification. At one point there was a staff member classified as an IT Analyst CL1 supervising a staff member classified at the higher classification of IT Analyst CL2. Furthermore, there was a sever line in the sand drawn between the full time and part time employees and which lead to communication breakdown and resentment between the two groups of employees.

3.2 We are not alone!

Throughout the university, there are many help desks, and just as many divisions with Technology Service in their name. As a result, public perception of our organization was skewed by the actions of other groups outside of our control. The Technology Services Help Desk needed to differentiate themselves from the various other technology service's groups and other help desks around the two campuses of Virginia Commonwealth University.

3.3 Quality and Consistence of Service.

Until around 2007, the statistics for the Technology Services Help Desk were dismal at best. The call answer rate hovered around 60% and first call resolution was not even measured. Public perception was low. This was caused by a disjointed leadership as well as a lack of formalized policy and procedure.

4. Before re-branding, we must re-vitalize.

Before re-branding makes sense, you must first put in place the foundation to support the new image you are creating. The first thing that needed to happen was to make drastic improvements in the public perception of the help desk. In order to make these drastic improvements, internal improvements had to be addressed first. Once the internal improvements were made, communication with our user base had to be established to work with them to insure that they were aware the changes going on and get them on board with the new organization.

4.1 Internal changes

Internally the Virginia Commonwealth University Technology Services Help Desk was a mess. Documentation needed to be created to have Policy and Procedures detailed. Next, the breakdown between the two groups of employees had to be addressed to get the teams working together. Also, metrics needed to be developed to accurately measure the success of the unit. Finally, the messy reporting structure had to be addressed.

4.1.1 Documentation and team building

The management of the Virginia Commonwealth University Technology Services Help Desk attacked the issue of Policy & Procedure documentation as well as the team building issue together. To do so, two committees were established and given the task of documenting the Policies and Procedures of the unit. There were two committees, one full time employee committee and one part time employee committee. The unique thing of the makeup of the committee was that the full time committee was chaired by a part time employee and the part time committee was chaired by a full time employee. Furthermore, once the two groups had their task complete, they would work together to finalize the policy and procedure document. Also, for the first time in the history of the help desk, meetings were held with a mixed attendance of both full time employees and part time employees.

4.1.2 Metrics

Historically the metrics gathered was used for reporting to upper management exclusively. This was not used for any form of real time measurements. This is what lead to the rather dismal 60% call answer rate. To rectify this, displays were put up in each employees cube to display current call statistics. (see Image 1)

It gives a visual indication of agents that are signed into the system, their status, average wait time, and number of callers in the queue. To make it more effective, if the longest wait time for a caller in the queue exceeds 2 minutes, the display flashes yellow. If the wait in the queue exceeds 3 minutes the display flashes red. This gives a quick visual signal that the calls are backing up and people need to address the callers. Since the implementation of the display, the call answer rate skyrocketed. Also, the displays proved very useful in distributing pertinent information regarding system wide issues. To accomplish this, yammer was installed and a private yammer group was created. Yammer is similar to twitter allowing a quick broadcast alert to be posted to the help desk yammer group and thus onto the displays in each cube.

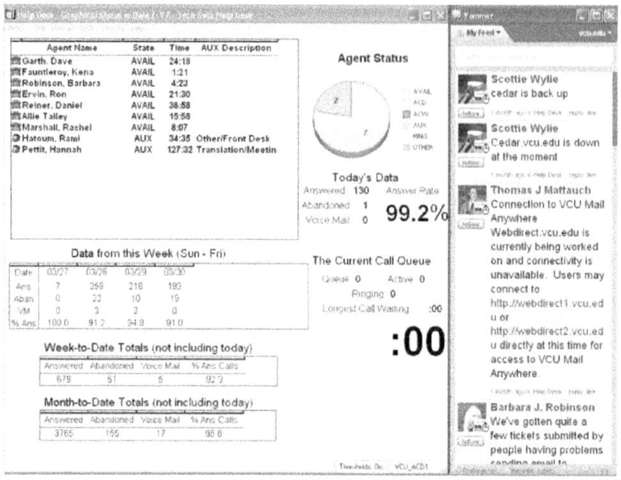

Image 1. Displays used in each employees cube.

In addition to the call displays, emphasis was placed on other metrics. Ticket to call ratio was a new metric that was being measured. It was determined that many of the typically easy user interactions were not being documented in a trouble ticket. This prevented management from accurately measuring staffing needs. Next, first call resolution was measured. To become a world-class support center, we had to insure that we were helping as many people as possible during their first contact with the center. Customer satisfaction was another critical metric to measure. Goals were set for each measurement, and on a weekly basis, management would review the metrics with each employee. In areas where the employee excelled, it gave management an opportunity to praise the employee. In areas where the employee fell short, it gave management a very passive tool to counsel the employee on what was needed to improve the short coming.

Being the nerve center of the organization, we took this as an opportunity to promote ourselves by taking several of the metrics we were collecting and passing them on to other groups within the organization. We started providing monthly customer satisfaction reports which were distributed to the manager's or directors of each technical team within the Technology Services division. We also provided a weekly report on aged tickets to give the managers of each team a quick overview of the tickets that they had in various ages from 0-30 days old all the way up to over 180 days old.

4.1.3 Org Chart Chaos

The reporting structure at the help desk was a mess. There were Part time employees who had a different reporting structure depending on where they were working that day. If they were on the walkup counter, they had one reporting structure and if they were at the call center, they had a different reporting structure. (See Image 2, In the image, FTE refers to Full Time Employee and PTE refers to Part Time Employee)

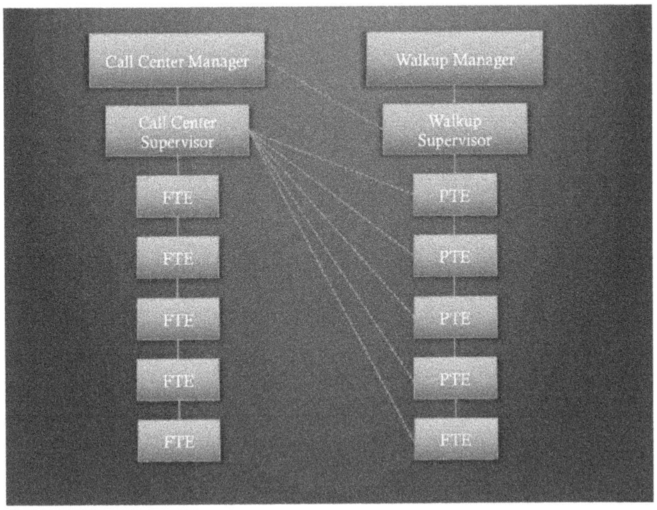

Image 2. Org Chart as it was before the reorg.

To address the issues this caused, the organization was redefined and streamlined with a more logical organization tree. (See Image 3.) This allowed for better communication, a single vision and a logical reporting structure.

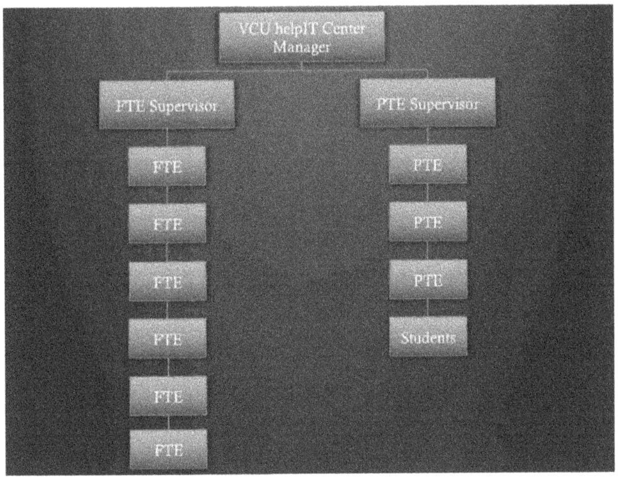

Image 3. Org Chart after the reorg.

Having the organization all reporting up to the same management structure improved communication and allowed for single management vision to be distributed to the staff. After having all of the staff aligned beneath one manager, the line in the sand was blurred. Next there needed to be a better team environment created between the two groups. To do this it was imperative that both sets of employees be trained on all areas of the help desk. Not only would this allow for a more team environment to be fostered, but also it would allow better coverage in areas when one of the areas is short staffed.

4.1.3 Team building

Now that the org chart was cleaned up and the reporting structure was improved, team building exercises needed to take place. The first concept was to perform team building outside of the office. We took this challenge using the "if you build it, they will come" approach. We set up an ongoing outing the first Tuesday of every month. The outings were designed to be fun and non-work related. We tried to mix up the outings to appeal to the masses (eg: Sporting functions, hot wing night, burger night at the local brewery, etc...) To address the staff that did not want to dedicate non-work time to a team building exercise, we also set up several lunch time functions (eg: Pot luck lunches, pizza parties, etc...).

4.2 External communication and buy-in

In order to improve the image of the help desk, the user community needed to be involved and communicated with regarding the changes going on. They needed to not only be informed of the changes, but they needed to feel that they were part of the change. One important thing that needed to happen was that while there were users within Technology Services, they were still external to the help desk and we needed to treat them as external users as well. User Group meetings were established to communicate with the departments and schools of the university. Finally, pilot projects were created and advertised throughout the departments and schools.

4.2.1 Internal is external

An important item in rebranding is getting cheerleaders for your cause. What better cheerleaders than those who work in the same organization as you. Within Technology Services at Virginia Commonwealth University, there are numerous technical teams. Historically, communication between the teams and the help desk was minimal. Communication was critical between these teams and the help desk. To do so, management from the help desk met with management from each of the internal technical teams to discuss methods for providing support to their user base. This opened up the lines of communication to allow for new policies and procedures to be established or existing policies and procedures to be solidified and modified insuring quality of service.

4.2.2 User groups

User group meetings were established to open the lines of communication with the end user. While the target was the end user, most who attended were localized support staff in departmental IT. This was good because it gave the help desk a platform to work with local IT to determine how best the help desk could support them while they supported their end users.

4.2.3 Pilot Projects

How best can you create a cheerleader for your department? Make them part of the solution. We had several new projects that needed to be implemented from enhancements to the ticketing system, to methods of communication with the user base. To help get the word out that we were not the same group that had low public perception in the past, we enlisted the support of the departmental IT support and in some cases the end users themselves to pilot some of these projects. To this day we use this as a tool to keep the user base in line with feeling like they are part of our solutions and as such have a stake in the success of not just the project, but also our organization as a whole.

5. It's time to re-brand

Now that that the public perception is improving and the foundation is set for continued success with new policies and procedures, everything is perfect right? Unfortunately that is not the case. What we discovered at Virginia Commonwealth University is that no matter how good you get, there are still those users that will associate you with your old image. As a result, our customer service surveys indicated that there was still a negative impression in many people resulting from occurrences in the past. To help combat that, we began a campaign to rebrand the help desk.

5.1 The logo

The previous logo was outdated using a corded mouse that appeared like it was purchased with a Gateway 2000 486 machine. (See Image 4.)

Image 4. Previous help desk logo

This logo utilized a color scheme that was not even part of the university image as well as outdated technology. As a result, a meeting was held to discuss rebranding the logo and a brainstorming session came up with not just a logo but a slogan. The logo was to utilize the school colors and incorporate an "IT" moniker. The idea behind "IT" was to create a play on words using the acronym for Information Technology. As a result, the help desk was now rebranded to the helpIT Center. (See Image 5)

Image 5. The new helpIT Center logo

Along with the new logo, a branding slogan emerged which would be spread amongst other units of Technology Services. The slogan was "We're IT". (See Image 6)

Image 6. We're IT is being used across the department

This allowed us to market many of our services under the "IT" campaign. At the helpIT Center we have two service arms, the getIT program and the fixIT program. (See Image 7) The getIT program is the program that Faculty/Staff and primarily Students use to purchase approved computers for use at the university or home. The fixIT Program is a full services repair shop at the university providing in and out of warranty computer repair work.

Image 7. The getIT and fixIT logos

5.2 The office

Next we had to improve our appearance to the outside world. The location of the helpIT Center is in the basement of the library on our academic campus. Prior to summer 2010, the entryway to the office was a single door and with a student body of over 32,000 students, plus over 10,000 faculty and staff, we would many times have a long line waiting for service. The desk space for the walkup counter was limited to two very cramped workstations. This had to change. A project was put in motion to widen the entryway and extend the walkup space to accommodate multiple workstations. (See Image 8) This offers us the ability to scale our staffing of the walkup counter to meet the need of the timeframe. During the summer when we are quite slow, we can have one or two staff members working at the counter, however if a staffing increase is needed, we can expand our staffing to meet the need up to potentially 6 workstations. Furthermore, we were able to meet the needs of our disabled user base by offering an ADA Compliant workspace. Finally, by opening up our entry way, we were given the opportunity to more boldly promote our center using signage behind the walkup counter as well as the large digital display at the entrance to our facility.

Image 8. The new entrance and walkup counter.

6. Going forward

Through efforts to improve our metrics and quality of service, rebranding was the final step in transforming our department from a substandard help desk to a world class support center. Through the process we learned valuable lessons in measuring our quality and consistency of service. The morale has improved through efforts to streamline the management structure and as a result our customer satisfaction has increased.

Managing iOS Mobile Devices

Kristen Dietiker
University of Washington
Box 356410
Seattle, WA 98195
(206) 616-9066
dietiker@uw.edu

ABSTRACT

Mobile devices are sweeping across campuses as students and faculty find new uses for them in learning, teaching, and research. At the University of Washington's Department of Surgery, a similar story is being told. There is great interest in deploying iPads in research and education among both faculty and staff. However, the tension between providing resources to meet faculty and staff interests and the requirement to meet institutional data security standards is difficult to manage. Similarly, the demands on IT staffs keep rising and it is difficult to find the financial and staffing resources to meet all requests. However, mobile devices make a strong use case in academia, and their use will continue to expand regardless if whether IT units are on board. At the Department of Surgery, managing the explosion of mobile devices could potentially be a complex and burdensome task, and iPad deployment could not proceed within the department until there was a security and management solution in place.

There are a number of different mobile device management solutions in the marketplace that were identified and compared. However, the department had a pre-existing installation of Casper Suite by JAMF Software that was used to manage the department's fleet of Macintosh computers. JAMF Software recently rolled out an iOS management component to the Casper Suite; using this solution, iPads can be centrally managed and security standards strictly enforced. After an analysis of other potential solutions, costs, infrastructure requirements, and technician training requirements, the Department of Surgery determined that leveraging Casper Suite to manage iOS devices was the best choice. However, with budget concerns impacting the ability to purchase test iPad units and additional Casper Suite iOS licenses, the deployment project was postponed to Summer 2011. The current timeline calls for building the iOS management infrastructure in Casper Suite in July and August 2011, and iPad deployment to an initial research unit in September.

Categories and Subject Descriptors

C.5.3 [**Computer System Implementation**]: Microcomputers. K.3.0 [**Computers and Education**]: General. K.6.2 [**Installation Management**]: Computing Equipment Management. K.6.3 [**Software Management**]: Software Selection.

General Terms

Management, Documentation, Security, Standardization.

Keywords

iOS, iPad, iPod Touch, Mobile Device Management, MDM, JAMF, Casper Suite

1. INTRODUCTION

1.1 Department Overview

The Department of Surgery is an academic department within the University of Washington (UW) School of Medicine. The department employs over 300 faculty, staff, researchers, and affiliated clinicians. While most faculty and staff are located at either the University of Washington Medical Center (UWMC) or Harborview Medical Center (HMC), some personnel are located at affiliated institutions. Research, Education, and Clinical Care are the three primary foci of the department. While the department is an academic unit, it is under the umbrella of "UW Medicine" and thus has strict data security requirements that govern the use of all departmental computing resources.

1.2 Information Technology Overview

The Department of Surgery IT Services Group (ITSG) is comprised of eight staff and student employees who maintain the network and domain infrastructure used by the department and who also provide technical support to departmental employees. Approximately 78% of the department's desktops are running Windows XP, and the remaining 22% are Macintosh computers. The department uses Microsoft Active Directory for authentication of both Windows and Macintosh hosts and provides additional Macintosh client management via JAMF Software's Casper Suite [1]. In addition, there are other campus IT groups that provide technology resources to departmental employees. The two main ones are UW IT and UW Medicine Information Technology Services. UW IT is the central university technology unit and provides network infrastructure and core IT services such as email, HR, and financial applications to the entire campus. UW Medicine IT Services provides the medical centers, School of Medicine, and other affiliate groups with clinical applications such as electronic medical records, and also manages the computing infrastructure in the medical centers. Both external groups provide limited support for mobile devices.

2. PROJECT OVERVIEW

2.1 Background

Due to Washington State regulations that regard cell phones provided to employees as a taxable benefit, and that also restrict the personal use of state property, the department has not provided or supported smartphones for faculty and staff. Palm PDAs were heavily used in the past, and were supported by ITSG, but the use of these devices plummeted as people bought personal smartphones. Given this rapid decline in use of PDAs within our department, and no requirement to support personal smartphones, there was no push to implement a management solution for mobile devices until very recently. However, the explosion of iPads among our user base over the past two years has created a huge demand for both device support and the delivery of services to mobile devices.

Recently, faculty began urging UW Medicine Information Technology Services to deliver clinical applications to mobile devices, as there are compelling examples that reveal the exciting future of mobile devices in medicine. For example, at the University of Chicago Pritzker School of Medicine, Internal Medicine Residents are equipped with iPads for clinical use [2]. In addition, there is great interest in utilizing iPads in medical education. For example, several other medical schools such as UC Irvine [3], Stanford University [4], and Brown University [5] are providing or requiring students to use iPads with electronic versions of their medical books and other course materials. Similarly, other groups across the University of Washington are deploying mobile devices in research and education; and as a national leader in surgical education, the Department of Surgery expects to be on the cutting edge of both of these areas. In addition to the interest in mobile devices for clinical and education use, other teams within our department are interested in deploying iPads in the collection and analysis of research data.

With these developments in mind, it has become increasing clear that maintaining the status quo in terms of requiring faculty and staff to purchase and support mobile devices on their own actually increases the risk of a data security incident for our department. If faculty begin using unsecured mobile devices to access and store protected health information (PHI) and other confidential information, the risks of data exposure from a lost or stolen device increase. And, as even our research teams utilize clinical data for research, the use of mobile devices in research also comes with a strict data security requirement. Thus it has become apparent that the department needed to implement a mobile device management (MDM) solution to provide secure devices to faculty and researchers in a way that facilitated use and also reduced the department's risk of data loss or exposure.

2.2 Constraints

Given the plethora of mobile OS's and hardware manufacturers, it was quickly realized that providing a MDM solution encompassing them all would be problematic for our small IT team and budget. It was determined that the practical course would be to focus on one platform that would enable the use of both in house and external apps, database input, and Internet access. Since UW Medicine IT Services was investigating clinical apps for iPads, it made sense to follow their lead and concentrate our efforts on the iOS platform. In fact, the iOS platform was heavily represented among the personally owned devices purchased by department faculty and staff, and several researchers had already approached ITSG with requests for iPads. Thus the decision to focus on iOS security and management was quickly made.

Financial considerations were also in effect. The department needed a method to deploy iPads to researchers quickly and cost effectively, with minimal user or technician training required. As there was no budget initially allocated to this project, actual implementation, including the purchase of test iPad units, was put on the back burner until the new fiscal year beginning in July 2011.

2.3 Requirements

A list of technical and practical requirements for managing iOS devices within the department was developed. In terms of technical requirements, the ability to manage the following features were required:

1. **Remote wipe:** Log into a web site and securely and permanently erase all data in the event of a lost or stolen device.
2. **Passcode lock:** Require and/or remove a passcode from a device.
3. **App distribution:** Publish both in-house and App Store apps to devices.

Practical requirements included cost, support requirements, integration with existing solutions, and technician training requirements. With minimal resources, the department needed an MDM solution that would require as little time for a technician to configure as possible.

2.4 Potential Solutions

A survey of available MDM solutions providing iOS support was made. As of April 2011, the following solutions were available or announced in the marketplace: [6]

Table 1. Mobile Device Management Solutions

PRODUCT	COMPANY
Absolute Manage	Absolute Software
Afaria	Sybase
AirWatch	AirWatch
BoxTone	BoxTone
Casper Suite	JAMF Software
McAfee EMM (formerly Trust Digital EMM)	McAfee
Mobile Active Defense	M.A.D. Partners LLC
Mobile Iron	Mobile Iron
Tangoe	Tangoe
TARMAC	equinix
Zenprise	Zenprise

All of the marketplace solutions met the department's technical requirements for iOS management: remote wipe, passcode lock and complexity, and app distribution. The majority of the solutions surveyed provided far more functionality than was required, including the support of alternative mobile platforms. Three solutions only supported the iOS mobile platform; these were Absolute Manage, Casper Suite, and TARMAC.

As the department already had an installation of Casper Suite to manage departmental Macintosh computers, the Casper Suite iOS components were included as part of already paid for maintenance upgrades, and that this solution met our technical requirements, ITSG quickly determined that the JAMF Software product was the most cost effective solution, even though it did not offer as many features as competing products, nor did it support non-iOS devices. However, as there was no mandate to support other platforms, that consideration was discarded. In addition, it was determined that Casper Suite would require the least amount of technician training and support, given the current familiarity with the tool. As it turned out, the licensing model for iOS devices in Casper Suite was less expensive than for our Mac OS X clients, and the department determined that it would be able to implement a fully functional and supported MDM solution for 15 iPads for under $250 (not including the cost of the iPads themselves).

With budget concerns impacting our ability to purchase test iPad units, the deployment project was postponed to after the start of the new fiscal year in July 2011. The current project timeline calls for building the iOS management infrastructure in Casper Suite in July and August 2011, and iPad deployment to an initial research unit in September.

3. PROJECT PLAN

3.1 Preparation

In order to use Casper Suite's MDM capabilities, several requirements must be met and technologies put in place first:

Apple iTunes: This is used on a workstation to activate, backup, and restore iOS devices and install iOS updates. In the case of an organization wanting to require MDM before allowing a user's personal iPhone or iPad to connect to a secure network, the individual continues to use iTunes on their home computer to activate, backup, and restore their device. For Department of Surgery iPad users, ITSG will use an IT workstation with iTunes installed to activate department-purchased iOS devices. This was considered feasible since it was a one-time procedure, and it was estimated that the number of devices would remain under 15 the first year. If a large number of devices are purchased in the future, however, this plan may need to be reevaluated.

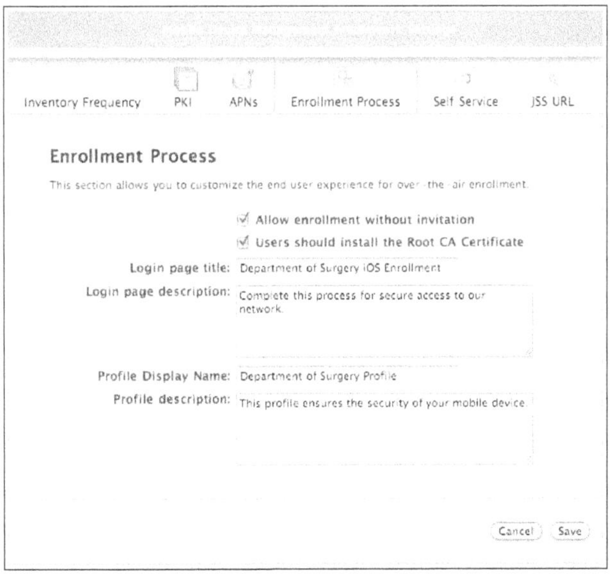

Figure 1. Configuring the Enrollment Process in Casper Suite

Apple Push Notification service (APNs): This technology is used to send notifications to devices, which triggers a check in with the MDM server. An organization must enroll in the Apple iOS Developer Program and get a Push Notification Certificate, which is then uploaded to the Casper Suite server [7]. In order to get a Push Notification Certificate, the organization must have at least one test iOS device available and give Apple that device's Universal Unique Identifier (UUID). The University of Washington has an Apple iOS Developer account, and once the new fiscal year begins and a test device can be purchased, the department will enroll the device and get the push certificate.

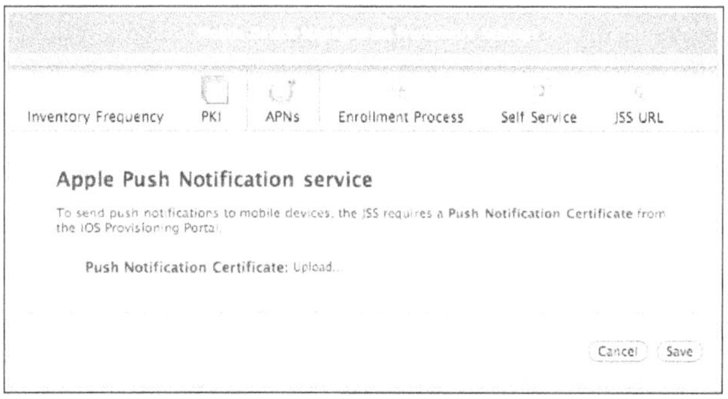

Figure 2. Uploading the Push Notification Certificate in Casper Suite

Public Key Infrastructure (PKI): This allows certificates to be pushed to iOS devices, allowing for secure communication between device and server. Casper Suite v. 8.0 and higher has a certificate authority built in, and it can also integrate with external CAs. The department is already running Casper Suite v. 8.1, so no configuration changes or upgrades are required. The option exists to use a self-signed certificate or a certificate granted from a CA; in this situation, it was determined that a certificate from the University of Washington Certificate Authority would be provisioned.

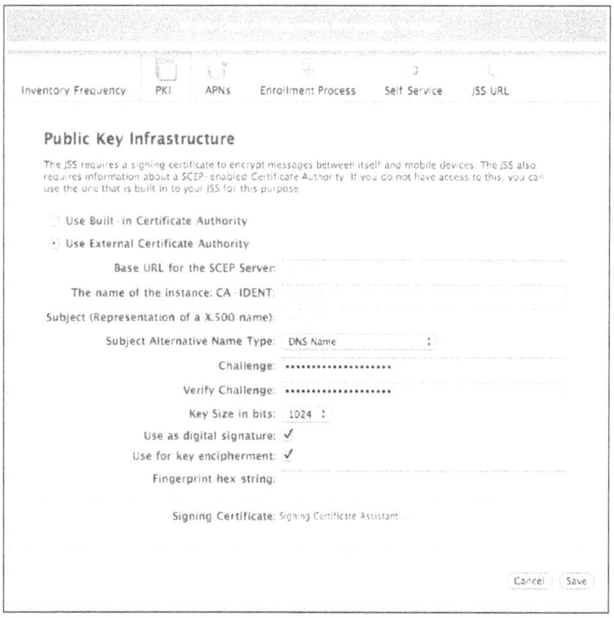

Figure 3. Configuring the PKI in Casper Suite

There are other configuration options to consider. The Department of Surgery is using the interval until July 2011 to determine the appropriate security policy and configuration settings to push to devices or groups of devices. An analysis of password complexity requirements would have the biggest impact on users; a default 4-digit PIN would be preferred by users, but some use cases might require a complex alpha-numeric device passcode. Additionally, other options exist, such as enforcing encrypted backups (when the device is attached to a computer with iTunes) as well as limiting access to device features and applications.

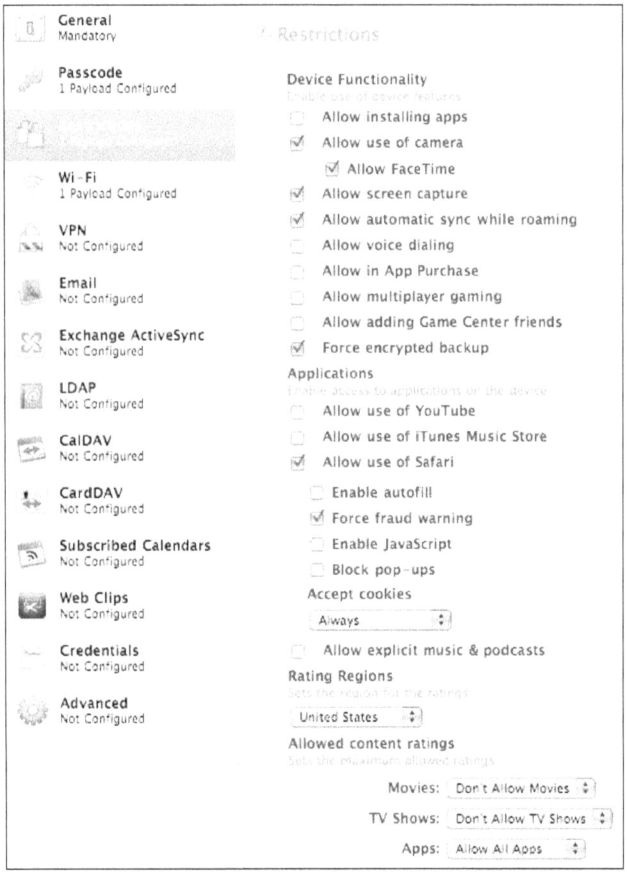

Figure 4. Configuring Device Restrictions in Casper Suite

3.2 Timeline

The project timeline calls for purchasing test iPad and iPod Touch units in July 2011 and using those device's UUIDs to obtain a Push Notification Certificate from Apple under the University of Washington's iOS Developer account. Once these are obtained, the Casper Server will be configured and different security policy and configuration policies will be tested. For example, testing and certifying the remote wipe capability is critical. Then, the results of these tests will allow ITSG to refine documentation, deployment strategies, and ensure that all technicians are familiar with the features and use of the administrative console. Finally, ITSG expects that a small group of users from various sections of the department will begin receiving iPads in September 2011 to test in various research and educational scenarios. They in turn will help us further refine the deployment and configuration policies in an iterative process.

4. Conclusion

The Department of Surgery at the University of Washington School of Medicine, part of UW Medicine, plans to implement a Mobile Device Management solution for iPads to enable their use by research staff and faculty in a secure way.

Other departments interested in deploying an MDM solution for iOS devices would be wise to evaluate Casper Suite carefully. However, it would likely be unsuitable for organizations needing to manage competing mobile platforms such as Android, Blackberry or Windows 7 Phone. While supporting mobile devices is difficult for many IT groups who are pressed for time and resources, the frenetic pace at which mobile devices are being adopted in academia make this a project worth undertaking, especially if the security of institutional data and computing resources is to be maintained.

5. ACKNOWLEDGMENTS

My thanks to the Department of Surgery IT Services team at the University of Washington School of Medicine and to those who read and made suggestions on this paper.

6. REFERENCES

[1] JAMF Software: Client Management Software for Macintosh Professionals. http://www.jamfsoftware.com/, (retrieved June 1, 2011)

[2] DOM iPad Initiative Increases Resident Productivity. *http://medicine.uchicago.edu/about/ipad.html*, (retrieved June 1, 2011)

[3] Incoming UCI medical students to receive iPads loaded with first-year curriculum. *http://today.uci.edu/news/2010/08/nr_ipad_100803.php*, (retrieved June 1, 2011)

[4] iPads to be distributed to incoming class by Stanford medical school. *http://med.stanford.edu/ism/2010/august/ipad.html*, (retrieved June 1, 2011)

[5] Textbooks Go the iTunes Route, but Buying by Chapters Might Not Save Students Money. *http://chronicle.com/article/Textbooks-Go-the-iTunes-Route/127590/*, (retrieved June 1, 2011)

[6] Comparison of MDM Providers. *http://enterpriseios.com/wiki/Comparison_MDM_Providers*, (retrieved June 1, 2011)

[7] Generating an Apple Push Notification Certificate. *http://www.jamfsoftware.com/libraries/pdf/white_papers/JAMFSoftware-Creating_an_Apple_Push_Notification_Certificate.pdf*, (retrieved July 14, 2011

Charting a New Course from Blackboard to Sakai

Beth Rugg
Ithaca College
953 Danby Rd
Ithaca, NY 14850
607-274-7349
erugg@ithaca.edu

ABSTRACT

Ithaca College is charting a new course in the sea of learning management systems leaving the turbulent Blackboard waters to find a safe port of harbor with Sakai. This paper will chronicle the issues that led us to begin charting this course, the initial departmental recommendation, how we involved faculty in the review and decision making process, the technical review process, the pilot and the implementation.

Learning management systems are foundational instructional technologies. Yet, the options are limited and not extremely competitive. For the past decade Ithaca College had flip-flopped between Blackboard and WebCT (not necessarily by choice) trying the patience of all involved especially faculty and IT support staff. After the last upgrade forced by the purchase of WebCT by Blackboard, and in light of significant licensing increases, IT administration looked for a way to get out of the turbulent waters and into calmer seas. As a result of a collaborative review and evaluation process, Ithaca College is implementing Sakai hosted by Longsight beginning May 2011 with campus-wide implementation planned for the Fall 2011. This decision and move is significant because it will be the first major enterprise application system that is open source and hosted by an off campus vendor. The decision made sense philosophically, pedagogically and financially. We believe this change will provide a more stable, robust, collaborative environment for the future and will share our process in this paper.

Categories and Subject Descriptors

H.5.2 [**Information Systems**]: Information Interfaces and Presentation – *user interfaces, user interface management systems.*

K.3 [**Computing Milieux**]: Computers and Education – *collaborative learning, computer-assisted instruction, computer managed instruction, distance learning.*

General Terms

Management, Documentation, Performance, Reliability, Human Factors

Keywords

Learning Management System, Evaluation, Process, Blackboard, Sakai, Vendor, Implementation, Pilot

1. INTRODUCTION

Ithaca College is a private college located in upstate New York with approximately 6000 students and 750 faculty members. The institution has five schools: Humanities and Sciences, Communication, Music, Business and Health Science and Human Performances.

Information Technology Services (ITS) is a central IT organization that supports both academic and administrative services and systems for the college. Technology and Instructional Support Services (TISS), a department within ITS is responsible for academic support. The academic support team within TISS consists of two instructional designers, a training and documentation specialist and a digital media services coordinator. Ithaca College uses Banner for the Student Information System.

ITS worked with Faculty Council on getting the move from Blackboard to Sakai reviewed and approved. The Faculty Council is comprised of faculty representation from all of the schools and is makes recommendations for the College faculty on all-college policies concerning curriculum, programs, grading, appointments, tenure, and promotions. The Faculty Council also acts as a liaison between the faculty and administration on matters of mutual concern.

2. HISTORY

Since 2000, the learning management system at Ithaca College has been in a state of flux. Initially, Ithaca College used Blackboard. After several years of poor support, IT decided to move to WebCT. WebCT proved to meet the college's needs and provided good support but was bought out by Blackboard in 2005. When Blackboard ended its support of WebCT, Ithaca College was forced to migrate to Blackboard Campus Edition 8 (CE8). This migration was completed by 2009. Blackboard then announced that it would end support of CE8 by 2013. Blackboard's roadmap projected another difficult migration from CE8 to Blackboard 9 (the first offering in the fully integrated product line). At that time, many of CE8's key features were missing from Blackboard 9 including the ability to cross-list courses, the question database and the file manager. Subsequently, Blackboard has bundled some of the missing features into version 9.1 and other premium packages. To retain required functionality, it was determined that Ithaca College would need to move to a premium Blackboard offering that would include Blackboard community features at triple the cost. Ithaca College decided to evaluate all options and break the cycle of vendor dictated upgrades.

3. INTERNAL REVIEW

In late 2009, Mary Jo Watts, the Instructional Technology Specialist administering Blackboard at IC, was tasked with doing an internal review of LMS options. Her analysis reviewed proprietary and open source alternatives and recommended that the college consider moving to Sakai, a community source offering developed by higher education for higher education. This recommendation was partially influenced by Mary Jo's experience; she had been an implementer for Sakai at Rutger's University.

3.1 Proprietary Options

Blackboard, Inc has a near monopoly over the proprietary LMS market and expanded their dominance in 2009 with the purchase of Angel. At that time, Desire 2 Learn (D2L) was its only other major competitor. However, D2L had been embroiled in a three-year-long multimillion-dollar patent infringement lawsuit. Blackboard's patent infringement allegations were nullified but the long term impact for D2L was unknown.

3.2 Open Source Options

Resistance to vendor lock-in and escalating licensing costs have led many colleges and universities around the world to choose open source learning management systems such as Moodle and Sakai over the limited proprietary options. Both products are developed collaboratively. Their code is open for modification, distribution is free, and the licenses are liberal. Both systems successfully support teaching and learning at a variety of institutions. The differences between Sakai and Moodle, however, are significant. They have different development practices, different architectures, and different target user populations.

Moodle core software development is governed by an individual, Martin Dougiamas, and includes teams of developers funded by the Moodle project, Catalyst Ltd in New Zealand and the Open University in the UK. Dougiamas is the ultimate decision maker.

Sakai, in contrast, is often referred to as a "community source" product because it has a formal governance structure. Original development of Sakai was done at the University of Michigan, Indiana University, Stanford and MIT and is now guided by the Sakai Foundation, a dues paying, member-based, non-profit alliance of universities, colleges and commercial affiliates. The Sakai project model was established to sustain the long-term development of an LMS that can scale to fit the technical and functional needs of institutions with large and diverse user populations.

There are important philosophical differences between Moodle and Sakai as well. Moodle is designed specifically to present course materials and activities to students using a social constructionist approach. Moodle encourages the instructor to organize course resources and activities by units such as topic or date. Sakai is referred to as a Collaborative Learning Environment [CLE] because it was built to support collaboration of all kinds-projects as well as traditional classes.

4. REVIEW PROCESS

Once the internal review was complete, the Director of Technology and Instructional Support Services brought the recommendation to Faculty Council. Faculty Council agreed to support the proposal if the proposal was supported by a faculty review team.

Further technical analysis was also required and an internal review team was tasked with gathering additional information about the technical options for locally hosting either Blackboard or Sakai or moving to a hosted option.

Committee review work was prioritized. The faculty review effort was the first to take place followed by the internal technical review. It was felt that if the faculty did not support the initial recommendation than there was no reason to have the technical review team start analyzing Sakai. The faculty review team was also informed that the recommendation had to receive not only their support but the support of the technical review team in order to proceed to an implementation phase. Some core team members were on both review teams including the Instructional Support team (Mary Jo Watts, Marilyn Dispensa) and myself as project lead. Having shared team members helped keep both efforts informed as to the progress of the other effort. The faculty review effort took place from May through June. The technical review took place from June through September.

Both committees ended up supporting the initial recommendation to move to Sakai. The technical review committee also recommended a vendor hosted solution, conducted a vendor analysis and made the final vendor recommendation.

Clear, effective communication was critical to the success of the review effort. ITS leadership acknowledged that it was not a neutral product and vendor evaluation. We acknowledged that we felt Sakai would provide a superior offering while maintaining costs and that we had the support staff available who already knew the product. All of these factors influenced the initial recommendation.

Some faculty misinterpreted our recommendation for a final decision. However, because we went to Faculty Council and had an approved methodology and asked for faculty volunteers, this criticism was diffused. Others argued that cost was a deciding factor. It was not. We would not have recommended an inferior product in an effort to save money. We did feel that Sakai offered a more robust collaborative environment at a similar cost to our version of WebCT CE8. If either review team did not support the recommendation then we would not have implemented Sakai at Ithaca College.

Making an internal recommendation and then getting that recommendation vetted by the faculty and a technical review team was risky and unusual. But, through open and honest communication and hard work, the risk paid off. At worst, if either team did not support the recommendation then all we would have lost was time while still gaining an understanding of faculty and system requirements.

4.1 LMS Faculty Advisory Committee

ITS sent out a call for participation to all faculty members. Over twenty faculty volunteered; the final team was composed of ten faculty with representation from each school and a range of LMS experience and skill levels. The group met from mid-March through June and reviewed the initial recommendation, learned about the options, met with vendors, worked within Sakai. After this analysis the faculty review team supported the recommendation to move to Sakai. Their support was mixed, some would have preferred to stay with Blackboard because the interface was more familiar and the migration seemed to be easier but they recognized the financial implications and the flexibility that Sakai provided the institution. In general, faculty appreciated being involved in the process.

A final recommendation was prepared and presented to Faculty Council in October.

4.2 Technical Review

The technical review team was charged with evaluating Blackboard Academic Suite 9 (hosted by Ithaca College); Blackboard Academic Suite 9 (hosted by Blackboard); Sakai hosted locally by Ithaca College; and Sakai hosted by a vendor. Particular attention was paid to administration functionality; system architecture; security; support; cost; the migration effort; authentication; and integration with the student information system (SIS), myHome, iTunes U, clickers, etc. Details of implementation, configuration and migration were not considered within the scope of the technical review and were undertaken in a separate project.

To perform the technical evaluation, the team:

1. Defined desired and required functional requirements and performed a comparative analysis,
2. Reviewed vendor responses to our Requests for Proposals (RFPs) from Blackboard (both local and hosted solutions), Longsight and another vendor (Sakai hosted),
3. Conducted on-site vendor demonstrations (rSmart and Longsight) for ITS staff,
4. Surveyed the ITS staff who attended the vendor demos,
5. Interviewed several references for each vendor,
6. Evaluated all survey and reference responses and made a vendor recommendation.

The ITS technical review team concurred with the recommendation of the LMS Faculty Advisory Committee that Ithaca College should select Sakai. In addition, the ITS technical review team recommended that IC choose Longsight to host and support Sakai. Blackboard 9.1 did not meet the college's administrative, digital media and non-academic needs. Blackboard 9.1 Academic Suite with the community and content modules would have met the college's requirements but at a significant annual cost increase. The new version of Blackboard was based on a different architecture and would have required time and money for hardware and programming. Blackboard, hosted, was prohibitively expensive.

Sakai was chosen because it satisfied the requirements of a flexible, robust LMS with limited increase to annual licensing costs. There is a stable community committed to its maintenance and development. However, it was determined that the infrastructure and technical expertise needed to run Sakai locally required the addition of staff and hardware and was advised against. A hosted solution was considered the best option and the team recommended Longsight because they were superior in the quality of their response to the RFP, their campus presentation and meetings, the ITS staff survey responses, and the quality and enthusiasm of their references. In addition, their hosting costs were significantly lower than their competitor.

5. CRITIQUE OF REVIEW PROCESS

In retrospect, the review process worked well for where we were at as an organization and as an institution but it did require careful planning, organization and communication. We admit that we did not do an in-depth review of all options nor did we solicit faculty input by conducting competing pilots of various products (e.g. Moodle versus Sakai versus Blackboard). We were up front with why we were making the recommendations that were made; we didn't try to hide our agenda and; with the LMS market being so narrow, making the recommendation for Sakai and then getting buy in for that recommendation made sense and made the process simpler. The faculty review was taken very seriously. ITS facilitated the review process by meeting with faculty, hearing their concerns, showing both options (Sakai and Blackboard) and gathering feedback. If the faculty had disagreed with our recommendation, we would have rescinded the recommendation and started again. Internally, one of our Instructional Technology Specialists would have preferred and competitive review process and disagreed with our methodology but was part of the technical review team and ended up supporting the recommendation.

6. IMPLEMENTATION

Once the decision was made to move to a hosted version of Sakai and funding was secured, the implementation project was initiated and a plan developed. The implementation process included initial installation, configuration and testing, followed by a pilot use phase involving select faculty using the system in actual courses, followed by refinements, modifications and bug fixes, followed by a release of the new system to run in parallel to the old one for an academic year, followed by a deadline after which all new courses will be run on the new system and none added to the old, and finally a planned date for all courses on the old system to be closed and the system decommissioned. (As this paper is written, we are in the middle of the pilot phase of the implementation.)

6.1 Timeline

The Sakai implementation is following this timeline:

1. The contract was signed in January 2011
2. The hosted development instance of Sakai for Ithaca College was available within 4 weeks of the contract being signed by mid-February 2011
3. Pilot participation criteria and duration was defined in February. The pilot would take place during Summer Session 1, May through June 2011
4. Faculty pilot volunteers were solicited in March
5. The production instance of Sakai was available to pilot faculty members in April for course development
6. Migration processes were defined and support was available by April
7. Limited integration with the Student Information System (Banner) was available by May 1st
8. The pilot was run from end of May through the end of June 2011
9. The go/no go decision will be made in early July
10. Assuming a "go" decision, full automation with the student information system will be available in July
11. Sakai and Blackboard will run in parallel for the 2011-2012 academic year
12. Sakai will be the only LMS available to faculty for the Fall 2012 semester
13. ITS will pay for the Blackboard license through 2013 in anticipation of needing the retrieve content for faculty

6.2 Contract

The review of the contract was straight forward involving the vendor, ITS, Legal Affairs and VP of Finance and Administration. No significant obstacles were encountered.

6.3 Initial Configuration

Sakai is the first major enterprise system to be hosted off site. The technical review phase showed that the vendor met all of the college's information security requirements and abided by current best practices for system administration, backups and redundancy. The initial configuration was set up within four weeks of the contract being signed. The initial instance used Sakai version 2.7.

After reviewing the initial configuration, we requested some customizations needed for our faculty to "group" rosters together. We knew from our Blackboard implementation, that many faculty members teach multiple sections of the same course and want to be able to "group" the roster information together so that the content is available in one section. For the Blackboard implementation, we had done custom programming between Banner and Blackboard in order to make this functionality available. We found that the functionality we needed in Sakai was available by using the CMI API developed by Rutgers University and we requested that that API be used in our instance.

In Sakai, users click on a course or project link and have a new tab open up. The tabs can spread across the computer screen. Another API was available that allowed for a listing of all course and project sites in one tab. When the user clicks on the link a third tab opens up. We felt that that API was easier for the users and requested that it be installed in our instance.

We also requested some custom language as part of the course creation process in order to make the choices clearer to faculty members. Our system administrator, working with the Longsight integrator, made these changes.

It took approximately one month for the development instance to be configured to our specifications and tested. The changes were put into production within one day of testing being completed.

6.4 Sakai Gains and Gaps Compared to Blackboard

6.4.1 Gains

With Sakai we have gained:

- A more collaborative course environment
- A collaborative project environment not associated with academic courses available to any faculty, staff or student group e.g. task forces, student organizations, review groups, working groups, project teams
- A shared file repository
- Drop box
- Wiki
- iTunes U integration
- Email archive
- Polls
- Citation list
- Easy access for guests
- Easy account creation process for guests
- The ability for faculty to easily make content publicly viewable

6.4.2 Gaps

6.4.2.1 Course Content

In Blackboard, the Course Content page is the primary tool faculty use to organize and share materials. Sakai offers all users the ability to upload files and folders and to share them instantly with no linking required in the Resources Tool. Almost every Sakai tool grants instructors and project site maintainers the power to share files via attachments. Many tools can be configured to allow students and site participants the same ability. For those who would like to maintain the functionality of Course Content, both the Modules Tool and the Web Page (HTML) Tool allow instructors and project site maintainers to organize course content in a way visually similar to Blackboard's Course Content page.

6.4.2.2 Grading Forms & Goals

These tools are used primarily for rubric-based grading with an emphasis on learning outcomes. While there is no exact parallel tool in Sakai, instructors can upload a .doc or .pdf of a rubric as an attachment in the Assignments tool for students. After grading, the instructor can fill it out and upload it to the graded assignment that is returned to the student. The total score can be added to a gradebook column manually.

Ithaca College is also examining the option of integrating iRubric within Sakai. iRubric is a comprehensive rubric development, assessment and sharing tool recently developed by a third party vendor that integrates with Sakai. Longsight is installing this tool on a development site, and, once Ithaca College has had a chance to review the tool, a purchase decision will be made.

6.4.2.3 Who's Online

The Meetings (Big Blue Button) tool can replace this functionality. Two hundred hours of use of Big Blue Button is included in the hosting price. Big Blue Button combines the ability to see who is logged into the meeting with multiple forms of chat-- text, video and audio (VoIP or phone-in). Instructors and project site maintainers can track their students' and participants' usage via the Site Stats Tool. However, the initial research and use of the tool by the project team yielded inconsistent quality and performance results. The project team has decided not to promote the use of this tool during implementation.

6.4.2.4 Notes

There is no direct parallel in Sakai but students can use a variety of tools to take notes including the HTML page or text box options in the Drop Box and Resources or the Blog Tool.

6.4.2.5 My Progress

Instructors and project site maintainers can track their students' and participants' usage via the robust Site Stats Tool. Instructors and project site maintainers can generate usage reports and share them with individual students and participants in the Drop Box tool or via a private note in the Messages Tool.

6.5 Migration of Content

Migrating content from Blackboard CE 8 to Sakai 2.7 is problematic. We had been told during the technical review phase that the migration could be done in an automated fashion. That information turned out to be incorrect. It can be done for certain "flavors" of Blackboard, Blackboard Learn for example. However, it cannot be done for Blackboard CE versions. Users will have to rebuild their content in Sakai. The time it takes for this rebuild process will vary depending on the complexity of the Blackboard course. Many faculty may opt to start from scratch since Sakai actually presents information very differently then Blackboard.

Unfortunately, many pilot faculty members did not migrate content out of Blackboard into Sakai so we have limited feedback regarding the migration experience. We expect criticism but we are prepared to help faculty as much as possible and have developed several tutorials detailing the migration process. Unfortunately, we know many faculty members will wait until right before classes to build their Sakai courses and will be frustrated by the difficulty of the content migration.

Tests and quizzes do not migrate. We are recommending that faculty use Respondus to help them migrate question banks. Respondus has a free 30 day trial that faculty members can download or they can use the Center for Educational Technology where it is installed on the Windows computers.

Course packs will also be problematic as they are typically sold to faculty for specific versions of Blackboard. The number of faculty who use course packs is small but those that do rely on them. We are asking that faculty who use course cartridges contact ITS for help in getting course packs that work with Sakai

Rubrics associated with the Blackboard gradebook will not migrate since there is not a comparable tool in Sakai.

The biggest obstacle to a successful Sakai implementation will be the content migration. It will not be easy and we expect faculty frustration. But, we are hopeful that once the transition is made, because vendors are not dictating upgrades and changes, long term the system will be more stable from a faculty perspective.

6.6 Integration

6.6.1 Integration with the Student Information System

Our integration with the Banner student information system takes place in several ways:

- The course, instructor and enrollment data is pushed to Longsight. Longsight then runs an automated job to integrate the data within Sakai
- Using the CMI API, faculty have access to all rosters and can combine rosters for the purpose of creating a course in Sakai
- Data for multiple terms will be available depending on the time of the year

6.6.1.1 Course, Instructor and Enrollment Data

Course, instructor and enrollment data is pushed from the Banner system twice daily for the pilot and will be pushed four times a day during normal production. Real time integration with Banner is possible but would require a significant level of effort by both Ithaca College and Longsight so the implementation team decided it was not necessary. The Sakai data will be up dated more frequently then we were able to accomplish with Blackboard.

If a student drops a course, the student no longer has access to the course, the student's name drops from the roster and gradebook and any student data becomes unavailable to the student and the faculty member. If a student re-enrolls this access is restored. The Sakai system does not do any hard deletes.

If a course is cancelled in the Student Information System and the instructor has already initiated the course in Sakai, the course remains in Sakai. If content has been added to the course then the course appears in the instructor and students' active course drop down list. The instructor can contact the System Administrator who can make the course unavailable otherwise nothing happens.

FERPA protected students need to contact the Sakai System Administrator to request an account since the email address is not automatically passed to Sakai. This process is the same as the Blackboard process.

6.6.1.2 Combining Rosters

Instructors have the option of combining multiple rosters for courses they teach into a single course in Sakai. This functionality allows instructors to manage course content in a single course. Based on our experience with Blackboard, this functionality was highly desired by our faculty.

The CMI API developed by Rutgers for Sakai provided this functionality. We requested this API for our Sakai instance and worked with Longsight to change some of the language on the course creation pages to make the process clearer. Because Ithaca College maintains these changes, when we cloned the development instance into production this work had to be redone by the Ithaca College system administrator.

This functionality allows for:

- Multiple sections of the same course taught by the same instructor to be combined together
- Multiple sections of the same course taught by different instructors to be combined together
- Different course to be combined together
- Labs and lectures to be combined
- Grad and undergrad courses to be combined

When combining rosters, the new course, by default, had the name of the first section e.g. if Bio101-01 and Bio101-02 were combined the new course was titled Bio101-01 even though the roster listed students from both sections. We thought this was confusing and provided instructors with the option of renaming the course. This option allows faculty to create courses that deviate from the standard naming convention but we thought that was a better option.

6.6.1.3 Academic Terms and Course Availability

The implementation team decided that the Sakai-Banner integration for the fall and spring terms will follow similar standards as had been used with Blackboard. When instructors log into Sakai, they choose what term they want to see a roster for. Course data will be available to instructors to initiate their Sakai courses after the add/drop period e.g. in April for the fall term, in November for the Spring term. Summer courses can be initiated in early March. January Winter term will be available in November. Special terms e.g. Occupational Therapy Winter term, will be available as soon as the Registrar's Office makes the term available.

A process has been developed between Ithaca College and Longsight regarding the processing of this data. Tickets into Longsight's support desk trigger the daily running of these jobs.

Course, instructor and enrollment data will be available for approximately one month after a term ends. Ithaca College will put in a request to Longsight to make a term inactive at which point students will no longer see the course in the active course tab. Instructors always have access to import content from an inactive course when initiating a new course.

6.6.2 Integration with our Web Portal Environment

Initial research into how Sakai would integrate with our web portal environment indicated an easy integration. However that proved not to be the case. The course creation process used code that forced the page out of the portal environment and there was concern about embedding the system in another system and the impact that that would have on learning. So, we were not able to integrate Sakai in our portal environment as originally hoped although Sakai does provide more opportunities for portal integration than Blackboard.

The instructional support team identified three "portlets" to be available within the portal system: announcements, messages and a site listing for any individual. The announcement and message portlets have already been developed by other institutions and should be easy to include and we will request that the vendor develop the third portlet. Once that has been done, it can be contributed back to the community. At this time, it is unknown if and when that work will happen.

6.7 Training and Support

Changing the learning management system has significant impact on faculty members. The instructional technology team hopes to minimize the impact by offering a wide range of support including one-on-one training, group workshop training, online task-focused tutorials and a web site devoted to Sakai. Workshops will begin to be offered in July in anticipation of fall roll-out.

It is anticipated that the majority of questions will be regarding the migration of data and the meta-organization of the Sakai site since it is so different then how Blackboard organizes data. We are still designing options to meet this need.

6.8 Pilot

In the spring, all faculty members were invited to volunteer to participate in the pilot. Twenty six faculty members responded from four out of the five schools at the college. The implementation team decided we wanted three types of pilot participants: 1) faculty teaching summer session I courses 2) faculty who wanted to be able to group rosters together for fall courses and 3) community members, including staff, who were interested in creating collaborative project sites not associated with academic courses. We had volunteers for all three categories and identified ten faculty members teaching during summer session I, eleven faculty members who wanted to group course rosters together and six faculty and staff members who wanted to create project sites. The majority of volunteers were accepted into the pilot and we hoped to have five to eight hundred students in the pilot group. Unfortunately the attrition was a significant and only five courses ended up being taught in summer session I to approximately fifty students. Several faculty dropped out of the pilot with no notice; others had their courses cancelled due to a lack of enrollment. The end result was a much smaller pilot group then we had hoped for. However, we did learn from the pilot group and uncovered some "bugs" that were fixed prior to roll out. One pilot faculty member actively solicited her students about their reaction to Sakai. Many students found it to be more robust then Blackboard although there were some complaints about the system being confusing (as one would expect with any change).

To date, the pilot has not uncovered any reasons why we should not roll Sakai out to the campus community.

7. CONCLUSION

Changing learning management systems is never easy. Faculty prefer static systems and resent having to put effort into learning new technologies that take time away from teaching and learning. At Ithaca College, we believe that by abandoning Blackboard and moving to a community sourced product developed by educators we can eventually get off the carousel of change dictated by vendors. We needed a more open, collaborative and cost effective environment and feel that Sakai offers a good alternative to Blackboard. Additionally, by moving to a hosted option, staff time has been freed up to concentrate on systems that cannot be outsourced.

The move from Blackboard to Sakai will not be completed until August 2012. However, so far so good. The pilot is taking place as this paper is being written and we are receiving positive feedback. The process of out-sourcing a major enterprise system has gone well and required less staff time than expected. We have had to contract for more support hours with the vendor but once the additional funding was secured ($2500) it was a simple process.

We have encountered some unexpected problems. We had been told that content from Blackboard CE 8 could be migrated using automated tools; that is not the case. We are also coming to realize that more faculty then was expected rely on the rubric tool in Blackboard and we are looking into a third party product, iRubric, to provide that functionality. We had hoped that Big Blue Button would fill the whiteboard gap but that product has yielded inconsistent results and, in general, will not be recommended to faculty. We are also concerned about the need for faculty to re-think their course organization. Sakai offers many tools and options and is more flexible then Blackboard. But, this flexibility may also cause the system to be more confusing.

The experience of outsourcing this system to Longsight has been extremely positive. We did not need to purchase servers, train staff, gain experience in new architecture and develop systems. We had the initial test instance up and running within two weeks of the contract being signed. It took an additional two months for the system to be configured to our functional requirements and have a base line of integration with our student information system. Pilot participants had access to the system within two months of the contract being signed.

To date, Sakai has had 100% up time; we have not experienced any system outages.

A new version of Sakai became available this spring. We will need to decide whether we put that version into production or continue with the current version, 2.7. The rubric tool we are looking at integrates with 2.7 not 2.8. Once we have had a chance to review the rubric tool we may then need to decide between the rubric tool and the upgrade. We are very concerned about minimizing changes to the environment because of faculty response.

Overall, the implementation has gone smoothly and working with the vendor has been a very successful collaboration. Although not perfect, the system is more powerful and flexible than our Blackboard installation for about the same cost. Longsight's support far exceeds Blackboard's support; in most cases tickets are resolved within twenty-four hours. We are not maintaining hardware and some Database Administrator and Programmer Analyst time has been freed up to work on other projects. So far, the Instructional Support team has been able to manage both Blackboard and Sakai, no new human resources have been added to assist with running these systems in parallel for the next year. Long term, we are hoping that the instructional team will have the time and tools available to help faculty members design courses that meet their instructional design needs and the expectations of the students.

8. ACKNOWLEDGMENTS

Many thanks to the members of the faculty review committee, the technical review committee and the project implementation teams especially Mary Jo Watts and Marilyn Dispensa.

9. REFERENCES

[1] Dispensa, Marilyn; Rugg, Beth; Watts, Mary Jo. *ITS Sakai Training and Documentation website.* https://sites.google.com/a/ithaca.edu/sakai/

The Circle of Internal Communication

Jean Tagliamonte
Vassar College
124 Raymond Avenue
Poughkeepsie, NY 12604
845-437-7743
jetagliamonte@vassar.edu

Chad Fust
Vassar College
124 Raymond Avenue
Poughkeepsie, NY 12604
845-437-7545
chfust@vassar.edu

ABSTRACT

It was apparent that the knowledge base in our ticketing system was both woefully out of date and hardly used. The problem was that nobody owned the process and the users of the system had been jaded by missing or out-of-date information. In this paper, we describe the process of cleaning up the out-of-date knowledge base and reinventing the process to encourage use of a valuable tool.

Categories and Subject Descriptors

H.5.3 [**Group and Organization Interfaces**]: Asynchronous interaction, Collaborative computing, Computer-supported cooperative work

General Terms

Management, Documentation, Performance, Human Factors.

Keywords

Documentation, Communications, Ticketing System, Knowledgebase, FAQ, Resources, Search, Support, Database

1. INTRODUCTION

We live in the information age. Knowledge is readily accessible and incredibly powerful. Those of us in the IT industry are incredibly skilled at using the wealth of research tools available to us to find the answers we are looking for. Fortunately for us, not all people possess the ability to master the Internet the way we have. You have likely heard of the web site "Let Me Google That For You" [1]. In our industry, we call that job security. It is easy to dismiss searching as something "anyone can do", but, in fact, it is not. It is a skill like any other. Some are naturals. Others will never master it.

Part of being a skilled researcher and consequently, a good troubleshooter, is knowing where to look. In higher education, that is where things get tricky. It is easy to find the solution to an MS Office problem or a tip for Mac OSX, but what about the hundreds of things that are specific to our campus communities? Every campus has unique network configurations, printing systems, card accounting, back-up servers, content management systems, etc. No amount of Googling will answer all of the questions posed to our help desks.

2. THE KNOWLEDGE BASE

2.1 A Sad Story

That is where knowledge bases come in. A knowledge base is defined as is a database providing the means for the collection, organization, and retrieval of knowledge and solutions to problems.

Most campuses use some kind of trouble ticketing system and many have built-in or additional knowledge bases. In our knowledge base, each item is called an FAQ or Frequently Asked Question. For each question in the knowledge base, there is a solution. These FAQs can be extremely helpful if properly maintained. Think of the wealth of information that can be gained by accessing issues that have been resolved. But, too often, knowledge bases are woefully under-used or out of date. In our experience, we have found that is due to the adage "garbage in, garbage out". We would like to share a little tale:

> *"Once upon a time, in a quaint little IT department, a new ticketing system was implemented. It was shiny. It was exciting. A few ambitious little geeks started filling the system up with everything they knew about everything! They turned issues into FAQs. It was awesome! All of the other workers had answers at their fingertips and added answers too. The happy little IT department ran like a well-oiled machine. Then one day, the little geeks got busy with other stuff and forgot about the knowledge base. The workers who were using it weren't finding what they were looking for or, even worse, they were finding out-of-date solutions. They grew frustrated after wasting their time trying to implement fixes that were no longer applicable. The workers stopped using the knowledge base. The IT department grew less efficient because knowledge wasn't being shared amongst the workers. Everyone grew bitter and hated the knowledge base. The knowledge base became old and dusty and was never accessed again."*

It is a sad story and one that is possibly achingly familiar. Many IT organizations have knowledge bases that are out-of-date, inaccurate and, essentially, useless. In our organization, the old information in the knowledge base had taken to seed like a neglected garden.

2.2 A Two-Part Problem

Part of the problem was that the knowledge base was supposed to be everybody's responsibility. What's everybody's problem becomes nobody's problem. Someone needs to own the process. This is a tricky proposition; the owner may not know every facet of the information to put in the knowledge base. The process thus requires participation from others, with someone still maintaining ownership.

Figure 1: Forgotten Knowledge Base

Another part of the problem is that if people have been burned by the knowledge base in the past, it is difficult to regain their trust. People will naturally continue to assume that they will not find the solution they seek or find one that is inaccurate and consequently a waste of time. (Figure 1)

2.3 The Data Solution

As the documentation and training coordinators of the IT department, we set out to solve these problems. Our knowledge exists as a compendium of FAQs within our ticket management system, called Web Help Desk [2]. FAQs are composed of questions and corresponding answers, from "What's the serial number for Filemaker Pro?" to "Which tools need to be run at the beginning of every semester in the Blackboard Transaction System?"

We took ownership of the data and determined to remove out-of-date information. Some of it was obviously expired. In other cases, we weren't sure if the text was still valid. Sometimes we knew the right person to ask. Other times we didn't. We instituted a bi-annual FAQs audit during which our user-facing consultants and technicians are asked to check the knowledge base for every call or walk-up they receive. If there is no relevant FAQ in the knowledge base, they're instructed to add one. If one already exists, they update it if necessary. As the curators of the FAQ system, we edit and approve all changes to maintain relevancy and consistency.

That took care of the "out with the old" problem. What about "in with the new"? We tried to make it as easy as possible for the support staff to participate. If they had a solution to add they could create a new FAQ from an existing ticket or email the solution for us to add. It could be as simple as a link or the email thread with the user. We didn't want anyone to feel they had to refine and edit the solution down to something consumable. That is where we come in. We simply asked our consultants to furnish us with the relevant info and forget about it. Making the process less onerous for overtaxed employees was key.

Information Update 3/28/2011
Update to everyone on the CIS and the accutalk student employee list.

Website

- Updated VPrint Drivers http://computing.vassar.edu/guides/vprint/students.html
- Updated to Mathematica 8 http://computing.vassar.edu/software/index.html
- Updated Training Events calendar to include upcoming events http://computing.vassar.edu/training/events/index.html
- Added a new section about Mobile Device Security http://computing.vassar.edu/safecomputing/mobile/index.html

FAQs
The following FAQs have been recently updated. Thanks for all the hard work and please continue to make FAQs from common issue tickets.

FAQ Number	Category	*Question
951	Email; Other	What is the size limit on email attachments through the Vassar Email server?
952	Moodle; Troubleshooting	Instructor can see his/her Moodle site, but students report that they can't find it.
953	Moodle; Troubleshooting	Instructor tries to add a new student to his/her Moodle course site, but gets this message: _"Can not assign this role to user "John Doe" because Manage metacourse capability is needed."_
954	Moodle; Troubleshooting	Instructor: I can see a file in my Moodle site's *Files* area, but my students say they don't have a link to the *Files* area.Link [http://moodle.vassar.edu/mod/resource/view.php?id=5025]
956	Card Office; Other	How do I operate a VSA machine
957	E-Mail Report	How do you turn off the email notification that pops up when you are working on another document/program? thank you!
955	Card Office; Hardware	Video cameras are down or some are showing a blank screen. What is the triage process?
783	Computer Store	Computer Store Budget Numbers and codes
769	Card Office; meal plan	Plans and Dining Bucks
772	Card Office; Other	Winter Break Configurations for Students to be done!!

Figure 2: Sample Communication 1

2.4 The Communications Solution

With the quality of information getting better and better, it was time to address the issue of trust. We needed a way to encourage the employees in our group to get used to accessing the knowledge base again as part as their process. It would be easy for them to assume the data in there was as useless as ever. We decided to address this problem with communication. We created a weekly departmental email that listed all new or updated FAQs in the knowledge base. That helped. People began responding to the email with questions about the FAQ or with new information to be added.

The weekly email grew to include web site updates and support related events (Figure 2). After a while it became apparent that the message didn't need to be weekly but could vary depending on the time of year and volume of traffic at the help desks. Depending on the flow of information, we may do the updates weekly, bi-weekly or monthly.

2.5 Other Processes

We wanted another process in place to ensure FAQs were being updated on a regular basis. We initiated a bi-annual FAQs audit as a fail safe. It is feasible to assume that during busy times, employees might not update as regularly as they should. During each two-week audit, the help desk support personnel are asked to review FAQs for every call or walk up they encounter. When a client approaches the help desk with a question, the support staff member will evaluate their problem and then check to see if there is an FAQ on the issue. If a relevant FAQ exists, the staff member should check it for accuracy. If they can find no applicable answer, the staff member will create a new one based on the successful resolution. Using this process ensures that the information in our knowledge base is rarely out of date.

We applied a similar methodology to our departmental web site. Three times a year, we have a web site audit, during which directors are responsible for reviewing, or having their staff review, the web pages that pertain to their departmental groups. They send their changes to the web administrator to perform the updates. It is unrealistic to expect one person to know everything that changes in the department and decide, without guidance, how those changes should be communicated to the community. Using this model, the web administrator is certain to have accurate information that they can convey in a voice consistent with the rest of the web site.

We also scheduled monthly meetings with the directors of the groups within our department. Though the curated knowledge base and web audits improved the quality of information drastically, we still want to be ahead of installations, migrations, and other infrastructure changes. In our meetings, we discuss upcoming projects, especially noting changes in availability of services and best practices. We then develop training and documentation plans and update the departmental site and FAQs as needed.

2.6 Moving Forward

The internal communication processes we have put in place are working well but there are a number of things we would like to see improve.

1. Our ticketing system has a number of limitations that we are working with the vendor to improve, including:
    a. The ability to fine-tune which groups can see which FAQs. This will give us the ability to use it for more information that is only for managers, end-users or high-level techs.
    b. The ability to easily export new FAQs and create links to them. Currently the system exports all FAQs to a spreadsheet and all of the links are created manually.
    c. Notifications for FAQs that are going to expire. Currently, we don't use the expiry feature in the system because we have had a number of FAQs expire unbeknownst to us and were no longer showing up in search results.
2. Sending our communication out in HTML format.
3. Turning our communication into an IT newsletter.
4. Possibly having features written by some of the field techs or managers.

3. CONCLUSION

In conclusion, this process works if there are some key factors are in place. First, it is vitally important to have only one or two people owning the process. Without ownership, the process will be nearly impossible to maintain. Second, it is essential that participants receive valuable feedback and confirmation that their contributions are being used. As soon as contributors begin to feel that their efforts are wasted, their participation level will decrease. Finally, the communications should be clearly written, easy to follow and with all necessary detail. Inaccurate, incomplete or confusing instructions are far worse than no instructions at all.

4. REFERENCES

[1] Website http://lmgtfy.com/

[2] Web Help Desk is the product used for our ticketing and knowledge base system. http://www.webhelpdesk.com/

This Isn't Your Father's Computer Lab: Computer Labs Redefined

Dan R. Herrick
Colorado State University
Engineering Network Services
Fort Collins, CO 80523-1301
970-491-3131
Dan.Herrick@Colostate.edu

ABSTRACT
The College of Engineering at Colorado State University supports 20 computer labs, but only three qualify as the "traditional computer lab" model, with the number of available seats as the selling point. Our computer lab offerings have primarily shifted to electronic classrooms, meeting rooms, virtual labs, and collaborative design spaces based on evolving feedback from students and faculty. We promote group work spaces such as our Engineering Design Studios, a diverse offering of meeting rooms, multi-purpose spaces and electronic classrooms with a computer at each desk for interactive coursework. The curriculum emphasizes group work, and our technology services team works to support the curriculum by providing students with spaces that facilitate collaboration. Web-based virtual computer labs allow students to connect from virtually anywhere. Smart cards, thin clients and virtual desktops allow portable sessions. Audiovisual technology is prevalent and accessible. Our instructional needs require these types of evolving spaces, which blend instruction, course work and social interactions.

Categories and Subject Descriptors
K.3.1 [**Computers and Education**]: Computer Uses in Education – *Computer-assisted instruction (CAI), Collaborative learning, Distance learning.*

K.4.3 [**Computers and Society**]: Organizational Impacts – *Computer-supported collaborative work.*

K.6.2 [**Management of Computing and Information Systems**]: Installation Management – *Computer selection, Computing equipment management.*

General Terms
Design, Human Factors

Keywords
Computer Lab, Computer Laboratory, Computer Classroom, Electronic Classroom, Design Studio, Studio Classroom, Internet Café, Technology Suite, Virtual Lab, Collaboration

1. INTRODUCTION
The focus on computer labs in higher education has shifted from a traditional, well-understood model to more flexible models to accommodate diverse needs from all users. Students and faculty need flexibility of physical spaces and technical capabilities. All users of the computer lab environment can be accommodated with foresight of design and flexible operating tactics.

1.1 Institutional Background
The IT environment, including the computer labs, at Colorado State University (CSU) operates under a highly decentralized model. Central IT groups serve the university's basic and overarching academic IT needs, such as Internet backbone and course management software, while each college, department and administrative unit provides more detailed IT needs as appropriate to its constituency.

The College of Engineering at CSU has 2,348 enrolled students and 109 faculty, approximately 10% of CSU's student population. Engineering Network Services (ENS) supplies academic and business IT services to the College of Engineering only. ENS has 9 permanent full-time staff and 25-30 part-time student employees. The ENS Labs Team includes one staff Computer Lab Manager and 10 student employees.

Within the College of Engineering, some departments support their own computer labs. There are 20 facilities directly managed by the ENS Labs Team and under the oversight of the Computer Lab Manager. There are 7 other departmental computer labs managed by individual departments, or jointly managed by the department and by ENS. Altogether, there are about 425 computer lab seats.

2. WHAT IS A COMPUTER LAB?
The widest definition of a computer lab is a room which contains many networked computers for public use [1]. (The "public", in this case, are the students and faculty of the Engineering College.) For a university, a better definition would be "at least two similar computers located in an area primarily used by many students to complete course work" [2]. Characteristics of computer labs include computers shared by many users, the availability of academic software packages to each user, and the philosophy of providing a general computing resource to university students.

For our college, the definition has evolved over time just as the physical spaces and the uses they have been put to have evolved. We now consider labs to include what we have typically regarded as classrooms, meeting rooms, video conference rooms, hands-on instructional labs, and even virtual computing resources. This expanded definition can be summed up as this: A computer lab is a space whose primary purpose is to support the instructional use of programs taught within the department or college, and is equipped with appropriate computing technology.

In part, this definition has arisen from the *roles* that the computer labs have been given by their users, and the *types* of spaces that the college or departments have supplied. A room can have multiple roles (and most of ours do), but one type.

2.1 Roles of a Computer Lab

In part, the above definition has arisen from the roles that the computer labs have been given by their users. It is important to note that a successful computer lab's roles are guided by its users; identifying the purpose(s) and defining the services to deliver to a computer lab are critically important when planning a new computer lab or servicing an existing one [3].

A room can have multiple roles, and most of CSU's College of Engineering computer labs do. Roles include individual work, such as study or homework; group work, such as group project work, team meetings, and electronic conferencing; direct instruction, such as lecture or hands-on instruction; and use of shared limited-use resources such as printers, scanners and software.

2.2 Types of a Computer Lab

The sponsoring department or college determines the type of computer lab by the space it grants to the room, the layout of the room, and the technology within. While a lab may have many roles, they are generally only one type.

Computer labs are typically broken down into three distinct types [4]: General Purpose Lab, Technology Suite, and Computer Classroom.

Within the College of Engineering at CSU, we identify seven distinct types of computer labs: General Purpose Computer Lab, Computer Classroom, Design Studio, Studio Classroom, Meeting Room, and Virtual Computer Lab.

2.2.1 General Purpose Computer Lab

The general purpose computer lab, also called an "open" or "drop-in" computer lab, is the most common type of computer lab, and the most archetypal. Typically, the room is organized with rows of tables with personal computers and is optimized to fit the maximum number of computer seats. The goal is to serve the widest possible clientele for the most academic-related general computing needs. The room is generally not reserved for classes or other purposes, so that students know they may use it any time the lab is open. An IT help desk is frequently housed in or located near to the general purpose computer lab.

The advantages of the general purpose computer lab are that it is the least complex to set up and maintain, and maximizes the number of available computer seats. Disadvantages include a lack of flexibility in roles and limited group work opportunities due to the structure of the space.

2.2.2 Technology Suite

A technology suite is a more specialized type of lab which normally has high-end workstations, sometimes with specialized equipment or software, for advanced work with technology like audio and video, high-end scanning or graphics, and color printing or plotting. Many schools offer a "media studio", which is an example of this type. Access to this type of lab is generally more restricted, although in many cases students may use it when classes are not scheduled in the room.

In our environment, we have deliberately chosen not to segregate this type of higher-end technology, and instead integrate it with the other computer labs. Plotters are located in one of our largest lab spaces, the Lockheed Martin Magellan Design Studio, and one of our computer classrooms. Color printers and scanners are distributed evenly through our highest-use labs.

2.2.3 Computer Classrooms

A computer classroom, also called an "electronic classroom" or "smart classroom", is set up as a typical instructor-led presentation room and has a personal computer at each desk. One or more projection systems are available in this room, along with white or chalk boards, or electronic interactive white boards.

A classroom with a single computer, or computers that are only for instructor use, is not considered a computer classroom.

A distinct sub-type of the computer classroom is the instructional or teaching lab. Instructional labs are organized so that instructors can maneuver easily about the room to direct or observe student activity at the computers. The room is used primarily for hands-on instruction, such as "lab" course sections that coincide with lecture sections, and are often smaller than a normal computer classroom. Frequently these labs are available for general purpose use when not reserved for a class section.

Computer classrooms provide a level of student engagement far beyond a simple classroom, with the addition of audio/video technology, classroom response systems ("clickers"), video conferencing, and computers at each desk. These technologies allow students to interact in real time with the instructor, providing valuable feedback to the instructor and enriching the students' learning experience.

Our faculty and students have expressed a pedagogical need for classrooms specifically equipped with computers for instruction. Computer classrooms of this nature are not generally available at CSU, and software licensing issues would prevent them from having all of the necessary software. While computer-based classroom instruction has been available in the College since the 1980s, both with mainframe terminals and UNIX workstations, the first desktop computer-based Engineering computer classroom opened in 1999. As of 2011, there are five computer classrooms in Engineering, and two more planned for 2012.

2.2.4 Design Studio

The design for the College of Engineering's main Design Studio computer lab comes from Lockheed Martin's Spacecraft Technology Center [5]. Essentially, an individual design studio consists of six computer seats around the periphery of the room or cubicle, a central conference table, a projector and a projection screen or interactive white board. The computers are at desks which have a large amount of surface area for study materials, and typically have large wide screen or dual monitors.

The individual design studios are modular and one room can hold several Design Studios. In our college, the Lockheed Martin Magellan Design Studios contains six design studios, and the Lockheed Martin Orion Design Studios contains four. Each design studio is available to be reserved by a group or small class.

The design studios are immensely popular with the students. They are versatile: Design teams or study groups can use the space, and without any special setup, it is ready for the next group or individuals. Individuals can use the computers while study groups use the table and/or the projection system. One disadvantage of the design studios is that they are less space efficient than a traditional computer lab.

2.2.5 *Studio Classroom*

The studio classroom is a specialized type of computer lab. Larger than a design studio but smaller than a computer classroom, it is a hybrid between the two concepts. Six or more (typically up to 20) computer seats are available at the periphery of the room, while a large conference table is in the center of the room. A projection system and optionally an audio system are present in the room. Other specialized audio/visual equipment, such as teleconference or video conference equipment may be present as well.

The studio classroom model lends well to smaller classes, lab sections of a course, or large study groups.

2.2.6 *Meeting Room and Lounge*

Computer-enabled meeting rooms are often placed inside or adjacent to a general purpose computer lab, and serviced by the same staff that support the computer lab. In our situation, there are three meeting rooms and one large study lounge, all of which contain at least one computer of the same configuration as the others in the nearby computer labs.

The meeting rooms can be reserved for group work or study, and contain a projection system. They provide a quiet work space in the midst of the computer lab environment. Meeting rooms can be a separate room or as simple as a partitioned space within a computer lab.

Lounges are popular with students, and we have one lounge populated with a small number of thin client computers, with furniture that can be easily arranged into a configuration comfortable for a group of any size. This provides a transitional environment from a full computer lab to a non-computer recreational space. Other lounges across campus frequently feature a computer kiosk so that students and visitors alike can use a computer for brief tasks.

There are fewer lounges and study rooms in our college now. Thanks to the more versatile and social nature of the other lab spaces, there is a reduced need for these dedicated casual spaces.

2.2.7 *Virtual Computer Lab*

A virtual computer lab is a computing resource which is connected via another computing device, and which has the same or similar software resources as a physical computer lab. The virtual computing resource may be a physical machine in a remote location, such as a server in a server room, or a true virtual appliance which runs software. It may be accessed via a web browser, via a specialized connection program, or by a remote communications protocol such as RDP.

The advantages of a virtual computer lab are that it does not take up a physical facility, and it can be accessed from a variety of computing devices (including mobile ones). In some cases, a virtual computer lab may be used as a supplement to a physical computer lab, but in general it is used in place of the same.

The Engineering "Virtual Lab" came online in 2002, providing remote access via a web interface to servers which had lab software installed. This student-funded initiative was intended to supplement access to lab software to off-campus students. The Virtual Lab uses technology from Citrix to provide a remote desktop experience to web users, or to "publish" an application [6]. Users may also connect from a desktop application rather than through a web interface. On the back end, a load-balanced "farm" of servers, identically provisioned with software, provides the desktop, software and computing power for the users.

The Virtual Lab continues today, and is used widely by off-campus from their own computers, by students on campus from their laptops and graduate students working from their on-campus office computers. Use of the Virtual Lab drastically changes where, when and how a student can access their course software, providing students much more control over their computer lab experience.

Although very successful, some significant challenges remain for the Virtual Lab. Because many graduate students are provided computers with insufficient computing power by their home department, they use the Virtual Lab as a means to gain that computing power. This puts a strain on the computing infrastructure of the Virtual Lab. Also, faculty have seen the Virtual Lab as a resource to be put to use for distance learning, presenting some logistical and support challenges for our staff, as well as unfunded capacity on this student-funded resource.

3. OPERATIONS

3.1 Purpose

The primary purpose of a computer lab is to provide general computing resources for students. More specifically, the purpose of a computer lab is defined by its type and roles (see above.) A design studio's purposes, for example, include providing a space for group work combined with computers to access their course work software. A key philosophy of the Engineering computer labs is that each lab provides more than one purpose. For example, a computer classroom's primary purpose may be for classes mediated by an instructor, but when classes are not in session, the room may be used as group work space, meeting space, or individual computer work space.

The Engineering course curriculum is typically very technical, requiring the use of technology, especially computer software, for maximum instructional impact and to complete assignments. The curriculum also heavily emphasizes group project work, and in their senior year, each Engineering student is part of a Senior Design Team, which completes and presents a unique final project. The Senior Design Teams, in particular, use the design studios extensively for their group work.

3.2 Funding

The college administration provides minimal funding for the computer labs. The college's funding contribution is limited to the physical space the lab occupies, non-computing features such as furniture, and the one staff position to oversee the computer labs.

All technology within the computer labs is funded by the Engineering Charge for Technology. This charge, paid only by Engineering majors, is in addition to a general university technology fee. As a result, the Engineering computer labs have a disproportionately high level of technology when compared to many other university colleges or departments, which the Engineering curriculum requires. The Engineering Student Technology Committee (ESTC), comprised of 75% students and 25% faculty, administers the funds raised from this charge. Approximately 40% of these funds are used to fund the computer lab equipment and wages for student computer lab support personnel.

3.3 Level of Technical Service

Another key philosophy of the Engineering computer labs is that of self-service or self-sufficiency. It is accepted by faculty that Engineering students already have a familiarity with the computing systems in place in the computer labs, and basic computer training is not offered by the college. Instruction in individual engineering discipline software is given in classroom sessions (either lecture or lab) by faculty or graduate teaching assistants, not by us. Indeed, our IT employees often know little about the operation of the software they support. (See section 4.2, Software.)

Audio/visual equipment in the computer classrooms is matched as closely as possible with university-standard "smart" classrooms, in terms of both equipment and operation. Written instructions are posted at each lectern or specialized audio/visual device in each computer lab, and operation of this equipment is offered to instructors individually.

Signage is an important part of providing self-service to the computer labs. Signs in key locations of each lab include help desk contact information, operating instructions for audio/visual and specialized equipment, lab policies, and alternate lab locations and hours. Care must be taken to maintain the balance of providing enough important information via signs without contributing to visual clutter.

The ENS web site [7] includes a wealth of information about operating the computer lab equipment, the computers and the software. The web site URL is posted prominently in all major signage. We present an overview of the college's computing resources annually to some Engineering Freshmen and some graduate student orientation classes. We also offer graduate computing seminars twice per year.

3.3.1 Personnel

Notably absent from the Engineering computer labs are help desks located in the labs themselves. Instead, we have a central Help Desk at its main office. (An auxiliary Help Desk is located in the Academic Village residence hall program space but is staffed only at peak hours by Help Desk workers.) Why? The number of computer labs we support (20) and the widespread distribution of the computer labs across campus would necessitate several help desks and result in mostly idle student workers.

Since there is no help desk or consultant station in the labs, our workers wear clearly identifiable name tags when in a lab, so that a user can approach them with problems or questions. Otherwise, users call, email or walk to the ENS Help Desk for support with the computer lab equipment.

3.3.2 Faculty Involvement

The faculty is highly involved with the computer labs in Engineering. They decide what software will be installed each year to the lab computers. The ESTC, which is composed of about 25% faculty, determines how student technology funds are spent, in the computer labs and elsewhere in the college. Engineering faculty drive the computer lab pedagogical needs, such as the design studios and group project work.

The college administration also uses the technology in the computer labs as a recruitment tool for students and faculty.

3.4 Reservations

Most of the computer lab spaces, from meeting rooms to classrooms, can be reserved at any time by any Engineering student, faculty or staff member. The reservations are accomplished by a self-service web-based system. Reservations do not have to be approved, but we monitor them for conflicts or other special needs. It is not necessary to provide a rationale for a room reservation; however, class sessions are given first priority. The university's classroom scheduling office does not schedule classes for the Engineering computer classrooms, so it is up to the individual departments or instructors to ensure that their classes are scheduled appropriately.

Limits to computer lab reservations have been imposed by the ESTC to ensure that no one group can unfairly dominate the times for the labs. Classrooms may only be reserved for up to 15 weeks at a time, to ensure that study groups do not take up class time slots for a subsequent semester, and the other labs may be reserved for up to 6 weeks at a time, to allow each group an equal chance at access in popular labs and time slots.

4. TECHNICAL FEATURES

4.1 Computers

Three types of computers are present in the computer labs: Workstation computers, personal computers, and thin clients. In addition, the labs are available for other computing resources.

Approximately half of the computer seats throughout the Engineering computer labs are workstation computers. These are personal computers which have advanced compute power and graphics, similar to what would be found in a technology suite [see section 2.2.2, Technology Suite]. Unlike a university computer lab which serves a broad audience, the Engineering curriculum requires a large number of computationally expensive software packages (see section 4.2, Software), which in turn require more advanced hardware.

A small number of personal computers, termed "projection PCs", are present in some of the classroom lecterns, when required to interface with specialized presentation equipment such as interactive white boards. These projection PCs are connected to remote computing resources (see below) and do not have the advanced computing requirements of workstations.

Approximately half of the computer seats are thin clients [3]. Thin clients provide a portable, server-based desktop session via a combination of smart cards and Windows Remote Desktop Services technologies to users. The Academic Village residence hall provides thin clients in each residence, which means a user can initiate a desktop session on the thin client in their room, and take that same session (with applications that continue to run uninterrupted) to any other thin client at CSU. This ultimate session portability provides students with great flexibility: Wherever they choose to reconnect to their session becomes their computer lab.

Instructors particularly like thin clients in a classroom setting. Whereas 30 personal computers in a computer classroom may have inconsistently installed or configured software, 30 thin client seats are guaranteed to have identical software. Also, the zero noise factor associated with thin clients allows for less audible distraction in a classroom setting.

A common feature of all computers in the labs is the accessibility of external ports for users, such as USB ports for USB flash drives and headphone jacks. While providing this type of feature has long been viewed as optional, more and more students consider this an essential feature of a computer lab, due to the ubiquity of portable file storage.

The computer labs are mobile device-friendly. Video cables are provided at each lectern, in meeting rooms and at other projection sites so that users may use their own device on the room's video (and, if available, audio) system. Wireless Internet access is provided in each computer lab, so that users with laptops and other mobile devices have connectivity. Wired data ports and electrical outlets are provided in the classrooms, for students with laptops. It is not uncommon to see students using their own laptop in a computer lab and connecting to the Engineering Virtual Lab.

4.2 Software

A normal university computer lab serves a broad audience and has limited specialized software, instead staying to the basic software such as office productivity software, a graphics manipulation package, and web authoring tools. The Engineering curriculum requires a broad array of discipline-specific software packages, and many computationally expensive software packages.

One of the characteristics of the Engineering computer labs is that the same software packages are available on every computer in every lab. Thus, it is not necessary to go to a particular lab to use a specific software package. This results in tremendous advantages for students, in that they can use a computer in any lab and be guaranteed a consistent software experience. Faculty benefit for the same reason, plus it allows instructors to teach from the most convenient location for them, and in some cases, present the same computer-supported class to two different locations with assistance from video conference technologies in the computer classrooms (see section 4.4, Video Conferencing).

4.3 Projection Systems

As a method to show information to a group, projectors are heavily utilized in the computer labs. In most labs, a user has the choice of projection from the supplied computer, or their own laptop or mobile device.

Projection surfaces are either electric screens which drop in front of white boards, or interactive white boards which are permanently mounted. Interactive white boards are used in 15 computer labs, and because they require special software, are directly connected to a Windows computer.

Interactive white boards are very popular with instructors and students. These devices are used in many schools as replacements for white boards, and display a computer desktop, often paired with presentation software such as Microsoft PowerPoint [8]. The white boards in use in our computer labs have productivity software which allow, among other features, taking notes directly into PowerPoint presentations and annotating presentations, drawings and screen capture.

4.4 Video Conferencing

Several Engineering computer classrooms and studio classrooms support video conference technologies. The primary supported video conference technology is the Access Grid [9], an open source project. Our computer classrooms have dedicated equipment to manage the Access Grid software, which supports group-to-group interactions only. Three of the Engineering classrooms are equipped with Access Grid technology, which allows for triple the number of students that could potentially interact in one combined virtual classroom.

The Access Grid, and other video conference solutions of this scale, requires a dedicated, trained operator during the video conference or class. Due to staffing limitations, we do not provide the operator for each class or conference, but will train an operator. This supports the spirit of self-service for the Engineering computer labs.

Personal video conference technologies used by computer lab users, such as Skype, Google Talk and Apple iChat, are unrestricted but not specifically supported. No lecture recording capability exists in our computer labs at this time, but the computer classrooms have the potential for it.

4.5 "Smart" Lecterns

Following the Colorado State University classroom standard, Engineering computer classrooms are equipped with "smart" lecterns, in which all of the audio/visual equipment is routed through a control system and video switcher. The interface is accomplished via a programmable touch panel, which is located on the top of the lectern. The programming conforms to the university standard, so that instructors can feel comfortable moving from an Engineering computer classroom to a university general assignment classroom. Control systems for wireless microphones are housed inside the lectern.

4.6 Printers and Peripherals

Feedback from students shows that printers are one of the most desired features of the labs. The distribution and feature sets of the printers are key. Printers are dispersed throughout the computer labs, at a minimum one to each lab or adjacent lab area, with 24 printers and plotters total. Printer models range from high-volume large workgroup printers to small workgroup printers, depending on their recorded usage. All computer lab printers are networked and tied into the college's print quota system. Lab printers are monitored by the HP Web Jetadmin software [10], and alerts are sent via email so that the labs team can respond quickly to printer issues. Printers are maintained by the Student Lab Assistants, part of whose core functions are to stock and ensure the smooth operation of the printers.

Large format plotters are located in two major areas and are used much less frequently than the other printers. Because plotting can be technically challenging and each plot uses up a large amount of a user's print quota, users are asked to consult with one of our employees before attempting to plot, but are not restricted from plotting on their own. Written instructions for plotting are provided on our web site, as well.

Scanners are provided in two distinct types: Network scanners (HP Digital Senders [11]) and computer-connected desktop scanners. Users can scan documents on the digital sender's flatbed or ADF feeder, and scanned documents are sent to a user's email address in PDF format. The network scanners do not require a connected computer to operate. This makes these scanners extremely advantageous particularly in labs which contain only thin client devices, which cannot support a scanner natively.

A small number of desktop scanners are available, located in the larger computer labs. Previously, a larger number of desktop scanners had been dispersed throughout the labs, but were ineffective for the casual scanner user because other users would "park" on a scanner-enabled computer for hours at a time. As a result, a limited number of "scanning stations" are now present in the labs. Each scanner is connected to a basic personal computer that contains only scanning software and is not connected to a network, which discourages a user from using it for any purpose than scanning and image manipulation.

5. CHALLENGES

5.1 Funding for Non-Computing Features

As mentioned previously, funding for the technology in the computer labs is provided by a separate technology fee. However, by charter this charge cannot be used to fund items or projects which are outside the definition of technology equipment (and the labor to support it). As a result, features such as furniture and chairs, fabric partitions, carpet and associated cleaning, lighting, heating and cooling, and other facility-related features must be funded elsewhere. In every survey of college computer labs, "ergonomic chairs" are cited by students as one of the most desired features not currently seen in the computer labs. Engineering students spend hours at a time sitting in these computer chairs.

In these times of leaner funding for higher education, such features are viewed as "luxuries" and are not funded. Even in better times, these features have been funded by gift funds or special projects rather than central college funding. A limited amount of technology funds are allowed to be used for furniture to support the computing equipment -- certainly not enough to keep these items on a regular replacement cycle. It is unlikely that this situation will change.

5.2 Food and Drink

One of the most universal signs posted in computer labs is noticeably lacking in the Engineering computer labs: "Food and Drink Prohibited". Our "No Food or Drink" policy was abolished in 2010. Before this time, this was the most enforced policy and the one that created the most friction between users and lab support staff. The college had been perhaps too successful in its goal of creating a computer lab space that students desired to spend time in; Engineering students spent a disproportionate amount of the time in the computer labs, and naturally wanted sustenance. The policy was impossible to enforce universally because the labs were open 24/7 were not staffed outside normal business hours. Confusingly, some labs did allow food and drink consumption while others disallowed it.

The direct result of allowing food and drink in the computer labs was to provide more funding for student workers to clean lab areas. Since the policy was changed, no complaints have been received about the cleanliness of the computer labs. We appealed to the students' shared ownership of the lab spaces, and they are noticeably responsible with their food and drink consumption.

5.3 Vandalism and Misuse

Very few acts of vandalism, or breakage of equipment, have taken place in the history of the Engineering computer labs. In part, this is due to diligent security efforts (including security cameras), but credit also goes to the users of the computer labs themselves, who maintain a stewardship mentality of the computer labs and typically treat the facilities with respect. Notably, the number of sign defacing has decreased to almost zero since the food and drink policy was changed (see section 5.2., Food and Drink).

Misuse of the computer lab equipment is always going to be a factor when serving students, no matter how responsible the majority are. In most cases, the misuse amounts to students unplugging audio/visual equipment or changing it to a different configuration. Normally the reason for this is unknown, but it's suspected that when help desk support is unavailable after hours and a projection system operation is not working (or not perceived as working) correctly, the user ingeniously devises a temporary solution which involves changing the cabling. This of course prevents correct operation for the next user. The solution for this, in most cases, is to hide or lock down the cabling so it is not accessible to the user.

5.4 Visiting Faculty

It is especially challenging to provide support for visiting faculty such as a guest lecturer or an instructor from another college. Because the visiting faculty member generally does not have an Engineering computer account, which is used for all computing access, one must be obtained for them and other access issues, such as swipe card access to the facilities, initiated. These operations may take extra time because they must be coordinated with other support entities. This challenges the labs support staff, which are staffed primarily with regard to regular maintenance rather than immediate response.

6. HIGHLIGHTED LAB FACILITIES

6.1 Magellan Design Studios

The Lockheed Martin Magellan Design Studios consists of a 3,700 square feet room subdivided by fabric partitions into six design studios. Each studio contains six workstation computers with wide screen or dual monitors, a conference table, a projector and an interactive white board. A wide central corridor opens into entrances to most of the studios, and houses the printers and plotters. There are three entrances to the room: The main entrance opens to the building hallway, another connects to the Lockheed Martin Stardust Studio Classroom, and another connects to the Lockheed Martin Viking Electronic Classroom.

6.1.1 Purpose and Layout

The original purpose for the creation of the Magellan Design Studios, created in 1999, was to provide group work space and computing power for inter-disciplinary student design teams [12]. Incorporated into the design were casual meeting areas and lounges, in response to students' concerns about the intense work and the need for study breaks. This was and remains a room dominated by the student personality: Flexible, containing as much technology as they can consume, and a space that allows for social interactions.

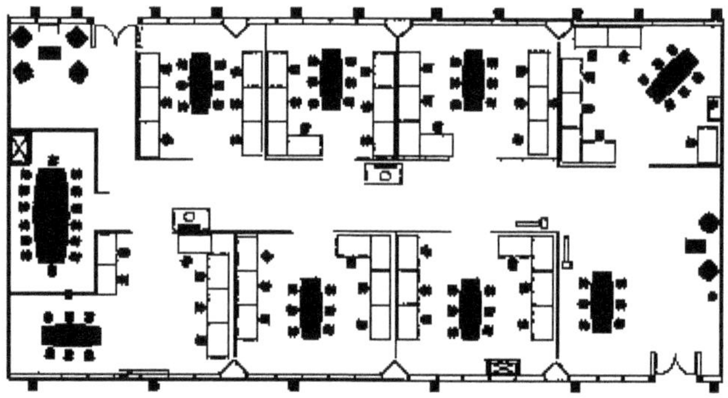

Figure 1. Original layout of Magellan Design Studio.

Originally, the room had seven studios, two lounges, two conference areas, and a help desk. (See Figure 1.) Over time, the needs and desires of the students changed and they were the driving force to split the room, carving out a computer classroom and a studio classroom, reducing the number of studios from eight (they had previously added one) to six, and removing the casual areas. (See Figure 2.)

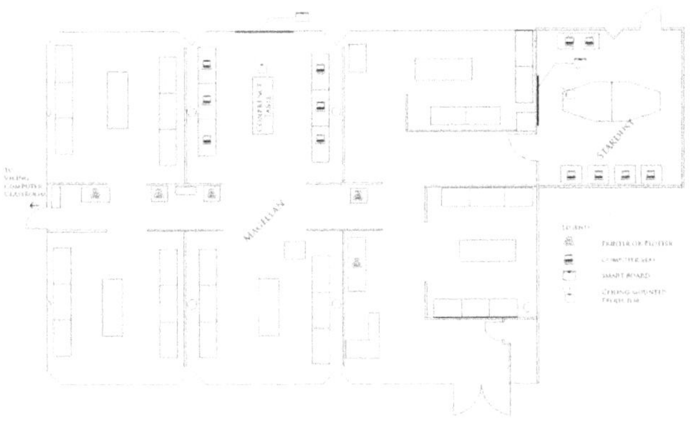

Figure 2. Current layout of Magellan Design Studio and Stardust Studio Classroom.

The current use of this lab is the same as the original, mostly design teams. This lab has traditionally been the most popular computer lab: even though computer seats were available in other labs (with the exact same computers), we would witness students waiting in line to use a computer in the Magellan lab.

6.2 Viking Electronic Classroom

The Viking classroom is the most popular of its kind. It connects directly to the Magellan Design Studios, but the main entrance is via the building hallway. The classroom consists of 34 thin client computer seats, three projectors, two wide projector screens, an interactive white board, an audio system, video capture cameras, hanging microphones, a wireless microphone system, a "smart" lectern, an Access Grid-enabled video conference system, and a printer. The projection system includes a matrix switcher, so that any source can be projected to any of the three screens. Sources in the lectern are a computer (for use with the interactive white board), a thin client, an instructor-supplied laptop, a DVD/VCR player, a digital document projector, and the Access Grid system (which includes the cameras and hanging microphones.)

The room has its challenges, as well. It was retrofitted from an existing, larger room and contains features such as support pillars that are poor for video conference uses. Because of its prime location next to the popular computer lab, students frequently use it as a "pass-through" location between the hallway and the Magellan lab, sometimes even when an instructor is presenting! Because it is often used by visiting faculty, it incurs more support calls due to the visiting faculty member's inexperience with thin client technology and the access issues mentioned earlier, which also results in the door being left propped open for convenience of the instructor and not closed properly after class. Because it serves literally every purpose of a computer lab, the technology can be a bit overwhelming to a new user of the instructional portion of the room.

6.3 Internet Café

This very popular computer lab was conceived and designed by Engineering College students to provide a social atmosphere for food and drink with casual computer use and meeting space [12]. The room has several design elements, including a computer "bar" complete with bar stools, a computer bench and tables with recessed computer monitors, and a separate meeting room with a projection system. (See Figure 3 for the layout.) This lab houses 25 thin clients and one personal computer (in the meeting room), two printers, and a network scanner.

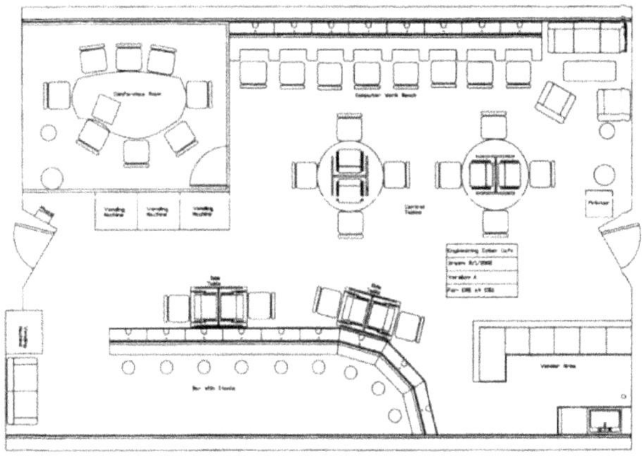

Figure 3. Internet Café layout.

It was originally conceived to be the one food-friendly computer lab in the college, and so contains vending machines and a food vendor area. While the need for a separate computer lab where food and drink is allowed has disappeared with the new food-friendly policy, this remains a popular computer lab. Its popularity can be attributed to its casual atmosphere, flexible seating (it's one of the three "generic" computer labs in our classification), and prime location on the first floor of the Engineering building. The room was designed with a 1950s theme, complete with neon clocks, bar stools and a working 1950s-era telephone.

The Internet Café has proved to be one of the most popular computer labs, and remains virtually unchanged from its original design in 2002.

6.4 Academic Village

The Academic Village is a "living and learning community" residence hall concept which opened in the fall of 2007. The College of Engineering partnered with CSU Housing and Dining Services to provide classroom and programming space in the Academic Village residence hall. Currently, the Engineering College maintains two classrooms, two meeting rooms, four design studios, a server room and an auxiliary help desk at the Academic Village. All computer seats in the Academic Village are thin clients, with the exception of some personal computers to support interactive white boards where they are available.

The computer lab facilities at the Academic Village have been very popular with the residents, thanks to their proximity and the fact that each resident has a thin client in their room, which allows a resident to carry a portable computer session from one thin client to another, anywhere on campus. Despite the high level of technology in the Academic Village, these computer labs have not been a draw for other Engineering students, likely due to the location across campus from the other Engineering resources.

7. FUTURE DIRECTIONS

7.1 Pervasive Computing

Weiser spoke in 1988 [13] of an era of ubiquitous computing, also called pervasive computing, which has yet to come to pass. The core idea of pervasive computing is that the actual computer is invisible to the user and yet the user can use its technologies everywhere. Portable desktop sessions, application publishing and virtualization, and the ubiquity of mobile devices (and the fantastic growth of their computing capabilities) seem to indicate that this era is close. The next generation of university students will have grown up, figuratively speaking, with a smart phone in hand and an interactive screen in every room. They will expect to have computing resources delivered to them at any time, without delay. The traditional computer lab model is as antiquated to them as the mainframe model is to computer users today.

7.1.1 Accommodating Mobile Devices

Mobile devices, mentioned above, are becoming more powerful and extensible. One limiting factor of laptops and other mobile devices is the graphics capability; software specific to the engineering disciplines, such as 3-D Computer Aided Design, Geographic Information Systems, and fluid or mechanical simulation software all require enhanced graphics capabilities that even low- to mid-range personal computers struggle to properly render. At some point mobile device graphics capability may catch up to the point where the graphics are at least "good enough" for students to use.

Even now, students use mobile devices to accomplish everyday computing tasks, and there is little reason to differentiate a laptop, a tablet or a smart phone, when providing access to a server-based software resource. It makes sense to accommodate these mobile devices because it reduces the demand for physical seats in a computer lab, which are always at a premium. We want to support expanding access to the Virtual Lab to users of mobile devices (while acknowledging a dependence on vendor-supported tools to enable this use.)

7.1.2 Continue Thin Clients

The use of thin clients in the Engineering College has expanded to six times its initial deployment from 2000. Given the low cost factor [14] of thin clients versus desktop computers, it is likely that further expansion of computer labs will feature thin clients. We are in the process of evaluating a replacement thin client infrastructure. Depending on the results of the evaluation, in particular the cost effectiveness of providing the same level of service and the ability to transport a session between a thin client and a user's own mobile device, existing workstation computer seats may even be replaced by thin clients.

7.1.3 Virtualization

The Engineering College has been slow to embrace virtualization, for practical reasons. (The benefits of server virtualization have been evaluated and found mostly lacking for this specific environment.) However, the college has reached a turning point where it makes practical sense to migrate many server-based services to virtual machines. Desktop virtualization has been utilized in the college's computer labs to a limited degree, and further use may be pursued, though for lab computers dependent on compute power it may not make practical sense.

7.2 New Facility

The Engineering College plans to open a new 122,000 square foot building, planned to open in 2013, which will include computer and non-computer classrooms, design studios, teaching laboratories, and research laboratories. It is expected that the lines between computer labs and classrooms, and between computer labs and teaching labs will continue to blur. The roles of the computer labs will be seen throughout diverse facilities and the challenge will be to help provide the services to students and faculty that computer labs have traditionally filled.

8. REFERENCES

[1] Computer lab. (2011, June 20). In *Wikipedia, The Free Encyclopedia*. Retrieved 23:32, June 30, 2011, from http://en.wikipedia.org/w/index.php?title=Computer_lab&oldid=435273009

[2] Hays, Malcom. ITCC RETREAT: Case Scenario – Group A, EdTech Connect, (2008, December 10). Retrieved June 23, 2011, from Missouri University of Science and Technology: http://edtechconnect.mst.edu/Group%20A.pdf

[3] Ritschard, M., (October 2009). Thin Clients: Make Them Work for You. Proceedings of the 37th Annual ACM SIGUCCS Conference on User Services; Association for Computing Machinery, New York, New York, pp. 41-45.

[4] Computer Labs. Retrieved June 23, 2011 from Pratt Institute: http://www.pratt.edu/academics/academic_resources/technology_resources/academic_computer_labs/

[5] College of Engineering Names Joseph Marcus the 2003 Honor Aluminus Award Winner, (2003, March 21). Retrieved June 26, 2011 from the College of Engineering at Colorado State University: http://www.engr.colostate.edu/news/index.cfm?id=111

[6] Citrix XenApp. Retrieved June 26, 2011 from: http://www.citrix.com/English/ps2/products/product.asp?contentID=186&ntref=prod_top

[7] Sun Ray Thin Client Information, (2011, March 2). Retrieved June 26, 2011 from the College of Engineering at Colorado State University: http://www.engr.colostate.edu/ens/info/sunrays/.

[8] Interactive Whiteboards in the Classroom, (2010, October 27). Retrieved July 1, 2011 from: http://rmtc.fsdb.k12.fl.us/tutorials/whiteboards.html

[9] Access Grid. Retrieved July 1, 2011 from: http://www.accessgrid.org/

[10] HP Web Jetadmin software – overview and features. Retrieved July 1, 2011 from Hewlett-Packard Development Company, L.P.: http://h20338.www2.hp.com/hpsub/cache/332262-0-0-225-121.html

[11] HP 9250c Digital Sender – Overview and Features. Retrieved July 1, 2011 from: http://h10010.www1.hp.com/wwpc/us/en/sm/WF05a/15179-15179-64195-12126-64404-3330619.html

[12] Ritschard, M., (October 2004). Building a Computer Lab that Students Will Love: Internet Cafés and Design Studios. Proceedings of the 32nd Annual ACM SIGUCCS Conference on User Services; Association for Computing Machinery, New York, New York, pp. 354-356

[13] Weiser, M., (March 1996). Ubiquitous computing. Retrieved 2011-06-19.

[14] Ritschard, M., (November 2006). Thin Clients: The Key To Our Success. Proceedings of the 34th Annual ACM SIGUCCS Conference on user Services; Association for Computing Machinery, New York, New York, pp. 343-346.

Trusted Computing Architectures for Mobile IT Infrastructure

Vijay Anand
Southeast Missouri State University
One University Plaza
Cape Girardeau, Missouri - 63701
(573)6512653
vanand@semo.edu

Jafar Saniie
Illinois Institute of Technology
3301 South Dearborn Street
Chicago, Illinois - 60616
(312)5673412
sansonic@ece.iit.edu

Erdal Oruklu
Illinois Institute of Technology
3301 South Dearborn Street
Chicago, Illinois - 60616
(312)5678814
erdal@ece.iit.edu

ABSTRACT

As computing architectures become mobile the physical ownership of data and security guarantees for that data is required to gain trust of the users of the computing architectures. In this paper we highlight security guarantees required to alleviate privacy concerns of the users of a computing service.

A hardware system entrusted with security is referred to as the trusted platform module (TPM). We highlight how security guarantees in an IT infrastructure can be met using trusted platform modules and should be an integral part of computing services along with other security constructs like firewalls, intrusion detection systems, anti-virus etc.

Categories and Subject Descriptors

K.6.5 [**MANAGEMENT OF COMPUTING AND INFORMATION SYSTEMS**]: Security and Protection – *Access controls, Authentication, Cryptographic controls, Information flow controls, Verification.*

General Terms

Management, Performance, Reliability, Security, Verification.

Keywords

Trusted, Virtualized, Mobile, Chain of Trust, TrustZone

1. INTRODUCTION

IT infrastructure has gone through a significant change over the last few years with considerable miniaturization of computing platforms. A typical mobile device has a fully enabled operating system which can replace a computer for almost all daily tasks of computing. With tablet computing taking hold and manufacturers experimenting with various operating systems the challenge to support a heterogeneous infrastructure is major. The other significant change in computing has been the advent of cloud computing through virtualization. This has reduced significantly the cost as well as management of computing resources. With these advances also new issues regarding security and privacy also arise. The primary challenges of privacy and security are:

- License management for a virtualized infrastructure is a significant challenge where the licensee wants to control the license.
- The issue of privacy of data in the cloud.
- Privacy of user data in a mobile computing device operating on battery.
- Malware attacking mobile devices which are limited in resources to guarantee security and privacy.

We contend that these elements of data security and privacy can be solved with the usage a trusted platform module (TPM) thereby making the TPM a critical component in the design of a virtual mobile infrastructure. A typical IT infrastructure with mobile devices is shown in Figure1.

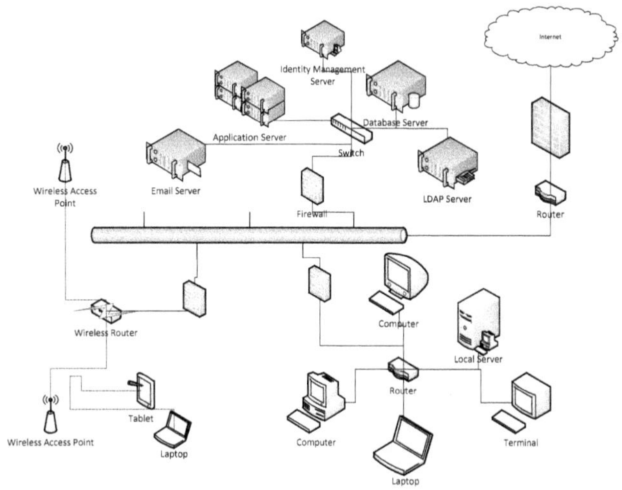

Figure 1. – Classical IT Infrastructure

The key aspects of security in this infrastructure are at router level, firewalls and software installed on all the servers and computers. Servers in themselves may have Host Intrusion Detection Systems (HIDS) and the subnet must have Network Intrusion detection System (NIDS)[10].

User data stored within the servers is protected with access and privilege controls, and ciphering systems. However user data which is not backed up to the server is still dependent on the user itself and may not be protected. Guarantees on the backed-up data are dependent on the way encryption is done at the server level. If the encryption system utilized is software-based it is prone to bugs and is a point of failure for the server storage of private keys. This is where the role of TPM in guaranteeing the key storage and ciphering functions is irreplaceable.

Although TPM-based guarantees are needed in a classical IT infrastructure the movement of local servers to a virtualized bank elevates the need for control of license management using a TPM. A typical example is that of a university where seats of license are limited and have to be timeshared.

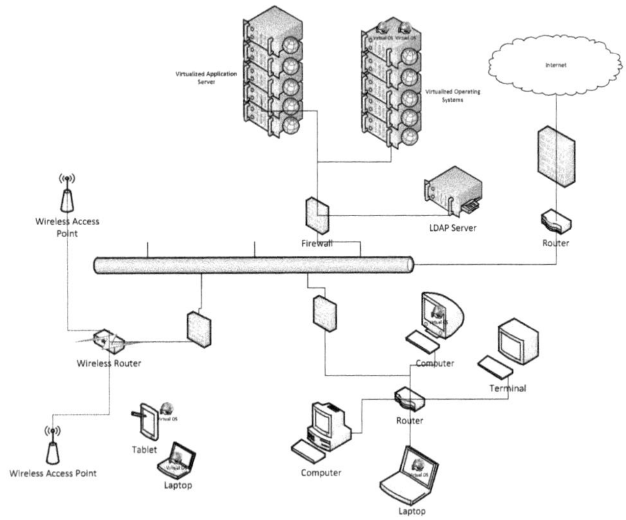

Figure 2. Virtualized IT Infrastructure

2. Overview of a TPM

The TPM provides a framework for encryption, random numbers and security features in an immutable hardware structure. Requirements for TPMs are described in the following subsections.

2.1 Chain of Trust

Chain of trust generally implies the transfer of trust rooted in some immutable hardware to the application component rendering a service in an operating system. This is referred to as the chain of trust since the execution process of various critical components of a computing system is guaranteed to execute in an uninterrupted manner and the immutable hardware trust binds all these components. An operating system goes through various components during its boot-up process and this trust is generally transferred from one component to another until the application service is invoked whose multithreaded execution is rooted in the single-threaded boot-up of the operating system.

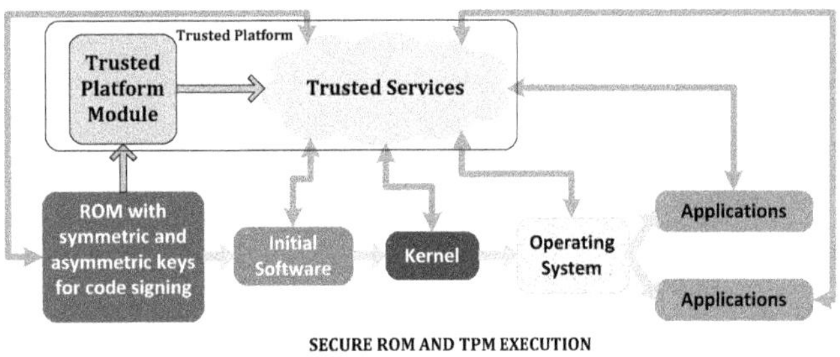

Figure 3. Chain of Trust

As shown in Figure 3, chain of trust assertion practically translates to the fact that each component is digitally signed and each component checks the digital signature of the next component. The trust of this digital signature is rooted in some immutable component which is the root of the chain of trust of the processor. The secure ROM thereby guarantees that the 'initial software' is always signed and verified [8] before execution is transferred to the 'initial software'. The 'initial software' then does the same in the operating system execution sequence. This assures that no malicious software can change the signed software. Since signing is limited to the software manufacturer, this generally guarantees a high level of trust on the signed software. There is a possibility to tamper with signed software and that will be discussed in the next few sections. The digital signature algorithm which is used has to be cryptographically strong. The parameters of cryptographically strong algorithms generally change with time and therefore with the increase in computing power, changes need to be made to guarantee the cryptographic strength of signature creation and verification.

2.2 Ciphering System

Secure transactions require data to be transmitted in an encrypted manner. Hence there is a requirement for having a ciphering system which supports most of the ciphering requirements with evolving cryptographic standards. A ciphering system generally consists of the following:

- A symmetric encryption system which provides on-board fast encryption
- An asymmetric encryption system which allows a system to communicate and share data with other systems in a secure way
- A hashing mechanism which is cryptographically strong. The strength of a hashing mechanism is generally measured with the birthday number.
- A random number generator which guarantees the random number is generated in hardware rather than in software.

Each of the above systems is discussed below.

2.2.1 Symmetric encryption

Symmetric encryption and decryption generally refers to the systems which are based on a secret key and the strength of the system is based on the secrecy of this key. If this key is somehow lost then the privacy of the system is compromised. The encryption/decryption algorithm has to be generally strong to defeat any brute force tampering of the encryption system. The most commonly used encryption system is the AES [9], which is considered a safe algorithm. Symmetric encryption systems are generally fast with very little time delay. The requirements for the TPMs are that the key is protected and there is no possible way to directly access this key from the public world.

2.2.2 Asymmetric Encryption

An asymmetric encryption/decryption system is based on the strength of the algorithm and the ciphering quality is based on the effectiveness of the algorithm. The public keys of an asymmetric algorithm are generally not kept as a secret. The quality of algorithm is based on the cryptanalysis of the algorithm and the best-known algorithms are RSA[14], ECC[15] The drawback of this type of algorithm is the computation power it requires and there is a noticeable delay for any encryption/decryption system. The requirement in the TPM module for an asymmetric system arises from the guarantee to keep the private key secret and the functioning of the algorithm tamper resistant.

2.2.3 Hashing

Hashing functions generally referred to as a one-way hash function are used in conjunction with encryption systems to create signatures for software components. A cryptographically strong hash is one in which it is computationally impossible to create a hash collision from two distinctively different data sets, whose complexity is measured by its associated birthday number. The most commonly used hashing mechanism is the SHA1[9] and other variants of the SHA[4]. The requirement of the TPM for the hashing mechanism is that it be computationally fast since hashing a big chunk of data can take considerable time in software.

2.2.4 Random Number Generator

Random numbers are used to create ciphering challenges in a secure communication infrastructure. Hence the requirement to create symmetric keys and challenges from random number requires a probability distribution of a random number which is difficult to predict [7]. The most commonly used random number is based on the average of the quantum shot noise of two oscillators. This removes the requirement of any software-based random number generation algorithm. The requirement from a TPM is to provide this random number service whenever requested.

2.3 Non-Volatile Storage

Non-volatile storage refers to embedded memory in the device which can be written to only once and cannot be erased. This sort of memory is generally referred to as One Time Programmable [5], [6] memory. The reason this is useful is because it gives a time slice progression of the device since data cannot be erased. It also provides another constant factor apart from the keys, and ciphering algorithms which software can use as a reference point to make critical decisions during execution.

2.4 Types of TPM

The various components of TCG[1]-based TPMs are shown in Figure 5. As can be seen there, the TCG based TPMs generally have most of the required TPM functionalities discussed in section 2. This architecture of implementation has mostly been adopted by the x86 architecture and these services are provided as a TPM co-processor to the x86 platform.

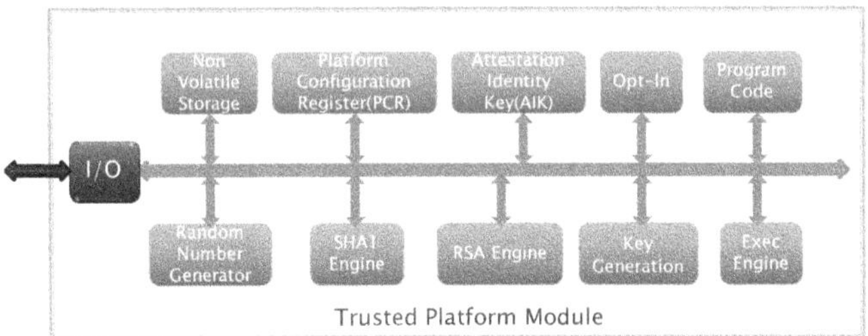

Figure 5. TCG-TPM Trusted Computing Module

TrustZone[3]-based architecture is based on the differentiation of two zones where the execution can occur in either of the zones, namely, the public and secure zone. This is a very interesting implementation because any peripheral is capable of existing in these two phases. The public world is orthogonal to the secure world in the sense that a public world cannot access resources in the secure world. This separation is based on the AMBA3 AXI bus fabric[2] which guarantees the public and secure world separation. The system designer has the luxury to design whatever peripherals need to be added to this system. The other factor is that the TrustZone architecture has been extended into the implementations of the core itself, which allows the processor to efficiently switch between secure and public world. A representation of the TrustZone operation is shown in Figure 6.

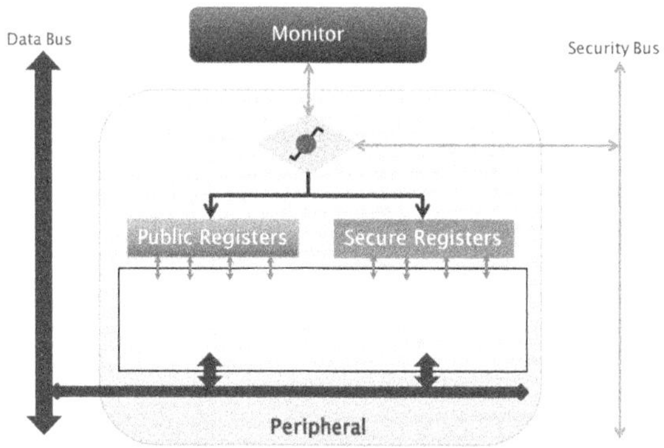

Figure 6. TrustZone TPM

3. Security in a Digital Infrastructure

Security in a digital infrastructure is of two types:

- Security of the computing resources: Computing resource in a typical IT infrastructure has the following components for securing the infrastructure.
  - Firewalls- A firewall typically controls the type of access particular network traffic has for a computing system. There are various kinds of firewalls, such as a network firewall where the firewall protects incoming traffic, and an application-level firewall where the computing system can limit the access of traffic to any application. They form the backbone of network security and the first layer of defense against any digital attacks.
  - Anti-Malware Software – Malware—also known as virus, worms, scareware, etc.—execute on a computing system and disrupt the normal working of the system. Anti-malware software is an application that detects and attempts to eliminate malware.
  - Intrusion Detection Systems – These systems watch out for trails of application execution in a computing system so as to find some atypical activity indicating some malicious intent. These are also referred to as signature-based firewalls. Intrusion detection systems generally come in two types, Network Intrusion Detection, which monitors the computers attached within its domain, and Host Intrusion Detection System, which is typically resident on the computing system itself and generally looks out for trails in that system..
  - Security of content: Content security deals with user identification and authorization. Such systems have various components, primarily:

- Identity Management systems, wherein the identities of those authorized to use the computing resources are validated.
- The data of users are protected by either VPN-enabled services or by a TLS/SSL-based session or both.

TPM in a virtualized infrastructure can be used to achieve secure communication, secure storage for key values used in ciphering, sealing content, hardware acceleration for ciphering , roots of trust and signature validation of executing processes. The roles of a TPM in such an infrastructure are as shown in Figure 4.

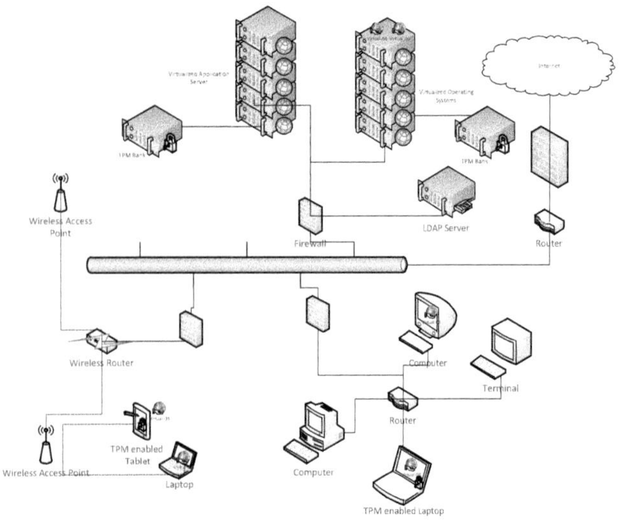

Figure 4. Proposed IT infrastructure

3.1 Secure Communication

Secure communication requires the use of asymmetric and symmetric keys, random numbers and hashing. The TPM either from the TPM bank, on server, or end computing resources provides these mechanisms by:

1) Ciphering Keys in the TPM which allow secure communication (SSL, IpSec) initiation and usage by hardware-enforced key generation and key usage. In any variant of TPM (TCG, TrustZone) the hardware guarantees provided can be used to prevent attacks on the key.
2) A hashing engine which provides real-time speeds for hashing large volumes of data. Hashing is critical to signature generation and validation in secure communication. In a virtualized environment when high multiple connections are being established and torn down, having such hardware guarantees is necessary.
3) Nonvolatile storage which acts as storage for keys for secure communication. Services based on the usage of keys enable users to maintain their privacy.
4) A random number generator, which plays a critical role in a virtualized service that, is based on secure communications where various communicating components authenticate each other using cryptographic challenge. In secure communication nonce (i.e., a number used once) and random numbers form the basis of key generation and usage which can only be provided by true random number generators. This feature refers to the unpredictability of guessing random numbers such that they are considered cryptographically strong [7]. Mathematical random numbers don't meet the cryptographic complexity of random number generation. TPM provides this cryptographically strong random number by choosing a source of entropy with its hardware random number generator.

3.2 Signature Validation

To ascertain that only validated (signed) assets are being utilized – TPM provides the only hardware-enabled guarantees for any signature validation. This is useful in the servers providing computing resources for applications that execute on the server.

1) TPM provides access to a hardware hashing engine whose performance is unmatched by any software-based system. When large amounts of data need to be hashed in real time for signature validation this feature becomes an absolute necessity.
2) The TPM provides roots of trust from which chain of trust can be created for validated assets. The roots of trust in a TPM cannot be altered once created and cannot be spoofed. This hardware guarantee is critical to signature validation in a virtualized environment when the signed assets need to be validated in real time before providing computing resources to the application.

3.3 License Management

User-enabled licensing information can be effectively managed by a TPM which can hold license information in hardware. The TPM can provide cryptographic guarantees better than software for license usage and propagation. It can also be used to remotely enable software forming the core of user enabled license management in a virtualized system. . Systems like Wibukey[13], Cryptosystems have similar constructs. The features for license management this user TPM provides are:

1) The TPM provides ciphering keys that can be used to encrypt licenses for secure storage of licenses. The access to these licenses is thereby restricted to the TPM owner who in this case is also the license owner.
2) The TPM provides non-volatile storage where licenses can be stored

3.4 Sealing

TPM provides a way to protect personal data on a device from either loss of the device or software attacks on it. The process of protecting external personal data is called sealing. The sealing process is internal to the TPM and guarantees that only the TPM which created the sealed data can unseal the data. This is useful in both networked storage in a virtualized environment and user storage for local data.

1) The TPM provides roots of trust which can be used to encrypt data. The TPM guarantees the protection of roots of trust and provides a hardware encryption engine which guarantees performance when data needs to be encrypted and decrypted.
2) The random number generator in the TPM allows the usage of a nonce for the encryption process and the and the number's true randomness allows the guarantees of sealing and unsealing.

3.5 Protected Content

Protected content can arise from DRM (Digital Rights Management) [16] or from personal data whose consumption is user-controlled, or from protected content created to be consumed by validated users of the virtualized framework [17]. By nature, DRM-compliant devices need to provide strict ciphering capabilities of content usage and monitoring. The TPM both at the server level and at the user device provides the framework to consume external DRM-protected content and create and consume internal content.

1) The secure execution engine in TPM provides a way to read the rights object in the DRM consumption [16]. It also allows the creation of rights objects for internal content.
2) Nonvolatile storage in the TPM provides a location to provision DRM keys with the hardware guarantees of the TPM to access these keys.
3) Protected content is encrypted and the TPM provides hardware-based encryption from the provisioned keys with real-time content consumption guarantees.

4. Conclusion

In this paper, we showed how TPM addresses the security goals and privacy of users of a virtualized computing system to facilitate secure services. We presented the case of using a TPM as an integral component of an IT infrastructure to solve various aspects of secure computing such as secure communication, secure storage, protected content, signature validation and license management. Although TPM is not widely used and many consumers don't demand TPM to be an integral part of the computing service, we present the case for the need of a TPM to be an integral part of secure computing.

5. REFERENCES

[1] TCG Specification Architecture, Overview Specification Revision 1.4 2nd,August 2007. http://www.trustedcomputinggroup.org/files/resource_files/AC652DE1-1D09-3519-ADA026A0C05CFAC2/TCG_1_4_Architecture_Overview.pdf

[2] ARM Security Technology: Building A Secure System Using TrustZone Technology, http://infocenter.arm.com/help/topic/com.arm.doc.prd29-genc-009492c/index.html

[3] A. K. Lenstra and E. R. Verheul, "Selecting Cryptographic Key Sizes", *Journal of Cryptology*, November, 1999.

[4] FIPS 180-2: Secure Hash Standard (SHS), http://csrc.nist.gov/publications/fips/fips180-2/fips180-2withchangenotice.pdf

[5] M. Johnson, A. Al-Shamma, D. Bosch, M. Crowley, M. Farmwald, L. Fasoli, A. Ilkbahar, B. Kleveland, T. Lee, T. Liu, Q. Nguyen, R. Scheuerlein, K. So, and T. Thorp, "512-Mb PROM With a Three-Dimensional Array of Diode/Antifuse Memory Cells", *IEEE Journal of Solid-State Circuits*, vol. 38, No. 11, November 2003.

[6] W.R.Tonti,"eFuse Design and Reliability", *Integrated Reliability Workshop Final Report* , Page(s): 1 – 32, October 2008.

[7] RFC4086 - Randomness Requirements for Security, http://tools.ietf.org/html/rfc4086, June 2005.

[8] Federal Information Processing Standards Publication 197 : ADVANCED ENCRYPTION STANDARD (AES), http://www.csrc.nist.gov/publications/fips/fips197/fips-197.pdf , November 26, 2001.

[9] RFC3174 - US Secure Hash Algorithm 1 (SHA1), http://www.apps.ietf.org/rfc/rfc3174.html

[10] A History and Survey of Network Firewalls, Kenneth Ingham and Stephanie Forrest, University of New Mexico, http://www.cs.unm.edu/~moore/tr/02-12/firewall.pdf

[11] Larry Rudolph, Infrastructure that Supports Pervasive Computing, *IEEE CS*, 2009 Pages 8 – 13

[12] Anirban Chakrabarti, G. Manimaran, Internet Infrastructure Security: A Taxonomy, *IEEE Network*, November/December 2002 Pages 13 – 21

[13] WibuKey http://wibu.com/start.php?lang=en

[14] R. L. Rivest, A. Shamir, L. M. Adleman, Cryptographic communications system and method, U.S. Patent 4405829

[15] A. Menezes, T. Okamoto, and S.A. Vanstone, "Reducing elliptic curve logarithms to logarithms in a finite field", *IEEE Transactions on Information Theory*, Volume 39, 1993.

[16] Content Management License Administration(CMAL) http://www.cm-la.com/licensing/download.aspx

[17] Universal Plug and Play (UPnP) http://upnp.org/sdcps-and-certification/

Can You Hear Me Now? Communicating to the Campus Community

Laurie Fox
SUNY Geneseo
1 College Circle
Geneseo, NY 14454
1 (585) 245-5577
fox@geneseo.edu

Andy Camidge
SUNY Geneseo
1 College Circle
Geneseo, NY 14454
1 (585) 245-5577
camidge@geneseo.edu

Kirk Anne
SUNY Geneseo
1 College Circle
Geneseo, NY 14454
1 (585) 245-5577
kma@geneseo.edu

ABSTRACT
The days of printed newsletters are long gone and our IT department uses a blend of email notifications, web page updates, and social media techniques to share information with the campus community. Determined to develop a communication plan that reaches everyone in the community, we worked with a team of students and staff to refine our procedures and deliver our messages in different ways to different audiences. This presentation offers ideas for communicating with your campus through a variety of channels.

Categories and Subject Descriptors
H.4.3 [**Information Systems Applications**]: Communications Applications – *bulletin boards, electronic mail, information browsers.*

General Terms
Management, Human Factors

Keywords
Help Desk, SUNY Geneseo, Communication, Announcements, Generational Differences.

1. INTRODUCTION
The days of printed newsletters are long gone and our IT department uses a blend of email notifications, web page updates, and social media techniques to share information with the campus community. Determined to develop a communication plan that reaches everyone in the community, we worked with a team of students and staff to refine our procedures and deliver our messages in different ways to different audiences. This presentation offers ideas for communicating with your campus through a variety of channels.

2. TYPES OF MESSAGES
When thinking about communicating to the campus community, we need to identify the types of messages that we intend to relay. We can typically group these messages into three categories: generic informational messages, announcements, and urgent news or situation updates.

SIGUCCS'11, November 12–17, 2011, San Diego, California, USA.

2.1 Generic informational messages
Generic informational messages let the community know about general news and information that is good to deliver occasionally to remind people about best IT practices. "Tips and Tricks", messages about backing up your important data, sales opportunities, software availability, lab hours, and contact information are all in this first category. These messages do not have any urgency, imperative or target audience. The world would be a better place if everybody knew the content of these messages.

2.2 Announcements
Announcements are notices of something new or changing. Depending on the content, there is at least one: a time factor, an imperative, or target audience. The availability of new software, time of a maintenance period, changes in a lab, removal of a service, and upgrade of a server are examples. Announcements often need to reach one or more target audiences by a certain time. Sometimes, the announcement also requires a reaction or action from the target audience.

2.3 Urgent news/Situation updates
Urgent news or situation updates are when the information is time-sensitive and need to reach a target audience in a timely manner. These messages are usually during an outage or service disruption and usually generated under very stressful conditions. Care and tact are required to insure that the correct information is relayed in a timely manner. In these situations, emotions can run quite high. Efficient and effective communications of urgent news and situation updates can reduce stress during the situation.

3. DELIVERING MESSAGES
For every type of message, we would like everyone to read every message we deliver. However, this is not feasible and requires us to consider delivering to target audiences the appropriate type of communication method for the message. We have to remember that communicating information to a variety of audiences requires different styles and media. Delivering your messages effectively is a moving target in both the style and the media.

3.1 The speed of change
Remember the days of sending out hard copy printouts of the email announcing something because too many people required something on paper before they read it? The speed at which our communications happen is exploding exponentially. Thirty years ago, email was just shared by a bunch of geeks in some research labs. Twenty years ago, the first web pages were just being served in a lab in Switzerland. Ten years ago, AOL Instant Messenger was just starting to take off. Five years ago, Twitter

was just a gleam in Jack Dorsey's eye. [1] Another way to look at it is, it took three years, two months and one day to reach one billion tweets. Now, it takes less than a week to generate a billion tweets. What is the next big thing?

3.2 Style, more important than you think

The style of a message conveys a lot of information and can either enhance or cripple your delivery of its content. Some of choices to consider are:

- Long-winded or not enough information
- Formal or informal
- Form letter or personal touch
- Fancy HTML with backgrounds or plain text
- Visual or textual (or aural)
- Very frequently or rarely
- Bulk mail or targeted direct mail

Each choice has a consequence. Depending on your message, you should consider each choice and determine if it is the right one for your message and your audience. Some of these style choices invoke a visceral reaction so be thoughtful.

3.3 Tools at our disposal

Geneseo has tried to stay current with the delivery of information to our community. We have a number of media outlets that we can use to deliver messages. Some of them are:

- Face-to-face communication (visiting people)
- Email/mailing lists
- Web pages
- Portal pages
- Wiki
- Twitter
- Facebook
- RSS feeds from Wiki, Twitter and Facebook
- Lab desktop wallpapers/screen savers
- Posters
- Bookmarks
- Postcards
- Cellular phones
- Telephone call tree

Each of these outlets has their specialty in the ability to deliver information and specific audience. For every message and audience, careful consideration should be made for each outlet.

3.3.1 Informational messages

Generic informational messages are not always critical for everybody to see. Reminding people to back up their important data is nice, but it is just a reminder. We use posters, bookmarks, postcards, desktop wallpapers, web pages, Twitter and Facebook to help blast the informational messages to as wide an audience as possible. We try to map the appropriate style to the medium used in such a way that is common practice. For example, tweets are not long and usually include a link for more information.

3.3.2 Announcements

Announcements are messages that we really want people to notice and read. We use web pages, email, wiki and face-to-face communication as the primary means to communicate announcements. We supplement these with Twitter, Facebook and RSS feeds to help spread the word.

3.3.3 Urgent News/Situation Updates

Depending on what services are affected, we use email or a telephone call tree get the message out to as many affected as possible. In an effort to reduce the impact of people wanting to know the status of a situation, we separate those working on restoring services from those asking for status updates. A single liaison or two bridges the communications gap and helps direct information in a timely fashion to the appropriate people.

4. MISCONCEPTIONS

It is easy to forget how technology could be difficult to understand for IT professionals. It is also difficult to see things from a point of view other than your own. We recommend that you check your assumptions often to make sure they are still valid. Things change and they change fast. What was important or worked yesterday may not work now.

4.1 "Build it and they will come…"

As the old movie quote from *Field of Dreams* states, build something and they will come to use it. This delusion is one of the biggest we face when we build something to deliver information to an audience and they have changed where, when and how they get their information.

Although you may believe you have communicated the message effectively, communication is a two-way activity. You must go out and verify that your message got through and change your tactics if it did not.

4.2 "Who are you again?"

Campus communities are very dynamic and have varying levels of long-term and short-term memory. Sending mail from a person's account may be the way it has always been done. However, people in the community do not know everyone and decide to read messages based on the sender. A random name from a stranger does not often drive people to read their messages, especially in these days of spam mailings.

We recommend that you set up a departmental account with an "official looking" address. Look into using PGP or other technology to electronically sign messages.

4.3 "What are you talking about?"

IT professionals tend to use jargon and local terms to describe things to the general community. What is "phishing"? What is a "DNS server"? IT is becoming more and more complex, making it more difficult to explain changes or problems.

4.3.1 Customer's Point of View

To avoid this pitfall, it is best to look at it from the customer's point of view and use their words to inform them. Think about services, not the technology that provides them.

4.3.2 Timing

Another way to avoid this pitfall is to deliver the message when it is convenient for audience and when they are prepared to listen. Only deliver messages to those who are affected by changes. Otherwise, the next communication may be ignored.

4.3.3 Accessibility

Finally, deliver the message in an accessible way. Provide a clear, concise tag/subject to indicate what the message is about. Edit your message down to short sentences. Put the most important information first. Do not use attachments. Be careful of colors, images or formats that cannot be read. Do not use technical terms, jargon, or acronyms. Provide easy access to more information via links.

4.3.4 Examples

Table 1 illustrates some of these techniques in developing subject lines for outbound emails. The originals were taking from emails sent last year as part of our normal communication of changes. The student team reviewed these messages and developed more informative subjects to replace the confusing original ones.

Table 1. Email Subject Comparison

Original	Improved
College's Main Phone number	College's Main Phone Number has changed to 585-245-5211
CIT Plans over curtailment	Computer updates will restrict your access to files temporarily between Dec 24th and Jan 2nd
*** ALERT *** Phishing Email SUBJECT: You have 1 new Alert Message!	* Warning * Email with the subject "You have 1 new Alert Message!" is a scam

4.3.5 Some statistics

The student team asked 50 students about CIT and found:

- 70% know very little about us
- 80% did not know about our news feed on our portal
- Only 12% knew about our Facebook fan page
- 49% read most of their email
- 74% say they never or rarely receive email from us
- 79% would read our mail if it was more clearly marked

In interviews with faculty, the students found that:

- Faculty didn't know they were getting mail from us
- Most faculty just briefly skim the messages

64% of small business executives said that they decide whether or not to open email based on whom it is from. – *Bredin Business Information (2007)*

55.9% of respondents cited knowing and trusting the sender as the primary reason for opening an email. – *Return Path (2007)*

78% of mobile email users are also regular users of social networking sites. – *Merkle* "View from the digital inbox 2011"

43% of mobile email users check email four or more times per day, compared to 29% of those who do not use mobile mail. – *Merkle* "View from the digital inbox 2011"

55% of those with an Internet-enabled mobile phone use it to check their personal email account. – *Merkle* "View from the digital inbox 2011"

13.36% of emails are opened by a mobile operating system or device. – *Merkle* "View from the digital inbox 2011"

4.4 "Email is for old people"

Although you want to send a message out to your audience, keep in mind there are probably many different audiences. "Email is for old people" and "I only use email to communicate with my parents" are examples of how generational differences influence media selection. In fact, it is worse than that. Instead of having 10 to 15 years to adjust, people are finding there are differences between siblings and their views of technology? Remember that Twitter didn't exist five years ago?

To avoid this pitfall, keep current with communication/media trends. Employ students to help get your message out and listen to them about how they are communicating.

5. CONCLUSIONS

Over the years, we have tried many techniques to get our word out to our community. There are a number of tried and true methods but we also need to acknowledge that media and style change over time and it is changing faster than ever.

6. ACKNOWLEDGMENTS

Our thanks to Susan Chichester, CIO and Director of CIT, for her support and our conference attendance. Thank you to everyone who contributed to this paper with ideas and proofreading talents.

7. REFERENCES

[1] Shabbir Akhtar. (2011, March) Jack Dorsey tweets about the beginning of twitter. [Online]. http://www.socialtrakr.com/2011/03/15/jack-dorsey-tweets-about-the-beginning-as-twitter-turns-five/

Successful Implementation of an Active Learning Laboratory in Computer Science

Hossein Hakimzadeh
Computer Science and Informatics
Indiana University South Bend
South Bend, Indiana, USA
1.574.520.4517
hhakimza@iusb.edu

Raman Adaikkalavan
Computer Science and Informatics
Indiana University South Bend
South Bend, Indiana, USA
1.574.520.4295
radaikkala@iusb.edu

Robert Batzinger
Computer Science and Informatics
Indiana University South Bend
South Bend, Indiana, USA
1.574.520.5042
rbatzing@iusb.edu

ABSTRACT
There is ample evidence of positive impact of active learning on student learning, attitudes, critical thinking, and retention. The traditional lecture-style classrooms are not suitable for group interaction or activities. Having an appropriate classroom with proper technology to support active learning is essential. In order to foster easier group interaction and collaborative learning, the authors have designed and constructed a new active-learning classroom inspired by the SCALE-UP classroom design. The classroom is specifically designed for group activities. Students sit around a collaborative station (each station can have up to five members). Each station is equipped with a large display monitor attached to a computer. The classroom walls are used as whiteboards for group activities. The authors have developed various timed group activities specifically for this course to enhance student learning. In this presentation, we will discuss how the use of proper technology, an active learning classroom, along with proper pedagogical approach can enhance learning, foster group activities, promote peer learning, and improve retention in gateway science courses.

Categories and Subject Descriptors
K.3.1 [**Computers and Education**]: Computer Uses in Education – *Collaborative learning.*

General Terms
Performance, Design, Experimentation, Human Factors, Standardization.

Keywords
Active learning, Active learning classrooms, Active learning pedagogical methods.

1. INTRODUCTION
At Indiana University South Bend, the university admission policy allows a significant number of at-risk students to enter college and be given a second chance [8]. As a result, the overall retention rate in introductory informatics and computer science courses can be as low as 50%. There are several reasons for these low retention statistics, chief among them are the lack of K-12 computer science preparation and inadequate mathematics and science preparation.

During the past two decades, to attract and retain students, the computer science education community has developed and experimented with a number of innovative approaches for teaching introductory computer science and informatics courses. These approaches include thematic courses such as those using games [2], computer security [16], simulation [15], computer graphics [3, 10], and robotics [7, 12]. Others [4], have obtained good results by introducing supplemental instruction and student mentors in early computer programming courses. Finally, a number of initiatives have used active learning approaches which promote working in small groups on hands-on activity [11, 17].

At Indiana University South Bend, our approach for dealing with student retention has been to design and develop a new CS0 course [1, 5, 6]. This course provides the students interested in computer science or informatics the opportunity to explore the required skills needed for the discipline in a controlled "incubator" like setting. The new course incorporates ideas from thematic courses as well as active learning to introduce the students to systematic and structured problem solving, working within small groups, research, data collection, reflective thinking, stepwise refinement, dialogue and discussion. Additionally, the students are exposed to introductory programming concepts such as variables and memory manipulation, conditionals, loops, modularization and code reuse, arrays, and objects.

The main motivation for creating an active learning classroom was to provide a rich interactive environment that fosters better student engagement, involves students in collaborative and cooperative problem solving, and promotes computational thinking. Developing the above skills in a freshman computer science course is of course challenging, especially in light of the fact that a significant number of students entering this course may be academically at-risk.

Given the above challenges, we felt that working in groups, will reduce the anxiety associated with being a new student, promotes peer learning, and at the same time increases their interest in computer science, and keeps them motivated.

Initially, the new CS0 course was offered in a traditional classroom as the active learning classroom was being planned and constructed. Although, the activities required students to work in groups, the traditional classroom configuration posed a constant challenge for the instructor. For instance, when students were asked to form groups of three or four, some did not even want to turn their chairs and face their team members. Similarly, the lack of a collaborative-workstation (e.g., common writing space and computer) kept students from having full-fledged interactions within groups. Thus, the new active learning classroom environment became central to the design and success of students in this course. The newly built active learning classroom is shown in Figure 1.

Figure 1. Active Learning Classroom.

2. CLASSROOM DESIGN

The decision to develop an active learning CS0 course warranted investigating related research in early science education [13], which led to the creation of the active learning classroom shown in Figure 1. During the course of our investigation we were excited at the success of the Student-Centered Active Learning Environment for Undergraduate Programs (SCALE-UP) designed and developed by researchers at North Carolina State University and adopted or adapted by more than 100 universities [14]. The original SCALE-UP, was designed for large enrollment science classes with 100 or more students. In CS0, accommodating 100 students was not a priority, given our traditional class sizes however; we did need to create a highly interactive and collaborative environment for the students. At the same time, the classroom needed to also allow the instructor to easily monitor and intervene when necessary. We also wanted the classroom to allow groups to write algorithms and draw flowcharts while solving problems. In addition, we wanted to maintain the instructor workstation to give mini lectures, and discuss and demonstrate computer programs.

Given the size of the room, several alternative designs were explored, and at the end the configuration shown in Figure 2 was adopted. The final design supports five collaborative-stations where each station can accommodate up to five students. Each station has a computer attached to a 46-inch LCD screen. This allows students to develop computer programs collaboratively.

One of the main issues we faced and which required several iterations was the ergonomic design and the height of the monitor. Since there can be up to five students at each collaborative-station we had to adjust the positioning of the display so that all the students, including those closest to the monitor can work with ease.

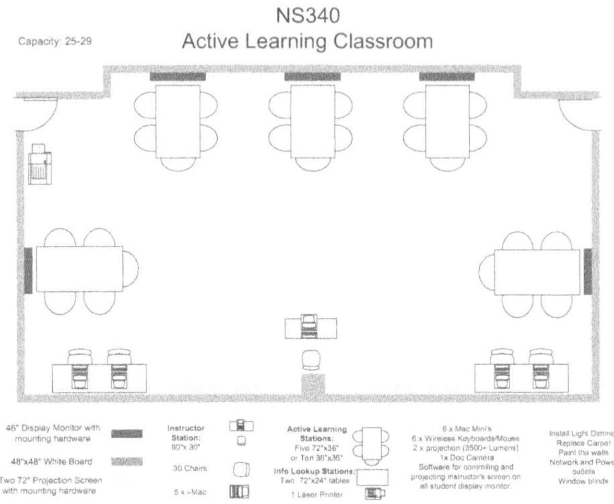

Figure 2. Classroom and Collaborative-Station Design.

To facilitate collaboration in algorithm development, flow charting, and other design activities, each collaborative-station needed to provide ample writing space. The first approach was to convert the entire the wall to a whiteboard by using a special paint. We used this approach during the first semester. Though it worked very well for group-work, it was hard to maintain and keep clean. A number of solutions were tried to no avail; therefore, in order to rectify the problem, we explored two alternative writing surfaces: 1) using glass as a writing surface and 2) using regular whiteboards. Though the glass was very easy to clean, the reflection of light severely affected the visibility of the writing. Thus, regular whiteboards were finally adopted. This approach has worked well, but students are now restricted to the size of the board and cannot work on the entire wall.

The classroom has an instructor station that can be used for lecture or demonstration. The configuration of the room as well as the arrangement of the collaborative-stations required two overhead projection units that allow students to follow the lectures with ease. Having two projection units has also improved the visibility especially when code components, typically with smaller font sizes, are demonstrated. The instructor station is also equipped with LanSchool classroom management software [9] to manage the collaborative workstations. This software can be used by the instructor to monitor student progress, help them fix bugs, provide directions and additional help. LanSchool enables the instructor to share his or her screen, or take the output from one of collaborative-stations and project it to the other stations for critique, analysis, or discussion.

At present the main disadvantage to using this classroom is the fact that the collaborative stations are not suited for conducting tests. Readers interested in constructing a similar active learning classroom can refer to www.cs.iusb.edu/active_learning_lab.pdf

3. PEDAGOGICAL METHODS

In this section, we briefly discuss some of the collaborative activities that are used to engage students in deeper learning.

The introduction of a concept can be based on a group activity where the students try to solve a problem even without knowing the programming constructs involved. For example, we ask the students to find the minimum of 10 numbers using the following procedure.

1) The instructor provides each team ten (1-inch square) pieces of paper with a number printed on each piece.
2) The students are asked to keep the pile with the printed side down.
3) The students are not allowed to see all the numbers at once.
4) Student groups are then given an extra blank piece of paper.
5) Students can see exactly one number at a time. After viewing a number they should put it back facing down.
6) Students cannot remember the numbers; however, they are allowed to use the blank sheet to write down exactly one number at a time. They can overwrite the existing number. In other words, the blank paper acts as a variable that can hold one value at a time.

This exercise develops their computational thinking as they have to compare one number to the other, step by step. This also makes it easy to explain the concept of variables, conditionals, assignment, and loops. After this, the instructor gives a short lecture (20-25 minutes). The lecture covers a specific topic for the day. For example, loops and various ways of implementing loops are discussed. The instructor then assigns a set of problems to be solved as a group. For example, find the sum of 10 user inputs. The set of problems provided typically require students to create algorithms and/or flowcharts, and then implement them using a high level language such as VB .NET.

Once the set of problems are provided, students are asked to form a group of two or three. Each group is then required to write the algorithm and draw the flowchart using the whiteboard. In order to promote full participation by all students, we ask one student to develop the algorithm and one student to draw the flowchart, and switch their roles with different problems. Once two groups have developed their algorithms they will be asked to switch places, and check each other's work and verify the workings of the proposed solution. This allows students to see and learn how the other team has solved the same problem. This also leads to discussions about efficiency and the use of different programming constructs for solving the same problem.

After this exercise, the teams are asked to return to their desk and translate their algorithms to a high level programming language. While writing the code we ask students to frequently rotate the keyboard to allow active participation by all. In addition, the instructor uses the LanSchool classroom management software to select the best solution from the student teams and broadcasts it to other students.

Each lab session, which is 2 hours long, is split into two phases. Depending on the problem, the time period for each phase is calculated. For example, the first phase can be 30 minutes and the second phase can be 90 minutes. In the first phase, students work individually to analyze the problem, identifying the inputs and output, and create the algorithm. During the second phase, students work as a group. In this phase, they compare each other's work and solutions. The first phase allows students to think and develop algorithms. The second phase allows them to learn from their peers and create the best integrated solution. They are also asked to implement the algorithm in the second phase.

The instructor visits all the teams during these activities. The instructor acts as an active listener and a passive participant. But the instructor helps the groups when they face a mental block that requires intervention. Sometimes the instructor just visits with the groups to make sure that all the students are actively participating. Based on our experiences, groups of two are most effective in engaging students. Although exams are typically an individual activity, some of the quizzes are designed as a group activity.

4. PRELEMINARY RESULTS

Although the results are preliminary, the initial indicators appear to be positive. Compared to traditional lecture style instruction, the active-learning strategies coupled with the use of the active-learning classroom have had several positive outcomes, including:

- Student engagement, both in-class and outside of classroom has improved.
- Attendance has improved significantly.
- Faculty feedback from CS1 (the sequel to this course) indicates improved performance compared to prior offering of the course.

As shown in table 1, student feedback (taken during the last two semesters of offering the CS0 course) indicates the effectiveness of active learning components in their learning:

Table 1. Effectiveness of Active Learning (n=43)

Course Component	Most Effective	Least Effective
In-class Active Learning Activities	74%	11%
Active Learning Classroom	56%	9%

In addition, 91% of the students indicated that their group members were helpful in learning the course material.

5. CONCLUSION

Active learning strategies have been shown to be effective in promoting student engagement, learning, and retention. In a traditional lecture-style classroom, students tend to remain as passive listeners. The mode of learning is mostly through a simplex transmission of information from the faculty to student. Studies have shown that a typical student today loses concentration and perhaps interest after approximately 10 to 15 minutes of traditional lecture. In contrast, active learning strategies break the session into a series of 10 to 15 minute activities, combining short lectures, individual problem solving activities, group analysis, peer learning, collaboration, brain storming, reading, writing, pair programming, and discussion. These intentional short duration activities are designed to keep the students engaged in learning.

Having an appropriately designed classroom with proper furnishing, equipment and technology to support active learning is an essential part of this learning model. In order to foster group interaction and collaborative learning, the authors have designed and constructed a new active-learning classroom inspired by the SCALE-UP classroom design. Students sit around a collaborative station, which is equipped with a large display monitor and a computer. Each collaborative-station is also provided with ample whiteboards for group activities.

Based on the authors experiences, during the past two years of teaching and refining this course, along with the feedback from students, as well as faculty who teach the CS1 course, we believe that the new CS0 course, with its new active-learning instructional model and classroom, successfully assists students with the gradual development of critical thinking, and problem solving skills, necessary to succeed in Computer Science and Informatics. We are encouraged by student feedback at the end of each term which reports that the majority intend to continue their studies in computer science or informatics.

As a further evidence of interest in the effectiveness of active-learning classrooms, our new classroom has been used by the mathematics department for the past two semesters, additionally, a number of computer science faculty has indicated interest in teaching their upper level courses. Furthermore, the classroom has been visited by a number of faculty and administrators at IU South Bend, and currently plans are underway to construct up to two additional active learning classrooms in the near future.

6. ACKNOWLEDGMENTS

This work is partially supported by Indiana University South Bend Curriculum Development Grant. Additional funding was provided by the Informatics program at IU South Bend.

7. REFERENCES

[1] Adaikkalavan, R., Hakimzadeh, H., "Problem Solving and Critical Thinking using an Active Learning Approach", The 11th Annual Midwest Conference on the Scholarship of Teaching and Learning SoTL, Indiana University South Bend. April 9, 2010.

[2] Barnes T, et al. "Game2Learn: Building CS1 Learning Games for Retention", ITiCSE '07: Proceedings of the 12th annual SIGCSE conference on Innovation and technology in computer science education, June 2007

[3] Batzinger, R., Hakimzadeh, H., Laboratory Exercises for A201 Introduction to computing. http://mypage.iusb.edu/~hhakimza/201_505/index.html

[4] D'Souza, D., et al. "Transforming Learning of Programming: a Mentoring Project", ACE '08: Proceedings of the tenth conference on Australasian computing education - Volume 78, January 2008

[5] Hakimzadeh, H., Wolfer, J., "Introducing a CS0 Class to Ease Transition to CS1: Another Attempt at Retention", INTERTECH'2009 - International Conference on Engineering and Technology Education, Buenos Aires, Argentina. March 8-11, 2009.

[6] Hakimzadeh, H., Wolfer, James, Adaikkalavan, R., ACS0: A Project Based, Active Learning Course; Work In Progress@, 2011 IAJC-ASEE International Associations of Journals and Conferences – American Society for Engineering Education, University of Hartford, April 15-16, 2011.

[7] Imberman, S, P, Klibaner, R, "A Robotics Lab for CS1" Journal of Computing Sciences in Colleges, Volume 21 Issue 2, Consortium for Computing Sciences in Colleges, December 2005

[8] IU South Bend Admission Rates, IU Institutional Research and Reporting http://www.iu.edu/~uirr/reports/compliance/doc/common_dataset/CDS_2010/IUSB_2010.pdf (Sections C and D)

[9] LanSchool Classroom Management Software, http://www.lanschool.com

[10] Matzko, S., Davis, T, A., "Teaching CS1 with Graphics and C", ACM SIGCSE Bulletin, Volume 38 Issue 3, September 2006

[11] McConnell, J, J, "Active and Cooperative Learning: Final Tips and Tricks (Part IV)", inroads – The SIGCSE Bulletin, Volume 38, Number 4, December 2006, pp. 25-28

[12] Pamela B. Lawhead, P.B., et al. "A Road Map for Teaching Introductory Programming using LEGO© Mindstorms Robots", ACM SIGCSE Bulletin, Volume 35 Issue 2, June 2003

[13] Prince, M., "Does Active Learning Work? A Review of the Research", Journal of Engineering Education, July 2004, Vol. 93 (3), pp 223- 231.

[14] Scale-Up Classroom design models. Student-Centered Active Learning Environment for Undergraduate Programs (SCALE-UP) http://www.ncsu.edu/PER/SCALEUP/Classrooms.html, http://scaleup.ncsu.edu/

[15] Stone, J, A, "Using a Machine Language Simulator to Teach CS1 Concepts", inroads – The SIGCSE Bulletin, Volume 38, Number 4, December 2006, pp. 43-45

[16] Taylor, B., Azadegan, S., "Moving Beyond Security Tracks: Integrating Security in CS0 and CS1", SIGCSE '08: Proceedings of the 39th SIGCSE technical symposium on Computer science education, March 2008

[17] Whittington, K., Yacci, M., "Active Learning for Classroom Management Model", Proceedings of the Informing Science & IT Education Conference, June, 2008. Accessed on the web http://proceedings.informingscience.org/InSITE2008/InSITE08p231-239Whit484.pdf

IT Collaboration Across Institutions

R. Mark Koan, Ed.D.
Phoenix College
1202 West Thomas Road
Phoenix, AZ, 85013
1-602-285-7855
mkoan@phoenixcollege.edu

ABSTRACT

Rapidly increasing demand for technology support services, and often shrinking budgetary and staff resources, create enormous challenges for information technology (IT) departments in public sector higher education. To address these difficult circumstances, the author helped develop a network of IT professionals from schools in a community college system and a research university in the same geographic region into a community of practice (CoP) that spanned the boundaries of their organizations. This collaboration allowed members from participating institutions to share knowledge and ideas relating to shared technical problems.

The author also collected data about the extent to which the community developed the factors that contributed to its development and the perceived value that the other leaders and participants attributed to the endeavor.

The results indicated that the group did coalesce into a CoP. The author also identified two crucial roles that aided this development: community coordinator and technology steward. Furthermore, the IT professionals who participated and the leaders from their organizations reported that developing the community was a worthwhile venture. They also reported that while the technical collaboration component was very valuable, the non-technical topics and interactions were also very beneficial.

Finally, indicators also suggest that the community made progress toward self-sustainability and is likely to continue. These findings suggest that other higher education IT organizations faced with similar circumstances may be able to follow this model and achieve positive results.

Categories and Subject Descriptors

K.6.1 [**Project and People Management**]: *Staffing*

General Terms

Management, Documentation, Performance, Economics, Experimentation, Human Factors, Standardization

Keywords

Community of Practice, Collaboration, Management.

1. INTRODUCTION

With two recessions in the past decade, information technology (IT) departments in higher education institutions have experienced a number of budget difficulties, straining the availability of resources for continued investments in existing infrastructure and services and limiting the ability to implement new technologies (Green, 2009). In the fall of 2009, slightly more than two-thirds (67.1%) of American public universities reported cuts in their central IT budgets, and though community colleges fared somewhat better with just under two-fifths (38.0%) reporting cuts, these figures are up substantially from 16.4% and 14.1% (respectively) reporting cuts just two years earlier (Green, 2009, p. 10). Although circumstances for public universities were slightly better in 2010, with "only" three-fifths (59.8%) reporting cuts to their central IT budgets, community colleges fared worse than in 2009, with the number of schools reporting cuts increasing to almost half (46.2%) (Green, 2010, p. 11).

At the same time, due to both annual enrollment increases in higher education for each of the last 15 years ("Digest of Education Statistics," 2009) and increased technology usage among students in higher education (Caruso & Kvavik, 2005; Kvavik, Caruso, & Morgan, 2004; Salaway, Katz, & Caruso, 2006; Salaway & Caruso, 2007, 2008; S. Smith, Salaway, & Caruso, 2009), the demand for technology services at colleges and universities has continued to rise (Green, 2009). Casey Green (2010), Director of the Campus Computing Project (in which all of the institutions in this study participate), said, "the demand for IT resources and services continues to rise, even as the dollars supporting campus IT resources, services, and personnel are cut from institutional budgets." (Green, 2009, p. 10) This situation has created substantial challenges for IT leaders and their staff at these institutions where they are asked to continue offering a wide range of high-quality, reliable technology services, expand access to and availability of those services, implement new technologies, and help drive innovation across the institution—all while their fiscal and human resources continue to shrink.

Technology continues to advance at a rapid pace and demand for technology support services continues to grow, but IT departments face many challenges in the midst of the unprecedented budget pressures their organizations face (Green, 2009). Stephen Laster, the Chief Information Officer (CIO) of Harvard Business School recently said, "IT is under pressure to cut its costs, and on the other hand, it is under pressure to deliver more services.... It's a double-whammy of a hit, in the environment in which the IT department is operating" (Grush, 2010). In these difficult economic times, it is critically important for IT leaders to look for ways to improve their efficiency and effectiveness, and find opportunities to grow the skills of their staff members (Cullen, 2008).

1.1 Context

One way to address the challenge of increasing demand and decreasing resources is to collaborate by developing what is known as a *Community of Practice* (CoP). The author is an IT director at one campus in a large research university. After working with a colleague at one of the community colleges in the same metropolitan area in the summer of 2009, it became apparent that both leaders and their respective institutions faced a number of common challenges. It also became clear that there was limited collaboration among leaders of the 10 campus-based IT departments in the community college district and even less between the community colleges and the university. In an attempt to help develop these relationships and create more collaboration opportunities among their institutions, these two leaders encouraged a few select IT professionals from their institutions to help form the beginnings of an interorganizational group, which would eventually develop into a CoP.

All total, there were 28 unique participants from six higher education institutions who participated in this collaboration. During the 2010-2011 academic year, the author worked with IT leaders and staff from these schools in strategic ways to help the group advance as a CoP. The goal was to strengthen and grow this potential community and as a result, facilitate improved IT practice at each of the institutions.

2. KEY CONCEPTS

2.1 Communities of Practice

The term *community of practice* is now in widespread use in the disciplines of knowledge management, organizational learning, and education, but as Cox (2005) also points out, there is considerable variation in its use. Lave (1991) views learning as situated in social practice and explains that it should not be viewed as a "process of socially shared cognition that results in the end in the internalization of knowledge by individuals, but as a process of becoming a member of a sustained community of practice" (p. 65).

Brown and Duguid (1991) also view learning as key to becoming a member of a particular CoP, which occurs through a process they call "learning-in-working" (p. 41). In describing that concept, they make an important distinction between canonical, abstract knowledge maintained and transmitted through formal organizational processes like documentation and training, and the noncanonical, ad hoc knowledge that practitioners actually use to solve real-world problems. They explain, "The communities that we discern are, by contrast, often noncanonical and not recognized by the organization. They are more fluid and interpenetrative than bounded, often crossing the restrictive boundaries of the organization to incorporate people from outside" (p. 49).

CoPs tend to serve one or more distinct purposes *within* an organization. As mentioned earlier, Wenger et al. (2002) describe four examples of strategic intentions for forming such intraorganizatonal CoPs. The existing literature seems to have less to offer about how CoPs function *across* organizations, but Wenger (1998) notes that CoPs which span organizational boundaries may be more beneficial in "in fast-moving industries… to keep up with constant technological changes." Powell, Koput, and Smith-Doerr (1996), in examining the biotechnology industry, also argue that "…when the knowledge base of an industry is both complex and expanding and the sources of expertise are widely dispersed, the locus of innovation will be found in networks of learning, rather than in individual firms." (p. 116). This suggests that interorganizational CoPs, may also prove valuable as learning networks and drivers of innovation for technology professionals as well.

2.2 Community Coordinator

A community coordinator (CC) is a member of the community who takes on a leadership role to help plan, coordinate and facilitate personal interactions, meetings and other activities whose purpose is to consistently advance the general health and organization of the CoP. Wenger et al. (2002), describe the role of a community coordinator as a critical one for the success of a CoP. In fact, they explain that, "a number of studies have shown that the most important factor in a community's success is the vitality of its leadership" (p. 80). They list the key functions of this role as follows:

- Identify important issues in their domain.
- Plan and facilitate community events….
- Informally link community members, crossing boundaries between organizational units and brokering knowledge assets.
- Foster the development of community members.
- Manage the boundary between the community and the formal organization, such as teams and other organizational units.
- Help build the practice—including the knowledge base, lessons learned, best practices, tools and methods, and learning events.
- Assess the health of the community and evaluate its contribution to members and the organization. (p. 80)

In more traditional settings, CCs are often tasked with managing the boundary between the CoP and the larger organization. When communities span boundaries, however, there are additional issues with which a CC must contend. Cross and Prusak (2002), note the role of a "boundary spanner" (p. 9) as someone who can help people make meaningful connections to other practitioners and communities across organizational boundaries. Wenger also acknowledges the importance of "the *boundary* leadership provided by those who connect the community to other communities" (Wenger, 1998). He does not, however, discuss the importance of a CC *within* a community when multiple organizations are involved. Nonetheless, making these connections is an integral part of developing an interorganizational CoP and increasing its value to its members and the organizations to which they belong.

2.3 Technology Steward

One way to support continued interactions among members of a community is to introduce specific technologies for facilitating ongoing electronic communication and tools for storing and accessing the artifacts produced by the community. Wenger et al. (2009) identify the person who does this for the community as a technology steward (TS) and describe the function of this role as a person who helps a community "choose, configure, and use technologies to best suit its needs" (2009, p. 27). This person is distinct from an IT support resource as he or she stays engaged with the changing goals and needs of the community and is typically also a member (pp. 25, 131). This role can be distinct from that of the community coordinator and may be performed by a different person.

Selecting tools that meet the need of interorganizational communities creates different challenges, such as "finding resources and support... bridging organizational boundaries... and establishing responsibility to the community." (Wenger et al., 2009, p. 31). When there is no budget allocated to specifically support such a collaboration, the selection is further restricted to existing tools within each participating organization or free options available to the community. Each of these options presents unique advantages and obstacles. One overall tip the authors provide is that the tool selection process be iterative and to "start with the simplest, least expensive solution that you think will work" (Wenger et al., 2009, p. 129).

Once a selection is made, Wenger et al. (2009), indicates that the TS often helps with installation, configuration, and adoption of the tool(s). The TS is also in a unique position to help new members gain access, learn to use the technology tools chosen by the community, and encourage their use among participants. It is important for the TS to raise awareness of the tool(s) with the community and "make the use of tools a legitimate topic of conversation, but keep it in the context of the work of the community" (p. 141). Finally, technology stewards can monitor the use of community technology tools. One way to do this, suggested by the authors, is to use Google Analytics, which can increase "the amount and quality of data available. That data can help tech stewards assess tool usage or community activity patterns. ...[and] can help [them] ground [their] observations with objective measures." (pp. 141-142).

3. FINDINGS

To better understand the development of the CoP, meetings with participants were recorded and coded, members were given short post-meeting questionnaires, and they were asked to take a brief online survey. A few key individuals were also interviewed after the collaboration had been taking place for several months. All but one respondent indicated that before this group started meeting, on average they met with other group members (not from their school) a few times per year or less often.

3.1 CoP Development

3.1.1 Domain

In the coalescing stage of a CoP the key domain issue centers on establishing the value of the knowledge being shared. Participants agreed that the knowledge sharing among community members was one of the most valuable outcomes of participation. At the end of the November meeting, one member described it as, "Very informative!" and went on to say, "The collaboration is beginning to happen."

Extensive, and sometimes fairly technical, discussions of IT practice challenges played a central role in the development of this community. When asked about the value of the meetings in an interview, one member responded, "I do think it's been valuable and I think today's meeting actually was indicative of it... we had a great dialogue; it was very technical." Indeed, the majority of the conversations during the meetings centered on the technical topics selected for each meeting and other day-to-day IT support challenges that community members faced. Wenger et al. (2002) indicate that during the coalescing stage, it is typical for core community members to try to help each other solve these sorts of common practice problems.

Though many of the conversations centered on technical topics, a number of discussions that took place during the intervention focused more on organizational or political issues participants faced. One member explained how being a part of this community helped with those situations.

> I know it's very valuable to us. Just as we sit and listen to what you're saying, it's reassuring and an affirmation to me because these are things I've discussed with our management team. Just last week I had a conversation talking about... change over the next several years... and I was almost laughed out of the room.... What you're telling me is you're doing it today.

These discussions about non-technical topics proved very valuable to participants. One member suggested after the November meeting that perhaps for our collaboration the "value might be counsel vs. content".

3.1.2 Community

In the coalescing stage of a CoP, the primary community issue is building relationships and trust among members. Based on their responses to post-meeting questionnaires and data in the transcripts, participants reported their sense of community increased over the course of the intervention, with members rating the average value of the latter two face-to-face meetings higher than the two previous meetings.

Another finding was that this community helped members feel less isolated. This finding was a recurring theme in the data. In the fourth face-to-face meeting, held in December, when asked about whether the community should continue during the spring semester, one member said,

> You have to be able to collaborate. It helps. You feel like your own island for so long and then to hear what you guys are all going through and, you know, come to different sites and see things, it makes a huge difference...

A campus IT leader echoed this sentiment and said of his staff who were participating that he wanted "...to make sure that they understand that we're not an island... we may have particular [college-specific] problems, but they're not a whole lot different from the [university] problems, or [another college's], or anybody else." Another participant described the growing interdependency and trust that had developed among members of the community like this, "We are all going to rely on each other. We're going to rely on you guys. We are going to rely on other schools."

3.1.3 Practice

Practice involves determining what knowledge to share and how to share it. Knowing what practice to share involved community members taking time to understand one another's work and challenges. It is also a key element in providing value to the members. As Wenger et al. (2002) discuss, topics must be relevant to the participants or the CoP will not be viewed as valuable by members or the organizations of which they are a part.

Though each meeting had a specific technical topic around which the community agreed to focus, discussions were often far-ranging and many other issues came up during each session. In the first face-to-face meeting, one participant said, "One thing to note... and I'm sure you've noticed it, we started out talking about [Office] 2010, but look at how many other subjects got mentioned just from the sharing aspect. You know, that's what happens".

Participants were vocal about which subjects were relevant to them and, through dialogue, negotiated which ones the community should address and when, as is characteristic of a CoP in the coalescing stage of development. In this case, their preferences appeared early on in the intervention. When asked in the second face-to-face meeting in October about whether or not the community should change its focus from Office 2010 to Windows 7, one member explained the need for a shift, "I think Windows 7 is a lot more valuable as far as what's going on currently today, because I know… we're not planning on any kind of 2010 implementation of Office probably for almost a year." As it turned out, due to unforeseen challenges related to Windows 7, deploying Office 2010 turned out to be further away than most initially thought, so the community decided to re-focus on Windows 7 deployment issues.

How best to share knowledge is another important practice element for communities to work through in the coalescing stage and was a topic of discussion for this group. In the fourth meeting, an expert, vendor-led demonstration on Windows 7 deployment, offered by a hardware manufacturer with a strong presence at a number of the participating schools was proposed. In response, one participant said, "To be honest with you, this sounds great but coming back in those first couple of weeks I'm more interested in seeing your SCCM [installation]." This signaled another shift in focus for the community and for the fifth and sixth meetings, SCCM became a central topic of discussion as a means to successfully deploy both Windows 7 images and Office 2010. Given this clear preference among members, the subsequent meeting was organized as an onsite demonstration of how SCCM was being used at one of the participating institutions and that meeting had the best attendance of any until that point. The same topic was discussed in the following meeting and had even higher attendance.

3.2 Leadership Roles

There were three distinct leadership roles that contributed to the development of this CoP – community catalyst, community coordinator and technology steward.

3.2.1 Community Catalyst

The first leadership role that is important for this sort of endeavor is not clearly defined in the current CoP literature. This role could perhaps be called a *community catalyst*, to borrow a term from Frank & Smith (1999). Without an individual stepping up and taking a leadership role to actually work toward forming a CoP, it would be hard to imagine a community coming together in this way. Though CoPs like this one, that span organizational boundaries, certainly have an organic element to their development and evolution, they are unlikely to form spontaneously without some individual or set of individuals acting as a catalyst.

Given that, it is worth considering the possible motivations for someone to assume this role. The author had previous experience with developing a successful CoP in his own organization and his research interests prompted him to explore whether it could also be done across organizations and if so, whether the value would outweigh the costs of participation. In other contexts, however, it would be important for a leader to envision the value of such an endeavor in advance, decide the circumstances were likely to make developing such a community worth the effort, and then try to launch an interorganizational CoP or ask someone in his or her organization to attempt it following the model outlined above.

The position of community catalyst does not currently exist in most institutions. This role could be performed by the community coordinator, but may also be distinct from it. Regardless, such a role is critically important in building a CoP that spans organizations. Someone must take on the initial responsibility of developing a vision for an interorganizational CoP, articulating that vision and a strategy for implementing it, and then taking that concept to parties who may be interested due to an alignment of interests and a willingness to work together on those common issues.

Certainly, such a role is not without challenges. One way to think of it is to contrast it with that of a more traditional IT project manager. In each case, the person has little or no direct authority over participants, but there are more differences than similarities. Project managers typically begin with a charge, executive sponsorship, budget, deadlines, and often even an assigned roster of team members. A community catalyst on the other hand, has none of these. He or she has a vision rather than a charge, has to develop leadership buy-in rather than receiving sponsorship, may have no budget, will typically be accountable for timelines the CoP agrees upon, and will have to recruit would-be participants by articulating a compelling vision of the value such an endeavor can offer.

Furthermore, a project manager is typically held accountable to an organizational leadership structure for delivering an objective. The objective is often given to his or her team, rather than developed by it and is one that typically comes with an assigned timeline and strict budgetary constraints. In an interorganizational CoP such as the one developed in this study, however, the community catalyst may be volunteering his or her time and will typically help develop the initial objectives, timeline and funding priorities (if there is any budget available) with the leaders of other institutions and participants, collaboratively. Over time, these tasks would transition to a more traditional community coordinator, but initially bootstrapping such a community into existence takes additional effort.

If institutions of higher education seek to adopt this model as a way of confronting skyrocketing demand for services in a climate of ever-diminishing resources, they might consider creating such a position, formally, to help drive this type of innovation. Someone hired to be a community catalyst could then adopt, and no doubt refine, the model offered in this study as a way to begin building an interorganizational CoP among institutions in a particular region. After the first such CoP is formed, he or she could pass the leadership to one or more competent community coordinators and begin building another.

3.2.2 Community Coordinator

Other, more clearly established roles also played a part in the development of the CoP. Throughout the 2010-2011 academic year, the author arranged meetings with the IT leaders and held monthly meetings with various IT professionals from participating schools. During the meetings, the CC facilitated interactions and asked participants to share knowledge or asked clarifying questions to help the dialogue continue. As a way to initiate the dialogue and keep it flowing, in a number of sessions the CC specifically asked each school to comment on the meeting topic, the current challenges the IT staff at that school faced relative to that topic, and solutions they might have to offer the community.

To help address time constraints, face-to-face meetings were scheduled over the lunch hour and food was provided during each meeting to make it easier for participants to take the time to travel to another campus and attend the community meetings. One leader commented specifically on the value of meeting over lunch in an interview, "....just having those conversations, having a little social time over lunch to be able to talk about this stuff, I am in favor of that."

Participants also had preferences regarding the format of the interactions, which is an important issue in the coalescing stage of a CoP. Despite the technical nature of this group, when the leaders were asked whether they preferred more technology mediated interactions and fewer face-to-face meetings which required travel for their employees, they chose face-to-face. One member expressed the common sentiment, "we need specific meeting times to get participation... if we do online collaboration 'when we have time', we never have time."

When asked via the online survey in November about ways to improve collaboration, one respondent said, "Stay on track with our monthly meetings and continue to grow our relationships with each other." This desire for continuing to meet consistently was re-affirmed later in the study. Members expressed their desire to continue meeting every month so as not to "lose momentum". At the end of the March meeting, individuals from two other institutions who had not previously hosted offered to host upcoming CoP meetings.

In an interorganizational CoP such as this one, the CC also acts in the role of boundary spanner, linking members across multiple organizations. One organization reported on previous internal efforts to reduce organizational silos, but that did not meet with success, "In the beginning, we actually tried this on our own campus, and it was a failure because people felt like they didn't need to get together." Based on that perception, they decided that collaboration with other campuses was a better strategy and became very engaged, core participants in this CoP.

3.2.3 *Technology Steward*

Another leadership role that contributes to successfully launching and sustaining a CoP like this one is that of the technology steward. A need for a communication channel and a place to store, organize and share information was acknowledged early on when one participant sent an email saying, "I would like us to all discuss a possible portal/blog/whatever, for us all to communicate through instead of email." Indeed, this need for a repository to support the community is articulated in the CoP literature and was expressed by participants over and over again. Another participant said, "No matter what content managing system you pick you can work with it. ...the important thing is that you commit to some tool. You make a selection at some point and you work with it."

The CoP began by using a Google Group created by the author, acting as TS for the community. Shortly after participants began meeting face-to-face, Google announced that it was changing the features of its Google Groups service, thus making it much less suitable for this collaboration ("Google Groups Announcements Page: Notice about Pages and Files," n.d.). Due to this change, the author, again acting as TS for the community, created a Google Site linked to a Google Analytics account, allowing for the collection of comprehensive usage data.

The Google Site was used for tracking issues and solutions for various technical topics, providing community member contact information, posting meeting notes, and facilitating file sharing. There were also links to a Google Calendar for scheduling community events. Information about technical topics discussed in face-to-face meetings was posted for all six participating institutions and two-thirds of the participating schools contributed issues and solutions to the site. The information on the site continued to grow throughout the study.

Participants used the technology tools to collaborate and share knowledge and found them valuable. One participant explained the value of this sort of shared knowledge repository for the technicians at his institution,

> I think... that we all have our own issue bin... on our own campus. What I'm hoping for and have set one of my goals is that... I have people read this and say look this is what other people are going through. Is your question in here?

When asked how he might explain the value to his supervisor, one of the other members described the value of the Google Site and of having access to the posted meeting notes that he could share with others from his campus, "I would use the site and I would explain it and the value we've gotten out of it. Plus even the notes we take home every month when we come out here."

3.3 VALUE

The potential value of developing an interorganizational IT CoP is considered from two perspectives, (1) the perceptions of the participants themselves and the extent to which they find value in the collaborative efforts of such a community, and (2) the perspective of the leaders who support the overall efforts of the community by allowing their employees sufficient time to participate.

3.3.1 *Participant Perceptions*

The data show that participants valued the knowledge sharing and collaboration, believed the time and effort involved was worthwhile, and believed the community should continue. Furthermore, they indicated the value increased over time. Members rated the average value of the last two face-to-face meetings higher than the first two.

One participant described the benefit of sharing knowledge about IT practice with colleagues by saying, "...our issue bin is now for all the schools and we go from there and that is such an asset. That's information and information is everything nowadays." During the December face-to-face meeting, one member summed it up, "The value is in the... tool... What we can save here by sharing, discussing, learning – might take us back and when we bump into something, the solution's already there." When asked how participants would justify ongoing participation to a supervisor in that same meeting, one respondent said, "Yeah, it would be very easy to explain. That the value is not necessarily in a cost savings, it's in a knowledge base. It really is."

Key informants were also interviewed to gather a more in depth view of their thoughts about the value of building and participating in such a community. Participants and leaders were unified in describing participation in the community as valuable and worthwhile. When asked about this specifically, one interviewee had this to say,

> I do think it's been valuable, I think today's meeting was indicative of it.... We had a great dialogue. It was very technical... you're not all alone in this... so when you can find somebody that comes to the table and says I'm seeing this... that helps you personally, I think, as an IT person. You've been struggling; you know

somebody else is struggling; now maybe you can work together. That's why I think it's beneficial.

This question of value also came up during the face-to-face meetings and one member described the benefit of meeting with colleagues to discuss issues, "You're not alone basically. You know there are other people with the same problems and with more problems than you even have and you feel better."

In an interview, another member described the value like this, "I don't think we could put a dollar amount on the value of it. That's how valuable it is. It's not only valuable, it's necessary. It's even more than necessary; it is going to be the key to progress..."

Although members clearly found value in the collaboration, it was not without a cost in terms of time away from other duties, exacerbated by fairly long distances to travel between campuses for face-to-face meetings. When asked about whether or not the value gained was worth the amount of effort required to participate, one community member said this,

> I would say two things about that. I would say, yes, there is enough value, because the value comes from what we contribute, more than what we take away. Because if we are all contributing, then we all know it is like a potluck. We all come with something, and there is something everyone is going to benefit from – that they [*sic*] are going to enjoy. And on the other side, we have to learn on our campuses that sometimes, on the layers below us, we have to delegate, because it gives some of those folks a chance to shine. And even if they don't do well, it's a chance to take them aside and say this is what you need to do next time, and they'll improve.

Another respondent said, "Overall, I would have to say yes, because we are starting to implement things... I noticed that many of us... are all talking the same language now, so that is an overall value, for me."

When asked about whether or not the group should continue meeting in the spring semester on the post-meeting questionnaire in December, every respondent said yes. When asked about whether or not the group should continue to meet in an interview, one person said, "It would be a huge mistake if we stopped". Another individual answered, "Yes. It's an information-sharing collaboration. All of those things help to make us more of an IT community, even though we are all different schools... We're going the same direction. We all have the same goals..."

3.3.2 Leadership Perceptions

Prior to the first face-to-face meeting, leaders from each organization were asked about the possible benefits of further developing this group, to determine whether or not they supported the overall goals of growing into a CoP. All of the leaders agreed or strongly agreed that collaboration could expose their staff members to new ideas, help them improve existing skills and develop new ones, solve common and unusual problems, and all except one respondent (who disagreed), agreed or strongly agreed with the idea that increased collaboration could help his staff improve processes. Knowing what other institutions are struggling with and exploring different ways people solve problems that many organizations face, emerged as important themes in discussions about the value of this collaboration.

One administrator, to whom one of the participating leaders in this study reported, when asked if the collaboration seemed valuable and worthwhile from his perspective replied,

> Oh god, yes! ...this is terribly important... It's not straight ROI, it is a return on strategy... where we start forming these partnerships... you don't know what's going to come out of it, so you just gotta see what the collaboration brings, so it's not a direct return, but I would say it's definitely very positive.

Key leaders of participating institutions were also interviewed to get a deeper understanding of their sense of the value of the collaboration among the various participating institutions. When asked about whether he found this approach valuable, one leader had this to say,

> Yeah, I think it's been valuable on a number of levels.... getting some of my techs, both the ones that participated and when they come back and share with the other techs... [that] other people out there are struggling with some of the same things and here are some tips I got, or even if it's they tried that thing we were going to try and it just didn't work, so let's not waste our time on that. So it's been real [*sic*] helpful from a technical knowledge standpoint, you know to get those tips or successes being shared and also to avoid going into the failures. The other thing that it has helped with is that there are different ways, not just the technology part of it, but different ways in which people communicate or operate or even document or share things... Learning to work together and share that knowledge and get to know people has been real [*sic*] helpful.

Responses like these demonstrate the perceived value of meeting with others and discussing common problems, failures, and solutions.

When asked about whether the benefits outweighed the 'overhead' costs of participation, specifically, one of the leaders responded by saying, "Oh, absolutely. I encourage them to do those kinds of things... Go take a road-trip and go see how these people do things... I think we get our time back ten-fold, with visits like that." The leaders clearly expressed their belief in the value of our collaborative efforts, and importantly, also affirmed that the value derived from the community was worth committing the resources and effort necessary for their institutions to participate.

4. Toward a Model of Developing an IT CoP

Much of the literature about communities of practice focuses on the theory about why they are effective or observations about the function they serve or results various communities have achieved, but little actually describes the process of how to create, develop and foster success in such a community, particularly one that spans multiple organizations. This study attempts to narrow that gap by providing guidance as to how a CoP can be built among higher education IT organizations, along with a discussion of some of the difficulties one might face in doing so.

This study offers a model for developing an interorganizational CoP among IT professionals. Here are recommended considerations for developing one, based on the research conducted for this study,

- **Solicit** support and input from leaders at other institutions
- **Plan** meetings and select initial topic(s) of shared interest

- **Identify and Invite** colleagues from other institutions to join
- **Establish** community coordinator(s) and tech steward(s)
- **Foster** relationship building and trust among members
- **Revise** topics as community interests become more clear or change
- **Monitor** leaders and participants to ensure community continues to provide value
- **Adjust** meetings, communication methods, and technology tools as needs change

Over time, with additional research in this area, this model can be further developed and refined.

5. Conclusion

As both private and public institutions of higher education struggle with difficult budget situations across the United States, operating in conditions where resources are incredibly scarce has become the norm. In technology, where the industry continues to expand and change rapidly, challenges are further magnified by staff cuts and shrinking budgets. One way for organizations to continue to succeed despite these difficulties is through collaboration with other institutions. By developing and documenting a model for building a CoP among the IT professionals at the institutions in this study, others may be able to foster similar communities with partner institutions and achieve positive results.

Technology is an integral part of the educational experience. Nevertheless, in the face of diminishing resources and ever-increasing demand for services, the IT professionals who support that technology face constant pressure to do more with less. Fortunately, they don't have to face that challenge alone. Interorganizational communities of practice can transform and improve the way IT departments do business. IT leaders may have little influence over the pace of technology innovation or the budget allocations they receive, but they can decide how to address those challenges. If they have the foresight and flexibility to encourage and support the IT professionals who work for them to move beyond institutional boundaries, they can find new resources and solutions to their problems. Collaborating more closely with colleagues from other organizations is a strategy for success in these difficult times.

6. ACKNOWLEDGMENTS

Thanks to Dr. Kathleen Puckett, Dr. Teresa Foulger, and Dr. Colleen Carmean without whom this research would not have been possible. Also, many thanks to the participants from various schools who contributed to and became members of the community of practice described in this study.

NB: This paper is condensed from the author's doctoral dissertation, available through UMI/ProQuest, Copyright pending.

Koan, R. (2011). *Collaboration Across Organizational Boundaries: Developing an Information Technology Community of Practice.*

7. REFERENCES

[1] APQC International Benchmarking Clearinghouse. (2001). *Building and sustaining communities of practice: continuing success in knowledge management.* Houston TX: American Productivity & Quality Center.

[2] Brown, J. S., & Duguid, P. (1991). Organizational Learning and Communities-of-Practice: Toward a Unified View of Working, Learning, and Innovation. *Organization Science, 2*(1), 40–57.

[3] Caruso, J. B., & Kvavik, R. B. (2005). *ECAR Study of Students and Information Technology, 2005: Convenience, Connection, Control, and Learning.* Boulder, CO: EDUCAUSE Center for Applied Research. Retrieved from http://www.educause.edu/ir/library/pdf/ers0506/rs/ERS0506w.pdf

[4] Cox, A. (2005). What are communities of practice? A comparative review of four seminal works. *Journal of Information Science, 31*(6), 527-540. doi:10.1177/0165551505057016

[5] Cross, R., & Prusak, L. (2002). The people who make organizations go--or stop. *Harvard Business Review, 80*(6). Retrieved from http://sixdegrees.wdfiles.com/local–files/reading-capital/people.pdf

[6] Cullen, A. (2008). *CIOs: Must-Read Research In Economic Downturns - Forrester Research* (p. 7). Cambridge, MA: Forrester. Retrieved from http://www.forrester.com/rb/Research/cios_must-read_research_in_economic_downturns/q/id/47455/t/2

[7] Digest of Education Statistics. (2009). *Digest of Education Statistics, 2009 - Introduction.* Retrieved April 13, 2010, from http://nces.ed.gov/programs/digest/d09/

[8] Frank, F., Canada. (1999). *The community development handbook: A tool to build community capacity.* [Ottawa]: Human Resources Development Canada.

[9] Google groups announcements page: Notice about pages and files. (n.d.). . Retrieved March 7, 2011, from http://groups-announcements.blogspot.com/2010/09/notice-about-pages-and-files.html?hl=en

[10] Green, K. C. (2009). Campus Computing 2009: The 20th National Survey of Computing and Information Technology in American Higher Education (p. 46). Encino, CA: Campus Computing.

[11] Green, K. C. (2010). Campus Computing 2010: The 21st National Survey of Computing and Information Technology in American Higher Education (p. 46). Encino, CA: Campus Computing.

[12] Grush, M. (2010, April 28). Higher education IT in the "new normal" -- Campus Technology. Retrieved May 10, 2010, from http://campustechnology.com/Articles/2010/04/28/Higher-Education-IT-in-the-New-Normal.aspx?Page=2&p=1

[13] Kvavik, R. B., Caruso, J. B., & Morgan, G. (2004). *ECAR Study of Students and Information Technology, 2004: Convenience, Connection, and Control.* Boulder, CO: EDUCAUSE Center for Applied Research. Retrieved from http://www.educause.edu/ir/library/pdf/ers0405/rs/ers0405w.pdf

[14] Lave, J. (1991). Situating learning in communities of practice. In *Perspectives on Socially Shared Cognition* (1st ed., pp. 63-82). Washington, D.C.: American Psychological Association.

[15] Lave, J., & Wenger, E. (1991). *Situated learning: Legitimate peripheral participation.* Cambridge England; New York: Cambridge University Press.

[16] Powell, W. W., Koput, K. W., & Smith-Doerr, L. (1996). Interorganizational Collaboration and the Locus of Innovation: Networks of Learning in Biotechnology. *Administrative Science Quarterly*, *41*(1), 116–145.

[17] Salaway, G., & Caruso, J. B. (2007). *The ECAR Study of Undergraduate Students and Information Technology, 2007* (No. 6). Boulder, CO: EDUCAUSE Center for Applied Research. Retrieved from http://www.educause.edu/ir/library/pdf/ers0706/rs/ERS0706w.pdf

[18] Salaway, G., & Caruso, J. B. (2008). *The ECAR Study of Undergraduate Students and Information Technology, 2008* (No. 6). Boulder, CO: EDUCAUSE Center for Applied Research. Retrieved from http://www.educause.edu/ir/library/pdf/ers0808/rs/ers0808w.pdf

[19] Salaway, G., Katz, R. N., & Caruso, J. B. (2006). *The ECAR study of undergraduate students and information technology, 2006.* Boulder, CO: EDUCAUSE Center for Applied Research. Retrieved from http://www.educause.edu/ir/library/pdf/ers0607/ERS0607w.pdf

[20] Smith, S., Salaway, G., & Caruso, J. B. (2009). *The ECAR Study of Undergraduate Students and Information Technology, 2009* (No. 6). Boulder, CO: EDUCAUSE Center for Applied Research. Retrieved from http://www.educause.edu/ir/library/pdf/ers0906/rs/ERS0906w.pdf

[21] Wenger, E. (1998). Communities of practice: Learning as a social system. *Systems Thinker, June.* Retrieved from http://www.co-i-l.com/coil/knowledge-garden/cop/lss.shtml

[22] Wenger, E. (2001). *Supporting communities of practice: A survey of community-oriented technologies* (p. 65). Retrieved from http://www.ewenger.com/tech/index.htm

[23] Wenger, E., McDermott, R. A., & Snyder, W. (2002). *Cultivating communities of practice: A guide to managing knowledge.* Boston, Mass.: Harvard Business School Press.

[24] Wenger, E., White, N., & Smith, J. D. (2009). *Digital habitats: Stewarding technology for communities* (1st ed.). Portland OR: CPsquare.

Orchestrating an Institution-Wide Transition to Google Calendar

Stephen G. Lewis
Lehigh University
EWFM Computing Center
8B East Packer Avenue
Bethlehem, PA 18015
(610) 758-3000
sgl3@lehigh.edu

Stacey Kimmel-Smith
Lehigh University
EWFM Library
8A East Packer Avenue
Bethlehem, PA 18015
(610) 758-3000
sek2@lehigh.edu

ABSTRACT
Since the late 1990s, Lehigh University utilized a group calendaring system named Oracle Calendar. Pressured by more advanced customer expectations, rising licensing costs, and an ever-increasing number of trouble reports, Lehigh University investigated the possibility of migrating to Google Calendar. Lehigh University ultimately decided to make the transition and it is pleased to share its experience with other institutions. In addition to the history of Oracle Calendar, this paper will address how Google Calendar was beta-tested, how clients were trained in its use, the mechanics of the actual transition, and the feedback received from customers.

Categories and Subject Descriptors
H.4.1. [**Information Systems Applications**]: Office Automation – *groupware, spreadsheets, time management (e.g. calendars, schedules), word processing.*

H.5.2. [**Information Interfaces and Presentation (I.7)**]: User Interfaces (D.2.2, H.1.2, I.3.6) – *training, help, and documentation.*

General Terms
Management, Documentation, Economics, Experimentation, Human Factors.

Keywords
Google Calendar, Oracle Calendar, Oracle Collaboration Suite, Corporate Time, Netscape Calendar, Corporate Software & Technologies, Lexacom, Steltor, ICS, PDA.

1. INTRODUCTION
1.1 Lehigh University Overview
Lehigh University is located in Bethlehem, PA and boasts an enrollment of over 4,700 undergraduates, 2,200 graduate students, 660 faculty members, and nearly 1,000 support staff. Both library and computer services are combined in one integrated organizational unit known as Library and Technology Services (LTS). LTS owns and maintains over 600 classroom and lab PCs while also supporting nearly 2,000 departmental PCs.

1.2 History of Electronic Calendaring
In the late 1990s, Netscape Navigator was endorsed by LTS as Lehigh University's official web browser. Navigator was part of a larger suite of software known as Netscape Communicator. Among other components, the suite included Netscape Messenger (an e-mail program), Netscape Navigator (a web browser), Netscape Composer (a WYSIWYG HTML editor), and Netscape Calendar (a group calendaring system). In 1997, LTS set up an experimental Netscape Calendar server and allowed staff members to evaluate the usability of the software. At this time, however, Netscape Calendar was not officially supported by LTS. Users were pleased with the functionality and use rapidly spread throughout campus. By 1998, there were approximately 350 trial users.

A malfunction of the experimental Netscape Calendar server caused corruption of the calendar data file; data was lost, and it quickly became evident that the vast majority of trial users had been using the system with production-level expectations. LTS later contracted with Netscape for full product support, moved the data to a production-grade server, and officially endorsed Netscape Calendar as the campus calendaring system.

Netscape licensed their calendaring technology from Corporate Software & Technologies (CST). The licensing agreement expired in December 1999 and Netscape elected not to renew it [1]. At this time, Lehigh University looked at a variety of replacement calendaring systems including Meeting Maker, Up-To-Date, and CST's Corporate Time. Lehigh University elected to license Corporate Time, the same platform on which Netscape Calendar was based.

In June 2000, CST merged with their sister company, Lexacom, forming Steltor. By this time Lehigh University had licensed a total of 500 Corporate Time users. In June 2002, Oracle purchased Steltor and assimilated Corporate Time into their Oracle Collaboration Suite, renaming it to Oracle Calendar.

Around this same time, Lehigh University was also beta testing the Sun Java System Calendar, a component of the University's recently acquired Campus Pipeline portal system. Testing revealed several deficiencies: a cumbersome interface, short session timeouts that were not configurable, and synchronization issues were a few problems that users reported.

In 2008, Oracle made preparations to discontinue the Oracle Collaboration Suite in favor of their new collaboration platform named Oracle Beehive. LTS found Oracle Beehive to be both difficult to administer and expensive to license. Lehigh University ultimately identified Google Calendar as a replacement for Oracle Calendar.

2. ORACLE CALENDAR

2.1 Operating Environment

Oracle Calendar consisted of a desktop client and an on-campus server. A web-based client was also available with a limited subset of features. Each licensed user had exactly one calendar. Users, with appropriate security rights, could view others' calendars and propose meetings. E-mail and pop-up reminders could be set as required. Additional calendars, such as for rooms and equipment, could be defined as "resources" within Oracle Calendar and scheduled by users.

Faculty and staff began using Personal Digital Assistants (PDAs) as early as 1997 to have their calendars readily accessible at all times. Nearly all of the early devices were Palm Pilots. Users would connect these devices to their computers via serial, and later USB, connections. A program titled Palm Desktop was installed on each user's PC and managed the synchronization of data. A proprietary plug-in to Palm Desktop, Oracle Calendar Sync, facilitated communication between Palm devices and Oracle Calendar.

Smartphones, especially the Palm Treo, became popular beginning in 2003. Senior leadership particularly appreciated the ability to access e-mail when away from their desks. Although e-mail could be accessed via a cellular data connection, calendar synchronization still required a hardwire connection to a PC. Attempts to synchronize a Palm Treo over its 2G cellular connection would often fail due to insufficient bandwidth. For five years, the Palm Treo remained the Lehigh University recommended PDA until Palm retired the product line in 2008.

LTS evaluated several different PDAs when the Palm Treo was discontinued. Windows Mobile, BlackBerry, and iPhone devices were tested under a variety of conditions. 3G cellular technology had become increasingly widespread in the late 2000s. LTS established a strategic goal of moving away from using desktop PCs to synchronize PDA calendar data in favor of over-the-air wireless synchronization. The iPhone, unless jailbroken, was not capable of over-the-air synchronization with Oracle Calendar. The Windows Mobile platform was deemed unsatisfactory by LTS for a variety of reasons. The BlackBerry Bold 9000, AT&T's first 3G BlackBerry device, won LTS endorsement as Lehigh University's recommended PDA in late 2008. Lehigh University utilized Nexthaus SyncJE to wirelessly synchronize BlackBerry devices to Oracle Calendar via the SyncML protocol. Approximately one year later, iOS devices were able to synchronize wirelessly to Oracle Calendar via Synthesis AG's ToDo+Cal+Sync. This new development allowed LTS to endorse the iPhone 3G, in addition to the BlackBerry, as recommended PDAs.

2.2 Concerns and Limitations

After using Oracle Calendar for over 10 years at Lehigh University, LTS staff were well aware of its drawbacks. The cost for end-user Oracle Calendar licenses was partially subsidized by LTS. Departments were assessed a per-user fee for each license issued. License reuse was not possible since removing a user from Oracle Calendar would delete all meetings created by that person, including those that resided on other users' calendars. Concerns over cost/benefit fragmented the University population. Well-funded areas, particularly administrative units, had no qualms investing in Oracle Calendar licenses for their staff. Areas with lesser funding, however, often opted not to participate in using Oracle Calendar. These departments typically relied on paper calendars or stand-alone desktop software. Individual students were not eligible to use Oracle Calendar except in cases where required for student employment. Lacking a common campus calendaring system made it particularly difficult to schedule meetings for groups of people.

In 2007 and 2008, synchronization issues between Oracle Calendar and PDAs became increasingly prevalent. Users would often find themselves unable to synchronize their calendars. Other issues included individual events disappearing and entire calendars duplicating themselves post-synchronization without known reason.

At this same time, users also began to expect more from the software itself. Many were no longer content with the limitation of having just one calendar. Instead, they wanted to be able to create multiple independent calendars on the fly. Users also desired a full-featured web interface, not the limited functionality that the Oracle Calendar web interface provided.

3. GOOGLE CALENDAR TRANSITION

3.1 Initial Testing

Lehigh University created a Google Apps for Education instance in summer 2007 and immediately began investigating the feasibility of replacing Oracle Calendar with Google Calendar. The decision to partner with Google Apps came about through the work of a steering committee that included LTS leadership and front-line positions consulting with groups outside LTS as needed (e.g., the university lawyer). A member of this team was charged with promoting Google Apps and training users, and a voluntary working group formed to advance toward this goal. Among its activities were creating a Google Apps web page, developing the wording and look/feel of the landing page for Lehigh Google Apps, refining the policies and best practices of the service, and training one another on the various apps. Two members of the six-person team provided most of the Calendar training during the Google Apps transition.

Encouraged by initial findings, the entire LTS Client Services staff transitioned to Google Calendar in early 2008. In summer 2009, the Athletics Department was shifted to Google Calendar. Athletics was particularly willing to beta-test Google Calendar since the costs of Oracle Calendar allowed only a subset of their staff to utilize the system. Google Calendar also made it possible for coaches and student athletes to share a common calendar. Feedback was very positive and LTS became confident that Google Calendar could successfully replace Oracle Calendar.

3.2 Pre-Transition Outreach & Marketing

LTS met with most departments to explain why transitioning from Oracle Calendar to Google Calendar would be beneficial to the University. Key messages reminded users that Oracle Calendar was deprecated, not fully web-based, costly, fraught with PDA synchronization problems, and a closed system that did not allow interaction with the outside world. On the contrary, Google Calendar was presented as fully web-based, free of licensing costs, reliable, more functional, and an open system. These meetings also included brief demonstrations designed to excite users by highlighting such features as Google Maps integration, SMS text message reminders, calendar layering, and the ability to embed calendars in web pages.

3.3 Departmental Transitions

Departments were transitioned one at a time over a six-month period. The transition steps were extremely labor intensive, as each user required a hands-on visit from an LTS representative. The process began with exporting data from Oracle Calendar in an ICS format. The ICS export then needed to be cleansed via a custom-written tool that removed the following fields from each event: X-ORACLE-EVENTINSTANCE-GUID, X-ORACLE-EVENTTYPE, UID, RECURRENCE-ID, ORGANIZER, X-ORACLE-CLASS, CLASS, ATTENDEE, TRIGGER, ACTION, RDATE. Without removing these fields, repeating events would not synchronize correctly to iOS devices. The cleansed data was imported to Google Calendar and LTS assisted users in setting up appropriate security permissions for their calendars. PDAs were reconfigured using the Google Sync client for BlackBerry devices and Microsoft Exchange emulation on iOS devices.

The final step was setting up a backup for clients. Oracle Calendar, since it was a locally hosted server, was backed up to tape. Google Calendar, a cloud-based solution, did not have backups accessible to the end-user. This meant that data was not recoverable in the event a user accidently deleted a calendar and/or a PDA synchronization critically failed. LTS authored a web backup utility that accesses each Google Calendar private URL and saves an ICS export to disk in the campus data center. Unless a user explicitly resets his or her private URL, it remains static even when passwords are changed. Although these backups are seldom needed, they become extremely valuable in times of crisis.

4. GOOGLE CALENDAR TRAINING

4.1 Training Timeline

November 2010 was the target date for completing the transition to Google Calendar. The optimal time for training clients, consisting mostly of non-academic staff members, was summer 2010. Twenty Google Calendar training sessions were held and 119 staff members attended. Each session, lasting approximately two hours, was held in a computer classroom so that participants could follow along with hands-on exercises. Many departments elected to attend staff training *en masse*. This allowed instructors to fine-tune the curriculum to individual departmental practices and needs. Each session generated follow-up calls to the instructor(s). These questions were often answered with a simple e-mail but were sometimes addressed with additional on-site training or the creation of web-based video tutorials.

4.2 Participants

Many if not most of the people affected by the Oracle Calendar migration were administrative staff—secretaries, coordinators, directors, and business managers, for example. As a group, their technical skills varied. During training, the "show of hands" method of data collection revealed that:

- about one quarter of the participants used the consumer version of Google Calendar
- most were unfamiliar with the concept of cloud computing
- many had mobile devices that they wanted to synchronize with their Lehigh Google Calendar

Participant experience with the consumer version of Google Calendar presented a challenge in training. While they had experience with Google Calendar, participants often had trouble grasping the difference between Lehigh Google Apps and consumer Google. For those who maintained a work schedule on consumer Google, the options for sharing the calendar, or importing it to Lehigh Google apps, were explained. Even though some participants used consumer Google, they were unfamiliar with the notion of cloud computing and most made use of only one or two applications (Calendar and Gmail).

Despite prior experience with Google, participants needed a general introduction to address gaps in their understanding of the service. LTS provided a summary of the suite of products offered, showed how the apps integrate, demonstrated the collaboration features, and explained the concept of cloud computing. Participants were advised that in the Google environment, new features and options appear continually, and often without notice. Trainers decided that discussion of synchronization with mobile devices was out of the scope of the training, and participants were referred to documentation and their computing consultants for assistance.

4.3 Training Materials

The training outline (see appendix A) attempts a brief introduction to Google Apps and thorough coverage of Google Calendar features such as setting customizations, creating calendars, creating and modifying events, different kinds of events, inviting others to events, and a broad range of other topics. A handout titled "Ten Tips for Using Google Calendar" (see appendix B) included features in Google Calendar that LTS trainers felt would be useful. Finally, trainers developed Camtasia or Jing-based videos for common questions and shared them on the Lehigh Google Apps Web site.

4.4 Participant Reactions

Generally, staff was comfortable in the Google environment and satisfied with the features that were offered. There were, however, some perceived shortcomings in Google Calendar:

- Viewing/managing large groups - Some coordinators need the ability to view many staff calendars one at time. Oracle Calendar offered a columnar view that staff preferred to the overlay view that Google offered.

In 2010, the "find a time" view displayed the calendars in rows, rather than columns. This has changed, and now Google Calendar also uses a columnar view. Unfortunately, it is still not as functional as Oracle Calendar's group view.

- Color-coding events - In 2010, Google did not support color-coding of events. This feature was rolled out in Spring 2011.
- Event view/text truncated - Participants lamented that the Google Calendar views often truncated the event details.
- Calendar printing - Google Calendar offers a print feature but the problem with views extended to the print environment. Not enough information was provided within the view (e.g., event details), and the timespan options were too limited.
- Backup/system down - For some staff, intermittent downtime, for even a few minutes, was deemed unacceptable. In 2010, Google Calendar experienced downtime system-wide of several hours duration [2], and staff found this unsettling.
- Customization - While customization is generally a positive feature, participants sometimes found individual customizations made it hard to predict others' behavior. For example, an individual can specify whether event invitations are displayed or not. This customization impacts others (and most staff preferred their colleagues display event invitations so that potential conflicts could be seen).
- Invite versus add - In Oracle Calendar, it was possible to simply add an event to someone's calendar. In Google Calendar, the concept of inviting a colleague to an event was new, and it was perceived (rightly) as less powerful since the calendar owner must accept the invitation.

4.5 Tough Training Concepts

Participants had difficulty grasping some key concepts in Google Calendar. In the administrative offices, the ability to keep a paper trail and to house data locally is valued. Oracle calendars are routinely printed out, and Microsoft Word documents are stored locally and sent as attachments. Google Calendar (and Google Apps in general) is intended as an online replacement for the physical paper item. It works because Google Calendar and Docs can be accessed from nearly anywhere, at any time. Yet, in Calendar training, participants really wanted to a) have a printout of the Calendar and b) store it locally. Similarly, in Google Docs training, participants ask how to send a Google Document as an attachment. The idea of a resource that is solely online, and not housed locally, can be hard for some staff to accept.

Google's customization options are extensive, and in a shared calendar environment this can be confusing. For example, secretaries who manage their boss's calendar typically have the highest level of permission for the boss's primary calendar. Bosses used to delegating calendar tasks would tell their secretary, "I'm getting too much email; please turn off notifications." Trainers had to explain that customizations are set by each individual user, even for the same calendar, so the boss should set his/her own customizations for that calendar. Staff who schedule meetings cannot always predict how individuals have customized a calendar notifications, or how/whether calendar invitations can appear.

The calendar display toggle can confuse users. Many Google Calendar users called to report that a calendar had "disappeared" from the main window. Trainers reminded users that calendars could be toggled on and off, but often it was necessary to remote into the user's computer to show how the calendar could be displayed and hidden at will.

Clients often are tempted to create multiple calendars. While it is possible to create calendars for types of meetings, for certain projects, or for any number of reasons, this practice can make it hard for co-workers to check availability for meetings, since in most cases they won't have access to all calendars. Trainers suggested that the primary calendar be used for scheduling purposes, or if other calendars are used, events that affect scheduling/availability should be duplicated in the primary calendar.

4.6 Follow-up and Calendar Adoption

Google Calendar statistics show that about 500-600 users access Calendar every day, and the seven-day usage is generally from 800-1000 users. About 350 people are currently backing up their calendars via the LTS-authored utility explained earlier. Every semester about eight general Google Calendar seminars are held, and about fifty users attend. Trainers are regularly contacted with specific questions about Google Calendar and specifically for help in taking it to "the next level" with more advanced features.

Most departments that formerly used Oracle Calendar appear to be using Google Calendar, and all indications are that they have the same functionality with Google's product. Adoption of Google Apps on campus is voluntary but Google Apps are slowly appearing in academic departments. Some campus services are using Google Calendar to support unique needs. In Athletics, coaches in tennis, lacrosse, and field hockey require their student athletes to maintain and share a Google Calendar containing their class schedule and other commitments. This facilitates scheduling athletics training, practices, and events. In the College of Education, the student employee schedule is maintained in a Google Calendar that is published to a Web page. Lehigh's Facilities Services maintains its boiler room staffing schedule (a 24/7, 365-day operation) on Google Calendar. Materials Science manages its equipment reservations (e.g., high-end microscopes) on twelve calendars that are available to members of a Google Group for reservations.

Plans for further marketing of Google Calendar are underway. The LTS newsletter will feature unique uses of Google Calendar on campus in future issues. In addition to regularly scheduled Google Calendar seminars, new training sessions such as "What's new with Google Calendar," will be offered periodically and video demos will be posted on the Google Calendar web site.

5. CONCLUSION

5.1 Post-Implementation Survey

Approximately one year following the Oracle Calendar to Google Calendar transition, users were solicited for feedback. LTS sent a survey inviting clients to rate various aspects of Google Calendar and how they compared to Oracle Calendar. Specifically, clients were asked to rate ease of access, reliability, feature set, and ease of use. Clients were also invited to share their own personal findings. See appendix C for full survey results.

Overall, Google Calendar was ranked higher than Oracle Calendar. The one metric that Google Calendar was not ranked highly on, however, was reliability. Clients indicated their frustration with occasional, but memorable, intervals where Google Calendar would become unresponsive for several minutes. This seems to happen about once or twice a month and is acknowledged by Google with cute error messages such as "oops, we couldn't load details for your calendar, please try again in a few minutes." On one occasion, Google Calendar was down for several hours in spring 2010. Other perceived drawbacks include difficulty in viewing many calendars at the same time, limited printing options, and an inability to mark events as tentative.

Clients expressed their pleasure with several aspects of Google Calendar. They particularly appreciated their ability to access the calendar from any Internet connection, their ability to create and layer multiple calendars, the ease of use, reliable over-the-air PDA synchronization, and the fact that the University now had a common calendaring system across departments.

6. REFERENCES

[1] Shen, Antony. "What happened to Netscape Calendar?" SillyDog701. 29 Mar. 2006. 11 May 2011 <http://sillydog.org/netscape/kb/calendar.php>.

[2] Siegler, M. G. "You've Got A Date With FAIL, It's On Your Google Calendar." TechCrunch. 28 Apr. 2008. 12 May 2011 <http://techcrunch.com/2010/04/28/google-calendar-down/>.

A. Google Calendar Training Outline

Note: This outline was prepared for Google Calendar trainers/instructors in Summer 2010 and may not reflect the most up-to-date features.

1. General Comments
    a. Lehigh Google Apps
        i. A domain-wide address book of all Lehigh University users exists
        ii. Calendars and documents can be shared within the Lehigh University domain and outside as necessary.
    b. Mobile device setup is not covered in this training seminar.
    c. Google is constantly improving their product. New features will appear without notice.
2. Google Apps Start Page
    a. Log in via http://www.lehigh.edu/google
    b. Calendar is just one part of a suite of interoperable Google applications
        i. Can be accessed from anywhere there is Internet access
    c. Password is synchronized to your Lehigh University e-mail password
    d. Cloud computing
        i. Explain the pros/cons
        ii. Reminder that Google may not be the best place for very sensitive information
    e. Gmail is not recommended at this time. Continue to use legacy campus e-mail.
3. Layout Overview
    a. General
        i. Google Calendar is part of the Google suite of applications
        ii. Personalization options and general setting in upper right corner
        iii. Most real estate devoted to the calendar/planner
        iv. Demonstrate event creation and "quick add" feature
        v. Demonstrate month calendar in left margin
    b. My Calendars
        i. These are calendars that you own or can edit
            1. Color coded
            2. Demo how to add
            3. Settings
                a. Show in list
                b. Unsubscribe
                c. Delete
    c. Navigating Calendars
        i. Create a dummy test calendar
            1. Add a calendar, choose add, choose create new calendar
        ii. Now multiple calendars exist
            1. Hide/unhide
            2. Display "this calendar only" feature
            3. Change colors
            4. Change name
            5. Settings
    d. Other Interesting Calendars
        i. US Holidays
        ii. Co-workers
            1. Search is similar to e-mail addressing auto-completions
            2. Example: Jake calls his calendar appointments
        iii. How to change the name of the calendar

            1. Suggest that clients keep username
            2. Name changes are per-user and not seen by anyone else
        iv. How to add, settings, etc.
    e. Planner
        i. Red line indicates current time
        ii. Events are associated with calendar colors
        iii. Weather
        iv. Overlay concept
        v. Empty calendar may show view at midnight
        vi. Different views
            1. Day
            2. Week
            3. Month
            4. Four-day view (customizable setting)
            5. Agenda
        vii. Quick custom view
    f. Right-hand column
        i. Users define what appears there
            1. Gadgets, tools, tasks, etc.
4. Configuring general Google Calendar settings
    a. Calendar settings, general calendar settings, apply to all calendars
    b. Country, time zone (set automatically by default)
    c. Date formatting
    d. Day of week start (Sat, Sun, or Mon)
    e. Option to show/hide weekends
    f. Default view of one week is customizable
    g. Custom view – demonstrate how to change duration
    h. Add location to view weather
    i. Show events you have declined
        i. If you can't go, keep it on the calendar
    j. Invitation options
    k. Keyboard shortcuts
        i. T=today
        ii. C=create
        iii. P=previous
        iv. N=next
        v. M=month
        vi. And many more…
    l. Offline calendar
        i. Works with only one calendar
        ii. Suggest to use in read-only capacity
5. Search calendar
    a. Search by keywords
    b. Searches all calendars you can add events to
    c. Searches active calendar or default one
6. Sharing
    a. Arrow, share this calendar
        i. Default is share with others within Lehigh University
            1. See free/busy status only
        ii. Can make calendar available to all others
    b. Share with specific people
        i. Fine-tune permissions based on role
    c. Share with non-Lehigh people
    d. Share with consumer Google accounts
7. Events
    a. Add event
        i. Multiple ways to add event
            1. Click on date/time area
            2. Click on "create event"
            3. Press "c" on keyboard
            4. Quick Add
        ii. Minimum information is event title
        iii. If more than one calendar displayed, event added to default calendar
            1. Dropdown box lets user select other calendar if desired
        iv. Assumes current date and next hour
        v. End time is one hour later by default
    b. Repeating events
        i. Very flexible
        ii. Go under weekly to specify individual days of the week
        iii. Change for one, all, or future instances
        iv. Note the repeating icon
    c. Other options
        i. Where (location will populate in Google Maps)
        ii. Which calendar
        iii. Duplicate/copy
        iv. Description
        v. Attachment
        vi. Guests
        vii. Privacy
            1. Private (busy) -vs- public
        viii. Quick Add
            1. Need title at minimum
            2. Add pm to times occurring after noon
            3. If date not provided, Google Calendar will create on next valid date at specified time
            4. Enter date without time to make all day
            5. Enter guest e-mail address to invite them
            6. Multiday events, type 8/2 – 8/4
            7. Repeating events, type yearly / monthly / weekly

8. Invitations
    a. Be careful when testing/training as everyone gets invitation e-mails
    b. Create event, search by e-mail, search by last name
    c. You can usually see the calendar of the person you are inviting to an event
        i. Unless they have made their entire calendar private
        ii. Some staff may not be using Google Calendar
    d. Check guest and resource availability
    e. Resources
    f. R25 (campus classroom scheduling system) does not interact with Google Calendar
    g. How to invite lots of people
        i. Contact list/e-mail nickname file
            1. Disadvantage is that these can't be shared with multiple users
        ii. Google Groups
            1. Flaky at best, you can try it for informal groups
        iii. Max of 500 invitees at a time
9. Notifications
    a. General Settings
        i. Automatically add invitations to my calendar
    b. Calendar-specific settings
        i. Click on arrow to right of calendar
        ii. Event reminders (pop-ups, e-mail, SMS)
            1. Minutes, hours, days
            2. As many as you want
            3. Can override for an individual event
        iii. Invite notifications
            1. Change, cancel, replies
        iv. Daily agenda e-mailed to your every morning
        v. SMS option for text messages (costs money)
        vi. Mobile devices
        vii. Shared calendars
10. Editing Events
    a. Reminder alarms
    b. Delete, edit details, copy to another calendar
    c. Delete, change for all, repeating events? Only this instance option.
    d. All events in series will change past events
11. Move an event
    a. Can drag/drop or change within details
    b. Copy to another calendar
    c. Change event owner
    d. Duplicate event, change/modify as needed
    e. All day events
        i. Can mark your calendar as available or busy all day
12. Printing
    a. Prints whichever view you have on-screen
    b. No way to print all details
13. Add Calendars
    a. Add by URL
    b. By searching name
    c. Import calendar (ical format)
    d. Browse interesting calendars (such as holidays)
    e. Sports calendars
    f. Lehigh resources

B. Ten Tips for Using Google Calendar

Note: This participant handout was prepared for Google Calendar training in Summer 2010 and may not reflect the most up-to-date features.

1. Add Lehigh University calendars
    a. Academic Calendar (registration deadlines, exam dates, breaks, etc) -
    b. Other Lehigh calendars
        i. See the list at - https://sites.google.com/a/lehigh.edu/lehigh-google-apps/Home/lehigh-public-calendars
        ii. Includes sports teams, facility hours, art exhibitions, etc.
2. E-mail your daily agenda to yourself
    a. See a demo at - http://screencast.com/t/MGQzNzE5NDM
3. Use the Google Labs gadgets
    a. These often preview new Google Calendar features
    b. Next Meeting – is a very helpful gadget that displays a countdown to your next scheduled event
4. Popular keyboard shortcuts
    a. C = create an event
    b. / = search calendars
    c. P = previous date range
    d. N = next date range
    e. A,D,W,M = agenda, day, week, or month view
    f. S = view calendar settings
    g. T = jump to today
    h. Z = undo last action
    i. X = custom view
    j. Q = quick add
5. Use the Quick Add feature
    a. Click on Quick Add in the upper-left corner or type "q" if keyboard shortcuts available
    b. Type in title of event
    c. General guidelines
        i. Almost any date/time format is okay, e.g. 1pm May 24, 10am 4/14, Friday noon, etc.

ii. Precede dates and times with "on" or "at"
    1. Example: Meeting on Friday at 3pm
iii. For all-day events, enter date only
    1. Example: Library Conference on 8/14
iv. Multiple date ranges
    1. Example: National Conference 9/23 – 9/26 in Atlanta
v. Annual event
    1. Example: Mom's Birthday June 19 yearly
vi. Weekly event
    1. Example: Tennis practice Tuesday 7pm to 9pm weekly
vii. Monthly event
    1. Example: Meet with boss first Tuesday of every month at 9am
viii. No date provided
    1. Quick Add will put the event at the earliest valid future date
ix. More info at - http://www.google.com/support/calendar/bin/answer.py?hl=en&answer=36604#text

6. What's the weather?
    a. Add weather information to calendar
    b. Settings -> General
        i. Enter your location
        ii. Enter preference for Fahrenheit or Celsius
7. Know event icons
    a. Question mark = event invitation requires your response
    b. Alarm clock = event has reminder set
    c. Overlapping rectangles = event repeats
    d. Padlock icon = private event
    e. Silhouette of person = multiple attendees at this event
8. Searching calendars
    a. Use consistent terms when creating events
    b. Search is performed on all calendars that are active/visible
    c. Use search options to limit by date, exclude words, etc.
9. "Quick Select" a custom calendar view
    a. You can create a custom view of your calendar on the fly
        i. Click and swipe over mini-calendar on left selecting the days you want
            1. Main screen will change to reflect your selection
            2. See a demo at - http://screencast.com/t/MzExMjY5
10. View multiple time zones
    a. Do you have clients in other time zones? You can add a time zone which will appear adjacent to the local time zone. Add via calendar settings.

C. Post-Implementation Survey Results

20% Response Rate (787 Surveys Sent, 159 Complete Responses, 12 Incomplete Responses)

Approximately one year post-transition, Clients were asked to rate Oracle Calendar (O) and Google Calendar (G) on a 4-point scale. Higher is better. Free-form commentary was also solicited.

Clients report positive experiences with:

- Ability to access Google Calendar anywhere there is an Internet connection
- Ability to create multiple calendars
- Ability to layer multiple calendars
- Ease of use
- PDA-friendly, reliable synchronization
- Scheduling with other staff members, since so many people are using Google Calendar

Clients report these concerns:

- Difficult to schedule large group meetings on behalf of others
- Difficult to view many calendars at the same time
- Event details do not display in agenda view; you must click on the individual event
- Inability to check other calendars without adding them list of "Other Calendars"
- Very poor printing options compared to Oracle Calendar
- Inability to mark events as tentative
- Access control is not as granular as Oracle Calendar (ex: private events hidden from secretary)

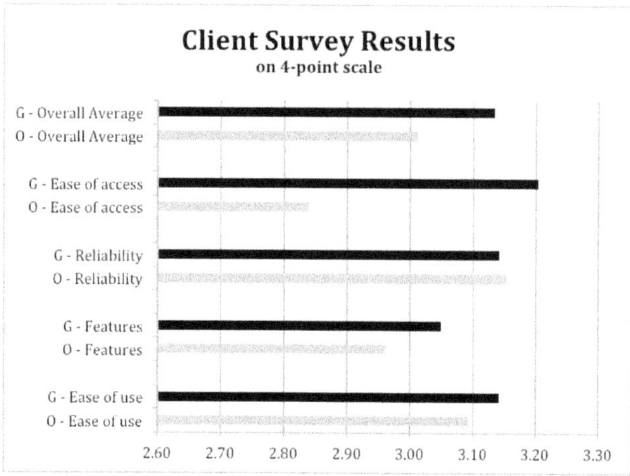

UR Mobile: There's an App for That

Melisa Tanger-Brown
University of Rochester
Rush Rhees Library G-138
Rochester, NY 14627
1-585-275-9162
Lisa.Brown@rochester.edu

ABSTRACT
In 2010 the University of Rochester partnered with Blackboard to implement a mobile solution for components of our web site that runs on iPhone, Blackberry and Android devices, as well as phones with web browsers. Popular areas of the web were implemented through an "app" solution that allows for multiple device support while keeping maintenance and development within our IT department to a minimum. We were able to leverage existing code from various services and areas of our web site and create a set of feeds that populate data into the mobile application. Blackboard maintains the actual device code and processing of the feeds which allows our IT team to focus on the data instead of the specifics of development of mobile applications and following trends in devices. This presentation will cover the decision-making process, the implementation, the on-going development and the end-user feedback.

Categories and Subject Descriptors
H.5.3 [**Information Systems**]: Information Interfaces and Presentation – *web-based interaction.*

General Terms
Design, Standardization.

Keywords
Mobile Computing.

1. INTRODUCTION
Learn, Discover, Heal, Create – And Make the World Ever Better.

The mission of the University of Rochester, along with its motto "Meliora" (meaning "Ever Better") provides those of us that work there with a clear understanding of how we fit in. Anytime we can provide more services or better services, we are enhancing the experience at the University. This project is just one such example of how this happens.

University of Rochester is one of the country's top-tier research universities which include a teaching hospital (Strong Memorial Hospital). We host more than 200 academic majors, more than 2,000 faculty and instructional staff and approximately 9,300 students. Learning at the University of Rochester is on a very personal scale with smaller classes, a low 9:1 student to teacher ratio and increased interactions with faculty.

Also included at the University are the Eastman School of Music and the Memorial Art Gallery.

The University of Rochester is also Rochester's largest employer with about 22,000 employees and envisions itself as a community that welcomes, encourages and supports individuals who desire to contribute to and benefit from the institution's missions of teaching, research, patient care, performance, and community service.

2. WHY GO MOBILE?
2.1 Strategic Planning
Four years ago, the Information Technology division worked with members of the University community to develop a strategic plan for technology. One of the top five items in the plan was to modernize our web presence and environment. The first few years of the plan focused on hardening the environment, however as those projects began to take shape, we began to look at modernizing the presence of the web.

2.2 Enhanced Cell Phones
Over the past two to three years, the number of enhanced cell phones has increased dramatically among the student population. In a student survey taken in 2008, less than 10% of students reported that they had an internet-capable phone (i.e. Windows PDA, Blackberry or iPhone). In a similar survey done in 2010, the number of enhanced cell phones had more than doubled with 28% reporting indicating that they had an internet-capable phone. This was during a time period where no campus mobile offerings were available.

2.3 Apple Incentives
For the past three years, Apple has been providing a free iPod Touch device with every Macintosh laptop purchase during its back-to-school sales. This puts internet-capable devices in the hands of more students, regardless of the functionality of their cell phones.

Ownership of internet-capable devices (i.e. laptops, cell phones and other such devices) among students was on an increase. According to a 2009 ECAR Study of Undergraduate students, almost 90% of students owned a laptop one year old or less and just over 50% owned some sort of handheld device which was internet-capable.

SIGUCCS'11, November 12–17, 2011, San Diego, California, USA.

2.4 Student Expectations

A student survey of undergraduates at the University of Rochester in 2010 contained requests to provide access to information via mobile devices. By this point, students expect to get their information on only on the web, but via handheld mobile devices.

All of these factors came into play in our decision to provide a mobile solution. The next decision was what format the mobile solution would take.

3. AVOIDING OBSOLESCNE

In deciding to move into a mobile world, an IT department must take into account many things: device compatibility, student desires, and future technologies.

"Because mobile technology is evolving at a rapid rate, the danger is that innovations based on any single technology could become obsolete very quickly." [1]

We didn't want to focus on any single technology, regardless of its current popularity. The next big things could be coming soon and in today's economy you don't want to waste efforts in one arena only to find out that you missed the boat.

"Because mobile IT is fast becoming a part of some professional practices, an institutional choice not to pursue mobility is increasingly untenable. Student expectations for mobility are rising, and mobile IT efforts are an important part of keeping an institution's online services competitive.

At the same time, the range of devices, formats, and tools—and the frequency with which they change—presents formidable challenges for institutions to navigate the many decisions about how and where to devote resources to mobile IT for maximum benefit." [2]

A decision was made to work with **Blackboard Mobile Central** to develop our mobile web presence. Blackboard provides the capability to take the most commonly used areas of your University web site and make them mobile-friendly.

The device specific application is built and maintained by the Blackboard mobile team and is supported on multiple platforms. Data feeds from common areas of the University's web site are provided in order to generate the dynamic information to the mobile application.

This is a versatile solution as the Blackboard Mobile team supports iPhone (along with iPod Touch), Blackberry, Android and Mobile Web. It is also comprehensive as the application has the capability of providing access data about Maps, News, Events, Directory Services, Athletics, Courses, Library, Images and Video. Within the Maps, you can provide data/information about bus locations, tours and availability (open/close) of places on campus. Data in the application is applicable to students, as well as faculty, staff, visitors, patients and alumni.

[1] Mobile Learning: Context and Prospects. Educause Learning Initiative. May 2010.

[2] 7 Things You Should Know About Mobile IT. Educause. Feb 2010.

This resulted in the creation of UR Mobile, an application that is available for iPhone, iPod touch, iPad and Blackberry, as well as available as a mobile web implementation.

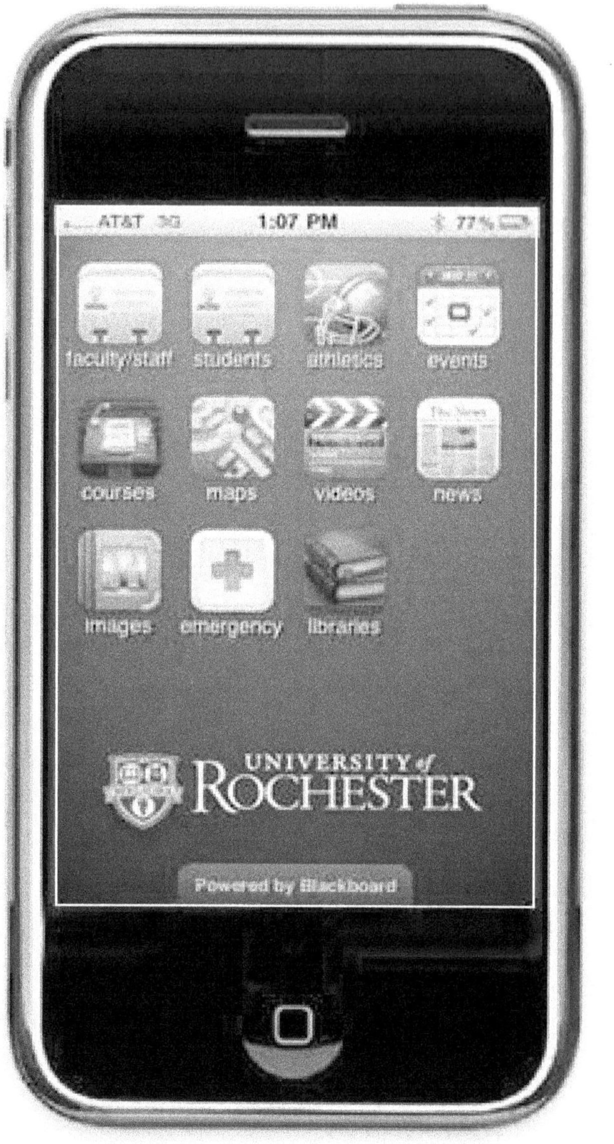

4. COMPONENTS

4.1 Directory

The Directory component of the mobile application allows the user to view information from your school directory.

Our first release of the application provided access to the public information in our newly-designed student directory. However, because our directory services for students are separate from faculty and staff, and the application only allows for one instance of the Directory component, we decided to make this component access our faculty/staff directory (once it was re-written) for our second release. This also allowed for efficiencies and added functionality with the Courses component.

The Directory component data feed is created by providing an XML web service that connects with our directory. The web service allows for a search and then delivers results.

4.2 Images

The Images component is a gallery feature. We took our homepage images and created an XML feed with caption information for this component. This allows us to provide users with a full experience of our campus by offering visual information about the programs we offer.

4.3 Athletics

The Athletics component provides news stories, upcoming schedules and past scores to users from your school's athletics program.

When we began this project, our athletics department was using a homegrown, database driven application to deliver this information to our web site. We simply needed to create XML feeds from the database in the proper format to drive the data in the mobile application.

In 2011, our Athletics program is transitioning to a vendor-based delivery and we will simply change our feeds to point to the vendor feeds for this same data.

4.4 Videos

The Video component allows you to connect to your campus YouTube channel and provide the same information via a mobile device. We connect this to the YouTube channel offered by our Office of Communications.

4.5 Events

The Events component provides information about upcoming events on campus to the mobile users. The list of events can be broken down by categories, providing you have different feeds for each category.

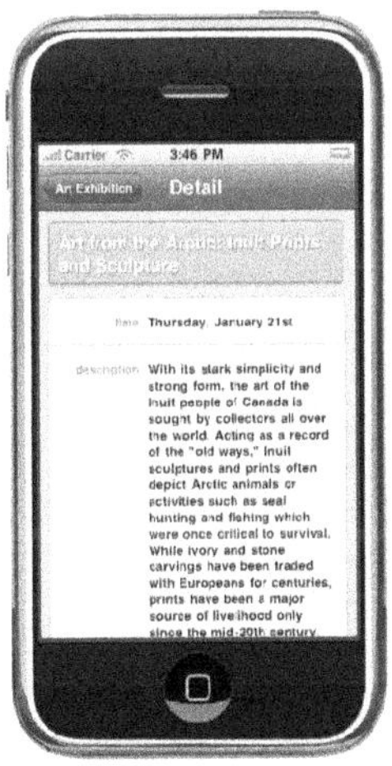

Our University Calendar system has the ability to provide RSS feeds for its various calendars. We provided these RSS feeds to the application and our events appear in the application.

A user can quickly get information about events happening on campus, as well as location information.

4.6 Courses

The Courses component has the ability to display information about courses taught at your campus.

As we were developing this mobile application, we were also redesigning our CDCS (Course Description, Course Schedule) database. Adding an XML feed from this database in a format compatible with that required for the application was a small addition to the project.

When a student looks up a course, they can see its offering for any upcoming semester, as well as the instructor of record and location. The application provides instant lookup via the Directory tool of instructor information, as well as instant location search in the Map tool.

4.7 Maps

The Maps component is a huge hit for users. By providing google style images of your campus, satellite coordinates, and an XML feed of your building information, you can provide mobile users with quick and easy access to finding their way around. The addition of the GPS capability in the mobile device lets the user figure out exactly where they are, relative to where they need to go.

Additionally, Maps has three plug-ins available: Tours, Places, and Transit.

Tours provides the ability to create virtual tours via your Maps. By providing satellite coordinates, you can take the user from location to location and provide commentary (visual, audio or text) via download. This provides the ability to offer virtual tours of campus or provide self-guided tours.

If the buses on your campus have GPS tracking, you can integrate this into your mobile application via the Transit plug-in. A user of the mobile application can see where the bus is located in real time and make sure that they get to the bus stop on time.

The Places plug-in allows you to designate services on campus within your Maps and let the users know if those locations are Open or Closed.

4.8 News

The News component gathers RSS feeds from whatever news areas you have on campus and displays them back to the mobile user. We were able to collect feeds from various news sources (Office of Communications, Medical Center Communications, Eastman School of Music Communications, Memorial Art Gallery, Simon School of Business, and Futurity) on campus and provide them in this one location.

4.9 Library

The Library component can link directly into your catalog using XML web services. However, at University of Rochester, we have four libraries with four distinct functions and we wanted to give them their place in this mobile application. Additionally, some of these libraries had already begun to create mobile web functionality.

Instead of using the Library component, we created a link to a new mobile web site that displayed all four libraries available. Each one was a link to that library's web site (either regular or mobile). This provided each library with a place in the application and took advantage of the work already done by their IT areas to provide mobile access to their information.

4.10 Emergency

A recently added component was Emergency. This provides phone numbers for common emergency information sources on campus. We use this to provide instant access to our Campus Security and our Emergency/Weather Hotline. For students with phone capabilities on their mobile device, this is an instant line to emergency services.

4.11 Mobile Learn

Because we are also a customer of Blackboard's Learning Management System, we have also begun investigating the use of Mobile Learn. In Spring 2011, we offered a pilot of the Mobile Learn capability to students via iOS over wi-fi. As a result of the pilot, we are contemplating licensing Mobile Learn to expand usage to 3G networks and other devices (Blackberry and Android). This will also allow us to integrate Mobile Learn into our Mobile application so that students will only need one mobile application to access all of their University information.

5. USAGE STATISTICS

We launched the first release of the application in mid-May 2010, after graduation and students had left for the summer. We decided to wait until back-to-school to advertise the application.

Within that first month, with no advertising at all, just word of mouth and emails to key stakeholders at the University, we had 320 active users and more than 1900 launches of the application.

Within one year of availability, we now have over 2600 active users of the application on iOS devices. [Statistics for Blackberry and mobile web are not available.] The application has been launched more than 27,000 times and averages 67 runs per day.

6. ACKNOWLEDGMENTS

Our thanks to the **Blackboard Mobile** team for their support in developing, maintaining, and continued enhancement of this application.

7. REFERENCES

[1] The ECAR Study of Undergraduate Students and Information Technology (2009). Educause Center for Research. http://www.educause.edu/Resources/TheECARStudyofUndergraduateStu/187215

[2] 7 Things You Should Know About Mobile IT (Feb. 2010). Educause. http://www.educause.edu/Resources/7ThingsYouShouldKnowAboutMobil/199797

[3] Mobile Learning: Context and Prospects (May 2010). Educause Learning Initiative. http://net.educause.edu/ir/library/ELI_SO/ELI3022.pdf

[4] 7 Things You Should Know About Mobile Learning (May 2010). Educause. http://www.educause.edu/Resources/7ThingsYouShouldKnowAboutMobil/204763

The Awkward Hallway: Getting Inside an Applicant's Head

Nathan Carpenter
University of Illinois at Urbana-Champaign
1304 W. Springfield Avenue
Urbana, IL 61801
1-217-265-6825
carpente@illinois.edu

Ryan C. Tucker
University of Illinois at Urbana-Champaign
1304 W. Springfield Avenue
Urbana, IL 61801
1-217-265-6813
tucker@illinois.edu

ABSTRACT

Hiring new student employees is a task that many IT help desks face every semester, and finding quality applicants can often be a chore. How do you pick the best candidates from a pool where everyone seems so similar?

The interview process at the CITES Help Desk at the University of Illinois at Urbana-Champaign has been designed to accomplish two things. The first goal is to get to know the applicant and ascertain whether they would be a good fit for the Help Desk. The second is to sell the Help Desk's role on our campus. If the applicant isn't buying our customer service philosophy, we can avoid later headaches.

Our three-part interview weaves together both these goals. Students are asked to complete a hands-on "technical" portion, a rapid-fire Q&A about IT services on campus and then answer some scenario based questions. Each piece gives us an idea of the applicant's knowledge, poise, attitude, communication abilities and customer service skills. But, we can also learn a lot about the applicant from the subtleties. Does the number of tabs they open in a browser matter? What does their choice of search engine tell us? Do they show composure during the walk down the long, awkward hallway on the way to the interview room? These questions and answers help us get into the head of the applicant.

This paper will explore the interview questions we ask and the answers that give us the best impressions of an applicant. We'll also discuss the little things that may go unnoticed that can add up to make the difference between hiring or passing on an applicant.

Categories and Subject Descriptors
K.6.1 [**Management of Computing and Information Systems**]: Project and People Management – *Staffing.*

General Terms
Management, Performance, Human Factors

Keywords
Interview, student consultant, logic, hiring, aptitude, customer service, technical

1. INTRODUCTION

Hiring student staff is a challenge that nearly every IT organization faces at one time or another. The application and interview are integral parts of the hiring process with each lending different insights into the applicant. The interview that is required to find quality candidates could range from simple and standard to in-depth and technical, depending on the quantity and quality of staff that is being sought. Creating a streamlined interview process with pertinent questions allows you to judge a candidate's worthiness but also allows you to convey a lot of information about the position. This helps both parties make an informed decision about the potential employment opportunity.

2. OUR ENVIRONMENT

The CITES Help Desk is the central IT help desk for the University of Illinois at Urbana-Champaign. We answer basic computing questions about inquiries about CITES services from faculty, staff (including campus IT professionals), students and retirees. Because the range of our customers' technical expertise is so large (but skewed towards the "average" user), we need students who are first and foremost good communicators who can provide excellent customer service. Technical expertise, in the traditional sense of troubleshooting hardware or network problems, isn't a requirement for applicants. We feel that the needed skills and knowledge can be taught. More accurately, technical aptitude is what we are looking for. The old phrase "We can teach you technical skills, but not people skills," is quite fitting.

Our student staff consists of more than 40 consultants and our turnover rate from year-to-year ranges from 10 to 20 students. We interview candidates during the semester prior to their start semester (i.e. students who are needed for fall are interviewed and hired in the prior spring)

3. THE APPLICATION

We post job openings on our campus Virtual Job Board as well as the CITES website. Interested students are asked to fill out an online application.

The application is divided into three parts. The first is basic demographic information and standard application fodder (name, address, year in school, resume attachment, references). The second is a self-ranking section where we ask the applicant to rate their knowledge on a scale of 1-5 on various categories such as Windows XP or CITES Express Email. The third section is a set of short answer questions that are fairly typical of applications (e.g. What experience do you have in customer support? and Rate your communication skills). Completed applications are saved in a database and reviewed by our primary Help Desk HR person when the time to hire students rolls around.

It should come as no surprise that a large number of applications are dismissed quickly. A student's honest answer that they are looking for an "easy" job will lead to a quick rejection. Some students rate themselves low across the board on the "technical" areas. Some, despite unlimited time to complete the application properly, have forms rife with typos and grammatical errors or just plain lazy answers. Since we're looking for motivated, technically leaning, effective communicators, answers that don't indicate that they would be such employees are easy nixes. If the application passes muster, the next step is the interview.

4. THE INTERVIEW

Our student interviews generally last between 45 and 60 minutes and are conducted by our Help Desk HR representative and a member of our student management team.

First impressions are key. We are looking for the same things as everyone else when an applicant arrives: Were they punctual? Were they appropriately dressed? Did they bring a pen and paper and other requested documents (perhaps a resume, if not included with the application)?

The first thing we do with the applicant is give a short tour of the Help Desk. This allows us to give a brief introduction to what we do and find out if the applicant has ever had need to contact the Help Desk.

The next stage is a walk down a long hallway en route to the room where we do interviews. We've dubbed this the "awkward hallway" as small talk sometimes never seems to take off, resulting in some uncomfortable silence.

Once in the interview room, we review a few Help Desk policies in an effort to further educate the applicant on expectations. Experience has taught us that we should provide a lot of information to applicants so they can make an informed decision about whether this is a job for them. We have hired some students who made it obvious that they agreed to a job they weren't expecting and quickly left our ranks. This isn't a benefit to anyone. Once our initial spiel is done, we're ready to begin the interview proper, which is divided into three parts.

4.1. Hands-On Portion

The first piece involves having the applicant sit at a computer and complete a list of tasks, each involving a CITES service. Prior to having the applicant begin the tasks, we tell them that they are allowed to use any help resource they have access to, including asking the interview team questions. There is not a time limit for completing the tasks, although we do warn that if too much time passes we will stop their progress so we can complete all pieces of the interview in the time allotted.

This is not meant to be a technical test. There is very little technical skill needed to complete the interview. Instead, these tasks allow us to see intangible qualities in action. How does the applicant search for information? What tools do they use? How organized do they keep the information they find?

Let's walk through the five tasks to see these questions in action.

4.1.1 Fix the machine's networking

Initially, the machine isn't able to connect to the internet because we have simply disabled the network card. This is literally fixable with a double-click if you know where to go. This first task is the most technical and it sets the bar for us. Some applicants seem to aimlessly poke around, while some open up the command line right away. Some go straight to browser settings. These are all extremes and none are especially desirable considering the applicant has done zero troubleshooting. We certainly don't want the hunt and peck method of troubleshooting, but we also don't want consultants who will jump to a more technical answer when a simple one should suffice. More than one applicant has disabled the Windows firewall with no reason to do so, and that's bordering on dangerous for customers. A good answer for us is to check the browser for an error message or open up the network properties and then go from there.

4.1.2 Set your security questions

This is perhaps the easiest task, but it provides important information. We use an on-line password manager at the University of Illinois. Within the password manager, you can save answers to two security questions. We ask the student applicant to find the application and set their two security questions. *HOW* they try to find it is telling. Very rarely does the applicant search for "CITES Password Manager" which is odd considering that exact phrase is in the task list. They may search for "security questions" or something similar. We're not saying this is "wrong", but in this case it's entirely ineffective due to how the information is presented and indexed on the website.

Seeing the tool the applicant uses for the search is also important. Many go straight to google.com for searches, which adds extra clicks and time. This can be maddening because a search bar is built in to the CITES website that uses Goggle search. Many times, applicants have to do two or three searches on Google because they neglect to type CITES or UIUC as a search term. Going to the CITES website to search is far more effective.

4.1.3 Name the five email services provided by CITES

This is a test of vocabulary and information processing. All five are listed right on a main email page on the CITES website. The challenge for the candidate is to process how the information is presented. An excellent answer rattles all of them off, noting that there is a different between Exchange 2007 and Exchange

2010. A bad effort would be suggesting that Thunderbird is an email service.

4.1.4 Set up the VPN

This is a test of the applicant's ability to find and follow instructions. There are no tricks here. Everything they need is listed out step by step. Most applicants make it through this one just fine, but the task does tell us more than just their ability to follow documented instructions. The process most commonly used to set up the VPN requires that the user leave the documentation page to download an installation package from our WebStore. This link does not open a new tab. How they manage tabs is another interesting intangible that by itself doesn't break the deal, but together with other little things may make a difference. It's also interesting to note how many applicants don't look at the entire page of instructions, trailing off around step 12 or 13 of 16. Giving customers incomplete steps won't do customers any good.

4.1.5 Update McAffee's virus definitions

This task is the only one that might require the applicant to go off to the wilds of the internet to find information and often leads to the most consternation. The simplest solution is often the best and here they only need to make a right-click of the mouse and select Update now. Leading customers to a "private" section of McAfee's site to download a file is certainly not the simplest solution (and a questionable one at best).

There are a few other interesting actions we note during the hands-on portion that can also contribute to our overall impression of their skills, but singularly don't affect our decision.

- Does the applicant listen to all the instructions? Nothing drives the interview team crazier than when an applicant dives into the tasks while we are still giving the instructions - not only because they should be listening but it means they've turned their back to us while we are talking, and that's not good policy from a service perspective.

- How fast do they scan a page and move their mouse? Understandably, different people consume information in different ways and at different rates. But, when an applicant grabs that vertical scroll bar and zips the page up and down looking for information it seems like an inefficient method for data collection. The same goes for how much they move the mouse around the screen. A lot of movement seems unorganized and scatter-shot.

- Do they repeat the same thing over and over with the same result? This is especially notable during the networking task, but does come up at other times. This shows more inefficient actions and doesn't translate well into providing good customer service.

Ultimately, the principle of Occam's Razor comes in to play with every task, and should come in to play with every customer inquiry. The simplest (or easiest to complete/understand) solution is *usually* the best one. Applicants who get to an answer but take a long road to get there indicate that we might need to invest more time in teaching them basic troubleshooting.

4.2 Rapid Fire

This section of the interview consists of one of the interviewers reading off a list of technical services that are on campus. From this list, the interviewee needs to respond in an immediate "yes" or "no" indicating whether or not our organization, CITES, supports that service. Overall, this section is not set up as a large determining factor in our opinion of the interviewee. We see this part as more of an information piece to help them better understand the job and scope of responsibilities. It helps us evaluate the applicant's awareness of campus and its technical services.

The interviewer will give a name of the service and a one or two sentence description of the service. We are then looking for a quick "yes" (CITES does support that service) or "no" (CITES does not support that service) from the candidate. Not only does this help the interviewee understand services that CITES support but how the structure in CITES is loosely built. We explain that not all services can be supported in the Help Desk, but must be transferred to other groups within CITES. This should also build a little confidence in the student that they have a large support structure behind them to help them assist a client. When discovering how many services the Help Desk support, some new student workers can feel overwhelmed.

The scoring in this test is mostly neutral. Interviewees would only get positive or negative points if they confidently got them all correct or confidently get them all incorrect.

This test only lasts as long as a student takes to say "yes" or "no". We review how they did afterwards and explain the answers. This portion of the interview should not take over 3-4 minutes to complete. If interviewee takes time to think about the prompt, they are missing the point of the Rapid Fire session thus ruining the spirit of "rapid."

4.2. Scenarios

Up to this point, we haven't let the applicant do much talking. The third portion of the interview consists of some conversation and scenario based questions. We start off with questions that allow the applicant to talk about themselves a little bit. Common topics include their hobbies and their ideal career. We then ask the applicant to relate a time when they received good customer service. They often relate a story where the person they worked with was nice or patient or offered them free items. Good answers should relate specifics about an encounter which would translate into their role as a Help Desk consultant.

We then proceed with some actual questions that have basis in real-life Help Desk questions. We usually select three or four from this list:

4.3.1 The Blu-Ray

We start the scenario by asking the applicant to name a movie. The first scenario supposes that the applicant is working in a big box store where they sell movies. The scenario is presented like this:

"Someone comes up to you and in their hand is a Blu-Ray copy of [the movie the applicant named]. They ask you, 'Will this play on my TV at home?' How do you respond to the customer?"

A really good answer to this question is a series of questions that would produce useful and informative answers. Many applicants answer with, "I would ask if they have a Blu-Ray player," We would prefer questions like, "Do you have a device that plays movies at home?", "How much did that device cost?", "How long have you had it?" which are much more effective troubleshooting questions. An applicant's ability to think in those terms is a definite positive.

4.3.2. Explain something technical

Because the Help Desk has such a large customer base, it goes without saying that our customers' range of technical expertise varies greatly. As such, we must be able to communicate technical ideas with varying degrees of complexity and language.

"Please explain a situation where you had to explain something technical or complicated to someone who was not savvy in that particular area. And, it doesn't need to be about computers."

Often we get answers along the lines, "I help my mom with computers a lot since she doesn't know much about them. I show her what she needs to do when she calls me, step by step." What we're shooting for here are very specific details - maybe even to the point that they are explaining that technical concept to us.

4.3.3. What not to do

We tell applicants that about 60% of our business is done over the phone, and that this makes for interesting challenges. Most of these calls are going to deal with topics that the applicant has already been exposed to in the interview, but sometimes the call concerns an obscure problem or service.

"What are some things that you should NOT do when the customer is asking you about an unfamiliar topic?"

Common answers here are, "I don't lose my patience," or "I don't tell them I can't help them." These answers OK, but what we're really driving at here is a demonstration that they understand processes. Great answers for us would be, "I wouldn't guess at an answer," hopefully inferring that they would use the help resources available to them thoroughly. "I wouldn't panic," or something similar shows that they would keep their cool. "I don't say, 'I don't know,'" is controversial since we want to manage customer expectations to the best of our ability but not a commonly accept customer service answer. "I don't get angry/frustrated" is common too, which is fine, but a bit obvious. "I don't NOT solve their problem..," is a nice try, but ultimately lacking substance.

The final two scenarios are fairly boilerplate questions about leadership experience ("Are you a leader or a follower?") and professional mistakes that they've made in the and how they learned from them.

4.3. Wrap-up

This concludes our prepared set of questions. It is now time for the applicant to ask us questions about the job. More times than not, they don't have any prepared or did not come up with any during the interview. This is not what we are looking for. We want a curious applicant that is educating themselves fully on the job that they possibly could be offered. We do not have a set of questions we are looking for. We actually want them to ask us anything to show us that they are still highly interesting in the position.

At this time we give them an anticipated of a call back and end the interview. This will be the second time we lead the applicant through the "awkward hallway". This can be very interesting no matter how the interview went.

5. HIRED?

Almost every time, the interviewers meet right after the interview so we are discussing it fresh in our mind. We go over each portion of the interview and how we thought they performed. We will point out their strengths and weaknesses as well as "quirks" that we noticed during the interview. These "quirks" can show us a lot about the student and they are familiar tells in the outside world interviews. They can be anything to yawning, no eye contact, lazy posture, interrupting, not listening to our instructions on the different sections, etc. We are looking out for the following personalities: Hotshot Helen, Overconfident Karl, No-confidence Nellie, Paycheck Pauly, and Homework Hugh. You probably have seen these types of students in your workforce or interviews.

We also talk about the interviewee's attitude during the interview. Our environment in the Help Desk is specific enough to warrant another paper so we won't go into much detail here. We need to make sure that those we are bringing in will mesh well with the other student workers. If the interviewee seems that they are extremely shy we may consider that they may not fit in well with all the outgoing students that work here. Not only are we looking to improve the Help Desk, but we are also not looking to set a student up for failure. There are some exceptions to that rule. If a seemingly introvert does excellent on all of the portions they will more than likely be given the job in hopes that they may "come out of their shell" in the office. But the rule does not flex the other way, such as an extremely friendly interviewee and would be great in our community but shows no technical talent they will not be highly considered.

Our hiring ratio is actually high with all the testing that we do. We would estimate that we hire 8.5/10 people who interview. We believe that most of the weeding out prior to the interview helps ensure that the in-person interviews are rarely a waste of time.

6. CONCLUSIONS

We find that most of the applicant's start working at the Help Desk knowing a clear set of expectations and having an eagerness to begin doing the job well. The next step in their career will be training which will introduce even more expectations and requirements. But, we feel the interview process does the job it's intended to do and the students we hire will be able to succeed in our environment.

The Windows 7 Build Key: Redesigning and Automating Image Deployment

John B. Tyndall
Information Technology Services
The Pennsylvania State University
University Park, PA 16802
(814) 865-2886
jbt8@psu.edu

ABSTRACT

The image deployment process requires a certain amount of effort, finesse, and luck to effectively execute. Manual techniques are prone to inefficiency and inconsistency, and commercial products necessitate costly software, server-side additions, or network changes; and likely, these tasks must be performed by specialized IT staff.

Dwindling resources and increasing demands are compelling IT organizations to do different with less. Technology is changing in the academic community, and IT service units must adapt by concentrating on other, more valuable initiatives. The Windows 7 Build Key (WBK) allows this by replacing the complication and redundancy of image deployment and configuration with a fully unattended procedure that requires only about 5 minutes per machine.

A bootable USB-based solution, the WBK is portable, easy, secure, and different from other approaches. Sensitive information like passwords, data, and the image itself are encrypted, allowing student/outsourced staff to build machines without disclosure or technical prerequisites. The WBK also takes the work out of image maintenance: out-of-box software or drivers are a simple drag-and-drop, and configuration is updated inside an XML file—no more finger-crossing with Sysprep. At the end of the build, users have a fresh installation of Windows 7 that is completely configured without any IT intervention. And even better, the computer can be rebuilt later without using the build key.

This paper presents a model for designing a zero-cost automated Windows 7 deployment strategy from build to login that doesn't require any changes to the network or large investment of time.

Categories and Subject Descriptors

C.5.3 [**Computer System Implementation**]: Microcomputers—*personal computers, portable devices, workstations*

SIGUCCS'11, November 12–17, 2011, San Diego, California, USA.

General Terms

Management, Performance, Design, Economics, Reliability, Security

Keywords

Active directory, automation, build key, deployment, group policy, imaging, ImageX, unattended, WBK, Windows 7

1. INTRODUCTION

The Pennsylvania State University is a public research instituion with 19 campus locations in addition to University Park, as well as several special-mission campuses throughout the state. While Information Technology Services (ITS) offers core technology, IT is mainly decentralized. As a result, each campus and college has its own IT staff and infrastructure and may or may not utilize all of the University's recommended services.

The Windows 7 Build Key was created as a low-cost, low-infrastructure, and low-maintenance image deployment solution designed to work across all of these distributed environments, regardless of systems management mechanisms or technical expertise. The WBK leverages the power of unattended installations to create an all-in-one dynamic and clean environment that maintains the features of traditional imaging without the headaches and time usually involved.

2. BACKGROUND

For several years, most Penn State IT organizations have used Symantec Ghost, the popular commercial disk-cloning tool, for developing and deploying administrative and academic images.

2.1 Symantec Ghost

Ghost allows systems administrators to customize a single computer and transfer an exact copy of it (i.e., an image of its current state) to another computer, saving the hassle and time of manually installing, configuring, and customizing each subsequent computer.

Ghost was a great time-saver; however, IT staff experienced several limitations. Unless (and sometimes even despite) using Microsoft Sysprep to remove hardware identifiers and incorporate drivers, IT staff needed to create and store separate images for each model of computer. Also, they had to split the image across multiple CDs or DVDs or use the Ghostcast functionality to deploy the image via the network (while unattended, this procedure necessitated the

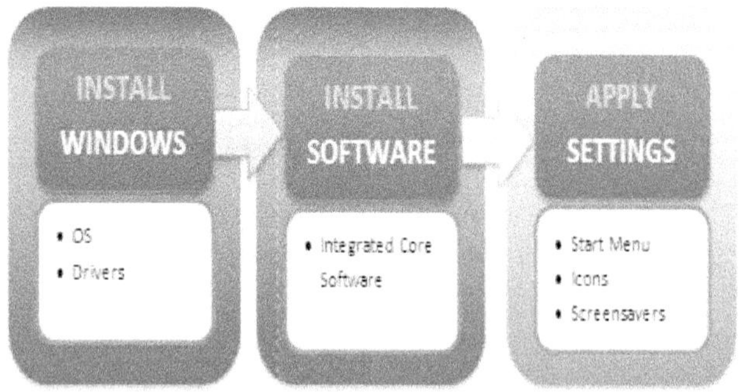

Figure 1: The Install Process

creation of network boot discs). Regardless of deployment mechanism, updating the image was also time-consuming; even a small change required modification to and resealing of the entire image. Furthermore, being a commercial enterprise solution, Ghost requires a costly license.

2.2 ImageX and Windows Imaging Format

To address certain limitations of sector-based image technologies like Ghost, Microsoft created the ImageX command-line utility and the accompanying Windows Imaging file format (**.wim**) [2]. As with Ghost, ImageX takes an image of the computer's current state and deploys it to other computers; however, ImageX uses file-based imaging, which—among other benefits—allows for direct modification of the image, much unlike sector-based images. This means that updates and drivers can be easily injected into the image. Originally released with Windows Vista, ImageX also works with Windows XP.

The WBK leverages the power of ImageX primarily because it is natively supported by the latest version of Windows (e.g., Windows Setup—`install.wim`—is itself an image) and also because it is freely available via the Windows Automated Installation Kit [1]; thus, IT departments can save the money spent on Ghost by using ImageX.

3. UNATTENDED INSTALLATIONS

Computer imaging is convenient because systems administrators can configure a computer exactly how they want it to be for the end user, then take a snapshot of it and deploy it to other computers. Regardless of whether the imaging technology is sector- or file-based, though, images must be maintained and constantly updated. Such revisions can be tedious, since even a small change—driver installation, software update, additional file, etc.—requires modification of the entire image.

The degree of difficulty to update images depends on the technology being used; however, in general, the less often an image is modified, the less chance there is for inconsistency.

The WBK addresses this limitation of traditional imaging by combining an unattended operating system installation with unattended and silent core software installations as shown in Figure 1; software and user-based settings are applied by group policies when the computer joins the domain.

3.1 Unattended OS Installation

An *unattended* installation is one that requires no user interaction. Using an unattended operating system installation instead of an imaged one yields the same effect of an image, i.e., automatic deployment, but provides a fresh OS environment as opposed to one that has been heavily edited. While imaged OS's are not necessarily bad, there is less chance for errors or complications when using a clean installation.

Systems administrators can perform unattended Windows 7 installations by incoporating an `unattend.xml` file. This answer file provides Windows Setup with common installation parameters (e.g., license acceptance, language and time zone settings, local user accounts, product keys if not using KMS authentication, etc.), as well as the ability to integrate commands (e.g., calls to batch files, registry settings, etc.). The Windows System Image Manager is included with [1] and provides an easy-to-use GUI for creating and editing `unattend.xml`.

The WBK uses an unattended installation of Windows 7 to obtain a clean operating system installation. An `unattend.xml` answer file is used to configure routine settings, set authentication registry entries, and call a batch file after autologin to kickstart the rest of the deployment process.

3.2 Unattended Software Installation

A *silent* installation is one that does not display any windows or messages. Most software packages include command-line arguments that allow system administrators to perform silent or unattended installations. For example, the Mozilla Firefox 4.0.1 installer is `Firefox Setup 4.0.1.exe`. Normally, a user double-clicks the file and clicks through the setup prompts until the software installs. Alternatively, Mozilla Firefox 4.0.1 can be installed via the command line as follows:

```
Firefox Setup 4.0.1.exe -ms
```

This command silent installs Firefox in the background without any of the standard setup windows. The `-ms` argument installs Firefox's default settings; however, additional arguments and/or configuration files can be used for a more advanced and customized installation.

Another common installer is the Microsoft Scripted Installer (**.msi**). The `msiexec.exe` utility is a standard Windows program that installs **.msi** files via the command line. Silent installations can be acheived with the `\qn` argument, and `\qb` results in an unattended installation with a progress bar.

Using unattended and silent installations is a powerful alternative to pre-installing applications on an image. In particular, these types of installations are useful for computer-dependent applications that cannot be pre-installed. The software's documentation should detail its silent and/or unattended capabilities.

The WBK build process integrates silent and unattended software installations to dynamically install applications that systems administrators want available out-of-box to their users. These installations occur during the Post-Installation Configuration phase, discussed in Section 5, and allow the same Windows installation to be used for multiple images.

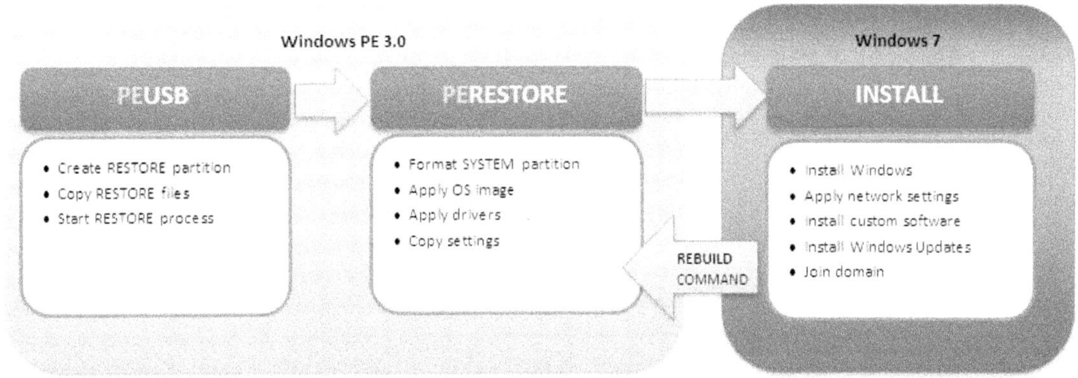

Figure 2: The Build Key

```
<CONFIG>
    <LabAcad>
        <BUILDING name="Harrisburg Library" code="LIB">
            <ROOM name="L1" ou="HarrisburgLibraryL1" subnet="14
        </BUILDING>
        <BUILDING name="Olmsted Building" code="OS">
            <ROOM name="L1" ou="OlmstedL1" subnet="146.186.88.1
            <ROOM name="L3" ou="OlmstedL3" subnet="146.186.84.0
            <ROOM name="E243" ou="OlmstedE243" subnet="146.186.
            <ROOM name="W14" ou="OlmstedW14" subnet="146.186.88
            <ROOM name="W101" ou="OlmstedW101" subnet="146.186.
```

Figure 3: Sample Configuration File

4. THE BUILD KEY

The Windows 7 Build Key (Figure 2) is a custom application used to automate computer image deployments. The installation phase is comprised of two environments: Windows Preinstallation Environment (WinPE) to copy and deploy the image, and Windows 7 to install the operating system. WinPE, available in [1], is a minimal version of Windows that can be extended into a powerful pre-installation environment for deployments, recoveries, forensics, and other uses. The entire deployment process is local—the OS image and setup files are copied from a USB flash drive, and all post-OS software installations occur on the machine itself; a network connection is required only if joining the computer to a domain and installing Windows Updates.

A USB flash drive is a portable, secure solution. Other imaging techniques may not require the need to carry around a build key; however, this solution allows non-systems administrators to deploy computer images. Because configuration data and even the image itself are encrypted, sensitive information cannot be compromised, and advanced technical knowledge and access are not required to execute a routine task. Computer deployment can now be easily outsourced to student staff or deployment teams, allowing systems administrators to concentrate on more important work.

4.1 Organization

The WBK is a bootable WinPE utility comprised of two custom applications to deploy an operating environment: PEUSB, which records machine settings, partitions the local hard drive, and copies the PERESTORE environment to a hidden partition on the local drive; and PERESTORE, which formats the system drive, applies the OS image, and installs drivers.

Four primary containers allow the WBK to be easily updated without manipulating the core setup image or the WinPE applications; they are encrypted using TrueCrypt [3], an open source encryption application:

- `config.data`
  Contains **`unattend.xml`** and XML configuration files for departments, buildings/building codes, and subnet information. Figure 3 shows one of these XML files. In this example, each room of a building has its own OU in Active Directory and subnet range; the mask and gateway are incorporated into the XML file so that all is needed when building a computer is the last octet of the IP address. Whenever IP network information changes, a building needs added, etc., an IT staff member can simply update the appropriate XML file.

- `drivers.data`
  Contains supported driver files, which are installed during Windows Setup. It is possible to inject the drivers into the image itself to reduce deployment time; however, the dynamic installation ensures that only drivers for that model are installed. This also makes model-based imaging obsolete, since drivers can be dragged-and-dropped into this container as needed.

- `image.data`
  Contains **`install.wim`**, which may or may not have been modified.

- `PSU.data`
  Contains a directory that is copied to `C:\Windows\PSU`. This folder is comprised of custom configuration files and utilities as well as a protected setup folder that automates the rest of the deployment process; source files for custom software included with the image are located here as well. Applications can be updated or added simply by copying the files to this container.

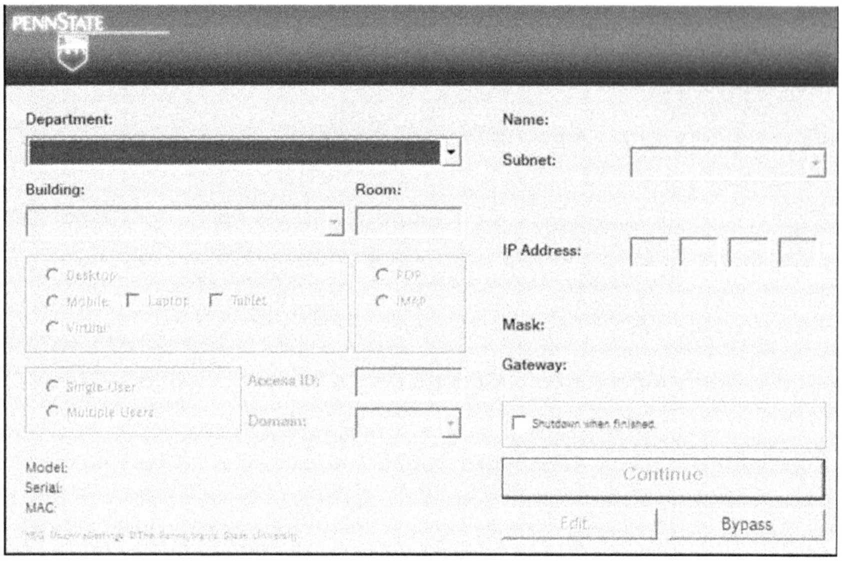

Figure 4: FacStaff Build Key Menu

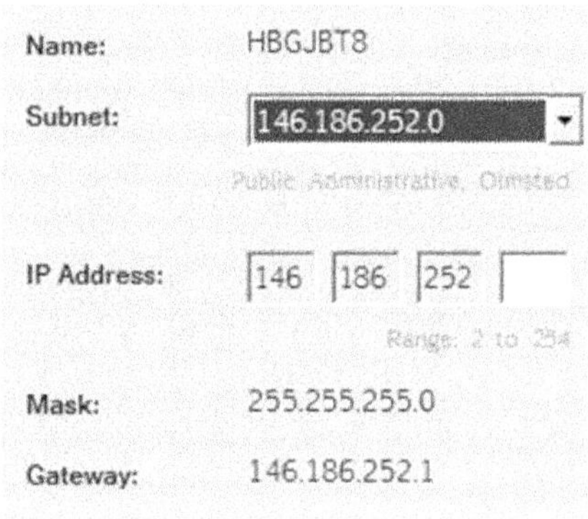

Figure 5: FacStaff Computer Name Generation

Figure 6: PERESTORE Environment

4.2 PEUSB

PEUSB is a custom Visual Basic application written for WinPE 3.0. This utility scans the destination computer for hardware inventory; unencrypts `config.data` to populate the WBK menus; creates a file with the machine configuration information; creates a small hidden partition on the local hard drive; copies the PERESTORE environment, other encrypted containers, and updated `unattend.xml` (with the new computer name) to that hidden partition; and then reboots the machine into the PERESTORE environment.

Figure 4 shows the main build key menu for faculty/staff computers. The dropdown menus are populated by XML files in `config.data`, and machine information from the inventory scan displays in the lower left-hand corner. When building a computer, a user selects the appropriate department and building, then enters the room number. He or she then selects a few settings about the computer: its type, whether or not to use POP or IMAP email, and whether or not the computer is for one or many users. PEUSB uses this information not only for inventory data, but to establish a consistent computer name. For example, Figure 5 shows the automatically generated name for a single-user desktop for JBT8 at the Harrisburg campus. As with lab/academic computers, the only IP information needed is the last octet if not using DHCP.

The menu also includes options to edit the generated computer name and/or networking information, or to completely bypass the build menu, installing a blank copy of Windows.

Filling out the information in this build key menu is the only physical interaction that is required by the entire build process. It takes about five minutes for the PERESTORE files to copy to the hidden partition, and the rest of the build process is completely automated.

4.3 PERESTORE

PERESTORE is a custom Visual Basic application written for WinPE 3.0. This utility scans the computer for the machine configuration files that PEUSB created; decrypts drivers.data, image.data, and PSU.data; formats the system partition; applies the operating system image; copies the <PSU> directory; copies the relevant drivers; sets its parition as hidden; and reboots the machine into Windows Setup.

This environment is completely unattended, so a status window displays the progress on the screen (Figure 6).

4.4 Windows Setup

Windows Setup is the standard operating system installation routine. Using the unattend.xml answer file configured with Windows SIM, Windows Setup is completely automated, but also customized with the appropriate computer name generated in PEUSB as well as the appropriate driver set from PERESTORE.

The install.wim image applied by PERESTORE has a filesystem in tact, so any additional settings or files (e.g., unattend.xml, user account pictures, <PSU> directory, etc.) can be copied before Windows Setup boots.

The WBK configures Windows Setup to execute a Post-Installation Configuration phase after the operating system has been installed.

5. POST-INSTALLATION CONFIGURATION

A computer image is convenient primarily because not only is the operating installed and customized, but so is the software suite.

The WBK maintains out-of-box imaging results by incorporating a series of unattended and silent software installations after Windows Setup. During this phase, network and machine settings are applied; custom software applications are installed; Windows Updates are installed; and the computer is joined to the domain. An email containing inventory and build information is also emailed to IT staff as well as an automated inventory system. Also, the entire build process from PEUSB to PERESTORE to Windows Setup to the Post-Install Configuration (PIC) is logged to a single file in a protected directory for review.

This process is also entirely unattended and requires no user intervention. Depending on the amount of customized software and updates, the PIC phase can take anywhere from 10-30 minutes. For example, Penn State uses a systems management tool to deploy software to academic machines; thus, these computers have a very small PIC phase with one or two installations. Faculty and staff machines need to have out-of-box readiness and have a larger PIC phase with several installations for a standard software suite.

5.1 RunOnce

RunOnce is a single batch file that controls the PIC execution flow. It calls the commands to set power and network settings, send email inventory information, perform unattended and silent software installations, and join the domain.

5.2 LockScreen

After Windows Setup is complete, the computer logs in locally using the local administrator account. Immediately afterwards, the auto-login feature is turned off, and the LockScreen utility starts before a user is able to interact with the desktop. This is a custom-built .NET application that locks the screen, allowing unattended installations and

Figure 7: LockScreen

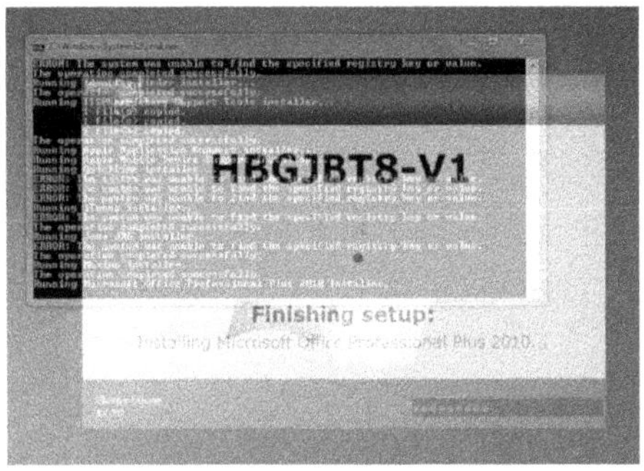

Figure 8: LockScreen *Debug* Mode

setup procedures to run uninterrupted without user manipulation or intervention. LockScreen displays a fullscreen dynamic status window (Figure 7); it terminates Windows Explorer and the Start Menu and also ignores common control keystrokes (e.g., CTRL+ALT+DEL, ALT+TAB, ALT+F4, etc.) and mouse-clicks.

LockScreen features a *debug* mode, which reduces opacity by 50% to view the background status while still maintaining protection (Figure 8). Also, LockScreen can be completely terminated; Windows Explorer and the Start Menu will be restored, but the PIC process will still continue until manually terminated.

5.3 Windows Updates

The WBK process uses a Visual Basic script to apply Windows Updates during the PIC phase after network settings have been applied and before the computer joins the domain.

Alternatively, ImageX provides the ability to inject Windows Updates directly into the image. This can reduce the time of the PIC phase and does not necessarily compromise the integrity of install.wim, though it will increase its size.

The dynamic method of the WBK maintains minimum image maintenance.

5.4 Installing Specialized Software

The WBK replaces traditional imaging with a fully unattended setup procedure that provides out-of-box readiness for most users; however, sometimes different classes of machines require different software sets. For instance, all education and psychology faculty might need SPSS, while IST faculty require Visual Studio, and staff assistants always re-

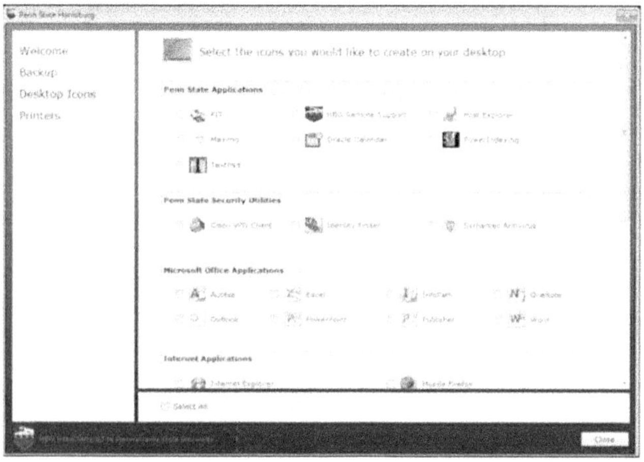

Figure 9: UserConfig: Desktop Icons

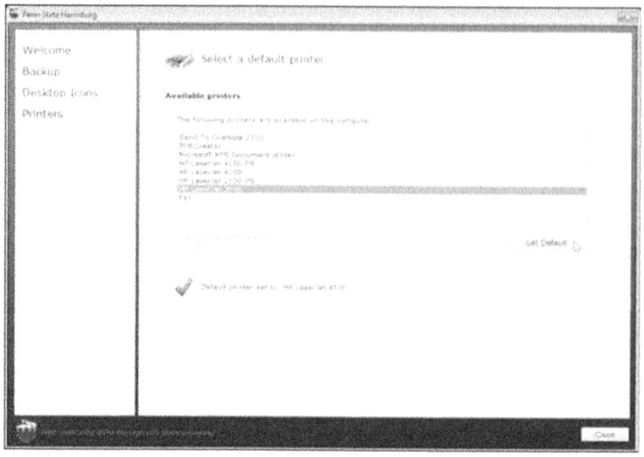

Figure 10: UserConfig: Printers

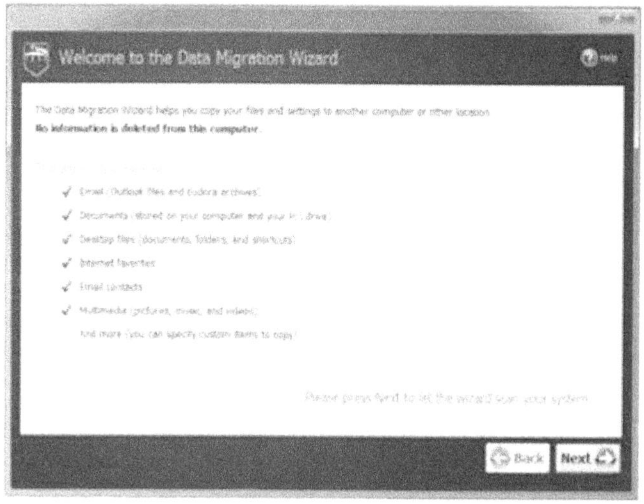

Figure 11: Penn State Data Migration Wizard

quest a mainframe client and financial software. Similarly, lab software varies depending on lab type (e.g., general purpose, engineering, humanities, etc.) or room. When the difference between machines is software, it makes no sense to create a separate image. Instead, after a common software suite is installed to establish basic functionality, these specialized applications can be deployed using systems management software or group policies after the computer joins the domain.

If using systems management tools, it is easy to create software distribution groups based on software packages and add machines to the corresponding groups. If using only Active Directory, a logical organizational unit structure and managed software installations/startup scripts achieve the same outcome. Either way, shortly after the computer finishes the PIC phase, the Deployment phase automatically addresses these customized installations. Established as policies, systems administrators do not have to worry about manually installing specialized software again, since any time the computer is rebuilt, the applications will automatically deploy.

5.5 Installing Printers

Dealing with printers can be cumbersome, as there are many different models with many different driver sets and installation types. To avoid manual printer installations, it is best practice to use networked printers that can be centrally managed.

With Windows 7, printers can be easily deployed with group policy without any extra scripting or configuration. The Print Management snap-in for Windows Server 2008R2 provides an easy-to-use GUI for installing and deploying printers. Deploying printers via policy allows the printer to be centrally managed on a print server so that all clients receive the same settings. As with specialized software installations, since printers are deployed via policy, IT staff will not need to manually visit each machine to install printers, because the printers will be automatically deployed.

5.6 UserConfig

UserConfig is a custom .NET application built to assist users with non-policy settings. This utility runs when the user logs in, and it does the following:

- Displays a welcome message and offers support information.
- Provides a means for users to read and accept Penn State's Computer and Network Security policy.
- Enumerates installed software and lets users choose which application icons they would like on the desktop (Figure 9).
- Allows users to configure backup options, network storage locations, and My Documents redirection.
- Allows users to select a default printer (Figure 10).

5.7 Maintaining User Data

The Penn State Data Migration Wizard (Figure 11) is a custom .NET application designed to help users migrate local

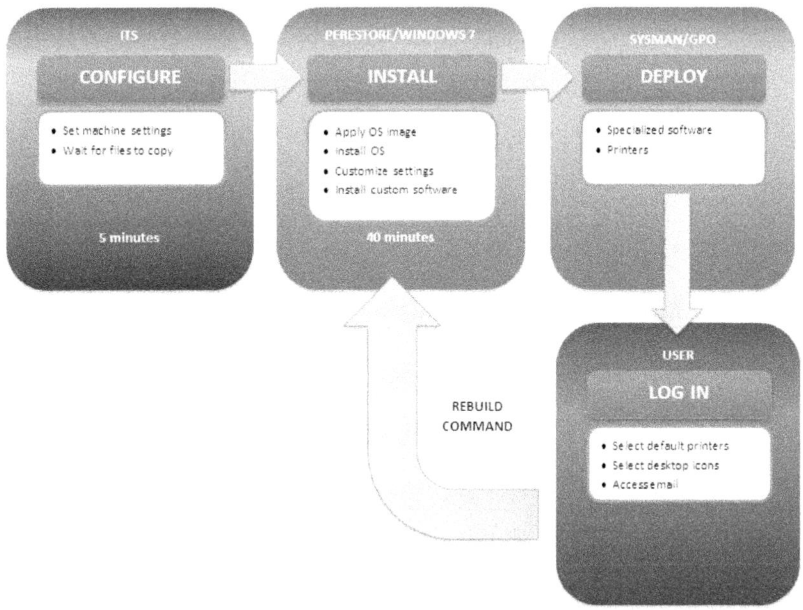

Figure 12: The Build Process

data to a network storage location. ITS centrally provides both Windows- and Unix-based network storage; many campuses and colleges also provide local area network storage. This application assists users with migrating their data to these locations.

Although each IT department establishes its own data storage policy, the WBK recommends the best practice of storing user data on the network. Not only is the data more secure in the event of a compromise or disaster, but data backup and restoration becomes almost a non-issue at the machine level.

Folder redirection is relatively simple to set up via group policy for Windows 7 and is a low-maintenance alternative to using roaming profiles. Once a setup like this is in place—like with specialized software and printers—computers can be rebuilt automatically since user data is on the network and automatically available when a user logs in.

5.8 Configuring Microsoft Office

Though Penn State provides web-based email, many IT departments encourage faculty and staff to use a local email client, particularly Microsoft Outlook. Penn State provides both POP and IMAP service, and many units also administer Exchange. Consequently, these IT staff members need to visit each computer to manually apply the proper email settings based on the type of email server their unit implements.

The WBK automates the email configuration process by utilizing the Microsoft Office Customization Tool (OCT). OCT is part of Microsoft Office Setup and can be accessed with the following command:

```
setup.exe /admin
```

OCT provides a group policy-like interface to modify the default installation of Microsoft Office and its components (e.g., Word, Excel, Outlook, etc.). Modifications are saved to an **.msp** file, which applies the specified changes when Office is installed. The WBK uses OCT to create an Outlook profile with Penn State's email settings. The appropriate settings are selected at the build menu (Figure 4) and then copied to the installation from PERESTORE. Thus, users can automatically log in to Outlook and access email without any IT intervention.

5.9 Rebuilding Computers

The WBK features the ability to rebuild computers without using the build key.

PEUSB creates a small RESTORE partition on the local hard drive, containing a copy of the PERESTORE environment (which includes the image, drivers, and software). Before the Windows Setup phase, this partition is marked as hidden; however, a simple command to set the partition as unhidden and active will reactivate the PERESTORE environment and result in the computer's automatic rebuilding. This command is easily deployed via systems management software or as implemented as a remote command. Thus, IT staff members only need to physically visit a computer once; should a computer need a rebuild, it can happen remotely.

Similarly, the RESTORE partition can be upgraded remotely with an updated image, new drivers, a different software suite, etc.

6. FUTURE WORK

The WBK is a production service that is used to deploy academic, administrative, and special-purpose computers from a single source. Its design not only allows easy modification by systems administrators, but also enables seamless use within a distributed IT environment such as Penn State.

An upcoming modification to the WBK is the design of a GUI to update the key's components. Currently, IT staff must manually decrypt the data containers, update the XML configuration files, drag-and-drop drivers and software source files, and adjust the installation batch files. An administrative GUI would make modifications much more organized and would also streamline the editing process.

Also, revisions to the WBK are placed on a deployment share, and IT staff deploy those changes to the key with a RoboCopy batch file; this admin interface would provide an integrated update process.

7. CONCLUSION

Particularly in the academic community, users are now becoming early adopters of new technology. As students and faculty adopt these innovative tools, IT service units must focus on new—and noticeable—initiatives and ideas. Time-consuming background tasks, like imaging and deployment, can no longer take hours per machine.

Accordingly, as IT departments must find ways of operating with tightening budgets and less resources, it is often a battle of doing *different* with less. By creating more valuable solutions that streamline lengthy procedures, IT staff can invest in the most visible aspects of higher education technology: the classroom and learning experience. Having the time to be more collaborative with peers and users, IT organizations can evolve from issue-resolvers to solution-providers.

The WBK is one such example of a solution-minded approach that saves IT departments time, money, and also allows them to concentrate on the important, rather than the immediate.

As shown in Figure 12, the WBK's build process is completely automated. IT staff need invest only 5 minutes per machine; the rest of the deployment is fully automated, and the user has a completely configured computer in about 30-45 minutes total.

This entirely free solution changes and modernizes the concept of traditional imaging by providing image-like results with a non-image, dynamic process. It is intuitive, secure, and easily updateable without compromising the end-user experience. Most importantly, not only can it deploy both academic and administrative machines from the same key, it is also easily extendable to work with any unit, campus, or university.

8. ACKNOWLEDGEMENTS

The author would like to thank the Systems Management group at Penn State for providing an early build key model. Also, the author appreciates the campuses and units who tested and implemented the WBK in their environments.

9. REFERENCES

[1] Microsoft Corporation. Windows automated installation kit. http://technet.microsoft.com/en-us/library/dd349343

[2] Microsoft Corporation. Windows imaging file format (wim). White paper, October 2007. http://go.microsoft.com/fwlink/?LinkId=92227.

[3] TrueCrypt Foundation. Truecrypt: Free open-source on-the-fly encryption. http://www.truecrypt.org.

Read, Write, and Present for ACM SIGUCCS Conferences

Trevor Murphy
Williams College
22 Lab Campus Drive
Williamstown, MA 01267
011.413.597.2231
Trevor.M.Murphy@williams.edu

ABSTRACT

The Association of Computing Machinery Special Interest Group in University and College Computing Services (ACM SIGUCCS) is made up of professionals who support and manage of information technology services at higher education institutions. SIGUCCS sponsors an annual conference that is drawn together by volunteers. The conference program takes the form of paper authors presenting their findings in 30 minute talks, as part of a panel, or in a poster session. Papers are presented on a variety of tracks such as management, technology, customer support, documentation and training, or instructional technology. The track titles can change over time. Attending and contributing to the SIGUCCS conference program is an opportunity for professional development. This paper seeks to demystify the process of contributing to the SIGUCCS conference program as a reader, author, and presenter and thus make the opportunity to obtain professional development through contributing to the SIGUCCS conference program easier.

Categories and Subject Descriptors

A.2 [**Reference**].

General Terms

Documentation, Human Factors.

Keywords

SIGUCCS, Program, Conference, Presenting, Authoring, Reading, Template.

1. THE ACM SIGUCCS CONFERENCE: AN INTRODUCTION

The Association of Computing Machinery (ACM), founded in 1947, is an organization that seeks to promote computing as a science and as a profession http://www.acm.org/. SIGUCCS, http://www.siguccs.org/, is one of 36 Special Interest Groups (SIGs) of the ACM and is made up of professionals who support and manage of information technology services at higher education institutions. The mission of SIGUCCS is to provide professional development opportunities for SIGUCCS members and other individuals in the field.

The SIGUCCS conference is a gathering of higher education IT professionals. There is a range of ways to engage with the conference program that extends beyond attending talks and networking with professional peers. Volunteer opportunities abound at SIGUCCS conferences. There are session chairs who introduce speakers, registration desk assistants, newsletter writers and assemblers, track chairs, and the core conference committee. Even the SIGUCCS board is made up of volunteers. This paper focuses on the role of the reader, and the author and presenter. These roles offer an accessible path to professional development.

2. READERS

Readers serve a vital service in the publishing process for author/presenters. Papers are better when constructive feedback is incorporated into the authorship of the paper. To the author, a paper's potential improvements can be near invisible. The goals of the reader are to help the author create the strongest paper possible to meet the standards of ACM, to be a real contribution to the paper's future readership, and to reflect well on the author. For this reason, multiple readers look over the paper and suggest improvements. Readers generally work in a given conference track. These tracks can include management, technology, customer support, documentation and training, and instructional technology. Tracks are overseen by a track chair who will organize the process of guiding drafts from the author to readers until the manuscripts are ready to be published.

One reason to be a reader is to explore and learn how professionals in a similar field at a similar institution are coping with changes in technology. It can also be a way to network with professional peers.

2.1 Three Different Types of Readings

When asked to read and edit a paper, the first thing that comes to mind is spelling and grammar. However, spelling and grammar can be left for last. First read the paper just for concepts and ideas or formatting. End with a spelling and grammar check. Each reading has a purpose. Furthermore, different readers have different strengths. Every paper would benefit from a strong concepts and ideas reader.

2.1.1 Concepts and Ideas

Looking at the ideas presented in the paper can help address coherency, information organization, and relevance. This type of reading ignores grammar, spelling, and formatting for the time being and focuses instead on the big picture. The reader asks questions such as:

- Is the title appropriate and clear?
- Are the subsections appropriate to address the topic in an organized fashion?
- If there are multiple authors, did they write the paper or do some of the authors really belong in the acknowledgements?
- Does the abstract lay out a problem, how it was solved, and why we should care in 250 words or less?
- Is there a section introducing the school size and setting so that readers may know the context and environment in which the problem identified in the abstract is being addressed?
- Does the paper have clarity and utility?
- What questions come to mind that remain unaddressed?
- If you were truly interested in this topic, what information do you really need or want to know?
- What content in the paper is extraneous, so obvious that it need not be stated, or off topic?
- Are the references appropriate?

If the reader asks these questions and poses them to the author, the future readers can be spared much confusion and instead be treated to well organized and thoughtful presentation of information.

2.1.2 Formatting

A formatting edit again ignores spelling and grammar for the time being. Instead, the reader asks if the paper's styles conform to the template laid out by the ACM (link to template). Some details to check include:

- No double spaces. Do a find and replace of the double spaces and replace them with a single space.
- Does the paper use the template styles, fonts, and spacing for the various headings, subheadings, and body text?
- Put the references in correct order which is in alphabetical by last name. This is likely not in the order in which they were addressed in the paper.
- Do the references conform to the Chicago Manual of Style author date system used by the social sciences and science disciplines?
- Does the paper conform to the page limit for the presentation type?
- Is the classification and description correct?
- Is the copyright statement correct?
- Is there any extra spacing not specified by the template. Generally, all the spacing is included in the styles of the template. Paragraphs or hard returns are not needed to provide the spacing between sections.

Since formatting is largely non-negotiable, there is no need to use track changes in Microsoft Word and identify for the author every instance of deviation from the ACM publishing format standard. It can sometimes be easier to make the formatting changes, save the document, and send the new appropriately formatted document to the author with a note about the formatting standards and some encouragement to make their future paper edits to the properly formatted version of the paper.

2.1.3 Spelling and Grammar

Finally, read the paper for spelling and grammar. Track changes is an appropriate tool in this situation as sentence structure and clarity can be achieved in any number of ways. Suggest alternatives that help clarify the topic and ask questions if the author's intent is unclear. The author's ideas need to be intelligible, but the task of choosing the language to achieve that purpose is up to the author.

2.2 Marking Papers Up

When it comes to marking up edited papers, use the tools that come with Microsoft Word or Adobe Acrobat Professional. Papers that have been reviewed can be sent to the author, track chair, and/or posted on the conference content management system.

2.2.1 Microsoft Word

Formatting edits are non-negotiable and the changes can be made and saved. All other edits can be made using the track changes feature of Microsoft Word. To illustrate this point, try find and replace double spaces with single spaces in a paper that used double spaces at the end of every sentence. As a result of all the replacements made in the paper, other comments and edits will be lost among the numerous notes indicating yet another double space that was edited to a single space. A better approach is to make the change, save the paper, and only then begin to track changes. You can note that you made formatting changes as a comment on the draft paper. Comments should be clear that they are about paper formatting, or the content.

2.2.2 LaTeX or Adobe Acrobat PDF

LaTeX users usually output and submit a PDF document. These PDFs can be marked up using the mark up tools in Adobe Acrobat Professional. Look closely at the PDF for formatting issues such as spacing, fonts, and header styles. Formatting errors can be less obvious in PDFs than in Microsoft Word documents. Compare the PDF with PDFs already published in SIGUCCS proceedings. Readers may have to consult the ACM paper template document to find the actual settings specified for the various template styles and communicate these settings to authors. Concept and idea edits as well as spelling and grammar edits in Adobe Acrobat Professional are as easy to make as in Microsoft Word.

3. WRITING

Authors contribute to the program by sharing problems and solutions they have encountered in the higher education IT environment. Not only do authors get a professional publication out of contributing to the SIGUCCS program, but they will also meet peers who are interested in the same topic at the conference when they present their paper. This network can prove valuable as the author continues to work in the area related to the paper topic.

When the call for proposals goes out soliciting abstracts for the SIGUCCS conference program, authors should not be intimidated by the prospect of writing a paper. Hard earned experiences should be shared. There are ways to cope with the anxieties of writing and presenting. First, it should be known that the program committee exists to support authors through the process of writing and presenting their papers. The program committee seeks to empower authors to produce their best work and they can be very helpful especially to first time authors.

Papers can be presented as a poster, full presentation, or as a panel. Ideally, the choice of paper type would be made based on the content. However, a first time author may choose to write a smaller paper for the poster track or to find a collaborator from a different institution to co-write and present the paper as a panel. Poster papers are two to four pages in length while full papers are four to eight pages long. Panel papers are three to five pages long. The program chair or chairs can help connect authors with other collaborators.

3.1 Idea to Abstract

An abstract is just a compact 250 word or less summary of your paper idea. A website that has good suggestions on how to write an effective abstract can be found at http://www.ece.cmu.edu/~koopman/essays/abstract.html. The website lists the parts of an abstract: motivation, problem statement, approach, results, and conclusion. It might also help to think about what track the paper would be in. The tracks are instructional technology, documentation and training, customer support, technology, management, and the poster track.

3.2 Writing the Paper

Once the abstract is accepted, it is time to start working on the paper. Start by downloading the ACM template. Replace the title and abstract sections with the real title and abstract. Break the paper down into sections and subsections that come to mind for the topic. Under each section and subsection write a brief summary of the topic. Remember, a mediocre draft can be edited to make it better. But a draft that isn't written can't be improved or shared with others. Authors should not censor themselves as they compose a draft. It might help to think of writing the paper as a series of emails on the topic to a friend that doesn't know much about the topic.

Also, consider that the program committee would rather see a mediocre draft and help the author through difficulties than to not hear from the author at all.

3.3 References

Authors should check at the college or university library for other work on their topic. Ask a librarian. Search the ACM database for previous SIGUCCS papers on the topic and reference them. This small bit of research can provide a fuller view of the paper topic.

3.4 Obstacles

Two common obstacles for authors are procrastination and being reluctant to ask for assistance. The program committee is interested in seeing authors successfully completing papers and presenting at the conference. Authors should then be candid and communicate freely with the program committee about any difficulties. Interventions and modified schedules with deadlines that guide the author through the writing process can be individually tailored. Lack of communication and procrastination leaves less time for any potential modified schedule to be put into place. Program committee members may well have suggestions on how to proceed that are genuinely useful.

3.5 Fill in the Details

As the paper writing progresses, add in the correct copyright information and paper classification.

4. PRESENTING

There are many tips on presenting. This is one site with tips: http://www.ece.cmu.edu/~koopman/essays/abstract.html. Creating the presentation ahead of time and practicing the presentation delivery are key to success. If the presentation is a panel, make sure to meet with your co-presenters to arrange how the content delivery will be divided up. Any slides, handouts, or posters should be stored in electronic form in a retrievable space on the internet or on an USB thumb drive. Authors commonly email presentation materials to themselves. A backup can salvage a presentation in the case of hard drive failure or material loss or damage.

Poster presenters draw attendees in and talk with them about a topic. Hands on props can be useful elements to add to a poster. Successful posters usually also have a unifying visual theme.

Authors would be well served to think of visual elements that help tell their stories. Photos and graphics can be helpful for presenting certain content. Stage fright can be coped with by focusing on a friendly face in the crowd and explaining to them the content of your presentation.

5. CONCLUSIONS

Contributing to an ACM SIGUCCS conference program as a reader, author, or presenter is a great way to join in the conversations of higher education IT profession. Successful ACM SIGUCCS conferences depend on the richness and vitality of the readers, authors, and presenters. Volunteers support, encourage, and guide authors through the process of sharing their research and experiences with others. Consider contributing to the program of the next ACM SIGUCCS conference.

6. REFERENCES

[1] Association of Computing Machinery. http://www.acm.org/.

[2] Association of Computing Machinery Classification System. http://www.acm.org/about/class/1998/

[3] Association of Computing Machinery SIG Proceedings Templates. http://www.acm.org/sigs/publications/proceedings-templates.

[4] Association of Computing Machinery Special Interest Group in University and College Computing Services. http://www.siguccs.org/.

[5] Koopman, Philip. 1997. How to Write an Abstract. http://www.ece.cmu.edu/~koopman/essays/abstract.html.

[6] Williams College Libraries Chicago Manual of Style Author Date System. http://library.williams.edu/citing/styles/chicago2.php.

Superstar Student Staff Teams

Karen McRitchie
Grinnell College
1119 Sixth Avenue
Grinnell, IA 50112
1-641-269-4531
mcritchie@grinnell.edu

ABSTRACT

It has been 10 years since the Student Technology Consultant program at Grinnell College began. It started with 10-12 students who answered phones at the campus Helpdesk and has evolved into a program that enriches the students learning and work experience for their future careers. A common issue for departments who utilize student works is keeping them engaged with their job. The students have to enjoy working as well as getting some kind of reward for their efforts. With small budgets, this can often be a challenge for the IT departments.

Once you hire the right people and they complete the training program, there are many other ways to keep them engaged in their work, so that you are able to benefit from their work during their tenure with the college or university. At Grinnell College, I have implemented a student leadership team, project leadership, certification programs, a special senior achievement, volunteer opportunities and social events which all contribute to the successful retention of the student staff. In 10 years, I have had only a a few students be terminated or quit their job with IT Services.

Explore the ways in which you can engage your student staff, keep them motivated and create an amazing team that will not only benefit the technology users on campus, but also give them opportunities for learning and experience that will benefit their future endeavors.

Categories and Subject Descriptors

K.6.1 [**Management of Computing and Information Systems**]: Project and People Management – *staffing, training.*

General Terms

Management, Measurement, Performance, Human Factors

Keywords

Management, Student Staff, Teams, Leadership

1. INTRODUCTION

Twelve years ago, they were just regular student staff, nothing special. They would show up, do the job and get a paycheck once a month. There were the usual employee performance issues: missing work, lack of motivation. It was just a job and they were managed by a style that suggested, "I am the boss, do what I tell you."

There was this talented pool of students, how do we make them useful for Information Technology Services, campus "customers" and ignite their talents so that they gain real-world work experience?

A creative management approach would be applied and the group would evolve over the next 10 years to a superstar team!

2. TECHNOLOGY CONSULTANT VISION

The student staff for Grinnell College Information Technology Services department is called Technology Consultants (TCs). They are utilized in supporting all technologies used on campus like audio-visual equipment, computers, software and technology services.

The Technology Consultant program provides service to support the technology needs of the campus community as well as provide job, project experience and learning opportunities for the student staff to benefit their future career endeavors.

3. ENGAGEMENT = PRODUCTIVITY

Engaged workers are productive workers and create less management challenges. It is important to create a student worker who will give the department a return on their training and work investment. The staff needs to stay engaged with their job, while providing benefits to the IT staff or campus community, otherwise it is pointless to even consider hiring student staff.

3.1 WIIFM—WHAT'S IN IT FOR ME?

There needs to be benefits for both the IT department and the students in order to create an engaged worker. Student staff positions do not always have the best funding, so there needs to be other rewards in performing their IT job. The generation who is working in this decade wants to be doing something that they feel is beneficial. They want direction and guidance to a point, but then they want to be able to work on their own. They want to learn new things and develop their skills for future endeavors. They want to enjoy their work and understand how their contributions affect the "big picture."

The IT department staff needs to analyze how they can utilize student staff by determining the support needs of the campus community and department. Students are often used to fill in the gaps in staffing and as a cheap solution to staff a helpdesk. They are bright, usually motivated and can be responsible—let them do tasks and projects that will benefit the department. For example, the networking staff might be able to utilize a student assistant or

SIGUCCS'11, November 12–17, 2011, San Diego, CA, USA.

the student staff could be trained to image and install new systems.

3.2 Create a Community

A community is more than just a team, it is a culture. Foster a community spirit within the student staff team and the IT staff if possible. This community or culture helps the student staff to belong to the department or team. They learn to rely on their coworkers and are less likely to "let them down" by showing up late or missing shifts. They contribute ideas and find ways to improve processes and policies. Provide some social events for the students. This past year, the TCs participated in origami sumo wrestling, a visit to a pumpkin farm and corn maze, pub night (food only, they pay for drinks), and even movie trivia contest and jeopardy.

3.3 Communication

This is probably the most important part of creating workers who are engaged. Communicate! Find what works for your group, email, blog, bulletin boards, texting, meetings and then listen to their ideas. Communicate to them what is going on with the department and how their jobs and projects relate to the support of the campus and the strategic plan. Let them know that their service is valuable and appreciated.

3.4 Fun

Fun can be part of the job and still remain professional. When a worker enjoys their work, they are usually an engaged employee and contributes much to the success of the team and projects.

Fun doesn't have to be expensive, it can be pizza together, construction paper cutout awards, cheap toys to give away and cupcakes at the helpdesk for the day.

3.5 Rewards

It is important to reward your staff for a job well done. Some institutions are able to provide pay raises for their student staff; at Grinnell College, the wage is frozen, so rewards have to be creative. Favorite candy bars, golden diskettes, opportunities for learning new things and most important, a thank you.

Intrinsic rewards are important, telling someone they have done a great job or entrusting them to do an advanced task, are ways to provide some intrinsic value to their work. Teach them skills that they can utilize in their careers after college. Provide opportunities for them to gain experience for their resume'. There are many ways to provide rewards within a small budget…be creative!

4. Hiring the Right People

At Grinnell College, hiring occurs at the beginning of each of the two semesters. Our application is electronic, we collect applications for about 2 weeks, and then the student leadership team scores each application. At least 4 people must review an application, then the scores are tallied and averaged to find those applicants with the highest scores; they will be invited to interview.

We receive approximately 60-100 applications each semester for 10-12 positions. The number of trainees is related to the number of seniors who are graduating. So if we need 25 total to cover the attrition due to graduation, we might hire 12 in the fall and 13 in the spring. We only accept applications from first or second year students, as that gives us the best return on our training investment since the students go on to work for 2-3 years.

This year we are utilizing an online service called Active Interview [1], where the applicant fills out part of the application with text and then answers are also completed with video. Multiple reviewers score the online applications to determine those we will actually interview. Testing has gone well with this service, however at the time of the conference, more details can be reported on the success of this project. The idea was to have the application be a "mini interview" and weed out those who did not want to put in the effort to apply.

Those who score highest in the interview process are hired into the training program and need to complete that program successfully before working for IT.

5. Basic Training Program

There are two components to the semester-long training program. Each component must be completed satisfactorily and then a final Consultant Test is administered to each trainee. The test is a hands on evaluation based on skills learned during the semester.

5.1 Workshops

There are eight workshops, held on Saturday mornings that are 2 hours. The trainees are allowed to only miss 1 workshop during the semester. The workshops currently are: win7, Mac OS, networking & campus services, digital media training, booby trap lab, customer service/expectations, problem solving, and an intro-like session that introduces them to their mentors and our facilities.

5.2 Mentor Sessions

There are 8 weeks of mentored shifts. The trainee works on shift with a certified mentor on a variety of tasks contained in a weekly guide. Each trainee spends a shift in the helpdesk, AV center and digital media lab so that they get an overview of all of the areas. The Saturday workshops correlate with the mentor guide tasks for the week so that things learned at the workshop are reinforced that next week.

6. Evolution of the Student Program

We had a decent, fairly common program for student staff. It provided quality staff to serve in labs and other facilities. The problem, however, is that students and staff on campus today don't need the same type of support that they did ten years ago. We used to have to help students copy files to CD or access the network. Today's students are digital natives and are able to function well with technology. The question became "where will we best serve our campus community?"

Along with service to the campus, "what opportunities could we provide to the TCs which would give them experience as well as the skills to benefit ITS without letting them just sit in the public labs?"

7. Planning Team

The TC program has always had a leadership team, which is a group of 5 students in leadership roles: administrative, training, AV Center and Helpdesk coordinators. A few others were selected to be a part of the planning team so that we had representation from newer staff as well as experienced. We went off campus for a day with lots of food and our creative ideas to discuss and reorganize our services and program.

8. Superstars!

There are many components to the current student staffing model. We kept those things that were working like our student leadership team and training programs, and we developed some additional opportunities and resources to evaluate and either discard them for better ideas or add them to the program.

8.1 Student Leadership Team

There are 5 TC Coordinators, each with a distinct role, yet also part of the general leadership team. We meet weekly in the dining hall during the lunch hour for general updates, communication and planning. The Administrative Coordinator handles daily operational tasks, making sure students show up for their shifts and are following procedures and policies. The AV Center Coordinator helps the AV Center director with scheduling, training and general AV operations. The Helpdesk Coordinator's role is the same for the helpdesk staff. The Educational Coordinators organize and help facilitate new staff training, continuing education workshops and public education.

8.2 Part-Time Leadership Positions

There are several other leadership opportunities for TCs who want to have a leadership role, but don't have the time to commit to one of the coordinator positions.

8.2.1 *Volunteer Coordinator*

—works with the IT director in the local K-12 school system to provide TCs as volunteers to work setting up computers, imaging, updates and working with teachers on application issues.

8.2.2 *Social Coordinator*

—This is our "cruise director" who helps plan and facilitate social events throughout the academic year. This past year we had a trip to the pumpkin farm, bowling, corn maze, origami sumo wrestling tournament, picnic and golden disk award dinner.

8.2.3 *System Administrator*

—oversees the two servers that we manage: AV Webcheckout server and our TC Database which is our intranet for scheduling, time cards, training and hosts our wiki.

8.2.4 *Application Development Coordinator*

—leads the App development team as we are trying out writing some iOS and Android apps which will assist at the helpdesk and internally. Eventually this team may work with other campus departments in app creation.

8.2.5 *Wiki Administrator*

—coordinates wiki contributions and content

8.2.6 *TechMap Coordinator*

—creates and maintains the LabStats Techmap that is published to the campus

8.2.7 *Lab Services Coordinator*

—manages the group of TCs who provide maintenance to the public labs

8.2.8 *Planning team participation*

—open to anyone as needed for program planning.

8.3 Additional Certifications

We provide several other certifications that allow the students to do advanced work.

- Mathlan—linux certification
- Mentor—allows students to work as mentors with new hires
- Facilitator—when completed, students can help develop and facilitate trainings and workshops
- Digital Media Specialist—works in the digital media lab with faculty and student projects
- Hardware—allows helpdesk staff to work on more advanced, non-warranty hardware problems.

8.4 TC+ Achievement

Finding a way to reward students without much funding is a challenge. We found that many TCs really enjoyed learning and taking on new responsibilities, so the TC + (plus) Award was created. [2] This was developed utilizing a group of TCs who aided in the planning. The purpose is to keep records of all learning and service opportunities while employed in the TC program and then senior year, presenting the TC with a leather-like portfolio containing all of their certifications and service. This is something that hopefully can be used for job interviews or as other records of their experience as a TC for Grinnell College.

Points (or in our case megabytes) are earned for participation and then accumulated for the TC + Achievement. The points differ based on semesters of service, so that someone hired in their first year doesn't have advantage over someone that was hired in their second year or went abroad for a semester. The details of the award are published on the TC bulletin board listed in References.

8.4.1 *Requirements*

- Must have Helpdesk or AV Certification
- Participation/Certification in 5 other areas from the following: mentor, mathlan, facilitator, digital media specialist, planning team, assistive technology assistant, wiki postings, a part-time leadership role, Women in Technology, Beanie team or App development.
- Community Service—part of the philosophy at Grinnell College is one of service and assisting the local K-12 schools with their technology needs is a way that we are able to contribute skills in knowledge to our community. The local K-12 schools has very little technology budget and only one person to handle their IT.

8.4.2 *The "Really Cool Faux Leather" Portfolio*

All of the certifications, workshops attended, workshops facilitated, times served as a mentor and participation in various areas are recorded and certificates created for the portfolio.

9. BENEFITS FOR ITS AND CAMPUS

We pulled the TCs from sitting in the public labs, where they were not very productive to areas that they could provide better service to the campus and ITS. Several new services have been created.

9.1 Helpdesk Services

The helpdesk is staffed in a way that allows the helpdesk students to go out on campus as needed to assist technology users. In the past, a TC sat in a public lab and helped those who came to them for questions. Helpdesk staff will now go anywhere that they are needed. If a student is in a physics lab and needs computer help, they call or text the helpdesk and someone will assist.

9.2 Mobile Support

We provide connections through Meebo chat [3] and texting, so if someone has a question or problem, they can use the Meebo client [4] on their smartphone, connect to the Meebo client online or text the helpdesk for assistance. We have to communicate the way that the digital natives communicate!

9.3 Lab Services

TCs are scheduled to provide semi-weekly maintenance to every public computer on campus. They check out computers, connections, peripherals, clean keyboards/screens, replace hardware as needed and even reimage systems. This assures us that problems are reported efficiently and systems are not "down" for extended periods. In the past, a computer might sit a week or two, broken, because students wouldn't report the problem to ITS. This step in preventative maintenance has reduced the number of broken things that the ITS staff need to fix and has reduced their work load as they can give general maintenance tasks to the lab services group. This group is also responsible for the IT posters in the labs and any necessary signage for equipment or services in the lab spaces.

9.4 Dorm Outreach

One of the needs identified by the planning team was that these digital natives, who are savvy about many aspects of computers and smartphones, still need help in a few areas. One of these needs is that they don't know how their computer works. They know how to get on Facebook and upload their photos, but they are less educated about viruses, malware, file organization, data.

Second, faculty assumes that students know how to use various "common" applications such as Microsoft Word and Excel. They need to know some basics, like how to set up a paper in Word or how to do a basic function for statistics class in Excel.

We have provided a service called Dorm Outreach. We have a 45 minute session every week in a different dorm lounge. Each session has a 15 minute presentation, then the rest is hands on or discussion. Some of the titles include "My computer runs too slow…", "I just need to type my paper in Word…", "Did I catch a virus?"

These are quick, task/project focused sessions, highly advertised, were students can come over for cookies and help with their computer.

9.5 Women in Technology

This year we teamed up with the CS department and created a "Women in Technology" group. The purpose of this group, which is for men as well as women, is to bring awareness to the low number of women seeking education and careers in a technology field as well as provide some education to the young women in our community. There are hundreds of jobs within the category "technology" as most often others think you need to be a programmer to work in a technology field. We are hoping to bring a speaker to campus, have an awareness event and do something with the younger girls in our community.

9.6 Assistive Technology Assistants

Another service that has evolved from the TC program is to provide assistance to the AT Coordinator and assist students using technology for accommodation. Follow-up with students who were given technology accommodations was difficult as the AT Coordinator has many other jobs. By hiring and training two students to assist with Kurzweil software, speech-to-text software and other tools, we provide better support and follow-up for those with learning and physical challenges.

10. YOU, TOO, CAN CREATE SUPERSTARS!

It is your job, as a manager, to provide the resources necessary to make your team superstars! Step out of "its always been done that way" to "let's try it out!" Sometimes things won't work, when we first started mobile support, the student on the cell phone just sat most of the time, so we had to advertise and market this service to our campus, especially the new students. It takes four years to change the culture, so the new students will find this type of support as a regular connection and utilize the service.

The TC program has existed at Grinnell College for 12 years and has evolved in many ways, but we were still stuck in the model of having students babysit labs. Once we realized that was not the best use of our resources, we evolved again, this time in many creative ways. The one mistake, we did too many changes at one time, it caused some bumps. One day, we had 7 people staffing the same space and doing nothing. However, this is how we learn and change direction in order to find our own superstars!

11. REFERENCES

[1] http://activeinterview.com/

[2] https://sites.google.com/site/grinnelltc/faq

[3] http://helpdesk.grinnell.edu/

[4] http://www.meebo.com/

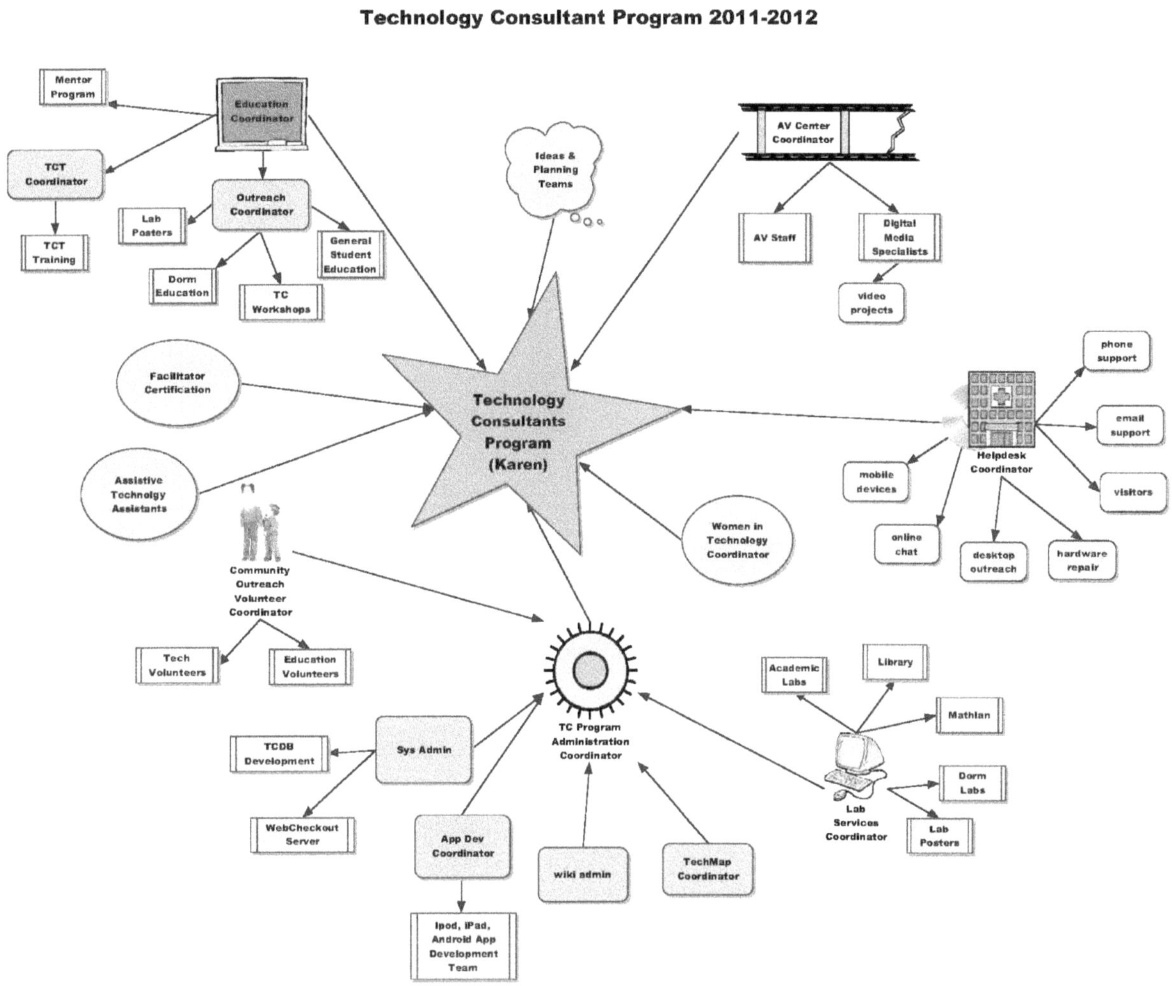

Table 1. 2011-2012 Technology Consultant Model

The Mission: Delivering Technology Information To Those Who Need It Most

Jace Laakso
University of Montana
32 Campus Drive
Missoula, MT 59812
406-728-2251
jace.laakso@umontana.edu

ABSTRACT
Administrative associates are often the hardest working people on campus. They're at the front lines and in the trenches answering difficult questions from faculty and students. If they want to learn about new technologies, they're often limited by their abilities, their schedules and their work environment. This disconnect can hinder IT's ability to function efficiently.

To address this need, Client Support Services at the University of Montana created a user group. Technology Associates Group, (TAG) meets once per semester to talk about upcoming changes in campus technology and systems, tools to help them use their office technology more efficiently, and new applications available for their department's students and faculty. We frequently have guest speakers such as the University President and the Registrar who are eager to meet staff they wouldn't normally encounter. They give insights into their technology use and/or what upcoming changes might impact TAG members.

At UM, approximately 200 staff are classified as administrative associates. They've enthusiastically embraced this group. At our first meeting, we expected just a few would attend. When over 40 registered we had to schedule a larger room and meetings have averaged that number ever since. Each meeting is held in a different campus building giving them a look at rooms and technology they often don't have the opportunity to experience. They also meet and interact with their colleagues and we serve refreshments setting a welcoming and comfortable atmosphere.
We have also created a TAG website for those who can't attend the meetings so they can view Camtasia recordings and minutes of the meetings.

It has been an overwhelming success. As one TAG member said in a recent survey: "I love these opportunities to interact with you face to face and build those relationships."

Finally, a tech-savy staff helps IT perform more efficiently.

Categories and Subject Descriptors
K.6.1 **[Project and People Management]**: *Training, Staffing*

General Terms
Management, Documentation, Performance, Human Factors, Standardization.

Keywords
Information, customer service, staff involvement.

1. INTRODUCTION
The University of Montana, located in Missoula, Montana has about 1300 staff, approximately 200 of whom interact on a daily basis with students, faculty and other staff. They are often at the "front lines" of service to the campus community. They are asked questions about technology or email or passwords. This often results in frequent calls to IT Central, our centralized computer help desk. To address the need for disseminating technology information to them, Client Support Services (CSS) created TAG in 2010. This user group is open to all administrative associates and meets once every semester.

TAG has its roots in an earlier effort to answer questions about classroom technology. In particular, the audio visual department, Instructional Materials Services, underwent a major transformation. Up until then it had been a part of the Mansfield Library. In 2002, the library decided to separate the media from the technology used to present it. This new department was renamed Presentation Technology Services. It became part of Information Technology and was no longer associated with the library. This change led to confusion for many and the questions arose: "What the heck is PTS?" In January 2005, two staff members began visiting departments to discuss presentation technology services available for their faculty and students. Later that year, a mailing list was created by looking in the campus telephone directory for likely staff members. The response to our efforts was positive. The mailing list continued to grow and by 2006, it became apparent this was a population that needed more information about other technologies impacting their jobs.

Additionally, in 1998, Central IT organized Technology Partners to address the need to communicate and get feedback from IT support staff in various departments. One major objective of Tech Partners was to provide useful information to their departments. Unfortunately, although Technology Partners continues to meet once per quarter, that information doesn't always reach their constituents in a timely manner.

In the spring of 2009 several focus groups were held to assess the critical technology needs of new staff and faculty. The result was the creation of a short Technology Orientation for new employees. After about 4 of these sessions, we realized it wasn't just new employees who were attending. Long time employees also wanted technology information or information about who to call for help.

For instance while some departments have their own IT support, most campus email service is handled by Central IT. Others felt that they were not included when information about network outages or exchange maintenance that could have affected them was sent out to the Tech Partners listserv. We discovered that quite often a lot of useful information was disseminated via the unreliable trickle down method. Some good information but some inaccurate information got passed along this way. We needed to deliver technology information in a better, more effective and consistent manner to administrative staff.

2. THE PROCESS

Beginning in early 2010 at the behest of the Associate CIO for IT, several meetings of IT staff were held. The consensus was that it was time to conduct a pilot project specifically directed at this unserved population to see if providing information to this group would help IT be a better organization. Would we see fewer service calls at the help desk? Would IT be able to do a better job if input was gathered from those who were farther away from the IT decision making processes? This pilot project would be a user group. For the first meeting in June, 2010 we invited as many administrative associates as could attend to a meeting where we would present information to help them with the many issues they faced each day. We initially called it AATUG for Administrative Associates Technology Users Group. We used the distribution list for an invitation and over 40 of the potential 200 administrative associates responded, more than we expected. We invited several IT folks to talk about new technologies and services such as Camtasia Relay, our new Academic Planner for students and recent upgrades and additions to our technology classrooms. We held the meeting from 3:00 to 4:30 PM, hoping it would be a good time for them to get away from their offices for an afternoon break with coffee, tea and cookies. Each meeting since has been held in a newly built campus building with a tour of the facilities including its new technology. Campus administrators such as the President and the Registrar are eager to present at future meetings.

3. THE NEXT STEP

We created a web site that provides information about upcoming meetings, minutes of previous meetings and links to helpful documents presented. We polled members for a new name that would be easier to pronounce and offered a prize to the winning entry. Response was quick and enthusiastic. Members voted for TAG.. This enthusiastic and quick response has been typical of all notices to the listserv, indicating that this new user group has been well received and filled a need for an unserved population.

4. SURVEY RESULTS

Surveys conducted after TAG meetings in March and June 2011 indicated that this program is a resounding success. When asked about the effectiveness in providing technology information, 100 % felt we were Very Effective (55%) or Effective (45%). On usefulness of information provided, 55% said it was Very Useful and 45% Useful. No one responded that these meetings were not effective or not useful. Further comments on what they liked least about the meetings: 75% had no comment; two had complaints about some presenters' inability to easily use the tech classroom equipment to illustrate their presentations; two complained about the room temperature.

When asked what they liked best it wasn't as easy to quantify:

The presenters are informal and don't talk over one's head (like some IT folks). You are presenting quite a bit of info that I have not been aware of: 'The SkyDrive' for example.

It's nice to have the meetings in different settings. I had never been in the new Education addition - so the tour afterwards was really awesome.

The presenters are very helpful and the question/answer is facilitated quite well! The new wing of the building Tour was very enlightening, and it would be a great thing if we could do that in some of the other buildings.

It is mind expanding.

I also appreciate that IT is taking the time to give updates to the administrative assistants so we can pass the info on to our departments. Another positive thing about the meetings is that they are fast-paced so each presenter holds my attention.

And the one that best sums up the general feeling of those in attendance: *I've had very good experiences working with IT folks, but we don't often see you. I love these opportunities to interact with you face to face and build those relationships. I also benefit from the interactions with the other TAG attendees. It's very beneficial in knowing how best to direct students and others on campus.*

5. TAG BENEFITS

There is often a disconnect between well-meaning IT folks who want to introduce a new email client or make a change that would be "better" for everyone. Those well-meaning ideas may not always be perceived as positive for those who end up having to make changes in their daily routines. The more information non IT staff members have about technology, the better they are able to answer questions from their students, faculty and colleagues. The more questions they can answer, the less time IT has to spend on minor issues.

In a sense, TAG members become partners with IT and this partnership has major benefits for both TAG and IT. We send notifications to TAG about system maintenance and upcoming changes to systems, helping them understand what IT does. In turn, TAG becomes more understanding of the complexities of the vast number of variables facing IT on a regular basis.

Since we began holding TAG meetings, recorded work orders at IT Central help desk have decreased by 20% (1028) from the previous year. While there isn't hard data to support the conclusion that TAG resulted in this decrease, it can be seen as a positive indicator of its success.

Moreover, the opportunity for TAG members to meet and talk to IT folks is valuable. It helps bridge the gap between the "Techies" who run the systems and those who actually use the systems. IT learns from TAG what technology information they might need and gains important insight into how IT is performing. In addition, TAG members have enthusiastically embraced the concept of being heard about their concerns and meeting with each other and sharing their thoughts with each other and with IT.

6. THE FUTURE

We continue to hold meetings and ask for TAG members' input not only for future meetings but also for issues by which they are affected. We will have a table for TAG at the second annual Technology Fair being held on campus in September. The TAG website will feature a photo of a TAG member each month with a short bio. We're calling it "TAG, You're It!" Finally, since TAG is all about administrative associates, we are asking them to participate in the process by having them join an advisory group to help guide the future.

A Comparison of the Usage and Experience of a File Sharing System with Different Operation Policies

Naomi Fujimura
Kyushu University
4-9-1, Shiobaru, Minami-ku,
Fukuoka Japan
+81 92 553 4434
fujimura.naomi.274@m.kyushu-u.ac.jp

Zen'ichi Hirayama
Kyushu University
4-9-1, Shiobaru, Minami-ku
Fukuoka Japan
+81 92 553 4588
hirayama@design.kyushu-u.ac.jpl

ABSTRACT

There are many kinds of file sharing systems used for various purposes in the world. At our University, we use a commercial product called Proself as our file sharing system. Proself has been set up under two different operation policies in our university. One is to provide an alternative to the practice of attaching files to e-mail messages in the e-mail system for our whole university. The other is to promote file sharing between specific groups such as laboratories, departments, and so on in one small campus. We have been operating two separate systems for about one year, and analyzed the usage to understand the differences between how these file-sharing systems are used.

We found that there are similar and different characteristics of usage in the two file sharing systems. The ratios of users against the potential users, the months actively used, file types uploaded and downloaded, and login time pattern over the course of a week are different between two systems. The login time pattern for a day is similar between two systems. JPG and PDF files are frequently transferred in the systems, but the order is different. Our analysis illustrates the difference of practical usage and gives us useful information to operate them in the future.

Categories and Subject Descriptors

H3.5 [**Information Systems**]: Information Storage and Retrieval – *On-line Information Services*

General Terms

Management, Measurement, Design, Economics, Reliability, Security, Human Factors

Keywords

File sharing, File usage, E-mail, Attached file, Analysis

1. INTRODUCTION

There are many kinds of file sharing systems used to exchange and share files at universities. There are commercial and free systems, on-line and off-line systems, and so on [1][2][3]. Common examples include:

- Google Docs that allows many users to access a file simultaneously.
- File server that allows a user to provide other users with the access permission to files.
- File exchange system for uploading and downloading files among users.

We think there were the requests to store and share documents such as dissertations, papers for SIGs and societies, presentation files, and papers to read in the laboratory. Our division uses groupware called Teamware [4] to share files among staff members and teachers. However, it is not used well because only staff members except teachers can upload document files into the system. Teachers can only download them by their necessity via Teamware.

Exchanging files by attaching them to e-mails is popular. Users often attach a huge file and/or numerous smaller files. Exchanging files this way creates problems when manipulating e-mauls and increases load on the mail server. In fact, this causes many servers to limit the size of e-mail.. Another issue is that users may feel anxious in sending secret or important files via e-mail.

To solve these two problems, we introduced the file sharing system called Proself that is a commercial product [5] under two different operating policies in our University. One is to minimize the number and size of attached files in the e-mail system for the entire University. The other system is used to promote file sharing in arbitrary groups such as laboratories, departments, and so on in our Ohashi campus. It was a independent university called Kyushu Institute of Design, and integrated into Kyushu University in Oct. 2003. We have still independent activities in Ohashi campus.

We have been operating these systems for approximately a year and analyzed the usage to see the differences in how these file-sharing systems are used.

2. File Sharing in Ohashi Campus

The Information Management Office uses the file sharing system Proself to share files in laboratories and minimize the exchange of files via e-mail in the Ohashi campus.

2.1 Number of Users

Table 1 shows the number of logins and the number of individuals in every month. The number of potential users is about one hundred including teachers and some staff members. The number of individuals is increasing gradually in Table **1**. About a fourth of the potential one hundred users have used the system recently. The peak of usage is January and February when teachers and students exchange their master and doctorate dissertations.

Table 2 shows the number of logins by the day of the week. Users access the system consistently during weekdays. While there is a decrease, users continue to use the system on Saturday and Sunday. Figure 1 shows the number of logins by hour. Most users access the system during working hours (8AM - 5PM), however users continue to use the system into the late evening and early morning typically.

Table 1. The number of logins and individuals Ohashi campus

Month	Apr.	May	June	July	Aug.	Sep.	Oct.	Nov.	Dec.	Jan.	Feb.	Mar.
Logins	133	99	72	64	102	67	106	77	88	198	152	102
Individuals	16	18	22	23	24	24	25	25	26	26	26	26

Table 2. Logins by the day of the week Ohashi campus

Day	Mon	Tue	Wed	Thu	Fri	Sat	Sun
Login	224	236	219	193	258	69	61

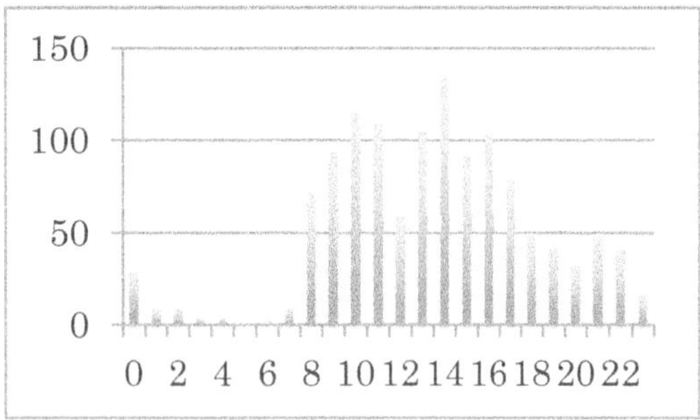

Figure 1. Logins by hour – Ohashi campus

2.2 Upload

Table 3 summarizes the number and size of files uploaded by month. October and August saw the most file uploads with significantly, and fewer files uploaded in September. We guess that some heavy users affect the statistics. The largest file, 1.3 GB, was uploaded in May. The average size of files varies between about 1 and 9 MB in Ohashi campus.

Table 3. Number and Size of Files Uploaded – Ohashi campus

Month	No. of Files	Sum (KB)	Max (KB)	Min (KB)	Ave (KB)
Apr.	490	1,830,513	298,831	12	3,736
May	599	5,508,369	1,313,239	18	9,196
June	627	1,711,873	204,360	2,590	2,730
July	475	1,724,975	157,106	996	3,632
Aug.	1,073	5,709,404	881,803	43	5,321
Sep.	358	1,656,541	391,252	0	4,627
Oct.	2,199	2,204,375	280,022	141	1,002
Nov.	969	3,424,561	490,007	3,402	3,534
Dec.	505	1,467,947	182,629	0	2,907
Jan.	662	4,319,708	688,419	0	6,525
Feb.	356	2,017,638	560,557	52	5,668
Mar.	402	2,083,379	193,473	8	5,183

Table 4. Download status of files in Ohashi campus

Month	No. of Files	Sum (KB)	Max (KB)	Min (KB)	Ave (KB)
Apr.	475	2,431,069	298,831	12	5,118
May	1,423	8,043,697	1,313,239	2,715	5,653
June	1,858	15,630,636	204,360	2,590	8,413
July	1,805	16,406,739	96,315	2,681	9,090
Aug.	1,715	8,174,075	881,803	43	4,766
Sep.	445	2,719,876	391,252	0	6,112
Oct.	3,444	7,903,958	158,684	141	2,295
Nov.	2,031	4,763,793	490,007	3,402	2,346
Dec.	1,329	4,092,955	182,629	8,168	3,080
Jan.	1,031	13,440,716	688,419	0	13,037
Feb.	1,297	4,006,850	561,104	52	3,089
Mar.	2,888	7,948,779	193,473	0	2,752

2.3 Download

Table 4 summarizes the number and size of files downloaded by month. We see the same pattern of the system used heavily in October and less in September. The largest file, 1.3 GB, is downloaded in May, the same month it was uploaded. File download numbers are higher than the upload numbers. This means that individual files are shared with multiple users.

2.4 Types of Files Shared

We analyzed the file types uploaded. Table 5 shows the top ten types of uploaded files. Table 6 shows the top ten file types by file size. Table 7 shows the top ten file types by average file size. JPG and WAV are the top two file types in Table 5. This means that many users exchange photos and voice recording from meetings and conferences. JWW files are used by free CAD software used by our Faculty of Design. Zip is the top file type in Table 6. This means some users combine many files into a single zip file.

Table 5. Top 10 File Types Uploaded Ohashi campus

Kind	No	Sum (KB)	Ave (KB)
jpg	3,022	5,054,903	1,673
wav	2,669	678,997	254
pdf	722	1,457,368	2,019
jww	605	35,121	58
doc(x)	514	1,201,065	2,337
zip	244	16,316,872	66,872
xls(x)	144	47,959	333
html	138	1,492	11
ppt	86	503,064	5,850
txt	85	539	6

Table 6. Top 10 File Types by Size Ohashi campus

Kind	No	Sum (KB)	Ave (KB)
zip	244	16,316,872	66,872
jpg	3,022	5,054,903	1,673
rar	9	3,872,460	430,273
wma	41	1,462,378	35,668
pdf	722	1,457,368	2,019
mp3	82	1,333,442	16,261
doc(x)	514	1,201,065	2,337
wav	2,669	678,997	254
al	48	515,028	10,730
ppt	86	503,064	5,850

Table 7. Top 10 File Types by Average Size Ohashi campus

Kind	No	Sum (KB)	Ave (KB)
rar	9	3,872,460	430,273
zip	244	16,316,872	66,872
wma	41	1,462,378	35,668
mp3	82	1,333,442	16,261
al	48	515,028	10,730
lzh	2	15,272	7,636
ppt	86	503,064	5,850
shd	34	114,121	3,357
doc(x)	514	1,201,065	2,337
tif	8	18,304	2,288

Table 8. The number of logins and individuals University

Month	May	June	July	Aug.	Sep.	Oct.	Nov.	Dec.	Jan.	Feb.	Mar.
Logins	164	136	144	1233	950	970	1066	970	1120	1132	1256
Individuals	15	20	38	401	510	594	672	718	771	811	847

RAR is the file type with the largest average size in Table 7. The average file size (430MB) of RAR files is larger than the average size (67MB) of ZIP files. This is likely because some users prefer the RAR file type for huge files since this file type is known for high performance when compressing file size.

3. FILE SHARING IN THE UNIVERSITY

Information Infrastructure Initiative has provided all staff members with primary e-mail service since July 2009 in Kyushu University [6] [7]. The file size for e-mail is limited to 300MB in total and 10MB for each e-mail. Therefore, we deployed the file sharing system Proself to provide an alternative to the practice of attaching files to e-mail messages in May 2010. Initially, the University Proself system had a file limit of 1 GB and a time limit of two weeks. The time limit was later extended to four weeks. After sufficient testing, we announced the system ready for general use in 4th August 2010.

3.1 Number of Users

Table 8 shows the number of logins and individuals using the University system by month. The number of potential users is about eight thousands including teachers and staff members. The number of individuals is increasing gradually. About 16% of potential users are now using the system. The number of logins has been consistent after we announced the service in August 4th.

Table 9 shows the number of logins by day of the week. Users access the system almost constantly on weekdays. While there is a decrease, users continue to use the system on Saturday and Sunday as in Ohashi campus. Figure 2 shows the number of logins by hour of the day. We see the same usage pattern as with the Ohashi campus system with heavy use during working hours and continued use into the late evening and early morning hours.

Table 9 Logins in the day of week University

Day	Mon	Tue	Wed	Thu	Fri	Sat	Sun
Logins	1582	1639	1779	1889	1579	351	322

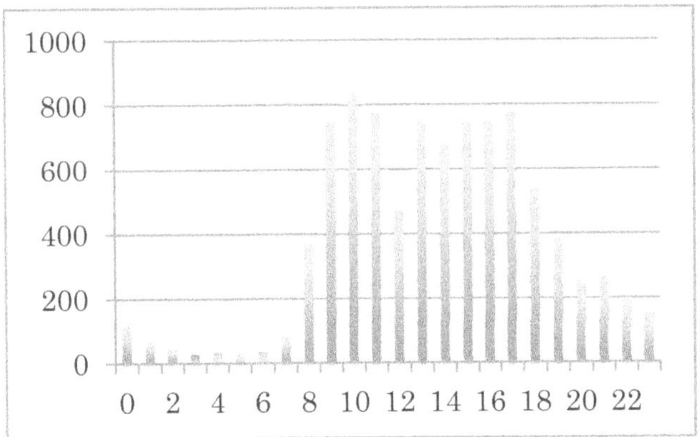

Figure 2 . Login in the hours in a day University

3.2 Upload

Table 10 summarizes the number and size of files uploaded by month. Users started to upload files after 4th August 2011. The system has seen steady use with the maximum size of a file increasing.

The average size of files varies between about 2 and 7 MB. It seems almost same to in Ohashi campus except May.

Table 10. Number and Size of Files Uploaded University

Month	Files	Sum (KB)	Max (KB)	Min (KB)	Ave (KB)
May	33	62,343	25,834	105	1,889
June	95	338,283	281,396	245	3,561
July	233	608,380	160,858	400	2,611
Aug.	6,144	17,360,399	589,761	0	2,826
Sep.	7,007	21,432,879	637,377	0	3,059
Oct.	6,129	21,945,076	847,327	0	3,581
Nov.	6,260	43,354,439	870,493	0	6,926
Dec.	7,235	29,351,922	969,295	4	4,057
Jan.	9,896	31,828,070	859,656	0	3,216
Feb.	8,265	35,559,731	940,026	0	4,302
Mar.	9,820	49,983,078	848,424	0	5,090

3.3 Download

Table 11 summarizes the number and size of files downloaded by month. Once the system was announced in August, users downloaded the most in March and the least in September and October. The maximum size of a file is gradually becoming larger. The number of downloaded files is several times larger than those downloaded in Ohashi campus. It comes from the difference between users in Ohashi and University.

Table 11. Number and Size of Files Downloaded University

Month	Files	Sum (KB)	Max (KB)	Min (KB)	AVE (KB)
May	102	157,887	25,834	105	1,548
June	361	767,486	281,396	245	2,126
July	606	948,621	160,858	400	1,565
Aug.	10,063	24,584,443	589,761	0	2,443
Sep.	6,679	51,305,263	637,377	0	7,682
Oct.	7,815	46,639,041	847,327	0	5,968
Nov.	11,589	67,715,452	870,493	0	5,843
Dec.	15,891	73,769,041	969,295	9	4,642
Jan.	19,098	63,672,524	859,656	6	3,334
Feb.	14,824	63,185,203	848,886	0	4,262
Mar.	29,256	133,926,92	848,424	0	4,578

3.4 Types of Files Shared

Table **12** shows the top ten file types of uploaded to the University system. Table 13shows the top ten file types by size. Table 14 shows the top ten file types by average file size. JPG is the top file type in Table **12**. This means that many users exchange photos frequently. The second and third most popular types are PDF and DOC. This means that many PDF and Word documents are exchanged via the system. While the number of PowerPoint files is not very high, (1,195), the average file size of these files (8.6 MB) is larger than those of other Office files types (DOC, XLS). We see this again with MP3 files in Table 14. The two files shared have the largest average size (154 MB).

Table 12. Top 10 File Types Uploaded University

Kind	No	Sum (KB)	Ave (KB)
jpg	16,229	30,965,250	1,908
pdf	9,051	27,285,271	3,015
doc	5,234	5,545,905	1,060
img	5,083	2,724,432	536
xls(x)	4,415	2,418,069	548
bmp	2,027	1,219,613	602
eps	1,238	2,065,977	1,669
ppt (x)	1,195	10,294,312	8,614
gif	936	3,378	4
Zip	921936	54,057,151	58,694

Table 13. Top 10 File Types by Size University

Kind	No	Sum (KB)	Ave (KB)
zip	921	60.765,238	65,977
jpg	16,229	30,965,250	1,908
pdf	9,051	27,285,271	3,015
ppt (x)	1,195	10,294,312	8,614
zip	142	6,708,087	47,240
doc	5,234	5,545,905	1,060
img	5,083	2,724,432	536
xls(x)	4,415	2,418,069	548
tif	794	2,225,120	2,802
eps	1,238	2,065,977	1,669

Table 14. Top 10 File Types by Average File Size University

Kind	No	Sum (KB)	Ave (KB)
mp3	2	308,262	154,131
Zip	921	60,765,238	65,977
ppt (x)	1,195	10,294,312	8,614
Wma	244	1,424,012	5,836
Gz	3	16,768	5,589
Dat	121	459,755	3,800
Afi	116	420,506	3,625
Pdf	9,051	27,285,271	3,015
Tif	794	2,225,120	2,802
Jpg	16,229	30,965,250	1,908

4. ANALYSIS

The system for Ohashi campus has the following characteristics.

- About a fourth of potential users are using the system.
- Users use the system more on Friday.
- Users use the system around the clock.
- The system was most heavily used in August and October.
- JPG and WAV are the most popular file types.

The system for the University has the following characteristics.

- About a sixth of potential users use the system. This is slightly less than usage at the Ohashi campus.
- Users use the system more on Thursday.
- Users use the system around the clock, similar to Ohashi.
- Users used the system more in November.
- JPG and PDF are the most popular file types.

The ratio of actual users against potential users is slightly different between in Ohashi campus and the whole university. The reason may be that we talked to many teachers and staff members at the Ohashi campus about how the system may be useful for them on a small campus.

Staff members work in the daytime, but teachers often work at all hours. As a result, the number of users accessing the systems never becomes zero, even late at night, early in the morning, and on Saturday and Sunday. PDF and DOC file types are shared frequently in Ohashi campus and University. We guess that documents for meetings are shared among users in both systems.

5. CONCLUSION

We are operating two Proself file sharing systems with different purposes and policies. The purpose of the Ohashi campus system is to share files in laboratories and provide an alternative to the practice of attaching files to e-mail messages. This system has a file size limit of 2 GB and no time limit. The University system has the single goal of minimizing the use of e-mail attachments to exchange files. It has a 1 GB size limit and four week time limit.

We found both similar and different characteristics of usage in two systems. The ratios of actual users against potential users, the months actively used, file types uploaded and downloaded, and weekly login patterns differ. The daily login pattern is similar. JPG and PDF files are frequently shared in both systems, but the order is different. These findings show the difference of practical usage and give us useful information to operate them in the future.

We have found that disk storage is not heavily used. So far, the ratio of disk storage usage is under ten percent of capacity. We expanded the service to all students in June 2011. We are planning to extend the file storage time limit. We may also consider charging users interested in more disk space and increased time limits.

Finally, it is useful for users who exchange files with companies for their research to use a file sharing system that is operated by the University. They are pleased with the system because they could not exchange large files in e-mail and used some free file sharing systems such as Lively Networking [1] before.

6. REFERENCES

[1] Lively Networking : http://www.lnet.co.jp/promotion/web/storage/

[2] Data deliver/Security deliver : http://www.datadeliver.net/

[3] The comparison of facilities in Free On-line storage : http://www.maciseurope.org/

[4] Teamware: http://software.fujitsu.com/jp/teamware/

[5] Proself : http://www.proself.jp/

[6] Kyushu University Primary Mail Service : http://www.m.kyushu-u.ac.jp/

[7] Naomi Fujimura, Keisuke Masuoka, and Yoshinori Masaki, Experience with Individual Receipt Confirmation System and the University Primary Mail Service, Proc. of SIGUCCS 2010 (Technical Session), pp.65 - 70, Oct. 2010

The Cultivation of a Help Desk Dashboard

Shereese Thomas
Help Desk Analyst
5221 Gullen Mall
799 Student Center Bldg
313-577-4198
Ae7694@wayne.edu

Adam Perkins
Help Desk Technician
522 Gullen Mall
799 Student Center Bldg
313-577-4778
Ck7939@wayne.edu

ABSTRACT

Wayne State University Computing and Information Technology (C&IT) Help Desk implemented a relevant, user-friendly, organized, inclusive, and aesthetically-pleasing centralized resource, the C&IT Help Desk Dashboard to connect our first-tier, student support staff to frequently accessed knowledge. This increased efficiency by decreasing incident escalations, talk time, and second-tier interruptions.

In developing the Dashboard (after its initial stint on a Blackboard course site), a Lead Help Desk Technician (HDT) was tasked with creating a simple HTML document containing links to various C&IT resources. The Dashboard's logic was written with PHP, or PHP: Hypertext Pre-processor, used in collaboration with a MySQL database. Using a WordPress back end, the Dashboard pulls posts from its database and publishes them on its front page. It includes an announcement system for timely communication of problems and important news to student staff. These technologies drove implementation of the timesheet notification system, login system, and our customer service survey results tool, allowing flexible access to data through user-specific variables.

In a short period of time, the C&IT Help Desk implemented a free, flexible, custom tool to help student assistants' access knowledge quickly to help customers. What began as a functional dashboard, including the ability to post announcements and search all of Wayne State's institutional documentation from a central location, evolved into a relatively complex web application using modern web technologies to streamline customer interactions. This increase in knowledge accessibility and integration decreased first-tier stress, increased organizational confidence and provided tangible benefits for customers and support personnel alike.

Categories and Subject Descriptors

K.6.1 [**Project and People Management**]: Training.

General Terms

Management, Documentation, Design, Human Factors

Keywords: PHP, WordPress, MySQL

1. INTRODUCTION

The Wayne State University's, Computing and Information Technology (C&IT Division) Customer Services Department is the face of IT for the university faculty, staff, and students. The IT Help Desk has historically operated on a limited budget. With a talented pool of staff and a limited budget, it comes to no surprise that this unit leverages off the shelf packages and rapidly developed middleware to create innovative, effective tools. These tools enable the student employees to meet and exceed the mission and strategic goals of the IT division.

In the previous paper on our Help Dashboard written by Ms. Thomas[1], an analysis was performed for the goals, learners, content and performance of the C&IT Help Desk. The results of this analysis assisted in the development and design of the original Dashboard in 2009 which was delivered by the learning content management system of the university, Blackboard. The justification was the fact that student technicians were currently using the resource for academic purposes.

The purpose of the Dashboard was not to instruct on call tracking or to assist with reporting statistics. The resource was designed solely for training on the resolution and escalation of WSU systems problems and issues. The documentation process is the primary function of Help Desk Technician and is necessary to keep a record of IT concerns for C&IT personnel and other technical support partners throughout campus. While the workflow of instructional design is the responsibility of the Help Desk Supervisor and Analyst, the success of the documentation process requires the Technicians to access the content quickly. The processes below were developed by using the principles of the instructional systems design model (ISD model) described in the evaluation references of this article.

2. PROBLEM STATEMENT

In order to provide solutions for Help Desk customers quickly and efficiently, the Help Desk Technicians needed to have a resource allowing access to troubleshooters and service catalogs; however it was apparent the resolutions and escalation instructions needed to be better communicated, organized and archived for systems troubleshooting as well as cases of system emergencies, updates and maintenance. The Help Desk full-time staff designed and developed a training "Dashboard" for accessing this information simultaneously. The team selected a non-term specific course in Blackboard for use as a dashboard. Such a course allowed for easy updating and addition of contents. The objective of the C&IT Help Desk Dashboard is to increase the number of issues resolved on first contact for WSU C&IT Help Desk customers by identifying the appropriate steps for resolving issues consistently and efficiently. Unfortunately, the delivery of the Dashboard using Blackboard caused several issues:

- Student technicians were not able to set the direct link to the Dashboard as their browser's home page.
- Help Desk staff did not have the ability to manage and maintain the local resource.

SIGUCCS'11, November 12–17, 2011, San Diego, CA, USA.

- Better customization and management of announcements was needed for archiving and referencing.
- Customization of searches for knowledgebase and other troubleshooting resources was necessary for quick access.
- Ability to customize the structure of the page and to manage web resources was requested by Help Desk Technicians.
- Use of the Dashboard for monitoring survey results for each student technician was useful for monitoring performance.
- Ability to customize security options, login and permissions in house was not an option in Blackboard.
- Creating a scheduling modification tool for Help Desk Technicians in order to eliminate traffic on the Help Desk email list.

3. APPROACH

3.1 Functional Assessment

The full time staff of the Help Desk, consisting of the Supervisor and Analysts conducted the initial evaluation of the Old Dashboard (figure1) while monitoring questions asked for day-to-day student technician support. The full-time staff expected to be working with tier 2 escalations and documentation but found themselves continually interrupted by student technicians on problems clearly documented on the C&IT Dashboard course on Blackboard as well as various WSU websites. The full-time staffs begin to look closely at the Help Desk Institute (HDI) surveys as well as call and wait times to analyze the performance of all technicians. It became apparent that the Dashboard's content and delivery needed to be independent of Blackboard. In February 2010 there were obvious deficiencies in training for the technicians' increased responsibilities. The HDI surveys indicated the knowledge of student technicians on supported services had fallen about 2 tenths from the previous year (Figure 4) as well as the quality in service averages measured in C&IT Help Desk customer responses (Figure 3). The experiences of Blackboard outages during the busiest time of the year caused the popularity of the Dashboard to lose momentum.

During the course of the Dashboard implementation, the Help Desk leadership set a goal to enable student technicians to operate independently because of expansion of duties and hours of operation where full-time staff would be unavailable. Consistent and reliable support was necessary for the Help Desk to provide university constituents with assistance during expanded hours including evenings and weekends. It was also necessary to integrate student technician training, development and changes in schedules into the new student technician management structure.

As a result, lead technicians were designated for each shift in order to compensate for the absence of the full-time staff during meetings, vacations and expanded hours. Soon after the leads were appointed, the lead student technician co-authoring this paper volunteered to assist in the creation of a Dashboard page and design the back end for a new stand alone web resource. This was necessary to facilitate the independence of the student staff. Without the lead technicians, it may have become necessary to add a second shift for a full time staff person. The contents of the previous version of the Dashboard were then migrated to a resource independent of C&IT supported systems with a new look and feel on a new Dashboard (Figure 2).

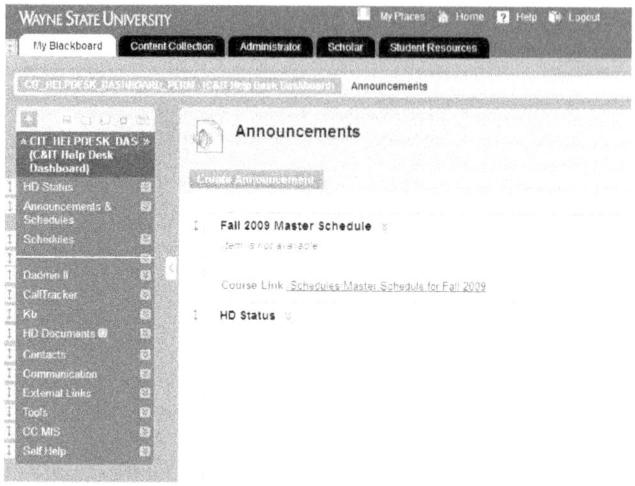

Figure 1. Old Dashboard

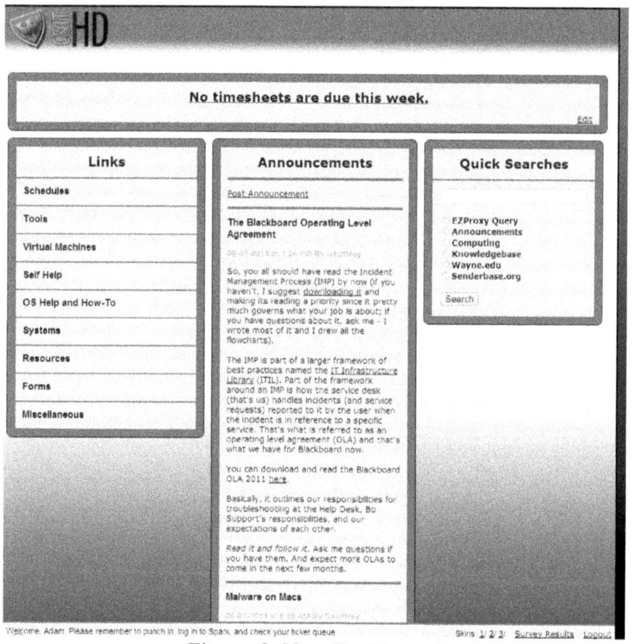

Figure 2. New Dashboard

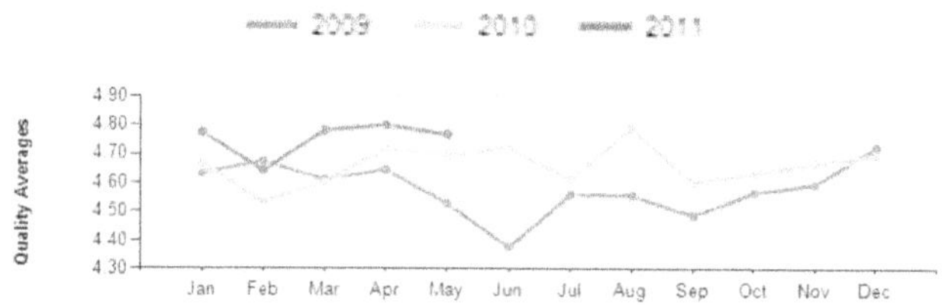

Figure 3: HDI survey Quality Average

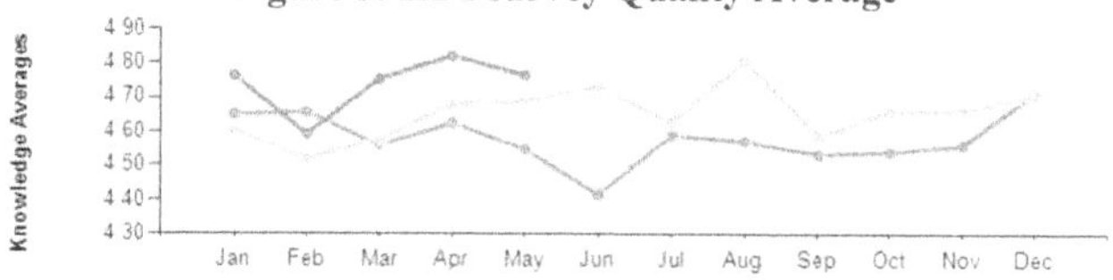

Figure 4: HDI survey Knowledge averages

The first noticeable milestone of the new Dashboard was the management of announcements. WordPress content management was used to create organize and archive announcements for C&IT

Help Desk support information for student technicians. The benefits of WordPress included user friendliness, search abilities and flexibility in the integration of these resources within the Dashboard. The fact that this was an open source content management system was the final deciding factor in its implementation. This feature allowed the web editing flexibility needed for the design of the Dashboard.

The roll out of expanded hours began just before the fall of 2010. C&IT Help Desk full time staff worked diligently to prepare training material to bring these student staff up to speed for this highly political change mandated by the Office of the Provost. Soon after the implementation of the new Dashboard in August of 2010, the HDI survey results reflected the increased knowledge and quality of student technician support for C&IT services. Both areas were increased by 2 tenths from the previous year.

3.2 Formative Feedback

Feedback was solicited from Help Desk student technicians after the implementation of the C&IT Help Desk Dashboard's first phase on Blackboard. The survey process was designed to make revisions to the Dashboard in phases after collecting results of the formative feedback for the dashboard. The primary purpose of the surveys was to begin the outcome based evaluation process for providing meaningful information to key players in Help Desk training. This formative feedback served the following purposes[2]:

- Ensures key players a strong voice in the design and management of training
- Become part of an ongoing service delivery data collection method
- Links continuous improvement to student technician and organization referenced outcomes
- Allows for the systematic evaluation and improvement of services
- Identify the potential areas of focus for C&IT Help Desk training

The process of compiling the results of surveys is an attempt to allow student technicians to utilize empowerment evaluation methods where they will help themselves by participating in the customization of the C&IT Help Desk Dashboard. The questions were written to reflect the attitudes of the Help Desk staff about the Dashboard content and delivery system. The responses were partly used to solicit anticipated outcomes in order to help the student technicians align their performance goals with the tools provided in the training Dashboard.

The Help Desk analyst in charge of training and development created a survey to reflect the attitudes about the content of the Dashboard in addition to offering suggestions about existing and future training modules. The Help Desk supervisor continued to be instrumental in the consultation of the needs of the student technicians primarily because he provides direction for Help Desk Analysts. The Help Desk supervisor also has an accurate assessment of the current skills of Help Desk student technicians. The Help Desk analysts continue to perform many of the functions of instructional design for the Dashboard in their assign areas of responsibility.

3.3 Creating the Page

Help Desk full-time staff set about the task of having a dashboard created. They requested the creation of a page with two central features: a section in which links to documentation and tools could be aggregated and organized by category, and an announcement section which would allow full-time staff to immediately communicate issues and outages to the student-assistant staff.

The section of the page containing links was originally written in straight-forward HTML and organized into a table which placed each individual link in a cell beneath a category to which it belonged. The list grew long and began to become cumbersome, extending twice as far off the page as other sections on the same page.

When the section, which took on the heading "Links," began to consume the majority of the page, it saw a change in format. Using JQuery, the "Links" section was re-written to display only categories by default. Headings were assigned the role of "parent" to the "child" links beneath it. These categories would then expand once clicked, revealing all of the links in the category which was clicked. This minimized the amount of space required by the "Links" section to create a more sensible interface which allows technicians to find documentation and tools more easily.

The announcement section, aptly named "Announcements," saw its start as a widget which displayed the Twitter feed of the C&IT webmaster. While this generally warned the student assistant technicians about major outages, it ultimately fell short as it did not allow full-time employees access to add new news items or issues, and because the content posted by the webmaster was geared towards the student audience and often irrelevant to the Help Desk's student assistants.

The Twitter widget was replaced by an implementation of WordPress running in the background from which the dashboard pulled-in posts. This enabled the Help Desk's full-time staff to post news items instantaneously and directly to the front page of the dashboard.

Another main section which would come to occupy space on the front page of the dashboard is the "Quick Search," section. This section contains a single field and six different search engines which display results relevant to their originating web-site. These engines allow the student assistant technicians to execute database queries to verify access to library resources, search previous announcements to the Help Desk Dashboard, search Wayne State University's central Computing website, search the Wayne State University knowledgebase for articles relevant to their issue, search all of the sites on the Wayne.edu domain, and to query Cisco's senderbase.org website for the reputation of email servers.

Other areas of content were also moved away from their old homes and onto the Help Desk Dashboard. The Help Desk's e-mail troubleshooter, which walks students through common issues associated with configuring a Wayne State email account, was moved onto the dashboard site, which, using inline frames and eventually AJAX, enabled it to move to a format which allows student assistants to follow it to the end without ever leaving the page.

More basic pages were added to the dashboard as well. Content which was once displayed on paper signs pinned across the office was moved into individual pages containing the same information. Help Desk work schedules, internal phone number lists, troubleshooters and lists of student records database forms were all included on the dashboard, on a single central server.

3.4 *Writing the Back-end*

As the Help Desk dashboard came into existence, it became clear that it would necessitate more functionality than simply the display of pre-written text. Once PHP was enabled and a MySQL database installed, dynamic and scalable functionality was well on its way.

The first task to capitalize on the advantages offered by these technologies was the announcements system. It is a simple WordPress blog installation which stores posts and user information in a MySQL database. The dashboard was written to integrate the WordPress announcements into it rather than writing a dashboard website with WordPress as its base. The page connects with the WordPress database, and displays the posts within it.

Early on in the project, full-time staff members expressed interest in a tool which would notify student-assistants that their timesheets were due and the date on which they're due. This manifested itself as a tool which full-time staff and senior student-assistants could edit, providing it with a date and a statement of whether or not it is a pay week. This data is then stored in the MySQL database and relayed to all users at the top of the dashboard.

Recently, it became necessary to provide student-assistants with feedback about individual callers. The Help Desk maintains a form which already solicited such information from callers. Full time staff created a database into which these surveys are now imported. By assigning individual fields in the database to individual variables in PHP, a tool was created which allows the dashboard to display surveys by month, allowing student-assistants to see how they're doing in calls.

In order to create the tool which returned to students these survey results, the database required user data which could be referenced to provide the proper student with their respective surveys. This necessitated the implementation of a login system which defines the individual users of the site, forces them to authenticate, and would open the door to dynamic tools catered to the individual users of the dashboard. The login system uses students' LDAP credentials, called AccessID at Wayne State, and password in order to authenticate and allow them access to their account. These credentials are also stored in their own MySQL database and referenced by necessary tools to authenticate and determine user-rights. It also allows for administrator pages which are only accessible to an account which is deemed to be an administrator of the site. One example of this is the page which allows editing of the timesheet notification system which is restricted to only allow the administrator to make changes.

4. RESULTS

Using the web resource "survey monkey", student technicians were asked to evaluate content on the original Dashboard. Questions were written to solicit input for additional training modules added to the Dashboard. The questions were focused primarily on:

- University organization structure
- C&IT division organization structure
- Service catalog for other campus support groups
- Escalation paths for C&IT subject matter experts

Student technician responses indicates the knowledge of university organization structure was only somewhat familiar for 62.3% while 37.7% reported that they felt they were familiar. None of the technicians reported that they were not familiar with university schools, colleges and divisions. Only 12.5% student technicians felt knowledge of university organization structure would not assist them in resolving Help Desk issues. The overwhelming response was a desire to learn about organizations within the university including the C&IT Division. In the follow up to this question, student technicians were encouraged to visit websites for any of the organizations to which they were not familiar. This would provide general information for the student technicians evaluators for subsequent interviews with stakeholders (Help Desk Supervisor/Analysts) and ensure that follow up be conducted efficiently.[3]

The content on the Dashboard's "self-help" area contains troubleshooters and catalogs for C&IT services including escalation paths and support details for Administrative Systems. Survey questions were used to evaluate the popularity of the self-help resources and determine with which strategies student technicians were most comfortable. Items evaluated included:

- Wayne Connect e-mail troubleshooter
- Resnet troubleshooter
- Administrative Systems catalog

Student technicians reported across the board that the troubleshooters were most useful and most familiar for assisting with resolutions of calls on first contact. The responses indicate 100% approval for the troubleshooting method of self help, while the service catalog received 37.5% approval for clarification of Administrative Systems issues.

5. FUTURE WORK

Upon conclusion of the content evaluation, Help Desk Analysts will continue to make revisions to self-help tools for their appropriate areas of responsibility. Follow up with lead student technicians in weekly briefings indicated there is no need to expand on the university organization structure training. It was decided there was no immediate need for the training module on organization structure because of the wealth of information on the WSU web site.

During the next major projects, Help Desk full-time staff providing direction to the student technician staff will be responsible for the implementation of operating level agreements for C&IT SMEs of supported systems. The results will include continuous development of the Dashboard by building on current standards to ensure that every call is consistently handled. Lead students technicians will continue to have input on the content and design of the Help Desk Dashboard, in addition to expanding on their own professional development through assisting in projects such as these. The cultivation of the Dashboard is proof of the growth in the development of the C&IT Help Desk student technician staff.

6. CONCLUSION

The evolution of the C&IT Help Desk Dashboard is a continuous process lead by the help desk full-time staff. The expansions of hours along with the ongoing technical improvements of the Dashboard are the direct result of the assignment of Lead Help Desk Technicians and their collaboration with the full-time staff. This phase of development has proven to be the biggest achievement of the C&IT Help Desk in the past decade. The next phase of evaluations on the Dashboard will allow technicians to review their individual student technician call statistics. As of now, student technicians are able to view HDI survey responses from their individual customers, but the future work will allow technicians to review they're monthly team statistics on call and wait times. Currently, results are set up to show HDI surveys responses for individual technicians from month to month on the new Dashboard (Figure 2). Over all HDI survey results are also available as shown in samples from figures 3 and 4 of this article. Individual statistics of the HDI surveys will require that student technicians take action for less desirable survey results and compile the findings of follow up responses in the call tracking system. Student technicians receive annual reviews where special recognition in surveys, emails and displays of exceptional leadership are acknowledged. The student technicians with outstanding reviews are considered for lead positions and pay raises.

7. ACKNOWLEDGMENTS

My thanks to: Rodrigo Reis: Help Desk Analyst & Geoffrey Sperl: Help Desk Supervisor

8. REFERENCES

[1] Thomas, S., (2009) *Make your Help Desk training interactive and interesting to your student technicians by allowing them to select, create and edit material on a training "Dashboard".* SIGUCCS '09 Conference, St. Louis, MO.

[2] Schalock, Robert, L. (2001). *Outcome-based Evaluation.* (2nd ed.) New York: Kluwer Academic/Plenum Publishers.

[3] Chen, Huey-Tsyh. (2005). *Practical Program Evaluation.* Thousand Oaks: Sage Publications

What's Growing on Your Keyboards?

Jason Wagner
University of Rochester
Lower Hoyt Hall
Rochester, NY 14627
1 585-275-0517
jason.wagner@rochester.edu

ABSTRACT
Thousands of users touch the keyboards and mice of public computers at the University of Rochester ever day. In conjunction with the University of Rochester Medical Center we set out to discover what the users leave behind. Samples were taken from the busiest computers on campus and tested for the presence of bacteria and viruses. A variety of cleaning products was also tested to measure the efficacy of cleaning methods.

Categories and Subject Descriptors
K.3.0 **[Computing Milieux]**: Computers and Education –*general*

General Terms
Management, Measurement, Documentation, Performance, Human Factors, Standardization

Keywords
Labs, Bacteria, Experiment, Cleaning Products

1. INTRODUCTION
The University of Rochester, located in Rochester, New York, is a private, tier-one research university with 5066 undergraduate and 3065 graduate students. The University is comprised of a teaching hospital and six academic divisions located across three main campuses. The primary academic divisions responsible for undergraduate instruction, with nearly 4500 undergraduates, are the schools of Arts & Sciences, and the Hajim School of Engineering and Applied Sciences, which combined are most commonly known as "The College." Our campus IT organization, "University IT", is the central IT organization for the university across our academic units.

University IT offers more than 550 public computers in labs, libraries, classrooms and kiosks spread across campus. Computers are replaced on a three and sometimes four year renewal cycle. The keyboards and mice are especially worn at the time of replacement. Despite regular cleaning, the keyboards are prone to retaining debris from users, including food particles, fingernail fragments, hair and dry skin flakes. During the height of the swine flu pandemic in the fall of 2009, University IT staff became concerned about identifying any pathogens present on public computing keyboards and the most effective means of cleaning the peripherals users touch the most.

2. EXPERIMENT DESIGN
KeyServer metrics were used to identify the busiest public computers on campus. University IT staff were provided with collection swabs and trained on proper sample collection techniques by URMC microbiology lab technicians. So armed, samples were taken from the keyboards and mice. Each sample was labeled with the location, time and date of the collection. Our control sample for the experiment was provided by swabbing a brand new keyboard and mouse which had been sealed in factory packaging until opened for this test.

The swabs were transported to the URMC microbiology lab where they were plated and incubated by technicians who reported the results.

The same techniques were used to test for the efficacy of the cleaning techniques.

We did not test for fungi.

Figure 1: Control (no bacteria present)

Figure 2: Goergen Hall Kiosk Sample, indicating the presence of normal hand flora including Staphylococcus epidermidis and diptheroids

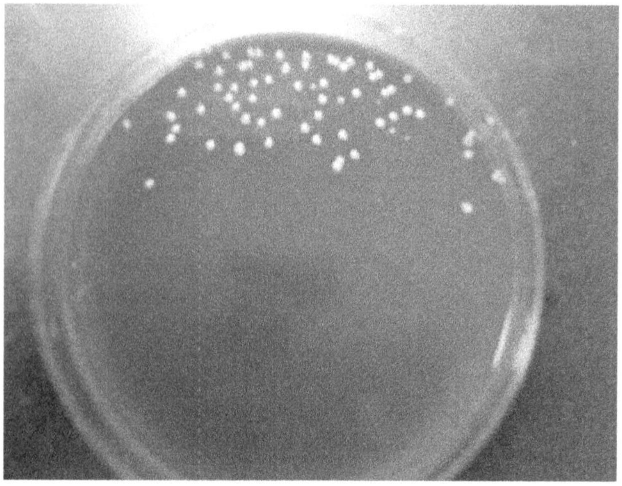

3. RESULTS

No viruses were detected on any of the keyboards or mice. Bacteria were detected on every sample. The colonies present included normal hand flora, including Staphylococcus epidermidis and diptheroids, a form of Corynebacteria that are non-pathogenic. No infectious pathogens or virulent strains of bacteria were detected. This was not cause for celebration however, as the bacteria detected may still cause illness for immuno-compromised members of the University Community.

4. CLEANING PRODUCTS

We compared three different cleaning products and techniques to kill the bacteria on the peripherals. These included both common household disinfectants and commercially available specialty keyboard cleaning sprays. Our results indicated that all the products tested killed the bacteria present.

We found that household disinfectant wipes were just as effective as a household disinfectant spray and paper towels. The specialty keyboard cleaner was also an effective agent, though it did cost more than four times the household products which provided the same bacteria free results.

As a cleaning control, we also tested an untreated cloth which wiped away the bacteria without any chemical agents. This method was not effective in removing all the bacteria present. Friction alone was an insufficient method for cleaning the peripherals.

5. CONCLUSION

Since our study was commissioned a variety of controls and techniques have been implemented to keep oft touched items clean. These include weekly wipe downs of the keyboards and mice using a disinfectant spray and paper towels, the installation of wall mounted hand sanitizer pumps in every lab and common public computing locations and user education using digital signage. University IT encourages users not to enjoy finger foods while typing on public computers and to use hand sanitizer before and after using a shared computer.

We've Been Over This Before! Tracking the Lifecycles of Scheduled Events

Nathan Carpenter
University of Illinois at Urbana-Champaign
1304 W. Springfield Avenue
Urbana, IL 61801
1-217-265-6825
carpente@illinois.edu

Ryan C. Tucker
University of Illinois at Urbana-Champaign
1304 W. Springfield Avenue
Urbana, IL 61801
1-217-265-6813
tucker@illinois.edu

ABSTRACT

One of the greatest struggles for our Help Desk was handling regularly scheduled events like account deactivations or the distribution of financial aid letters. Year after year slightly different versions of these events caught us off guard causing confusion amongst the staff which in turn led to poor customer service. We were exclusively reactive to these situations. Our responses were not standard and would pass without a proper dissection of how the event should be handled in the future.

A series of events made us realize that a passive reaction could not be our action plan. The Help Desk got slammed with a variety of issues that we had seen before, but yet we couldn't respond in a quick and consistent way. We didn't have documentation that recalled all the actions we previously took. We needed to come up with a way to track these events so that we could keep ourselves and our colleagues aware of events and figure out how to deal with issues before they hit the Help Desk.

The Lifecycle and Problem Tracker was our solution to this problem. Using our campus wiki, we devised a series of templates and a calendar that would allow us to track re-occurring events. Liaisons were assigned to these events and departments so that we could meet with various stakeholders before an event happened to ensure that the information we gave our customers was accurate. Templates allowed us to keep canned text and knowledgebase solutions in a single location to make deploying them a snap. We could also track unexpected issues and keep ticket counts and follow-up conversations so they could be easily accessed in the future or used in a post mortem.

This system has allowed us to be agile, responsive, transparent and generally less frustrated with issues that shouldn't be causing us or our customers any stress.

SIGUCCS'11, November 12–17, 2011, San Diego, California, USA.

Categories and Subject Descriptors
K.6.1 [**Management of Computing and Information Systems**]: Project and People Management – *Life Cycle.*

General Terms
Management, Measurement, Standardization

Keywords
Lifecycle, request, incident, problem, reactivity

1. INTRODUCTION
"Insanity is doing the same thing over and over again and expecting different results" - often misattributed

A common notion is that the most challenging aspect of IT support is its unpredictability. We don't know when things will break. We don't know exactly how new services will be accepted by our customers. We don't always know how decisions made by our colleagues outside of IT will affect us. These uncertainties put us in the position of being reactive. On the other hand, a great deal of our business is very predictable. We reset a lot of passwords at the beginning of a semester. We allow new students to start using their accounts in the spring and we turn off old students' accounts in the fall. These cyclical tasks might be considered "easy" since we face them regularly. While the nature of our work demands us to be reactive to customer questions, we should know answers to these "easy" tasks inside and out because we've handled them before.

2. THE PROBLEM
Herein lies the problem: What happens when scheduled events that should be handled easily constantly cause hiccups in support? At best the Help Desk is left with frustration and at worst we find ourselves providing inadequate support to our customers. The CITES Help Desk has found itself in this position more than once. An event we knew was coming turned into a support headache. We needed a way to track both these events and the completely unpredictable occurrences so we could attempt to reduce frustration in the future.

2.1. An Example
A lot happens between the time a prospective student applies to our university and when they step foot on campus as a freshman. Even looking at the process from a strictly IT viewpoint there

are many moving pieces that all have to fall into place to make for a seamless event. An ID has to be created and subsequently claimed by the (at this time prospective and perhaps undecided) student. They need to establish passwords so they can sign up for housing, orientation sessions, financial aid, placement tests and an array of other important services. But since they don't yet have access to all services (they don't have a campus email account, for example), they have to wait to be informed of their availability later.

The general process is the same every year. The *specific* processes differ almost every year and this is the source of continual (and growing) frustration. Documentation written for a given year may change the next. Processes that Help Desk might *assume* would (or should) not change may do so anyway.

Examples of changes that we've seen with the prospective student intake process include:

- Deadlines and activation dates
  Example: This year we activated student email accounts in April. Last year we activated them in mid-May. This was done to ensure that emails sent by campus groups reached the students at their @illinois.edu addresses.
- Processes, some managed by CITES, some not
  Example: The email system used by undergraduate students changed from one that was internally supported to an outsourced option. Students now had to physically sign up for an account. Previously, students had an account automatically provisioned.
- Notifications, some managed by CITES, some not
  Example: Emails sent by Housing or Admissions would be sent prematurely. In turn, this would cause an increase in IT support tickets as certain tasks may not have been completed yet. Perhaps students hadn't yet claimed their NetID or the students admission status hadn't yet been propagated to our IT systems
- Ownership of data and processes
  Example: The entirety of the student orientation process was moved from the Office of the Dean of Students to Admissions. This was not clearly conveyed to the Help Desk which resulted in several misdirected inquiries.

3. THE SOLUTION

What we lacked was a way to keep track of all these changes from year to year. We had to rely on our memories or archived email to fill in the blanks of why last year's event went so poorly. It may seem elementary to create a repository of events, but one did not exist. We had to create one.

The Lifecycle and Problem Tracker was designed to keep events, both planned and unplanned in a central wiki space. We could record all kinds of data about unplanned events, such as:

- When something happened, and not just the date, but specific time. Quite a few ill-timed emails have gone out at 4:45 PM on a Friday which resulted in students not being able to receive help from the Help Desk or the office that sent the email until the next day, or in some cases, the following Monday
- Triggering events
- Common customer questions or concerns

After the event had been completed, we could flesh out our data even more if a post-mortem was conducted. We could therefore add:

- Contact points for follow-up
- Number of tickets generated
- Suggestions for future events

For normal, cyclical events that were scheduled, we could add them to a calendar and be proactive as they approached. Using previously collected data, we could meet with stakeholders both inside and out of CITES to ensure that all parties understood what would be happening and be made aware of any relevant changes. Doing this should eliminate many of the frustrating "surprises" that seemed to pop-up year to year because it was assumed that nothing had changed. In turn, we could be much better prepared to assist our customers with issues as they came up.

4. RESULTS

Since this is such a new process for us, it's difficult to say how effective it will be. We've already discovered a challenge, which is actually recording the events in a timely way. Even a few days can affect perception of an event and mis-information can be propagated. To combat this, we're working to develop workflows that ensure that information about incidents are captured in a timely manner and that the documentation is as accurate as possible.

But as we build up a healthy history of events we should be able to see, at a glance, where an event should be going. Unplanned events can be triaged quickly and accurately. The data no longer sits in the ticketing system or an email client. It's accessible and searchable by everyone who might need it. Time and again we notice when our jobs are helped along with effective tools, accessible knowledge and proactive actions. Our customers reap the benefits of all these things and their IT life on campus becomes just a bit easier.

Which Web Solution Is Best for You? A Decision Tree

Debbie Durant
IT-Client Support & Services
University of Delaware
Newark, DE 19716
(302) 831-1992
debd@udel.edu

ABSTRACT
This poster explains the different Web hosting options UD offers, along with criteria to help users decide which option best meets their needs.

Categories and Subject Descriptors
H.3.5 [INFORMATION STORAGE AND RETRIEVAL]: Online Information Services -*Web-based services.*

General Terms
Management, Documentation, Design, Human Factors.

Keywords
Content management systems, Web, hosting

1. INTRODUCTION
The University of Delaware has offered server space for colleges, departments, and organizations dedicated for websites since the dawn of the World Wide Web in the mid-1990's. Since that time, Web pages and sites have become more elaborate, and more structured hosting options are now available to the University community. These include Drupal and WordPress servers maintained by central IT. This decision tree was developed specifically to help faculty determine which service or services would be appropriate to meet their hosting needs.

2. HOSTING ENVIRONMENTS
2.1 Drupal
Our central IT Drupal service includes three servers: a test server for testing upgrades and patches; a development server, and a production server. Most sites develop their own themes, although there are a few pre-designed UD themes available. Users can modify themes and content but cannot install modules that are not approved for use by central IT.

2.2 WordPress
Our central WordPress service includes a test server and a production server. We have a selection of themes (9 so far) from which the user can choose, which range from very simple to highly customizable. Any theme can be set to show the UD Branding header and footer, or not, as needed.

2.3 Static HTML
Our main Web site continues to be hosted on a Solaris server. This traditional web-publishing option includes one server and allows users to publish their site using Static HTML and Javascript. Perl is available and server-side includes can be used for easy template-based designs.

2.4 Google Sites
The University participates in Google Apps for Education. IT supports users who create Google Sites as part of the GoogleApps @UDel.edu program.

2.5 Non-IT Supported Hosts
Colleges, departments and other units are not required to host their sites on the central IT servers, so other Web servers exist on campus but are not supported by central IT. There are also organizational units who contract their hosting with outside providers. This poster does not address non-IT supported environments.

2.6 Sakai
Sakai is used as the learning management system for the University of Delaware. It also has a project management component, so that faculty and staff at the University can create projects for collaboration purposes. It is possible to share Sakai content to the public, but using it for this purpose is most relevant to the course management function.

3. CRITERIA
Faculty requesting Web hosting space are often unclear about what would be the best option to choose when selecting a Web site environment. We developed this tool to help faculty decide which tool would most closely meet their requirements.

Primary decision: Why do I want a Web site?

Choices: Presentation of Information vs. Collaboration

3.1 Presentation of Information
If Presentation is chosen, it is assumed the site will be open to the public. If it is public and represents an official University organizational unit, it should have the UD branding header and footer. If it is for non-official business, it should not. At the time this chart was created, the branding was not available for Google Sites. Therefore those who need that feature are directed to Drupal, WordPress or Static HTML.

Organizations that need Presentation sites are not always skilled in website creation, and often do not have access to individuals skilled in web development. So the tree directs these people to WordPress, which is easier to learn for non-technical users. Others who need larger and/or more complex sites are directed to Drupal, which is highly customizable and suitable for larger installations.

3.2 Collaboration

If Collaboration is chosen, the site owner needs to decide if the site will be viewable by the public. Both Google Sites and Sakai have the ability for sites to be kept private. However, if public viewing is involved, Google Sites is generally the better choice. Drupal has collaborative features as well, so if the collaboration is to be coordinated with a Presentation site, Drupal should also be considered. The WordPress installation recently upgraded to version 3, which will allow more collaboration than the previous version in our implementation.

If a collaborative site does not need to be open to non-UD viewers, then usually the decision is whether to use Sakai or Google Sites. If all members of the collaborative group are knowledgeable about Sakai, then a Sakai project requires little training. Google Sites operates differently, and creating the first site often calls for training and/or experimentation.

4. CONCLUSION

The purpose of the decision tree is to give our faculty users a visual reference to make it easier for them to decide on a web platform. None of the choices shown are black-and-white, however: there are occasions when a different tool may be selected, if other parameters are included. For a large proportion of our audience, this tool has helped us to help them determine their web hosting environment.

5. ACKNOWLEDGMENTS

Thanks to the members of the IT-Client Support & Services Web Presence team for their contributions and editing.

Figure 1. Decision tree for selecting web hosting environment.

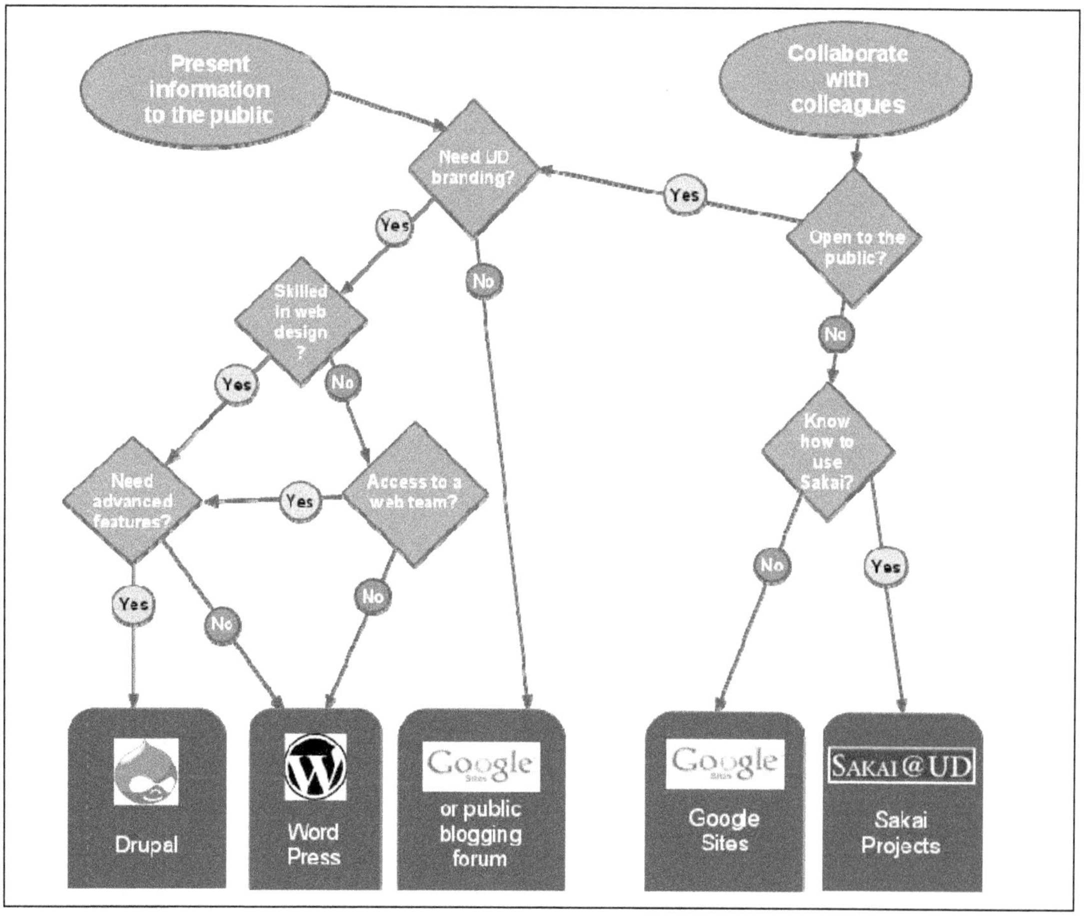

Physical Security and Data Projectors

Nason Simpson
Pima County Community College
4905a E Broadway Blvd
Tucson AZ, 85709
1-520-206-4811
nasimpson@pima.edu

ABSTRACT

Technology is expensive, especially when we talk about data projectors, which can cost anywhere from $400 to upwards of $4000.

In this paper, we will outline some of the security measures Pima Community College has taken to reduce the theft of these high visibility assets.

Categories and Subject Descriptors

K.6.5 [**Computing Milieux**]: Management of Computing and Information Systems – *Security and Protection.*

General Terms

Documentation and Security.

Keywords

Physical Security, STOP Tag(s), theft reduction, Pima Community College (PCC).

1. INTRODUCTION

At Pima Community College, we dealt with a significant issue with theft of projectors. On average, we had about 4 projectors stolen each year. Over the last five years before implementation of security measures, we had 22 projectors stolen. With an average cost of $800 this translated to roughly $18000. In these financial times, this is a significant part of our budget.

Immediately after the implementation of our high visibility security efforts, we saw an immediate drop in projector theft. We have been using this updated security model for three years, and in those three years, we have had 5 total thefts, this works out to just over 1 theft per year. In short, these efforts have saved us about $8000 so far.

2. THE ISSUE AT HAND

2.1 The Problem

Technology theft is a lucrative business. Often items can be resold for hundreds of dollars, making high risk targets like projectors an easy target. In the past, Pima College has absorbed the cost of the theft. A majority of our projectors are ceiling mounted in classrooms, yet undoing the mount has not proved to be an obstacle. Dozens of people stream through each class room every day. In these tough financial times, it has become apparent that we need to do all that we can to reduce theft. As we outlined above, PCC, was dealing with a significant loss of projectors due to theft.

This is something that is being universally recognized across the nation. The need for cheap and effective theft reduction practices.

Additionally, not only does the theft of a projector cause immediate revenue loss due to replacement, but also staff time lost in filing police reports, dispositioning, and ultimately installing and configuring the new projector.

2.2 The Solution

We needed a highly effective means of reducing theft. We chose to pursue a high visibility solution.

We combined two tactics, "STOP Tags", and Branding that produced a highly visible and effective means of reducing theft.

2.3 STOP Tags

These asset tags are manufacture with an indelible "tattoo" underneath the metal tag (http://www.stoptheft.com/site/index.php) . This is so that, if the tag is pried off (which takes up to 800 pounds of force), there is still a brand-like "tattoo" identifying it as stolen property. Removal of both would make the item unsightly and suspicious. The implementation of these is both quick, and simple, taking roughly two minutes per unit to install.

Additionally, each tag number is entered in to a database that is maintained by STOP and can be searched any time on line, by anyone. This makes identifying recovered property as simple as searching the number on STOP's website.

2.4 Branding

Branding projector units by using an electric branding iron with a customized name plate is both highly visible, and the resulting mark is extremely difficult to remove. (http://www.highlandwoodworking.com/craftmarkcustommarkbrandingironelectricheat.aspx)

This process is simple to learn, and takes only 2 minutes per unit.

The process does not harm the projector, as the application of heat is quick, and highly localized. Typically, the brand is pressed on to the projector for about 3 seconds and then removed. This produces a deep and well defined mark. This is repeated in 1 or 2 other places on the unit, depending on model and available area.

Once the brand has cooled, a small stencil is placed over the area, and it is spray painted fluorescent orange. This greatly enhances the visibility and readability of the brand.

Similar to the STOP Tags, removal of the brand proves difficult and renders the unit either unusable or very visibly damaged. Either way, making it no longer easily marketable.

2.5 The Result

As stated in the introduction, the combination of these efforts yielded an immediate drop off in crime that has maintained for 3 and a half years.

As stated above, our theft numbers went from over 4 projectors every year, to just over 1 per year.

The saved money from reduced theft has easily paid for the increased security efforts, which total about $8 per unit. Our institution has paid for roughly 400 STOP tags for projectors, and this is easily eclipsed by the $8000 in saved revenue.

2.6 In Summary

In summary, these efforts have reduced theft, saved money, and eased work load on our staff. These high visibility measures have proven effective, and easy to implement, providing no steep learning curve or major policy change.

3. ACKNOWLEDGMENTS

I would like to thank my colleagues at Pima Community College IT for providing me much help in gathering information for this paper as well as supporting my efforts.

Specifically, I would like to thank Theresa Roach at the PCC Department of Public Safety for providing all of the crime statistics used in this paper.

4. RESOURCES

STOP tags: http://www.stoptheft.com/site/index.php

Branding Irons:
http://www.highlandwoodworking.com/craftmarkcustommarkbrandingironelectricheat.aspx

Sun Ray Self-Help Guide

Dan R. Herrick
Colorado State University
Engineering Network Services
Fort Collins, CO 80523-1301
970-491-3131
Dan.Herrick@Colostate.edu

ABSTRACT
Having deployed Sun Ray thin clients throughout our computer labs, computer classrooms, a residence hall, some administrative offices, and some graduate student offices, we were faced with the challenge of disseminating basic usage information for these unfamiliar devices, particularly in the public areas. To assist with this, we developed a large format poster which introduced the devices, provided quick tips and answers for common problems, and basic usage information. As one aspect of our communication efforts around the Sun Ray devices, these posters have had a significantly positive impact.

Categories and Subject Descriptors
K.3.1 [**Computers and Education**]: Computer Uses in Education – *Computer-assisted instruction (CAI).*

K.6.1 [**Management of Computing and Information Systems**]: Project and People Management – *Training*

General Terms
Management, Documentation.

Keywords
Computer Labs, Documentation, Instructions, Signs, Thin Clients.

1. INTRODUCTION
Sun Ray thin clients are deployed throughout the College of Engineering at Colorado State University (CSU), in computer labs, computer classrooms, a residence hall, graduate student offices, and administrative offices. These are disparate environments with a wildly varying level of user expertise with computer systems in general, much less potentially unfamiliar computing devices such as the Sun Rays.

We attempted several methods of communicating correct usage and operation, including troubleshooting, of the Sun Rays to users, but were ultimately most successful with a large format poster placed throughout the public areas.

1.1 Thin Client Overview
For those unfamiliar with a thin client, and our Sun Ray implementation of thin clients, Ritschard's explanation [1] is a helpful reference. Essentially, a thin client is a computing device with a "thin" layer of hardware and software which connects a user to a server-based desktop session.

One of the primary advantages of the Sun Ray thin clients is the portable desktop session made possible by a smart card, which is integrated into Engineering students' school ID cards. Users insert their smart card into the Sun Ray device, log in and obtain a desktop session, and begin their work. When they are done using that particular station, rather than log out, they can simply remove their card and the session is stored on the server for later use. The user can return to their desktop session and all of their work in progress by re-inserting their card into any other Sun Ray on campus. Smart Cards also override a locked session, which allows students to reclaim an "abandoned" computer seat.

Users have the choice of a direct connection to a Microsoft Windows desktop session or a UNIX desktop session (from which they can initiate a remote Windows desktop session). The Windows desktop is provided by a farm of servers running Windows Server 2008 R2. The UNIX desktop is Solaris using the IceWM desktop.

2. TECHNICAL AND GENERAL USAGE CHALLENGES

2.1 Logon Screen and Desktop
Originally, the Sun Rays connected to a UNIX desktop, from which the user could work in UNIX or initiate a remote Windows desktop session. Feedback from users indicated that nearly all users preferred the Windows desktop to the UNIX desktop, and, in fact, most users simply considered the UNIX desktop a "speed bump" on their way to Windows.

To improve graphics performance over the network and to reduce the load on the UNIX servers, the Sun Rays were configured in "kiosk mode" so that they could directly connect a user to a Windows session without the intermediate step of the UNIX session. However, because some Sun Ray users used the Sun Ray's UNIX-based logon screen to directly connect to an X-session on Linux workstations, a compromise was reached. The Sun Ray administrator designed a new logon screen that allows the user to choose one of two Windows environments or the "Classic Sun Ray" environment (e.g., the UNIX desktop). (See Figure 1.)

2.2 USB Devices
The new kiosk mode operation of the Sun Rays had one important drawback: USB device functionality, for example to connect USB flash drives, did not function on the Windows servers. As a result, users were not able to use USB flash drives on the Sun Rays under the Windows desktop, as they were able to under Classic Sun Ray mode.

The workaround is to log in under Classic Sun Ray mode to access a USB device, copy the files to a shared network drive, and then log in to a Windows desktop.

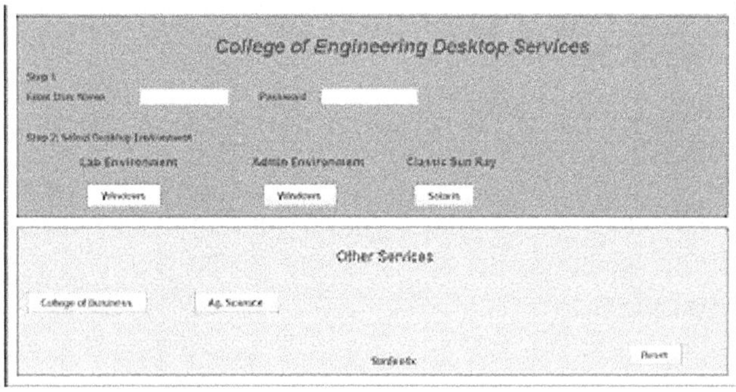

Figure 1. New Sun Ray logon screen.

2.3 Power Save Mode

Another touted advantage of thin clients is their extremely low power consumption [2], and this feature of the Sun Rays manifested itself by going to low power mode and causing the attached monitor to go dark. It often appeared to users as if the station was powered off, causing them, in some cases, to skip the station to look for one that was obviously powered on. The solution is to tap a key on the keyboard or to move the mouse, which will wake the screen.

2.4 Network Errors

Because the Sun Rays have no local operating system, a network connection failure is a critical error. The built-in firmware for the Sun Rays displays error messages that are only meaningful to a systems administrator or someone trained in interpreting them. (See Figure 2.)

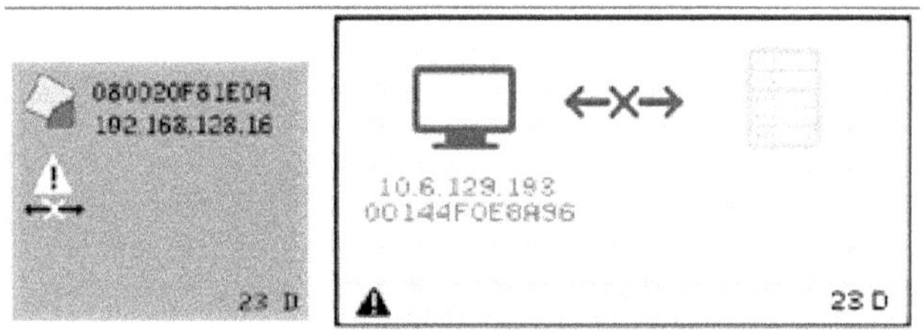

Figure 2. Sample of Sun Ray error display.

2.5 Locked Station

Users have the ability to lock a Sun Ray station, much like a Windows computer. In order to preserve privacy, the Sun Rays were set to automatically lock the screen after a specified timeout (determined by lack of input from keyboard or mouse). Some users would forget to log out and walk away, leaving a locked session for the next user. Many users did not realize that they could disconnect the previous user's locked session, without administrator intervention, through a series of keystrokes.

2.6 Audio

The Sun Ray 2FS units feature a headphone jack on the front of the device. Due to the way the devices are flat-mounted to desks in some of the classrooms, this jack is not immediately obvious. Also, the Sun Rays have specific Sun keyboards with extra keys such as volume control, which do not function in kiosk mode. As a result, users were often confused as to how to adjust the volume through software.

2.7 Nature of the Thin Client

It is difficult to concisely convey, to the user, the nature of a thin client and its nuanced differences when compared with a traditional desktop computer. The load-balancing features of the Sun Ray connection service connects a user initially with the least-loaded server, but the server to which they were connected to has no guarantee of staying that way. Because other users are using resources on the same physical server, a user initiating a software process that consumes a large amount of memory, processor power or network bandwidth which will cause other users on the same server to perceive that the server has slowed down. The only workable solution (short of terminating users' load-intensive processes) is for a user experiencing this delay is to log out of the server and then to initiate a new logon session, ensuring a connection to the least busy server at that moment.

3. COMMUNICATIONS METHODS

Most of the education for users came from the Engineering Network Services (ENS) web site [3], which contains sections on basic Sun Ray usage, troubleshooting, and usage tips. Two significant problems were evident in this communication model: (1) Users are not predisposed to read informative web pages unless directed to do so specifically, and (2) Users must have logged on to a computer in order to access a web page. (This is like including the instructions for operating a key inside a locked chest!)

In-person communications are used frequently, by computer lab and other IT staff. In the computer labs, requests for help are initiated on a reactive rather than proactive basis. This led to built-up user frustration with the Sun Ray devices, and the infrequent nature of personal contact with lab personnel caused many users to give up on the devices rather than seek a solution. Additionally, in-person communications are inefficient to reach a mass audience, such as computer lab users.

Users, for whom a Sun Ray was their primary desktop computing device, would often receive only basic instruction on its use, and, when a problem came up, they only had verbal instruction (sometimes received months prior) to fall back on.

Periodically, mass e-mails were sent to the Engineering users with updates to IT services in the college. Text such as "What are these Sun Rays?", along with a link to the ENS web site for further information, was included.

Even with the above methods of more traditional communications, it was clear that the users were not getting the information necessary to effectively use the Sun Rays. To address this, the "Sun Ray Self-Help Guide" poster was developed.

4. COMPOSITION AND DESIGN

First, the most common usage issues (outlined above) were compiled and solutions or workarounds developed for each issue. Each of the issues was explained more completely on the ENS web site, but concise answers were needed to provide a "quick and easy" solution for users.

The communication style of the poster is casual, with a question-and-answer format. Most of the section headings are phrased as an incomplete question with keywords, e.g., "Got Headphones?". These section headings were framed to draw attention to the particular keyword for the problem the user was experiencing. Figure 3 shows the current computer labs version of the poster.

Microsoft PowerPoint was used to create the poster. Graphics elements were included to help identify the parts of the equipment, and the on-screen error messages. The important operational features of the Sun Ray (Card reader, power LED, USB port, and headphone jack) were labeled. Figures at the bottom right of the poster showed the on-screen error messages;

as they were visual in nature, they were not easily described. The ENS and Sun logos were used to help users associate the brands with the Sun Rays.

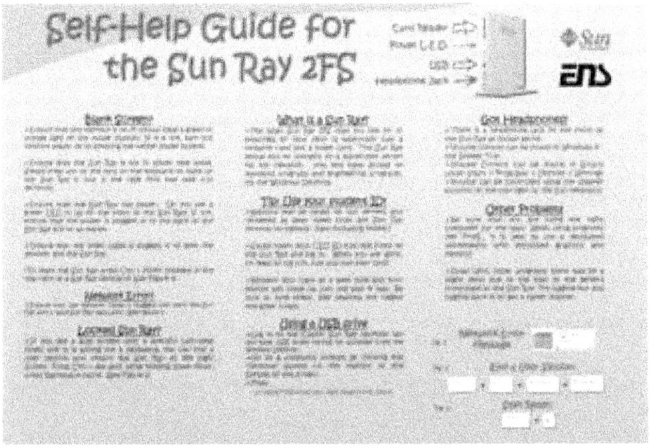

Figure 3. Current revision of poster.

The posters were designed and printed in large format, 36" by 24", on a color plotter on 20 pound bond paper. The paper poster was then glued to a poster board backing. The resulting hard-backed posters were hung on walls in prominent view in each computer lab which featured Sun Rays. Smaller versions, modified for the specific environment of non-computer lab users, were distributed to administrative and graduate student offices.

4.1 Revisions

An "administrative" version of the poster was also created, with only very minor changes (replacing "student" with more generic user terms).

The poster had to be revised for the switch to kiosk mode to address some functional differences in operation. During that revision, some headings were changed, sections were re-ordered, and small passages were re-worded. Figure 4 shows the original poster.

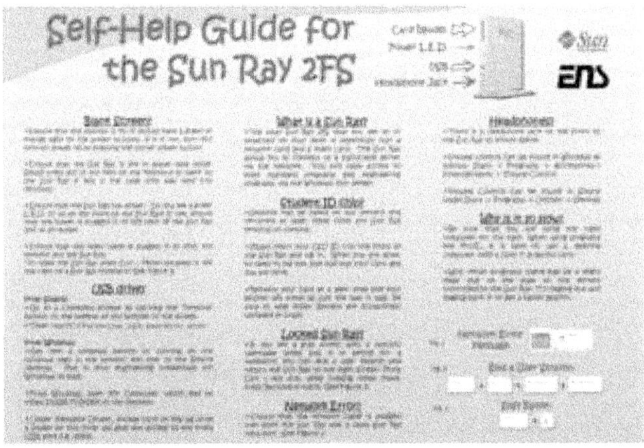

Figure 4. Original poster.

5. IMPACT

The posters received very positive feedback from computer lab users, both on the information presented and the presentation style. Their size makes them hard to miss, and students have been seen to stop and study the poster before continuing on to a Sun Ray seat.

Although the posters were vastly reduced in size for office users, feedback from this group has been positive as well. Some Sun Ray office users taped the sign to their wall or desk and still refer to it.

The number of in-person requests for help and help desk ticket requests with the common problems has dropped significantly.

With continued feedback from Sun Ray users, the posters have been modified slightly from their original design.

Overall, when used concurrently with more traditional communications such as a web page and in-person instruction, the posters have proven to be an effective communications tool.

6. REFERENCES

[1] http://www.oracle.com/us/technologies/virtualization/036088.pdf. Sun Ray 2 specifications.

[2] Ritschard, M., (October 2009). Thin Clients: Make Them Work for You. Proceedings of the 37th Annual ACM SIGUCCS Conference on User Services; Association for Computing Machinery, New York, New York, pp. 41-45.

[3] http://www.engr.colostate.edu/ens/info/sunrays/. Engineering Network Services, Colorado State University.

A Space Just for YOU: Specialized Learning Centers

Laurie Sutch
University of Michigan
206 Hatcher Graduate Library
Ann Arbor, Michigan, 48109
011 734 647-7406
lasutch@umich.edu

ABSTRACT
Technology is ubiquitous in the lives of our students, faculty, and staff, and often they are expected to "just know" how to use it for academic purposes. This doesn't always mean, however, that they really know how to transfer technology skills to their research. Since the 1990s, the University of Michigan Library has been supporting this knowledge transfer at the Knowledge Navigation Center (KNC) and Faculty Exploratory; in 2008 we began serving primarily undergraduates in a similar facility called the TechDeck.

Open to the entire university community, over 70% of KNC clients are graduate students who are scanning articles for their teaching or research, creating posters or web pages, or formatting their dissertations. The Exploratory was specifically designed for faculty, to help them explore and apply new technology in their teaching, research and professional communication. In addition to consultations, faculty attend workshops on creating web pages or presentations, or manipulating images.

Developed with the needs of undergraduates in mind, and located on the busy first floor of the Undergraduate Library, the TechDeck is open evenings and Sunday afternoons. The Tech Suites across the room from the TechDeck include the Brainstorming Room (with a CopyCam, whiteboards and projector), the Presentation Practice Room (with a video camera and screen capture software), and the Editing Room (with editing software and media conversion decks). The same professional and student staff operate all three facilities, creating more flexibility in scheduling, more seamless service, and a student staff with a broader range of experience and knowledge. This in turn enables the library to provide a higher quality service.

This poster session will highlight the similarities and differences between these facilities and discuss staffing models to support them all.

Categories and Subject Descriptors
K.3.1 **[Computers and Education]** Computer Uses in Education.

General Terms
Management, Human Factors.

Keywords
Software skills, technology facilities, computer coaching.

1. INTRODUCTION
Different populations on campus have different needs for the same technology – a graduate student wants a web page as a portfolio for possible employers, a staff member needs a page that serves internal uses, an undergrad student has to create one as a class project, and a faculty member want to display his or her research to the world. They each have different outcome needs, so can they all find the appropriate support? Additionally, technology is ever-changing, and keeping up with new tools is a challenge for everyone. Where can members of the campus community go to update their technology skills?

At the University of Michigan Library, we have created different facilities for these various users. At the **Faculty Exploratory** in the Graduate Library, faculty members get one-on-one attention in a faculty-only environment, so they don't feel uncomfortable learning next to a student that is in a class he or she is teaching. The **Knowledge Navigation Center**, also in the Graduate Library, provides support to all - students, faculty, and staff. Each facility is located near the main reference desks, so if there are research questions, they are easily referred. The Library's **TechDeck**, located on the main floor of the Undergraduate Library, is open late in the evening and has a poster printer for students presenting in class.

The facilities were not created in a vacuum; the Library surveyed other campus units for information on how and what they did, and incorporated solutions for perceived needs of the campus community. While originally the Faculty Exploratory and Knowledge Navigation Center were separately managed and staffed, by the time the TechDeck was created, they were consolidated into one staff. By combining the management of these facilities, staff and software are consistent between the various locations, so if a user moves from one to another, they can continue to get the support they need.

As we look to the future and consider the needs of incoming students as well as current students and faculty, we continue to adapt our services to meet those demands while maintaining the quality of services that the campus has come to expect.

2. FACULTY EXPLORATORY
In 1997, the Office of Academic Outreach at the University of Michigan (UM) was charged with promoting and supporting distance education at the University. While the "early adopters" of technology were well served by existing facilities and programs, there was nowhere for the large number of less computer savvy faculty. Realizing that the institution could not offer distance learning programs if faculty did not feel

comfortable with the technology on their own desktops, the Office of Academic Outreach, in cooperation with the University Library, created the Faculty Exploratory.

Its central location and proximity to other library resources such as the Knowledge Navigation Center and the reference desk on the second floor of the Hatcher Graduate Library made for an ideal setting, and when Academic Outreach dissolved in 1999, the Faculty Exploratory became part of the University Library.

In addition to providing walk-in or by appointment opportunities, the Exploratory also offers a variety of technology workshops, both scheduled and "on-demand." Rather than teach all that a software program can do, Exploratory workshops focus on what a faculty member needs to know to perform the task they wish to complete: put a syllabus up in the course management system, create a poster or presentation for a conference, manipulate images or graphs to put into a publication.

Since UM faculty are both Macintosh and Windows users, both platforms have been offered from the beginning, first with PC cards installed in Mac towers, and now with Mac minis using Terminal Services. This allows patrons to choose the platform with which they are familiar, and replicates what they will find when they try to accomplish the task in their own environment. There is also space for laptop consultation, scanners, and a media conversion station, so faculty members can capture a clip to add to a PowerPoint presentation, or work with their own movies.

3. KNOWLEDGE NAVIGATION CENTER

Created by the University Library, the KNC opened just a few months before the Faculty Exploratory, and similar to the Exploratory, the KNC provides one-on-one assistance to faculty, students and staff to help users integrate technology into their daily academic work. Over time and as technologies and library services have changed, the main areas of focus have shifted. Now they are: text and image scanning and manipulation; bibliographic management software; web content generation; presentation creation (PowerPoint, posters, and other page layout); and dissertation formatting. Though open to the entire university community, over 70% of Knowledge Navigation Center (KNC) clients are graduate students: scanning articles for their teaching or research; creating posters or web pages; or formatting their dissertations.

When the Faculty Exploratory became part of the Library, this created new opportunities for partnerships, particularly with the KNC. Staff in the KNC found they were answering the same questions over and over; creating a workshop series targeted at the large population of graduate students allowed those typical questions to be answered to the whole group, and post-workshop follow up questions in the KNC could be more in-depth and specialized. In the fall of 1999, the first workshops in the *Digital Dissertation Series* were held in the Faculty Exploratory, cosponsored by the Knowledge Navigation Center. Still held today, these workshops target graduate students who need software training to support their varied roles of student, researcher, and instructor, and include sessions such as "Using Microsoft Word Effectively for Your Dissertation," "Preparing Your PowerPoint for a Dissertation Defense or Job Talk," and "Creating Conference Posters with Illustrator".

The workshop series feeds into KNC consulting, providing an outlet valve for people who find that workshop content has been too advanced, too basic, or has not addressed their particular needs or concerns. The KNC has four Macs and five Windows machines, again providing a comfortable platform for the patrons. There are also two high-speed automatic document-feeding scanners and two flatbed scanners. Patrons can drop in, or are encouraged to set up appointments for more complex questions.

4. TECHDECK

The last component needed to complete our suite of services was a facility that specifically served the unique needs of undergraduate students [1]. In addition to traditional end of term papers, nowadays students may be required to create a web page, shoot a video, or print a poster as well. In late 2008, the University Library created the TechDeck, located on the busy first floor of the Undergraduate Library. Like the KNC, the TechDeck has both Mac and Windows computers and flatbed scanners; uniquely, it also has a large format printer that can be used for a fee. Students come to the TechDeck not only to learn how to create posters, but also to create web pages for class, edit moves they have recorded, add multimedia to PowerPoint presentations and much more.

Undergraduates do not need assistance 9-5, but rather evenings and weekends. With this in mind, the TechDeck is open evenings and Sunday afternoons during the academic year. Because the TechDeck is staffed primarily by undergraduates, students coming to use the facility benefit from peer-to-peer assistance from student workers who understand their needs or who may have even taken the same class.

Particularly in the TechDeck, many students come in "just to use a computer" and are happily surprised at what they end up learning because it is staffed by knowledgeable experts, thus educating more and more students "just in time" as they need it, rather than in a specific workshop "just in case."

In addition to the TechDeck, another set of resources was added on the first floor of the Undergraduate Library. The Tech Suites across the room from the TechDeck include the Brainstorming Room (with a CopyCam, whiteboards and projector), the Presentation Practice Room (with video camera and screen capture software), and the Editing Room (with editing software and media conversion decks). These reservable rooms have mobile furniture that can be reconfigured to meet the needs of the groups using them.

5. STAFFING

Managed separately until 2006, the KNC and Exploratory also maintained separate student staffs until 2008. Currently there are three professional staff members associated with the facilities: the Academic Learning Facilities Librarian (program director), and two Instructional Technology Librarians, one who is a generalist, and one that focuses on multimedia in teaching and learning. Typically the Instructional Technology Librarians do not staff the facilities, but rather are "on call" for complex questions and they are the primary workshop instructors. In addition, during the academic year there are approximately 20 part-time student staff members that come from all academic levels and from a wide variety of departments and courses of study. Users indicated that the staff's familiarity with the demands of various academic disciplines is an advantage in its ability to provide effective technology support.

Since appointments are not required (though encouraged for specialized help), there are generally two staff members in both the TechDeck and the KNC. A professional staff member is housed in the Exploratory, and since it is often tied up for workshops, only one student staff member is scheduled there. Appointments in the KNC and TechDeck are only allowed when there are two people scheduled, so the other person can assist walk-in patrons. Having a single staff that can work in any location creates more flexibility in scheduling, more seamless service, and a student staff with a broader range of experience and knowledge. This in turn, enables the library to provide a higher quality service.

6. CONCLUSION

In the past 15 years, we have taken opportunities to strengthen and make our services more relevant within the context of user needs and the emerging uses of technology in research, teaching and learning. By providing multiple facilities for different groups, we can satisfy their varying needs, offering the entire campus population the appropriate technology support. Knowing your institution and your constituents can help you determine what types of support may be appropriate. Understanding the importance of fostering and facilitating communication with other similar campus units is key, and can help you identify commonalities as well as gaps in service.

7. REFERENCES

[1] Alexander, L., Sutch, L. A., and Tuckett, H. 2009. The tech deck. *College & Research Libraries News*, 70(9), 508.

Raising the Bar – Cell Phones the GGC Way

Susan M. Kerr
Georgia Gwinnett College
1000 University Center Lane
Lawrenceville, GA 30043
678-407-5823
skerr@ggc.edu

ABSTRACT

Georgia Gwinnett College is the newest 4-year campus in the University System of Georgia. It opened its doors in August 2006 with a mission to maximize the use of technology toward enhancing instruction, collaboration, and student engagement. To that end, a cell phone program was initiated that provided a data capable smart phone to every faculty member and qualifying staff. Faculty were not responsible for holding office hours but instead were instructed to develop a "Technology Covenant" with their students. This Covenant indicated methods and times of proper communication that included text messaging, phone calling, and appointment scheduling. Since that time, the GGC Cell Phone Program has equipped over 600 cell phones or phone stipends to faculty and staff for enhancing student engagement and communications across campus. This paper will present outcomes, pros, and cons of supporting this initiative.

Categories and Subject Descriptors

C.1.3 [**Other Architecture Styles**]: Cellular architecture (e.g. mobile; C.2.1 [**Network Architecture and Design**]: Wireless communication; C.5.3 [**Microcomputers**]: Portable devices (e.g. laptops, personal digital assistants)

General Terms

Measurement, Standardization, Verification.

Keywords

Cell Phone, Cellular, Mobile, Student Engagement.

1. INTRODUCTION

Georgia Gwinnett College opened its doors on August 18, 2006 as the nation's first four-year public college founded in the 21st century and the first four-year public institution created in Georgia in more than 100 years. In less than three short years, the Commission on Colleges of the Southern Association of Colleges and Schools (SACS) granted Georgia Gwinnett its initial accreditation. The College was instituted with standards on innovative use of educational technology and commitment to an integrated learning experience that develops the whole person. GGC's focus is on a face-to-face classroom experience with portable technology solutions allowing students to learn, study, and work both on and off campus.

Upon its inception, GGC's Office of Educational Technology (OET) implemented a cell phone program intended to support the mission of the College by providing student access to instructors via cell phone calling, text messaging, and email. Smartphone technology was provided to all faculty and various administrative personnel to support this initiative.

Since the program began in 2006, data has been collected through various surveys providing evidence supporting the cell phone program's influence on increased retention rates and student engagement. The program has now become a foundational element of the GGC culture.

2. PROGRAM DEVELOPMENT

2.1 Initial Deployment

The GGC cell phone program began with a partnership between Sprint and Rave Wireless. A Rave Wireless store was brought onto campus to facilitate the purchase and support of cell phones. All faculty and administrative positions with a title of Director or higher qualified for the program, which included an option of a GGC-provided cell phone or a $50/month stipend added to the employee's monthly income. GGC-provided phones were equipped with a pooled number of minutes coupled with unlimited text and data.

2.2 The Technology Covenant

Faculty at GGC have a couple of anomalies that separate them from most faculty in traditional colleges and universities. First, they are not tenured faculty but have yearly renewable contracts. Second, they are not required to post office hours. Instead they are asked to provide a "Technology Covenant" with their students.

This Technology Covenant is a syllabus section describing how they plan to utilize technology with the class. Appropriate forms and times of communication are itemized for students to know how and when their instructor prefers to be contacted. The use of cell phones allows the instructor to be free from the confines of their office environment and enables engagement with the student population at higher levels than would otherwise be possible.

2.3 Explosive Growth

GGC began in 2006 with 118 juniors and 10 full-time instructors. In 2007, the student headcount increased to 788. Every year since has seen student enrollment growth nearly doubled.

Table 1. Student Enrollment Growth

Year	Headcount	FTE	% Growth
2006	118	76.2	-
2007	788	695.6	668%
2008	1563	1374.3	198%
2009	2947	2621.7	189%
2010	5380	4882.2	183%

As one would suspect, this increase in student enrollment has also prompted a similar growth in faculty. In 2007, 72 additional full-time faculty were added along with the first group of 4 part-time faculty. On average, the size of the faculty has increased approximately 60% each year since 2007.

Table 2. Instructional Faculty Growth

Year	Full-Time	Part-Time	Total	% Growth
2006	10	0	10	-
2007	82	4	86	860%
2008	105	10	115	134%
2009	124	43	167	145%
2010	193	131	324	194%

As the number of students and faculty increased, staff members showed more interest in using cell phones to support their unit's missions. Vice Presidents were given discretion to decide which of their staff members needed cell phones. For some functional areas, Sprint "hotspots" or "MiFi" devices were also purchased to support access to email and web services from remote locations.

2.4 Providing Support

Due to the explosive growth of the cell phone program, we had to update our support model. After the first year, Rave Wireless was no longer able to support the growing demands of the cell phone program. While Sprint continued to be the carrier, provisioning and supporting the phones became the responsibility of Support Services, a branch of the Office of Educational Technology (OET).

As Support Services began to assume the provisioning and support responsibilities, it became increasingly important to build strong relationships with Sprint's public sector account representatives, engineers, field care representatives, local store managers, and others involved in product development and support. While GGC took ownership of the purchase, deployment, and basic trouble-shooting of each device, hardware malfunctions became the responsibility of a few hand-picked local stores that were certified service centers.

2.5 Recent Additions

In 2010, the introduction of the iPad and other mobile tablet devices once again pushed the boundaries of the cell phone program. Support Services was asked to provide support for these devices, which meant broadening the array of vendors to include equipment and service from AT&T. A new AT&T satellite phone was purchased and deployed to enable communications from GGC's Outdoor Adventures program as they took student trips to remote locations not serviced by traditional cellular devices.

3. RESULTS

3.1 The Good

In all but a few cases, survey results from an annual Educational Technology Faculty Survey have shown consistent growth in the percentage of faculty who rated cell phone usage as several times a week or daily.

Table 3. Cell Phone Usage Survey Data

Question	2008 %	2009 %	2010 %
Read GGC Email	79%	82%	91.8%
Accessed Calendar	73%	82%	90.2%
Accessed Contacts	66%	58%	84.9%
Used Text Messaging	56%	67%	80.9%
Had Phone Conversations	64%	89%	71.2%

Similar growth has been demonstrated in a separate Annual Faculty Survey taken each fall. One section of that survey is dedicated to cell phone functionality and support. In this survey, faculty are asked how they ranked the cell phone's contribution in support of their teaching activities, student engagement and mentoring, research activities, and service activities. The results are shown in Table 4 below, with percentages showing those who indicated either Agree or Strongly Agree to cell phone impact.

Table 4. Cell Phone Functionality Survey Data

Question	2008 %	2009 %	2010 %
Support Teaching	67%	80%	76.4%
Support Student Engagement and Mentoring	71%	80%	84.2%
Support Research	39%	52%	57.7%
Support Service	62%	73%	69.2%

One valuable indicator on how well an institution is doing with student engagement is reflected in the student retention rates. Compared to all other state colleges within the University System of Georgia, GGC's retention rates have been higher every year since it began following the first freshman cohort in 2007. In fact, the 2008 freshman cohort retention rate even surpassed the average of the other state universities within the System.

3.2 The Bad

As GGC has experienced explosive growth in the student and faculty populations, staff growth has increased only slightly. With over 500 cell phones and over 50 tablet devices being supported, Support Services struggles with the manpower to provide adequate support. In addition to managing the devices, we must also manage the overall account. Certain services that cost additional funds cannot be totally blocked on all devices, so each bill has to be itemized in order to pass along personal charges to the end user. Support Services is not adequately staffed to facilitate this level of accounting.

In addition to human capital, the economic downturn has also taken its toll. When the program began, members of the cell phone program were allowed to upgrade their devices on a yearly basis. We can no longer provide annual upgrades due to the high number of program participants, higher costs for devices and plans, and a restricted budget. As a result, user satisfaction with the entire support process has been reduced. This has caused Support Services to begin an initiative aimed at managing customer expectations.

A final challenge stems from the multiple device formats on the market. Until June 2010, GGC utilized the Zimbra email system for all faculty, staff, and student email. Not all phones were compatible with Zimbra. Phones with their own specific OS would usually not sync with the email/calendar/contacts of Zimbra. Blackberry users also struggled. Even though GGC deployed a Blackberry Enterprise Server (BES), there were frequent problems with syncing the Blackberry devices and the Zimbra system. Obtaining access to and performing adequate testing on the range of devices from Windows OS, Palm OS, Android, Blackberry, and iPhone proved difficult if not impossible.

4. FUTURE PLANS

GGC will continue to promote the cell phone program, though aspects of the program may change. Additional staff is necessary to provide adequate support and ensure accounting issues are resolved. For instance, in the future part-time faculty may only be offered the phone stipend option. Although this places the burden of communication more squarely on the shoulder of the faculty member, it reduces the amount of risk involved with issuing equipment to part-time faculty members who are employed only seasonally with the College.

Sprint's partnership with Blackboard Mobile will allow students and faculty the ability to view Blackboard portal and classroom content on their cellular and tablet devices. A plan is in place to develop a Sprint ID to offer tailored services on all GGC-provided phones. That service will also be extended to others who have a qualifying phone that can receive the Sprint ID capabilities.

5. FINAL CONCLUSIONS

Although there are certainly challenges with supporting a growing and dynamic program such as the cell phone program, survey results indicate what GGC hoped would be true – the implementation of a ubiquitous cell phone infrastructure and culture significantly enhances student engagement and therefore adds to student retention and ultimately student success.

Faculty are also learning more about how to best incorporate the cell phone in their communication efforts with students. In earlier stages, some faculty initially made themselves overly available to students with little to no restrictions. They found themselves tethered to the devices as students called or texted at all times of the week and weekend, expecting immediate feedback. These faculty are now finding a better balance. Through the use of the Technology Covenant, they have learned to specify times and days of availability to define student expectations regarding communication.

Staff members are finding cell phones as valuable as faculty, though their use supports an entirely different function. In a survey of staff done in 2010, 47.3% of those who responded either agreed or strongly agreed that they needed a cell phone to do their job well. In a separate question, 61.4% agreed or strongly agreed that they actually use a cell phone to support their job responsibilities. However, 34.6% of these staff members reported having a GGC-provided device. This demonstrates a need to potentially expand the program to even more staff members.

An anonymous faculty comment in the 2010 Educational Technology Survey best sums up the growing mentality toward the cell phone program: "This is a great support to enhancing communication with students. Students may call or text me anytime and they seem very comfortable communicating with their professors in this way." As this comment suggests, cell phones have indeed become a huge part of the culture of GGC.

6. ACKNOWLEDGMENTS

Thanks to Linda Gilbert, Juliana Lancaster, Austen Krill, and Lily Hwang for their assistance in providing data provided in this paper.

InnovatEDU a Collaboration to Reduce Higher Ed Security Risk

George F. Claffey Jr.
Charter Oak State College
55 Manafort Drive
New Britain, CT 06053
860.832.3890
gclaffey@charteroak.edu

Harry J. Regan
ETC Support
Woodbridge, CT
regan@etcsupport.com

ABSTRACT

Twenty-first Century institutional leadership involves a combination of fundraising, enrollment management, facility planning, setting discount levels and a never ending balancing act managing the needs and expectations of students, faculty, staff, the community and, of course, the Board. The skills required for effective leadership require both a broad reach and intricate, detailed knowledge in order to achieve and maintain successful operations. IT security is one more concern on the pile of the leader's responsibilities. While the requirements for successful leadership have increased, decreases in budget funding, state or federal support, and endowments are requiring innovative, budget-friendly solutions for addressing IT & data security.

Categories and Subject Descriptors

Legal Aspects, Management, Measurement, Security, Standardization

General Terms

Management, Measurement, Documentation, Security, Legal Aspects, Verification.

Keywords

Higher Education Security Training, InnovatEDU, FERPA training, GLBA Training, DCMA Training, Anti-Virus, Phishing, Trojan Horse.

1. InnovatEDU: Securing Data and Enabling Change in the Risk Adverse Culture of Higher Education

Twenty-first Century institutional leadership involves a combination of fundraising, enrollment management, facility planning, setting discount levels and a never ending balancing act managing the needs and expectations of students, faculty, staff, the community and, of course, the Board. The skills required for effective leadership require both a broad reach and intricate, detailed knowledge in order to achieve and maintain successful operations. IT security is one more concern on the pile of the leader's responsibilities. While the requirements for successful leadership have increased, decreases in budget funding, state or federal support, and endowments are requiring innovative, budget-friendly solutions for addressing IT & data security.

Over the past ten years, advances in technology have allowed institutional leaders access to a wealth of new information to help guide decision making. Advances in analytic tools have allowed us to trend data, look for at-risk students, identify possible donors, and review the profile of an incoming class to help set next year's discount rate.

While technology has provided valuable information to help the institution, its ability to cripple an institution is just as great, if not greater. At the end of the day, buildings can be repaired, classes rescheduled, systems restored from tape, but a security breach of your student/alumni data will damage your institution's relationship with its students and alumni possibly causing them financial harm through identity theft. The loss of trust between the university and its student body will take years to repair.

Security is not a technology problem, it is a Presidential responsibility.

While a president may delegate authority for student housing crime to the campus police department, it is ultimately the President's responsibility to ensure a safe academic environment for students, the same holds true with information security. While controls can be administered by a Chief Information Officer, it is ultimately the President who holds the responsibility to protect student information and his/her name will be the one on the front of the local and national news

Over the past two years, there have been a number of disturbing developments in information security. Along with the proliferation of connected devices – the iPhones, iPads, smart phones and web-enabled everything—came an evolution in the way cybercrime was practiced. The frightening reality is: cybercrime has become commoditized. The black market cost of an "identity" plummeted from about $100 per identity to about $2

– and what that means is that for criminals to make serious money, they need volume.

In the wake of a security breach, history has shown that grant funders and the federal government often require additional and extensive audits following such a catastrophic event. Recent Gartner data shows that on average, an institution should expect to pay approximately $150 per identity breached. A relatively small breach of 10,000 records could easily cost an institution over $1,500,000 in direct student mitigation expenses. The greater cost are "hidden"; related to the less tangible cost to rebuild the relationship with the students and alumni. In fact, if not handled correctly, these relationships may never be rebuilt.

Identity theft has become so common, that the FBI no longer investigates identity theft incidents that are below 100,000 records. What is the ideal place to get volume? Student records in higher education.

At the same time, the evolution of virtualization and cloud computing have made things more abstract and removed from legacy security protocols. In the same floor space that once contained a single server, it is now possible to host four, eight, a dozen or even more virtual servers – each logically independent and capable of providing the same services - with the same security flaws - as their non-virtualized counterparts. Moreover, if an attacker can compromise the management system (aka the Hypervisor), he can exploit the vulnerabilities of the four or more servers on that virtual host.

Human nature makes us enthusiastic about implementing technology without fully thinking through the architecture and implications of design decisions. In performing security assessments and forensic investigations, we find evidence to suggest that networks and systems are often "assembled" for functionality rather than "designed" to incorporate both operational and security concerns. Often, security features are left out of a network "until we're ready for production". This is not an indictment of the technical staff – middle and senior management are just as culpable. We see system testing cut short to meet an expense or schedule milestone, with technical decisions being made based on resource availability rather than engineering criteria. Exceptions to accepted practices are often routinely granted, and plans to subsequently review these exceptions are ignored or forgotten. When the next project comes along, some of these exceptions and compromises create unwelcome "surprises" in critical networks and systems. Legacy system flaws are often left un-patched because "it will be replaced soon". Test systems with copies of live production data are forgotten about, while process data flows don't get updated when the application base changes. For example, transaction data is staged on Server A so it can be picked up by Process X, however only Process X was discontinued two years ago and that data is left orphaned, sitting on some machine waiting for a process to run – or for a hacker to find it. This phenomenon is independent of the size or sophistication of an organization. We have witnessed these scenarios in small private institutions and large state systems and everywhere in between. The common denominator is people. This becomes the "80-20 rule" of the 21st Century. While good engineering and operational practices are generally followed, they are not always followed despite what the project management office and senior management may believe.

Cyber security suffers from a similar dilemma that campus police face: "How do you secure an environment that is "open" in nature?" The educational environment is one of openness, sharing and collaboration. The battle between openness and control is often at the core of security breaches in educational institutions.

Rather than dig a moat around our campus and protect the drawbridge, information security must be layered to conceive for possible breaches of a single layer. It is through a combination of personnel, data, business process analysis, and technology that our information security will improve. The cost, disruption, mitigation and overall risk of holding confidential and personally identifiable data rests with the President. It will require a shift in culture and presidential leadership to provide major improvements.

Traditionally, cyber security focused on providing a gatekeeper or "firewall" between the outside world and the campus environment. Hackers are shifting their tactics and are no longer trying to compromise the firewall but rather compromise the end users. Disguised as a card from Hallmark, Citibank statements, eBay purchase, or local tech support, hackers are becoming exceptionally effective at convincing users to provide their username, password, and other private information in the name of opening or accessing something online.

Most disturbing, however, is the shift in tactics from attacking the infrastructure to attacking the user. Why waste time figuring out how to penetrate the firewalls when you can trick a user into loading a software agent to carry out the attack from the inside? Rather than attacking the central database, it is much easier for hackers to steal the credentials of the folks who have legitimate access—the Financial Aid Officer, Registrar, Admissions and Business Office staff.

The size of your institution doesn't matter and neither does the brand, quantity, and strength of your firewall. If your students and staff unknowingly give away their confidential access information to cyber criminals, then you are likely to be just minutes away from a disastrous breech and millions of dollars in restorative costs.

If we define a data breach as any unauthorized access of information, does it matter whether the perpetrator comes through an elaborate hack of the firewall and application server or if they just borrowed a USB device? Is it any less of a breach if a hacker is able to get an unsuspecting faculty member to click on an attachment in an innocuous looking email that caused malicious software to be installed on their computer?

Information security is NOT a technology problem, it is an institutional problem. Earlier it was stated that the problem was people – the solution is also people. Our best defense is to equip our end users with training to help them understand how to safeguard their information and that of our students.

The information technology (IT) department can help. By bringing together representatives of technical and business staff, the IT department can identify the "blackspace" where sensitive business data is stored, where business processes require, create, and move critical personal data.

All over the United States, Presidents and Chief Information Officers, including myself, have witnessed a disturbing increase in hacking. The common denominator is people. While good engineering and operational practices are generally followed, they are not always followed, despite what project management officers and senior managers may believe.

So how can a school really assess its security program and protect itself?

The most important and primary matter that you need to grasp is that your staff, students, and faculty are the weakest security links. It is not a hole-in-the-firewall or an exceptional hacker that will cause irreparable damage, rather, it is the admissions counselor who lost a laptop with student data while on a trip, the student worker in the registrar's office who just wanted to look up a friend's grades, or the janitor who threw out bags of carbon copies of credit card transactions.

Even if all security protocols are followed and all the appropriate layers of security are in place, the risk is often found outside the boundaries of these protections. For example, work at home arrangements often involve sensitive data being moved outside the protections that are in place on campus. Protecting confidential data after the data moves outside the campus protections depends on the individual employee's knowledge of security best practices and the individual's ability to independently implement security best practices.

InnovatEDU: A Higher Education Solution to a Higher Education Problem

As the person in charge of your institution's safety, the largest positive effect to your campus's security posture will be through efficacious training of faculty, staff, and students. Your definitive action to require this training will prove to provide the broadest security impact to your institution's vital data, and will also be one of the least expensive controls that you can implement. In as little as a one hour online course, faculty, staff and students can gain a basic understanding of how to protect and identify social engineering attacks and learn how to effectively safeguard data.

Secondly, you must recognize that what needs to be protected is the data, not the infrastructure. The infrastructure only plays a supporting role in the protection of information assets.

Our best defense is to equip our end users with training to help them understand how to safeguard their information and that of our students.

InnovatEDU was born out of both the CT Distance Learning Consortium, a higher education consortium serving over 130 P-20 institutions and Charter Oak State College, Connecticut's premier higher education institution. InnovatEDU was designed to allow higher education professionals a "thought incubator," in which to take some risks in the relatively "risk averse" higher education. Through its peer based design, these risks would be spread among the participants in InnovatEDU. After multiple conference poster sessions, a common theme emerged. Higher education is a laggard in comparison to its corporate peers in security posture and protection of critical data. Many solutions involved combinations of deep engineering expertise and firewall/IPS/IDS devices. After mining various security audit documents, findings, and advice, first project for InnovatEDU crystalized – "Provide Security Training for Higher Education Faculty and Staff." This project was combined existing teaching and learning resources with outside security expert services to create a higher ed for higher education product. It also leveraged Charter Oak's 35+ year model as a completely online institution.

Today, InnovatEDU raises awareness about information security and security training in higher education.

Topics include:

- General Cyber Awareness
- Anti-virus Software and Updates
- Remote Access Security
- Social Engineering
- Effective Password Management
- Phishing

The course is designed in an online format offering training "anywhere, anytime." Perhaps more importantly is the availability is the pedagogical design. The course was designed in a "mastery format" which educates and then quizzes participants in knowledge they recently learned. Should a participant, select an incorrect answer, the course provides a new teaching moment using different examples and situational simulations to help reinforce the correct action and or answer. In essence, you cannot complete the course without scoring 100% on all of the quizzes.

Software tools such as Lectora and Raptivity have added multiple "game simulations" to help engage students in "active learning" exercises designed to reinforce and provide multi-modal learning opportunities.

In addition to the pedagogical design, a dashboard allows CXOs to see who has taken the course or more presently, who hasn't taken the course. This 45-60 minute training is designed to mitigate significant institutional risk, at some campuses it has become a requirement to take and pass the security course before receiving your initial login.

We hope that you will explore www.innovatEDU.org and demo our first collaboration, an online "security foundations" course designed at training higher education faculty, staff, and administrators in security awareness, protection of confidential information, and internet best practices.

Windows 7 – Trials and Tribulations

David Dean
Lewis & Clark College
0615 S.W. Palatine Hill Rd.
Portland, OR 97219
503-768-7257
ddean@lclark.edu

ABSTRACT

Giving up on something you know in order to risk the unknown usually proves to be a challenge. It is customary to have created a comfortable atmosphere of using what's now considered the old, but there is a demand for the new. So now is the time to learn, explore and ultimately understand the new. This new version of Windows is radically different from the old version. It requires much time, patience and planning, which in the Information Technology world is something we do not have. This requires us to collectively pool our experiences together and collaborate to achieve our goals.

Windows XP has been around for a long time and most have become comfortable in developing and deploying it. Windows 7 offers a substantial upgrade from Windows XP in regards to features for users, but not necessarily for image developers. Image developers are discovering that creating a Windows 7 image is not an easy process compared to using Windows XP. It requires undergoing extensive test trials, researching new approaches to conduct old tasks, and giving up on features that can no longer be achieved using this new operating system.

At Lewis & Clark College, we have migrated all of our PC computers and dual-boot labs to Windows 7 64-bit from Windows XP. We overcame many obstacles while striving to meet our goals. This paper will highlight the in-depth process it took to develop and deploy a Windows 7 image for our environment, including the researched documentation and resources that assisted us through our endeavor.

Categories and Subject Descriptors

C.5.3 [COMPUTER SYSTEM IMPLEMENTATION]: Microcomputers
D.4.0 [OPERATING SYSTEMS]: General

General Terms

Design, Management, Reliability.

Keywords

Windows 7, deployment, sysprep

1. INTRODUCTION

1.1 Lewis & Clark College Overview

Lewis & Clark College is a private college located in Portland, OR. With an enrollment of approximately 2,900 undergraduates and 1,500 graduate & law students, Lewis & Clark's Information Technology department supports and maintains approximately 400 lab computers. Seventy-five percent are Apple computers where as the other twenty-five percent are PCs. Thirty percent of the Apple lab computers are setup in a dual-boot environment. All computer lab PCs & dual-boot Apple computers are running Windows 7 64-bit Enterprise. Lewis & Clark College previously ran Windows 7 64-bit Professional, but has acquired a Microsoft campus agreement that allowed us to upgrade all Windows computers on campus to windows 7 Enterprise. This also gave us the licensing to install Windows 7 on Apple Computers.

1.2 Scope

The information provided in this paper focuses on Lewis & Clark College's computer lab environment. While the configurations and process we have created for the college are comfortable to us, these items may or may not be relevant to other institutions. This framework can easily be expanded upon and modified to fulfill our evolution as well as fellow universities of Windows 7 development and deployment.

2. PREVIOUSLY IN WINDOWS XP

Information Technology departments have had many years to solidify their Windows XP development and deployment. There are many variations of the process, which are based on, but not limited to user and organization: needs, demands, policies and size. Lewis & Clark College process was basic in comparison to much larger universities. Our process has been simplified to be described in the following items.

2.1 Customizing the Desktop

Customizing the desktop was pretty straight forward process for Lewis & Clark. Initially, we would go about doing an OEM install of Windows XP and creating a local administrator account. From this account we would personalize the user interface, install and configure applications, install machine specific drivers, and configure the machine settings that were expected for each computer lab. Once all was complete, cleanup and optimization is accomplished by removing temporary files and trimming down the size of the user account to assist with profile loading speed.

2.2 Setting the Default User

The user environment for the computer lab has been prepared and is almost ready for new users to access. Windows XP offered different ways to disperse account settings and configuration, but the one that was adapted for Lewis & Clark was to select the Administrator account that was configured and copy it to the Default User account, which is where new accounts pull settings from when they are created. We also use Faronics Deep Freeze on our computers so we tell Deep Freeze software that it's ready to be deployed.

2.3 pGina

For our Windows XP images we used a program called pGina to allow users to authenticate to our computer lab using their ldap credentials and create custom login screen specific to our college.

2.4 Symantec Ghost

Lewis & Clark uses Symantec Ghost to manage its deployment of PC computer images for computer labs. Once we have copied our profile to the Default User account, we boot the computer to connect to our Ghost Server and create an image from that computer. Once that image has been created, we then configure the server to deploy the said image to the computer lab that it was created for by booting the computers in that lab to connect to the Ghost server and then sending the image to the computer lab once they are all connected. After the image has been deployed, we boot the computer lab to the Administrator account, set its computer name, and then freeze it.

3. WINDOWS 7 IMAGE DEVELOPEMENT

Microsoft presented an operating system worthy of an upgrade from Windows XP with Windows 7. When Windows 7 was first announced our I.T. department was eager to get its hands on it and dive into the features it had to offer. Upper management decided on the timeline for Windows 7 deployment, we began to build a master image of the operating system. Of course, we began by mimicking what we did previously in Windows XP. We found that what once was mastered was no longer relevant. Microsoft had eliminated our previous method to enhance a more proper formal method known as Syprep for image development and deployment.

After we discovered our old method no longer worked, we began researching the correct method of deployment. However, Microsoft had not issued any documentation on Windows 7 deployment until several months after its release. There were many exchanges of tips and tricks across different forums and blogs on figuring out the method, but no formal guide seemed in sight until we discovered a blog by Brian Lee Jackson, which is now a part of itbros.com[1].

This blog had compiled information from the author's personal experiences and information provided by commentators of the blog in establishing a visual guide of the method of sysprepping a Windows 7 machine. While not all the information was applicable to us, it gave a solid starting point on our endeavor. We spent several months researching, testing, and learning this method and customizing it to fit our instructional needs. Our image creation roadmap is illustrated throughout this section and we highlight some of the challenges we incurred in developing it.

3.1 Creating an Answer File

The first item introduced to sysprepping a windows 7 machine is creating an answer file. An answer file is described as a file that contains the settings and configurations to apply to a Windows image during installation. This file is commonly named unattend.xml. It's a file that holds values of variables that is used in the scripting process of sysprep. Sysprep will customize our Windows environment to the values set in that file. We create this file by downloading and installing Windows Automated Installation Toolkit (WAIK) on a workstation other than the reference computer. We then launch Windows System Image Manager.

3.1.1 Windows System Image Manager

Windows System Image Manager is the application provided by Microsoft to create an answer file for our Windows 7 image. It provides a graphical user interface to easily customize an answer file to our needs. In order to develop the answer file we need to import a catalog file from a Windows 7 DVD or an iso file. Answer files created are specific to the Windows 7 version used for the master image we are creating. For example, an answer file built using a catalog file from a Windows 7 32-bit could not work with a Windows 7 64-bit image. The following are the sections of the answer file that we add components to.

3.1.1.1 Generalize

The generalize section of answer file will prepare our Windows 7 installation to be imaged. The component we add to this section is amd64_Microsoft-Windows-Security-SPP_6.1.7600.16385_neutral. From this component we set the SkipRearm value to 1.

3.1.1.2 Specialize

The specialize section of answer file, defines machine-specific information for the image for example, configuring network settings, international settings, and domain information.

The first component we add to this section is amd64_Microsoft-Windows-Deployment_6.1.7600.16385_neutral. From this component, we will run a synchronous command to set the administrator account to be active using the path "net user administrator /active:yes" and setting the value WillReboot to "Never. "

The second component we add to this section is amd64_Microsoft-Windows-Security-SPP-UX_6.1.7600.16385_neutral. From this component, we will set the SkipAutoActivation to "true."

The last component we add to this section is amd64_Microsoft-Windows-Shell-Setup_6.1.7600.16385_neutral. From this component, we tell CopyProfile to be true. This will tell sysprep to copy the Administrator account to the Default User account. Set ShowWindowsLive to false, and set the TimeZone to Pacfic Standard Time.

3.1.1.3 oobeSystem

The oobeSystem section allows us to define settings that are applied during the first-boot experience for end users, also called Windows Welcome. oobeSystem settings are processed before a user first logs into Windows.

The first component we add to this section is amd64_Microsoft-Windows-International-Core_6.1.7600.16385_neutral. From this component, we set the values of the default languages used in our Windows 7 image by setting InputLocale, SystemLocale, UILanguage, and UserLocale to the value of "en-us."

The second component that is needed is amd64_Microsoft-Windows-Shell-Setup_6.1.7600.16385_neutral. From this component, we will set the following values: RegisteredOrganization to our college name, "Lewis & Clark College," and RegisteredOwner to "Authorized Lab User." The AutoLogon property will be set to enable the Administrator and log into the account automatically. The values set are: Username to "administrator," LogonCount to 5, Enabled to "true" and Password to our admin password.

The next property is FirstLogonCommands. These commands will run when the administrator account is logged into the first time via command line. Each command has to be executed in a specific order which will run synchronously. The First SychronousCommand CommandLine value will be set to "cscript //b c:\windows\system32\slmgr.vbs /ipk XXXXX-XXXXX-XXXXX-XXXXX-XXXXX" The Xs represent our Windows 7 Enterprise key. The values Order is set to 1 and RequiresUserInput is set to false.

The second SychronousCommand CommandLine value will be set to "cscript //b c:\windows\system32\slmgr.vbs /ato" This prompts Windows to attempt online activation. The values Order is set to 2 and RequiresUserInput is set to false.

OOBE Property will be defined by the following values: HideEULAPage to "true," NetworkLocation to "Home," and ProtectYourPC to 1.

Lastly, under the UserAccounts property, we are going to actually have Windows create a local administrator account. The following properties will be defined to tell windows to create the account: Action to "AddListItem," Description to "Local Administrator," DisplayName to "Administrator," Group to "Administrators," and Name to "Administrator."

Once finished, We save the file naming it "unattendlabs.xml".

3.1.2 Set Computer Name

After creating the answer file, we have to edit it to remove a line in order to prompt the computer to change its computer name. We will open the file in notepad and remove the following line: <ComputerName></ComputerName>.

3.2 Installing Windows 7

One thing we found upon installing Windows 7 compared to Windows XP is that it's considerably faster to install, but we can make it even faster by installing Windows 7 from a flash drive.[2]

We proceed through the normal process of installing Windows 7 on the computer where we are going to create our image. The issue is finding a computer desktop configuration we can use for multiple computer configurations instead of having to go through this process for each specific configuration. Most institutions it seems use Dell computers for their environment. We have had the most success with using the Dell Optiplex 980 and Optiplex 755 for our base images that we created for both our Dell Laptop and other desktop configurations.

Once the installation is complete, the computer displays the welcome screen inquiring about creating a username. This is where we boot into audit mode to begin customizing our image. We boot into it by hitting ctrl+shift+f3 from the welcome screen. This will reboot the computer and load 'audit' mode.

3.2.1 Audit Mode

Audit mode is designed to customize a Windows installation before deploying the computer to a user. This mode we are able to install applications, add drivers, execute scripts, and customize our user experience. Traditionally, we create a base image that contains the base environment we want applied to all other image configurations. We create a ghost image of our base and then deploy it to other lab configurations that need further customization. The user account that audit mode boots into is the built-in administrator account.

3.2.1.1 Disable Sleep

When in audit mode, we found the built-in administrator account is disabled. This caused conflicts when we were working on the computer and we walked away from working on it and returned the computer decides to go to sleep. Upon, waking we found that we were locked out of the computer because the account is disabled and in order to get back into the account we had to do a hard boot. Two options are available. One was enabling the administrator account, or second was to disable sleep for the computer, but not the monitor. We chose the second option.

3.3 Image Customization

As stated prior, we create a base image for our lab computers that has specific profile customizations, scripts and applications. Lewis & Clark College is highly centralized in regards to lab computing. It is important to us that all students, staff and faculty have the same user experience in all computer labs so they are familiar with navigating these computers no matter where they are. Besides our base image, we have 9 different Windows 7 lab configurations we have to develop. We will highlight some unique things we do in image customization for each other the following sections.

3.3.1 Install Applications

To ease our customization process and reduce redundant navigation on our master image, we install all applications first. It saves on time to configure the default programs for each of file type used while configuring Windows settings. Many of the file types can default to several different programs will install on our master so it's important we specify which file type goes where.

Additionally, we configure the current user and the all user profile to eliminate unnecessary folders and provide quick access to the application shortcuts. Both of these we configure when we are customizing the profile, but it makes it easier if all of the applications are pre-installed beforehand.

3.3.2 Install Drivers

For our base image, we do not install any drivers. This process we conduct only when configuring each specific lab configuration due to the hardware being varied for each lab.

3.3.3 Profile Customization

To assist in profile customization, we create a folder named "GodMode.{ED7BA470-8E54-465E-825C-99712043E01C}." This provides a single place to access all Windows settings without needing to browse options and folders in the Control Panel. This is a much more of an interactive way of configuring a profile and the Windows OS. Many other institutions configure these settings primarily using scripts, registry edits, and group policy that level of configuration is not necessary for our scope quite yet, but we are on our way by slowly evolving to it and learning how it can benefit us. We have had to learn and move to these models more since moving to Windows 7.

3.3.4 *Scripts*

In order to complete our profile customization, some settings need to be done during the unpacking process. We conduct this through shell and visual basic scripts. We keep these scripts and other profile customization files in a folder called management on the root directory of the system drive.

Our domain service authentication is managed via Active Directory. Our computers need to join the domain in order for users to log into them. The answer file does offer a way to join the domain, but we found that it lacked certain options that are needed in order for the machine to be setup in AD properly. We use a batch script that calls NETDOM to join the machine to the domain, but Windows 7 no longer has NETDOM pre-installed. We had to download Remote Server Administration Tools for Windows 7 with Service Pack 1 (SP1) and enable it from Windows Features under Remote Server Administration Tools.

This script not only joins the machine to the domain, but also adds certain domain users to the local administrators group and runs a registry edit to set the default domain.

Furthermore, it was found that customizing the taskbar application icons proved to be a great challenge due to the dramatic change from Windows XP and Windows 7. It took a lot of time and research into figuring out the process to create the taskbar we wanted users to have. While now there are guides to do this, originally when we were testing Windows 7 no one knew how. We slowly pieced together into a vbs script, which we refined later researching online[3].

Getting back to our shell script, we copy this taskbar script to the default user startup folder so that every domain user will get the same taskbar arrangement that we specified. Once completed, our script performs clean up of applications and deletes itself. This script is set into motion by executed by a registry edit before running sysprep that tells the script to run once after a reboot.

3.3.5 *Profile Cleanup*

Even previously in Windows XP, we need to clean up the user profile since it contains many unnecessary data that was used for updates and installations and we want to have fast loading user profiles. We access the hidden appdata folder listed under the user profile and proceed to go folder by folder to remove temporary or unneeded user customization files and folders for each application. We typically try to get our profile under fifty megabytes, but for computer labs it proves it to be a challenge.

3.4 Group Policy

Group Policy is a way to customize the environment of users and machines on the network or on a client computer. Global Group Policy provides a way to centrally manage and configure Windows, software and profile settings where local group policies is a more basic version that is designed to configure on a single computer.

3.4.1 *Global*

Lewis & Clark is still in the introductory phase in managing machines through global group policy. We hope to migrate to this model soon.

3.4.2 *Local*

We have limited the number of local policies that need to be configured. The only policy we definitely have to configure due to our AD environment is setting disable machine account password changes to enabled. This is due to having Deep Freeze installed on the machines. Additionally, we removed the extra step needed to logging into a computer by disabling the requirement of pressing control, alt, and delete to log in.

3.5 Running Sysprep

Sysprep prepares our custom installation so we can create an image of it to deploy to multiple computers.

3.5.1 *Scripts Used*

A couple of scripts are to prepare for cleanup of the sysprep process. On our image we needed to create a folder called scripts in the following directory: %WINDIR%\Setup\. We create a CMD file within that directory named SetupComplete.cmd. We edit this file and place the following line in it:

del /Q /F c:\windows\system32\sysprep\unattend.xml.

This deletes our xml answer file when sysprep is complete because the answer file will contains user account passwords.

We also place a shell script in our management folder in run the sysprep and execute our FIRSTRunOnce regedit for joining the domain.

3.5.2 *Answer File Placement*

In order for sysprep to run the answer file needs to be placed at the following location:

c:\windows\system32\sysprep

3.5.3 *Executing Sysprep*

When we are ready to create our master, we execute the custom shell script that calls sysprep using this line of code

sysprep /generalize /oobe /shutdown /unattend:unattendlabs.xml.

Sysprep will execute and shutdown the computer.

3.5.4 *Create Image*

Currently, Lewis & Clark uses a Ghost server to capture our computer images. Many others use ImageX and Windows Deployment Services. Once the computer is booted off, we plug in a flash drive that tells the computer to connect to our ghost server and automatically join a capture session. Then we capture the image from the server.

4. WINDOWS 7 DEPLOYMENT

All of our images are stored on our ghost server. When we are ready to deploy, we setup a deployment session through Ghost.

We boot all client computers we want to reimage to connect to our Ghost server and then from the server, send the image to all the client computers. Once the transfer is completed the client computer reboots and begins to unpack itself.

4.1 Image Un-packing

We found since we have pre-configured the image to execute our needs there is not much for us to do but wait until it's ready for us to name it.

4.1.1 Setting Computer Name

Lewis & Clark rely on several reporting tools to gather information and manage these computers. These tools rely on the computer name to differentiate each client. It was important us to specify each individual computer name. By removing the line of code from our answer file relating to the computer name. Windows Setup will prompt the user to type in a computer name. This is the only setup item we interact with through the unpacking process.

4.1.2 Loading Admin Profile

When sysprep completes and loads our administrator account we specified in our answer file, it will execute our script that joins the client computer to active directory and a variety of other items specified prior. We will then reboot the computer and then auto login again into the administrator profile.

4.1.3 Freeze it

The last item we must do to complete our deployment is to freeze our computer. Once all client computers have loaded into administrator profile a second time, we connect to our deep freeze server and tell all the client computers to freeze and reboot. From that we are done.

4.2 Outstanding Issues

Since we have deployed Windows 7, we still run into issues we have not been able to overcome. While there are little problems here and there, we highlight the following obstacles that are identified as ongoing issues not just for us but for Windows 7 deployment community as well.

4.2.1 First Login Profile

Windows 7 and Deep Freeze combination has raised an issue of when a new domain user's profile is created for the first time it takes about two and a half to three minutes for the user to log on. Using the sysprep process, we have not discovered a way to speed up the login process or alternative way to deploy. We hope that a solution will be made soon because we may revert back to Windows XP until a solution is found.

4.2.2 Language Bar and Keyboard Layouts

Our institution, with the field of studies we offer and our student population, requires a versatile mutli-lingual computer lab environment. The Macintosh operating system and Windows XP it is fairly easy to deploy language options for the computer labs, but Windows 7 sysprep has decided to eliminate the ability to deploy language options altogether from their copy profile process. Our Windows 7 environment has been unable to offer these options to our users.

5. CONCLUSION

Lewis & Clark found that migrating to Windows 7 was fun and rewarding experience. Our users are grateful for the change to a new and exciting environment. Changing the way our deployment and understanding how that worked was taxing. We wish that we had more time to prepare for our rollout to avoid as many bugs as possible, but we have no regrets.

We wrote this paper knowing that there will be someone who has not built a Windows 7 image before and wants a resource they can go to see all the collected knowledge of references and read about our experiences to greatly increase the speed of their rollout of a Windows 7 image.

6. REFERENCES

[1] Jackson, Brian. "Sysprep Windows 7 Machine Start to Finish." *The IT Bros*. 28 Jan. 2011. Web. <http://theitbros.com/sysprep-a-windows-7-machine-%E2%80%93-start-to-finish>.

[2] Jackson, Brian. "How to Install Windows 7 From Flash Drive / USB Stick - The IT Bros." *The IT Bros - We Know So You Don't Have To*. 27 Jan. 2011. Web. <http://theitbros.com/install-windows-7-from-a-flash-drive>.

[3] Jackson, Brian. "Taskbar Icons with Windows 7 Sysprep - The IT Bros." *The IT Bros - We Know So You Don't Have To*. 28 Jan. 2011. Web. <http://theitbros.com/copy-taskbar-icons-windows-7-sysprep>.

Investigating and Implementing Mobility

Fred Morris
University of Maryland
Office of Information Technology
College Park, MD 20742
01-301-405-7392
fred@umd.edu

Chris Higgins
University of Maryland
Office of Information Technology
College Park, MD 20742
01-301-405-5190
chiggins@umd.edu

ABSTRACT

The University of Maryland College Park is in the fourth year of a program to investigate the uses, advantages, pitfalls, costs and impacts of mobile devices in the pedagogical and social activities of a major University.

Categories and Subject Descriptors

K.3.1 [**Computers and Education**]: Computer Uses in Education

General Terms

Experimentation, Human Factors, Measurement, Security

1. Origins

In 2006-07, The University of Maryland College Park was working on methods to introduce prospective and new students to the technology on campus. Ms. Barbara Gill, then-Director of the Office of Undergraduate Admissions (OUA), was holding discussions with the late Dr. Jeff Huskamp, the University's Vice President and Chief Information Officer (VP/CIO) in the Office of Information Technology (OIT),.. The conversations centered on piloting a program that would provide a small group of newly admitted students with a device that could be easily integrated into their daily lives and enhance their experience at Maryland. With the release of the iPhone and iPod touch, it was clear the right devices were available with built-in wireless and a common stable operating system. The pilot plan was called the Mobility Initiative.

The goals of the Mobility Initiative were to:

- Enhance the classroom learning experience.
- Promote interaction between faculty and students.
- Provide students with a tool to help them manage their time and navigate the campus (physical and administrative environments).
- Enhance the personal safety of our students.
- Create an impression about the university's world class status through innovation and technology.

The plan was drafted and proposed to the Office of the Vice President and Provost (OVP/P) to enhance the Maryland experience for these students by offering these mobile devices as part of the scholarship. At the same time, discussions were ongoing regarding the increasing popularity and general utilization of mobile devices on campus. It was an obvious choice to combine the two topics.

The major stakeholders agreed that the Mobility Initiative should be undertaken. Its charter was to investigate what mobile devices were available, which were making an impact and what effects and changes, if any, their use could have on student and academic activities. Stakeholders became OVP/P, OUA and OIT. OIT played a central role in the pilot as it was recognized that a) the devices are, in fact, computing machines, b) IT infrastructure was likely to be impacted, c) OIT staff possessed required technical proficiency to assess and troubleshoot an IT environment that included the devices and d) OIT staff possessed the programming and web skills to adapt and/or create applications and content for consumption on the devices. Selecting the Banneker Key and Maryland Incentive Award Scholars as the pilot group was clear since they represent the most talented and most deserving students admitted to the university.

The three initial stakeholders decided that the day-to-day responsibility for the pilot should rest within OIT. In consultation with Admissions and the Provost, as well as with OIT management, the VP/CIO chose two OIT staff members to serve as co-project managers. Concurrently, the Director of Admissions assembled a Steering Committee of 28 members, comprised of deans, faculty, administrators and staff from a number of academic and support departments (such as Information Sciences, Engineering, Physics, et al.). The committee was charged with providing guidance, faculty input, feedback on progress and products and the like.

2. Planning

Following meetings with the steering committee, the project managers set about assembling two teams to define the initial course of the project: a planning and decision group and an operational team. The planning group was made up of staff from OUA, including the Director, the project managers and, as needed, the VP/CIO. In weekly meetings, they discussed and

SIGUCCS'11, November 12–17, 2011, San Diego, California, USA.

planned the specific strategies and efforts of the project. Also with this team rested policy decisions such as which devices to include in the project, how to handle lost or stolen devices, and the frequency and content of participant meetings.

The operational team was drawn primarily from groups in OIT that had direct involvement in getting the project running. Members were recruited from Academic Support (to bring expertise on faculty needs and use of technology in the classroom), Networking and Telecommunications (for contributions in adapting the devices for use on the campus wireless network and for testing/expanding wireless coverage in classroom locations projected for use by pilot students), User Support (for defining and implementing the support needs of project participants), Portal and Web Services (to provide expertise and manpower for web development of content required by the project) and from Data Administration (to organize and maintain the SharePoint site created to be the repository for minutes, records, and documents generated in the project). We also included a faculty member skilled in surveys and assessment. Meetings for the operations group were held bi-weekly.

3. Early Steps

An early decision by the planning group was the choice of devices to offer participants. The options were constrained by factors such as: a) the budget provided by OVP/P, b) the number of students in the pilot, c) the availability of the devices, d) the tools available to customize/program the devices' operating system and applications, e) the "wow" factor of what was being offered, and d) participants' family practices of cell phone and budget. Based on the above factors, the planning group decided to present participants with a choice.

We offered either an iPhone (making clear the monthly charges were the responsibility of the student) or an iPod touch. These units were nearly identical in most of the project's considerations covered above while enabling participation in the project without incurring an ongoing, monthly expense. Based on our available funds, we were able to offer each device with the maximum available storage space.

With two devices identified, discussions with Apple and AT&T began. As AT&T both sold the device and provided the service, iPhones were purchased through this vendor. iPod touches were purchased through Apple. Negotiations with AT&T resulted in discounted service plans and waived fees for those in the project. AT&T agreed to send representatives to campus for the distribution period so that students could collect their units and activate the accounts at the same place and time. We also invited AT&T to begin a schedule of weekly sales/support visits to our campus technology store (http://oit.umd.edu/techstore). Their agreement to do so resulted in direct support for students' AT&T accounts as well as the opportunity to offer the iPhone for sale in an on-campus location.

Providing mobile computing devices necessitated providing uses for the units in the form of web services and custom applications. As part of the development of the development the Portal and Web Services group produced mobile versions of the University's student portal and the Networking group built a specialized configuration to enable use of the iPhone and iPod over the University's secure Wi-Fi network. OIT's Academic Support group began work on a mobile app to access the University's online Learning Management System and obtained licenses for an app which turned the devices into classroom clickers. The project team also became aware of the efforts of a faculty member in the Department of Computer Science. He and his graduate students were developing an app suite for mobile devices that had components such as a campus map, a GPS-tracked campus bus schedule, the schedule for Washington, D.C.'s Metro bus and subway system, a geolocation marker (for tracking where a car or bike was parked) plus a proof-of-concept one-button emergency notification app. We contracted with the faculty member to create an iOS port of his suite and released it as one of the first group of apps created specifically for the project.

Other campus partners were brought in to the initiative to provide needed services. OIT Communications handled publicity, both on campus and to state and national news media outlets. The Terrapin Technology Store handled distribution of the devices, University Communications assisted with Maryland logos and graphics, and OIT Human Resources began the search for a dedicated, experienced iPhone software developer.

4. Year One

The first year of the project was the "how do we actually do this?" year. After summer preparations were completed, the deals were done, the classrooms' communications were enhanced, organizing began for the student meetings. We had decided to hold weekly, non-mandatory meetings covering a range of topics and presenters including training on the devices and the apps, presentations by faculty on the use of the devices in projects and research, and group discussions on device and app use personally and academically We also arranged for a Help Desk analyst to attend the sessions to provide any requested technical assistance.

The "official" website for the Initiative was released in the summer of the first year. We chose this mechanism, http://mobility.umd.edu, as the method by which participants would inform us of their device choice. For that first year, we had 142 students in the program. 100 chose the iPod touch and 42 chose the iPhone.

One special course was developed with support of the Initiative and in cooperation with the project's managers, Apple, Inc. and the College of Computer Science. This course is a 3-credit class, taught by an Apple Senior Software Engineer, on developing applications for iOS, the operating system that runs iPhones, iPod touches and now the iPads. Subsequent semesters have been taught by faculty from Computer Science with the class registrations remaining higher than the available openings.

Our concentration in year one was how the students used the devices in and out of class. At meetings, we shared cool apps that we discovered and queried the students on the ways they employed their devices. We heard about faculty that welcomed the use of devices in class and about those who prohibited it. Students took part in a usability study in which they gave feedback and opinions about the look, feel and operation of the apps provided by the project. We strongly encouraged regular feedback from students on how existing apps could be improved and, more importantly, what apps did they want that we didn't provide.

By the end of the fall semester, we found we had exhausted the need for weekly participant meetings. Attendance had decreased and we had added in other activities such as a web-based, mobile customized set of pages detailing University history. A faculty member and her graduate students in the School of Information Sciences tested a scavenger hunt activity with the Initiative students. Based on clues placed on those web pages and related sites, the student participants used their devices to locate and visit campus locations that taught the history of the University. The regular meetings were not reinstituted during the spring semester; rather communications and contact was done primarily through email, forums and surveys.

Through those forums and surveys, our takeaways from the first year were:

- Students liked using the devices as productivity tools – clicker, email, news
- Students are most enthusiastic about interactive learning on the device (scavenger hunt)
- Students do not see the devices replacing laptops but rather there is a place for a mobile device (on the go content; directions) and a place for a laptop (research)

Conclusions based on these comments told us that development for the initiative continues, must look at:

- Which content is appropriate for mobile app and web development
- How content of existing web pages should be re-formatted

5. Year two

Our first year assessment also pointed to a clear deficiency in the project. The population chosen to receive the devices, while engaged and helpful, consisted of students from a wide number of majors and colleges. There was no group of participants, no cohort, through whom we could get satisfactory information on the impact the devices had on learning in the classroom. Without a consistent band of students taking the same class, run by an engaged faculty member taking advantage of access to the devices, we were unable to assess how well the project fulfilled the goal of enhancing the classroom experience.

Two strategies were adopted to address the situation. The first was based in the realization that we needed to work closely with faculty to begin thinking about how a class of their students using iPhones and iPods could take advantage of the resource. This also focused on an examination of the potential changes faculty could incorporate into their courses made possible by having a class with anytime, anywhere connectivity. We sought to learn some of the advantages and risks and whether the faculty considered the experience a net positive or net negative.

To assist with identifying and recruiting faculty, we partnered with the University's Center for Teaching Excellence (CTE). The CTE (http://cte.umd.edu) is a faculty-led organization focusing on the improvement of undergraduate education. Programs they run and resources they offer give them a unique relationship with many University faculty. Alongside CTE, our project managers began reaching out to faculty, gauging interest in taking part in the project and encouraging participation with us.

As a result of this very successful partnership, the Initiative sponsored 6 faculty to attend CTE's Summer Institute for Teaching and Learning with New(er) Technologies dedicated to examining the use of mobile devices in the classroom. Faculty chosen for the Institute brought ideas of how to use the devices in their class plans. Through consultation and technical work between the sponsored faculty member and OIT's development staff, custom applications were created and implemented during the following academic year.

The second strategic action enabled the program to "create" single class cohorts and utilize the apps built for the Institute faculty, the Initiative itself, in addition to commercial apps. The Initiative purchased 66 iPod touches and set up a loaner program. Faculty were able to obtain mobile units for all the students in a given class (for which the students had to sign a document of liability to receive one). Devices could be borrowed for a few weeks or a full term depending on the project requirements and the availability of the devices. The apps requested by the instructor were loaded on the iPods, giving us an opportunity to see the impact of using mobile devices in a guided pedagogical process.

Feedback from instructors and students told us generally that a) students generally liked using the devices but sometimes thought they were extraneous to the project, b) there were minimal technical issues in implementation after the initial set up, c) activities outside the classroom were most effective in structure and impact, and d) students overall could see the benefit of using mobile devices for their classes.

6. Years three

The Initiative continued to grow in its third year expanding beyond the initial set of scholarship students to include a new program in Digital Cultures and Creativity. ,The 55 students in enrolled in this program received iPads as their mobile device in lieu of iPod Touches or iPhones.

As in year two, we continued to engage faculty to work to incorporate mobile devices in their teaching and learning activities. Faculty involvement increased with additional specific implementations of mobile ideas and applications being developed and used. The partnership with CTE has continued as well including ongoing funding for support of mobile learning faculty in the Summer Technology Institute. Additional faculty are creating environments for using mobile devices with the support of the Initiative.

Moving beyond the testing and beta stages for our campus developed apps, the program managers publicly released a number of the tools and apps that had been developed for the Initiative. Two years of testing, troubleshooting, refining and improving them made them ready to share with the campus public as a whole. This was an opportunity to provide the University benefits gained as a result of the ongoing efforts of the program and the Initiative team continues to release and promote new apps that had their beginnings in the Initiative.

In an effort to benefit from input by students not specifically in the participants group, the Initiative, the Office of Information Technology and the Department of Computer Science sponsored a Mobility Contest. Students were invited to design, create, test, and present apps of their choice with the three entries judged best receiving cash prizes. In a multi-step process, over 30 entries were initially received with more than 100 student participants from around campus. During the year-long development process the field narrowed to 10 projects and 30 participants. The winners were named in March 2011 with JamMyJam, a social music app taking top honors.

7. **Impact and lessons learned to date**

As we move into the fourth year of the initiative we can look back and see an evolution of the project and clear impact on our campus.

When the initiative began the iPhone had recently been introduced and few students had smartphones or personal digital assistants (PDAs) when the came to campus. Those students in the initiative were pretty unique on campus. Today, however, over half of our students have an app-phone, an iPod Touch, or a tablet device. The apps, mobile web sites, and wireless access points available to students have tremendously increasing usage. It is common for the students to use their devices in class for research and interactivity.

Similarly, development of mobile apps and web sites began with OIT programmers and in a highly specialized programming course. It has expanded to an open support of student development and numerous courses for a variety of mobile operating systems. The focus on individual app development has grown to a focus on building a mobile enterprise environment for ubiquitous access and development.

Probably the greatest impact is evident with our faculty and their courses. With the efforts to incorporate faculty into the initiative we have seen a tremendous growth in the use mobile devices for class activities both in and out of the classroom. Projects have ranged from the use of clickers, to in-class back channels using twitter, to data collection, to multimedia interviews.

Overall feedback in all aspects of the initiative has been favorable. For students, feedback has come from participant surveys, analysis of support trouble tickets and monthly student discussions and indicates devices are increasingly common Ifor personal and academic use but do not yet take the place of a laptop for more robust computing. Comments have shown that taking notes on the small iPod/iPhone keyboard is distracting and more difficult in class than typing on a full-size keyboard or handwriting. Those using iPads do not share the same feeling about not taking but still prefer laptops for papers and more involved projects. More popular have been the apps created to make learning about campus easier for new students. Location and map apps, transportation schedules, event notices and access to online learning and assignment tools have been very well received.

8. **What's Ahead?**

With year four underway we are exploring the different areas of mobile learning, and the mobile enterprise environment. For instance the release iPad and other tablet devices has the potential to influence the academic environment in a meaningful way. The larger screen provides more room for content, graphics, and interactivity. New tools (such as FaceTime for video connections and communications, and SkyGrid for new conglomeration) open additional areas to explore.

The Initiative will provide some focus in the coming year is eTextbooks and open content. Discussions among various campus stakeholders (e.g., faculty, the University Book Center, the Administration, and students) will be held to offer students mobile options in place of printed textbooks.

As mobile devices of varying sorts become more commonplace, the initiative will no longer need to focus on the individual but rather programs and the enterprise. The concepts of the mobility initiative are coalescing with a new project on blended learning and our new general education program.

Ubiquitous Computing

Matthew West
Lewis & Clark College
0615 SW Palatine Hill Road
Portland, OR 97219
+1 (503) 768-7251
mwest@lclark.edu

ABSTRACT

Ubiquitous computing takes computation from the desktop environment and moves it into every area of our lives. Instantaneous information and computation will be distributed over an array of small wireless networked devices. These can be embedded in daily artifacts such as appliances, light switches, stereos, cellular phones, and watches. This capability will revolutionize computation, allowing it to take place anywhere and at any time. Rather than accessing data only via a monitor and keyboard, one might access data via voice-activated commands and view it on a neighboring wall. Computation will be everywhere. Such technology will allow doctors to access medical histories during surgery uninhibited or help an architect inspect blueprint changes on site. For such a revolution to occur, however, an infrastructure and affordable technology needs to be established. This presentation will consist of a history of ubiquitous computing and an examination of current research developments. Advancing battery technology, wireless protocols (Bluetooth, IEEE 802.11, and LTE), applications, current examples, and social implications will be discussed.

Categories and Subject Descriptors

H.5.2 [**Information Interfaces and Presentation**]: User Interfaces – *input devices and strategies, interaction styles, standardization, theory and methods, user-centered design*; F.1.2 [**Computation By Abstract Devices**]: Modes of Computation – *interactive and reactive computation, online computation*; C.2.4 [**Computer-Communication Networks**]: Distributed Systems – *distributed applications, distributed databases, network operating systems*.

General Terms

Experimentation, Human Factors, Standardization, Languages, Theory.

Keywords

Ubiquitous Computing, Pervasive Computing, Mark Weiser.

1. INTRODUCTION

Over the past few decades, computers have become increasingly important in people's daily lives. Business people and computer aficionados are no longer the sole users of computers. People everywhere use the Internet and have tapped into a massive database of knowledge made up of a network of commercial, business, personal, and governmental information. The migration to the Internet due to affordable computers and Internet access will cause the emergence of a new paradigm of computing. Ubiquitous computing will enable a world where the monumental computer on a desk ceases to exist as a central link to information, but perhaps a wallet would hold all of a user's personal information as well providing access to the Internet. A user may have a refrigerator that tells them when items inside expire. Imagine that user then walking into a grocery store and having all the sale items that match their shopping list display the price and location of each deal on the shopping cart's display. These are small examples of the potential of ubiquitous computing.

1.1 Definition

Ubiquitous computing is a method of enhancing computer use and efficiency by making multiple computers available throughout a physical environment while having them essentially invisible to the user. The goal is to recess computers into the background of life, much like electricity has been. We no longer think about using electricity, we just do. This kind of relationship needs to be established with computers in order to create a more comfortable computing environment.

Some examples of potential ubiquitous products are clocks that find the correct time after power goes out, paint that dusts itself, walls that selectively dampen sounds, and keys that can beacon when lost. [18] Defining what isn't Ubiquitous Computing can help as well. Examples of what isn't ubiquitous computing are personal digital assistants (PDAs), tablet computers, and laptop computers. Even though these are Internet-enabled portable devices, they do not understand the context of their environment and react correspondingly. Another example of what isn't ubiquitous computing is virtual reality. Rather than integrating the computer into the user's environment, it tries to integrate the user into its computer-made environment. [19]

Mobile computing seems similar on the surface, but it is not ubiquitous computing, either. Mobile computing deals more with the hardware implementation of many of the core networking ideas of ubiquitous computing such as wireless network hardware protocols, global IP addressing, IP security, and roaming between data networks. Though ubiquitous computers will use these aspects of mobile computing, they are not the same. Mobile computing is neither a subset nor superset of ubiquitous computing, and they share many complementary goals.

1.2 History

Ubiquitous computing started out as a research program headed by Mark Weiser (July 23, 1952 – April 27, 1999) at Xerox's Palo Alto Research Center (PARC). It was first envisioned as an answer to what is wrong with personal computing. Computers are too hard to use, too complex, too isolating, too dominating, too big, et cetera. What started out as research led to creating a new field of computer science that speculates on a physical world filled and invisibly interwoven with sensors, activators, displays, and computational elements embedded seamlessly in the everyday objects of our lives. These objects would also be connected through a continuous wireless network. [17]

Ubiquitous computing will be the third major trend in computing history. The first major trend was the Mainframe Era (1950s-1980s). In this era experts and students ran computers behind closed doors away from the eyes of the public. When this era began, computers were so expensive and scarce that many people were forced to share one mainframe computer. The first relationship between humans and computers was thus defined as many users to one computer. In 1984 the number of people using personal computers surpassed the number of people using shared computers. This marks the second phase of computing. [18]

The Personal Computer Era (1980s-1990s) exposed computing to the masses and brought computers to many households. The computer became a personal tool. The computer on your desk was no longer a terminal, but your computer with your files on it, thus creating a relationship of a single user to a single computer. This personal attachment created a new relationship with the computer. It was no longer just a work tool, but a place to save writings and memos, to write a note to a friend, or to play a game. The main problem with this relationship is that interaction with the computer occupies all of the user's resources as they use it. An analogy can be made to an automobile. Both PCs and automobiles are relatively expensive special use items that require total attention to operate them. [17] The PC era pigeonholed the idea of computing to be time spent at a desk typing at a computer. Ubiquitous computing is working against this solitary definition and is trying to expand the use of computers to more diverse areas of our life.

The Internet provides the transition from today's computing paradigm to ubiquitous computing, and merges the ideas and practices from both the Mainframe and PC era, called the Transition Era. A large-scale client-server relationship exists where PCs act like web clients and mainframes become web servers. This massive interconnection of personal, public, commercial, business, and government information creates a background for ubiquitous computing. [18]

In the Ubiquitous Computing Era computers will be saturated in our physical environments and connected through a worldwide wireless network. [20] Our relationship with computers will change to many computers to one user. Some of the computers that we would access in a day could be very similar to the ones we use today. Some would be similar to the hundreds of computers, network devices, and servers we access in a few minutes of web browsing. Others will be embedded into walls, chairs, clothing, light switches, and books. We will access and use them without thinking. Though filling the world with networked mini-computers won't be easy or fast, embedding them into our daily artifacts is not farfetched.

Almost all stereos, televisions, radios, microwaves, refrigerators, and automobiles have some sort of circuitry in them. If they had an Internet server connected to them, they would have access to millions of sources of information. Stereos would be able to download play lists on request. You could turn on your microwave from work so that you could have a hot meal when you walked in the door. A car could be able to signal to your garage door to open when it was in your driveway. The possibilities are endless.

Embedded computers may be thought to be analogous to two other ubiquitous technologies of the past. Writing was once used solely as a tool to record and relay information to someone. Now writing can be found on billboards, clothes, furniture, cars, and buildings. We see it everywhere, yet it does not steal all of our attention. Writing lies in the background of our lives, but we use it regularly without thinking. The same can be said for electricity. We have learned to live with electricity; it becomes so second nature so that we hardly even think when flipping a light switch to brighten a room. It exists everywhere, yet it is so commonplace that electricity disappears from our lives. [20] Mark Weiser states a similar goal for ubiquitous computing: "Its highest ideal is to make a computer so embedded, so fitting, so natural, that we use it without thinking about it."

1.3 Initial Applications

Weiser and his research group came up with the first concrete ubiquitous applications between 1988 and 1994 at Xerox PARC. They called their initial incarnations "Pads, Tabs, and Boards." The idea behind their creation was to create an environment where people could collectively take notes and brainstorm together. Each board (eventually called LiveBoard) is used like a blackboard except that it is networked, and anyone with access to the PARC LAN can join in on a group discussion and add their own input through their pad or tab. The PARCPad is a miniature computer that is about the size of a page of paper. It is used for personal note taking and to add comments to the LiveBoard. Each PARCTab is about the same size as a post-it note and is used in a similar fashion. Pads and tabs were designed to eventually become a disposable computer.

An ActiveBadge was created for each user as well. The ActiveBadge is a beacon and identification, and is used to route the data from the wireless network to each device the user is communicating with. Many companies and classrooms today use a similar system for an array of reasons. Weiser envisioned that each user should have one badge, a couple of boards, tens of tabs, and hundreds of pads. [19]

Weiser's creations were the first step of envisioning ubiquity. There are many problems that need to be solved to enable technology to be immersed and used in the daily lives of users. Hardware, software, and people's perceptions of computation need to adapt to the needs of a ubiquitous computing environment.

2. TRANSITIONING

In order to establish a ubiquitous computing environment, an infrastructure of hardware, software, and communication must be engineered and integrated to provide adequate support. To achieve this goal, standards need to allow devices to dynamically share data, applications, and resources like printers, data storage, and computation. Distributed wireless networks and protocols are essential to allow small devices to communicate. Pervasive and accessible wireless networks must be provided to enable devices to have network connectivity. Communication mediums need to be coordinated so digital devices do not interfere with each other's transmissions. Various levels of networking protocols provide this coordination between our current wireless and cellular technologies: 802.11, 802.15, CDMA, GSM, 3G, and LTE.

For small devices to be able to function on a usable level, they also need to consume little power. The key approach to reduce power consumption is to reduce the clocking frequency of a processor and increase parallelism. [19]

There also needs to be a shift in the way users approach technology. Rather than using a multi-function desktop computer to help complete tasks, for example, a user may have to use many smaller single-use devices in conjunction with each other to gain a desired outcome. In order for these social elements to change, the underlying technology will need to progress to a point where computing can become ubiquitous.

2.1 Wireless Networking

2.1.1 Network Types

The structure of a wireless network can be organized in a similar manner to wired networks. The notions of local area networks (LANs) and wide area networks (WANs) both exist, but a new type of network has recently emerged: the personal area network (PAN). Wireless WANs (WWANs) are high power and have ranges measured in kilometers. These are used mainly in cellular communications. Wireless LANs (WLANs) cover distances from ten to a few hundred meters, consume a large amount of power, and are used to primarily network laptops. In the past, wireless networks were not often used due to high prices, low data rates, occupational safety concerns, and licensing requirements. [15] Most of those issues have been dealt with and many contemporaries use wireless communication on a daily basis.

Wireless PANs (WPANs) connect mobile devices carried by users to other mobile and stationary devices nearby. The PAN is the most crucial part of a ubiquitous network because users will primarily access their information using devices in the PAN. PANs are low power and the range for such a device would be about ten meters. [8] Due to the short range of WPANs, there are many ways to implement them including: radio frequencies, electric fields, infrared waves, and ultra-high-frequencies waves. [21]

2.1.2 Protocols and Standards

There are many options for implementing the physical layer of a network. As well, there are many options for choosing a protocol for the data link and medium access layers of a WPAN. The current WLAN protocol is WiFi, and has been used in many products for laptop wireless networking. Unfortunately, WiFi products consume too much power and have excessive range for many PAN devices. [21] The Institute of Electrical and Electronics Engineers (IEEE), the European Telecommunications Standards Institute (ETSI), and the 3rd Generation Partnership Project (3GPP) have created a set of protocols and standards to manage the wireless spectrum.

Cellular communication technology and wireless data communications are used concurrently but have completely different infrastructures and standards sets. ETSI has set the standards for 3G (or UTMS), our current cellular voice and data protocol, as well as LTE (Long Term Evolution), the next generation cellular protocol standard. 2G, CDMA, and other older GSM technologies are becoming less common and will soon be migrating to the LTE standard. [1]

IEEE has set standards for WLANs and WPANs. The 802.11 specifications are dedicated to WLAN technology and are what has standardized what we call "WiFi" today. The 802.15 specifications are designed for personal wireless devices. Bluetooth is an example of an 802.15 technology that was initiated as a means to connect cell phones to laptop computers. [21] Bluetooth's current use includes interconnecting a wide range of devices including: headsets, printers, phones, computers, and music devices. The standards encompass both the physical and data link specifications involved in implementing the technology, but are unfortunately incompatible with each other.

For a wireless PAN to be useful in ubiquitous computing, devices should be able to dynamically detect and use services provided by printers, displays, routers, and other resources. More ambitious goals should allow using shared office printers, receiving a menu, pulling lecture notes off of a LiveBoard, or paying for gas. Spontaneous networks and service discovery are essential to the usefulness of PAN devices. Just as a web browser is able to point to any web page, a wireless device should be able to access innumerable services anywhere. There are many higher-level protocols in development at companies, research institutions, and universities that provide the needed transport systems and service discovery that will aid in communication between ubiquitous devices. [21]

2.2 Battery Technology

For small, wirelessly enabled devices to be able to function as Weiser envisioned, battery technology needs to be advanced to a point where batteries can be embedded in small objects and provide power for the life of the object. The amount of power and the way the charge is discharged from a battery affects the life of the battery. As well, if devices will be used on the person, the battery size and weight need to be considered, as it's the bulk of any mobile device. [10] These constraints need to be considered when developing devices for a ubiquitous environment.

Even though most contemporary laptop and tablet computers have a battery life of less than ten hours, battery technology has advanced to the point where small wireless devices can be powered for a length of time on the magnitude of years. Sensor networks, radio frequency identification tags (RFID tags), and proximity readers are examples of devices that have low-power, long-life needs. Though more work needs to be done on battery technology, we are at a point where successful ubiquitous computing devices with low power needs can be designed and built.

2.3 Context-Aware Computing

Many of the requirements to establish a ubiquitous environment have been met by today's wireless and battery technology, but applications must also evolve in order to fulfill Weiser's vision of ubiquity. Applications will have to be location and context aware, requiring applications to learn and compute dynamically. Context-aware computing involves detecting, identifying and locating user's movements, routines, and actions while using this information to provide relevant data that may help the user with their actions. [14] The user can exist in many contexts in many different ways, even if they are doing the same activity in the same location. Since contexts depend heavily on the user's needs and application, context awareness needs to be dynamic and adaptive. Knowing the context of the user leads to being able to improve the application, particularly the interaction with the user.

Research and work in context-aware computing will be very useful to advancing applications to the level of sophistication that is needed for a ubiquitous environment. Kristof Van Laerhoven and Kofi Aidoo created a system to teach context to applications. Experiments were done with a small device with ten sensors on it. The sensors are used to measure light, humidity, temperature, and sound. The system merges the output from these sensors and maps the context description given by them to a description given by the user. [2]

Taking the raw data from these sensors and transforming it to a meaningful data structure by preprocessing the data with small routines can construct cues for applications. Cues are significant for fast and accurate context recognition systems. Experiments implemented with ten sensors have provided interesting results.

Simple activities are recognized within ten seconds with an accelerometer on the leg or hip. Learning about the location of a user with light sensors proved very efficient, especially when cues, such as frequency of light, were used. Research is currently being done on placement of sensors on clothing and devices, grouping of sensors for clustering, and redundancy of sensors to make the system robust. [2]

For context awareness to be effectively user-friendly, it is necessary that the system receive feedback from the user whenever the user can or wants to give it. Therefore the system needs to be self-taught, which previously has only been implemented in special cases such as playing chess or go. The likelihood of computers becoming truly context aware in the near future is slim, and it will probably take on the order of years to implement context awareness efficiently enough to be used in a ubiquitous environment.

2.4 Ambient Intelligence

For ubiquitous computing to be successful, not only does an application need to be intelligent, but also does the environment in which devices exist. Ambient intelligence can be defined as computational intelligence that exists in both the physical and digital environments. Most of the work in this field originally stems from work in artificial intelligence. Much like Weiser envisioned, ambient intelligence should be predictive and require minimal user intervention to get computation done.

Many of our daily activities currently recess into the background of our lives. Doors open for us at markets. Toilets flush for us when we leave their proximity. Taps dispense water with the wave of a hand. Similarly, ambient intelligence envisions that information will appear on a nearby television, watch, walls, and other displays as needed. [14] Children will be warned when crossing streets, tourists will be directed to nearby attractions, and advertisements will appear while we walk by.

Similar to context-aware computing, ambient intelligence is a difficult problem to solve. While there have been advances in the fields of computer vision, speech recognition, and gesture detection, predicting what people need in an accurate, sensitive, and quick manner is still far off. [14] Such small accomplishments in both fields prove how difficult it is to engineer applications and environments that can predict human action.

2.5 Monitoring

Monitoring, tracking, and recording devices will be needed to provide the cues for both contextual awareness and intelligence in order for applications and environments to be aware of context and comprehend activities. For example, there have been developments in ubiquitous computing to aid elderly or infirm patients who need minimal care. The reason for the interest in helping the less able is that there are explicit needs that can be identified for these groups. [14] Monitoring heath statistics, dispensing medicine on a regular basis, and tracking patient or asset locations are activities that could be monitored by such a system. The biggest concern with this area of technology is privacy. Most projects that have been developed are sensitive to privacy and ethical issues that surround the monitoring of people.

Issues of privacy, context, and motive are not easy to solve and may end up overwhelming the field of ubiquitous computing. Though there have been great advances in wireless and battery technology, creating and monitoring contextually aware applications and environments have not developed to the point where Weiser's vision of ubiquity can be completely realized. Ubiquitous computing technology is still in the beginning stages, as we have much work to do to in distributed systems management, human computer interaction, and sociological computing.

3. SOCIAL IMPLICATIONS

For ubiquitous computing to become successful, it has to be embraced by the public as well as the business markets. There are many design issues to be worked out in order to allow computing to take place anywhere and anytime. Not only will computers have to adjust to human interaction, people must adjust to computers. Just as cellular phone ethics have evolved with widespread use, so will ubiquitous computing ethics. With computers being everywhere, our social interactions and environment will change as well.

Computers have been designed primarily as devices to be used by a solitary person and can interfere with social encounters. When two people try to share a computer the social interference becomes apparent. Experienced computer users usually expect technology to have a negative impact on social interactions. Even within a highly technical community, most users believe that computer use decreases social activity. [6] If computers are to be everywhere, then they need to be passive in a social environment or facilitate social interactions.

Humans prefer to have relationships with humans rather than machines; therefore ubiquitous computers may unexpectedly inhibit rather than facilitate social interactions. Unfamiliar devices may trigger negative stereotypes that are strong enough to overwhelm other information that a user has about another human counterpart. Devices that are hard to share may make their users seem disagreeable and withdrawn. Certain kinds of familiar human-machine interactions, like writing or speaking, must be utilized in order to minimize this effect. These familiar communication forms may avoid some of the negative impact. Since our current devices, even cellular phones, have not been designed to support social interaction, they can make users appear unattractive. [6]

Given the importance of social relationships in our lives, we will only adopt devices that support, rather than inhibit such relationships. If ubiquitous computing is to be successful, it needs to support human social life. The task of programming a computer to understand, interpret, and speak languages is still not complete; it will take on the magnitude of years before computers will understand spoken intonations and contexts of all our human languages.

Ubiquitous computing will change the environment in which we work, live, and play. Ubiquitous systems allow people to be reached at any time anywhere. It will also make available useful personal information, including present location, but individuals need ways to communicate only with trusted users. Individuals also need ways to politely avoid interruptions when they can't communicate. Ubiquitous devices will have to incorporate new social functionality before they will become favored among users. Designers of successful ubiquitous solutions will incorporate the mechanisms behind interpersonal satisfaction and collaborative productivity. By designing for social computing applications, they will move ubiquitous computing away from social hindrance and toward social acceptance. Without social acceptance ubiquitous computing cannot be successful.

3.1 Privacy

One of the most contentious issue involved in developing usable ubiquitous computing systems is that of reasonable privacy for the user. There are costs and benefits of using a ubiquitous computing environment. From one perspective, ubiquitous computing has the potential to positively transform the interaction, safety, efficiency, convenience, and productivity of a user. Ubiquitous computing environments also have the potential for abuse. Users indicate a fear and general unease over the lack of control of information in such systems. [9]

Privacy in a ubiquitous computing environment is a difficult problem to solve, as there are different perceptions of privacy and its role in computing for every user. To address these issues, researchers have proposed using a privacy risk model where users selectively disclose information such as e-mail addresses, shopping history, or locations. [9] A privacy risk model helps designers consider the specific group of users, potential risks and benefits, and the type of feedback users will be giving the system.

Privacy, a social issue, could stand in the way of the widespread success of ubiquitous computing. No analysis can predict every potential use for a piece of information. The design issues revolving around privacy are integrated into social, legal, technical, and market issues. [9] Privacy risk models will help with designing and understanding social issues as trends move towards ubiquitous computing environments.

4. CONTEMPORARY EXAMPLES

The transitional phase of ubiquitous computing is far from over, as much of the research and fieldwork being done has yet to bear any major advances in mainstream consumer technology. Many of the advances in ubiquitous computing are happening in university and research and development labs. Due to the complexity of ubiquitous computing, many projects are spending time and effort on technology that provides a ubiquitous computing environment. In contrast, some projects are focusing on a single end goal or product using ubiquitous computing theory to implement their work.

4.1 Higher Education and Research Labs

4.1.1 Palo Alto Research Center

The Palo Alto Research Center (PARC), a Xerox company, pioneered ubiquitous computing and has been on the forefront of research and development of post-personal computer information services. Intelligent Mobile Computing, one of PARC's focus areas, researches wireless networking, client server architectures, and multi-device interaction which has resulted in the invention of context-aware services that can anticipate a user's situation and proactively provide contextual information.

PARC employs a holistic approach to their intelligent mobile computing following three major cornerstones in their research: contextual intelligence, "proactivity," and security. Current case studies being conducted include work with consumers, businesses, and the defense sector. [12]

4.1.2 Georgia Institute of Technology

The Ubiquitous Computing Research Group at Georgia Institute of Technology focuses their research on building and evaluating ubiquitous computing applications and services for daily routines. Topics that the research group focus on include: automated capture and access to live experiences, context-aware computing, home services, natural interaction, software architecture, security policy, and technology for individuals with special needs.

BrailleTouch, a recent invention by the group, is an eyes-free mobile text input technology based on the Perkins Brailler. BrailleTouch allows for a non-sighted user to dynamically enter information into a touch-screen based device, a hurdle for many Braille users. Many recent projects include: managing asthma through in-home probes, domestic energy consumption awareness techniques, creating dynamic physical buttons for touch-based interaction, and studying autistic behaviors through integrated sensing and visualization. [7]

4.1.3 Arizona State University

The Center for Cognitive Ubiquitous Computing (CUbiC) at Arizona State University is an interdisciplinary research center focusing on assistive, rehabilitative, and heath care applications. While ubiquitous computing has many applications, the center has chosen to serve the needs of physically challenged individuals by empowering them with ubiquitous technologies in order to enrich their lives.

CUbiC's projects are diverse and numerous, mostly focusing on enabling individuals with physical disabilities to better function in environments that currently pose great challenges to them. Some examples of more classic ubiquitous applications include sensing and identifying activity using wearable sensors, recognition and identification of a person based on face and speech biometrics, and enabling computer interaction using only feedback from a user's eyes. [4]

4.1.4 Carnegie Mellon University

Carnegie Mellon University's Computer Science program is one of the pioneers of ubiquitous computing. They have identified specific areas of research to work on in order to further Weiser's view of ubiquitous computing: smart spaces, invisibility, localized scalability, and uneven conditioning. Smart spaces consist of embedding computing infrastructure into a building's infrastructure, thus enabling mutual sensing and control of both infrastructures. Invisibility, an ideal expressed by Weiser, helps the ubiquitous computing environment meet the user's expectations while rarely presenting surprises. Another important factor in ubiquitous environments is scalability. As smart spaces grow in sophistication, so will the intensity of interactions between a user's computing space and its surrounding increases. Finally, in order to maintain a ubiquitous environment despite a lack of smart spaces, the user's computer environment must mask these uneven conditions between environments.

Carnegie Mellon's current projects are broad and well funded. Numerous professors are working towards a proactive and distraction-free ubiquitous computing environment. In collaboration with Intel, Carnegie Mellon is also working on a way to create a seamlessly mobile computing environment to allow a user to access their computing environment regardless of location and machine type they are using. Carnegie Mellon pioneered the creation and use of wearable computing and continues to research the topic. [11]

4.2 Private Sector Applications

4.2.1 Sensor Networks

Sensor networks are distributed wireless autonomous sensors that report physical data such as temperature, sound, vibration, or pressure. Each network is made up of independent sensors and microcontrollers that use a wireless mesh topology to transmit the data being collected. DASH7 and ZigBee are the two dominant standards being used in sensor networks, both of which function at low frequencies and power in order to preserve the deployment time of the network of sensors.

DASH7 is currently being used extensively by the United States Defense Department and uses an open source network stack. DASH7 has gained a large part of the wireless sensor network market due to its open nature and industry support. The current products offered are tags (assets, sensor, license plate) and readers that can add most benefits to security and asset tracking. [5]

4.2.2 Inferred Information

Just as one can read a sign or clock in passing, data can also be represented in an inferred manner. One can look outside to view inferred weather information, but that option does not exist for much data. In order to infer more complex information, data can be represented by a gauge, a changing icon or color, a graph, a location map, or a number.

Ambient Technologies produces a few products that can be configured to infer information. The Ambient Orb is a glowing ball that displays a different color depending on the real time information fed to it. There's a special use case where Ambient Technologies created an Energy Orb to be used by utilities to show the load on the grid, manage demand, and avoid blackouts. Just by looking at a simple color on a desk, one can infer information at a glance that may otherwise require a more intrusive way of gathering the information. [3]

Another project, the Data Fountain, uses real time currency data to provide a physical representation of the markets. The information displayed is the value of the Yen, the Dollar, and the Euro. The height of the water burst in the fountain represents the current value of each currency. Using water as a substrate illustrates the interconnectivity of the currencies while allowing the viewer to enjoy the sights and sounds of moving water. Just as advertising is ubiquitous, real time information will be displayed in an unobtrusive way in our lives. [16]

4.2.3 Home Automation

As technology becomes more pervasive in the home, the home network grows to encompass communications, entertainment, security, convenience, and information. There are a variety of protocols that are being used to control home automation devices: Z-Wave, X10, Insteon, and Zigbee. These are solely the protocols, a variety of manufacturers create the actual home automation devices that are then controlled by a central home controller. Though home automation is a relatively new product niche, there are a variety of devices being made.

A camera can be used to track your property or as a video door phone, for example. A dimmer can be attached to any outlet and controlled by a central controller. Audio systems can distribute music to any room. Door handles can scan for fingerprints rather than requiring the use of keys.

Home automation has matured to a point where a home filled with interconnected technology is plausible. The Ubiquitous Home project has pioneered a laboratory that mimics the environment of an actual home. Cameras and microphones are in every room and there is a live-in robot that provides home services. Though the technology in the Ubiquitous Home isn't as widely available as other home automation devices, one can envision the home as a plausible way of living in the future. [13]

5. CONCLUSION

Ubiquitous computing will revolutionize human interaction and use of computers, but the revolution will not happen overnight. Ubiquitous computing as defined by Mark Weiser will not exist for a few decades. There are too many issues that need to be resolved before computation can exist everywhere. Currently technology can handle a simplified ubiquitous environment in a controlled setting, but does not have the infrastructure or mass appeal needed to disperse inexpensive network-enabled computers. Computers are already immersed in our environment, but are self-contained. All types of manufacturing and commercial markets need to adopt the idea of embedding products with a network-enabled device. Once this happens consumers need to realize the potential for ubiquitous devices.

The infrastructure of hardware, software, and communication capabilities is currently unable to handle a truly ubiquitous environment. As shown, the technology for creating ubiquity is currently developed, but there are hundreds of issues to be solved in multiple industries to make ubiquity a realistic goal. In addition, many wireless networking, computer user interface, and artificial intelligence solutions will need to be implemented in order for ubiquity to be used on the level Weiser envisioned.

The possibilities enabled by utilizing an interconnected network are endless. Shipping companies could have packages sort and ship themselves much like packets are sent over networks today. A stockbroker could store his portfolio in his watch and do active trading with it on the New York Stock Exchange whether or not he was in New York. TVs could track viewing habits and actively recommend shows depending on a person's taste. Ubiquitous devices will enable today's computation and communication to occur in a familiar fashion like voice recognition or writing rather than via keyboards and mice.

Until distributed networks gain the sophistication and robustness to handle constant human interactions on a level we are familiar with, we are stuck with booting up, typing, pointing, and clicking. Computer systems are constantly changing to catch up with user's needs, and current technology trends show that ubiquity may be realized utilizing technology we have available today.

Ubiquitous computing is the optimal choice for making computation easy to access and use, but may interfere with our lives in ways we do not yet expect. Everything in life is a balance, and when one problem is solved there is always another to take its place. There is only one way to find out if ubiquitous computing will work for the world, and that is to try it. All of the major computer companies have started investing large amounts of research and money into creating useful devices to distribute computation, just as all major computing companies invested in networking twenty-five years ago. Now, there is wireless network access available in almost all public spaces. Who knows what research about ubiquitous computing will bring?

Twenty-five years from now we might have a computer-filled environment silently aiding all of our computation needs. Computation as we know it constantly changes, evolves, and will eventually become ubiquitous computing. Until then the only communication with computers we will have is the ominous glare of a screen, the sound of speakers, and the clicking of our fingers.

6. ACKNOWLEDGEMENTS

The author would like to thank G. Michael Schneider of Macalester College for piquing his interest in ubiquitous computing. Without his advising, the author would never have been exposed to this area of computer science. The author would also like to thank Kelly Wainwright of Lewis & Clark College for suggesting the submission of the paper to SIGUCCS 2011.

7. REFERENCES

[1] 3rd Generation Partnership Project, *About 3GPP*. http://www.3gpp.org/About-3GPP/

[2] Aidoo, K., Van Laerhoven, K. 2001. Teaching Context to Applications. *Personal and Ubiquitous Computing*. 5,1.

[3] Ambient Devices, *Platform.* http://www.ambientdevices.com/cat/platform.html

[4] Center for Cognitive Ubiquitous Computing, *About CUbiC.* http://cubic.asu.edu/

[5] DASH7 Alliance, *What is DASH7 Technology?* http://dash7.org/index.php?option=com_content&view=article&id=9&Itemid=10

[6] Dryer, D. C., Eisbach, C., and Ark, W.S. 1999. At What Cost Pervasive? A Social Computing View of Mobile Computer Systems. *IBM Systems Journal.* 38, 4.

[7] Georgia Institute of Technology, *Ubiquitous Computing Research Group.* http://home.cc.gatech.edu/ubicomp/

[8] Heile, B. 2011. *Overview of 802.15 Projects.* Technical Report. IEEE. http://grouper.ieee.org/groups/802/minutes/2011-March/802%20workshop/802-15%20Heile%20r0.ppt

[9] Hong, J.I., Ng, J.D., Lederer, S., Landay, J. 2004. Privacy Risk Models for Designing Privacy-Sensitive Ubiquitous Computing Systems. *DIS '04 Proceedings of the 5th Conf. on Designing Interactive Systems. 91-100.*

http://dx.doi.org/10.1145/1013115.1013129

[10] Martin, T. L., Siewiorek, D.P. 1999. Non-ideal Battery Properties and Low Power Operation in Wearable Computing. ISWC '99 *Proceedings of the 3rd IEEE Int. Symp. on Wearable Computers.* 101-106.

[11] Mobile and Pervasive Computing Research, *Mobile and Pervasive Computing Research in the Computer Science Department at Carnegie Mellon.* http://www.csd.cs.cmu.edu/research/areas/mopercomp/

[12] PARC, *Intelligent Mobile Computing.* http://www.parc.com/services/focus-area/intelligent-mobile-computing/

[13] Robles, John R.,Kim Tai-hoon. 2010. Applications, Systems and Methods in Smart Home Technology: A Review. *International Journal of Advanced Science and Technology.* Vol. 15 (February, 2010).

[14] Rogers, Y. 2006. Moving on from Weiser's Vision of Calm Computing: Engaging UbiComp Experiences. *UbiComp Conference.* (2006,) 404-421.

[15] Stallings, William. 2006. *Data and Computer Communications.* Prentice Hall, New Jersey.

[16] van Mensvoort, Koert, *DataFountain.* http://www.koert.com/work/datafountain/

[17] Weiser, M., Gold, R., Brown, J.S. 1999. The Origins of Ubiquitous Computing Research at PARC in the Late 1980s. *IBM Systems Journal.* 38, 4 (May 1999), 693-696. DOI=http://dx.doi.org/10.1147/sj.384.0566

[18] Weiser, M. 1996. *Ubiquitous Computing.* http://nano.zerox.com/hypertext/weiser/ubihome.html

[19] Weiser, M. 1993. Some Computer Science Issues in Ubiquitous Computing. *Communications of the ACM.* 36, 7 (July 1993), 75-84.

DOI= http://dx.doi.org/10.1145/159544.159617

[20] Weiser, M. 1991. *The Computer for the 21st Century.* Scientific American (1991), 94-104.

[21] Zimmerman, T.G. 1999. Wireless Networked Digital Devices: A New Paradigm for Computing and Communications. *IBM Systems Journal.* 38, 4 (May 1999), 609-617. DOI=http://dx.doi.org/10.1147/sj.384.0566

Team Mission: Solutions for Managing Software

Gordana Brouilette
University of Alberta
AICT
Edmonton, AB T6G 2H1
(780) 492-5564
gordana.brouilette@ualberta.ca

Cynthia Dooling
Pima Community College
Information Technology
Tucson, AZ 85709
(520) 206-4809
cdooling@pima.edu

Cheryl Stahler
Bloomsburg University of Pennsylvania
Technology Support Services
Bloomsburg, PA 17815
(570) 389-4685
cstahler@bloomu.edu

Cindy Stewart
University of Alberta
AICT
Edmonton, AB T6G 2H1
(780) 492-1345
cindy.stewart@ualberta.ca

Janice Tulloss
Information Technology
University of NC Greensboro
Greensboro, NC 27412
(336) 334-5401
janice_tulloss@uncg.edu

ABSTRACT

Managing educational software involves processes, tools and issues. There is a need for balance between faculty, staff and student satisfaction and the tools and methods utilized by administrators to acquire and distribute software.

At the University of Alberta we strive to reduce the cost of software by negotiating and obtaining volume site licensed software from a variety of software suppliers. It is true that acquiring discounted software leads to a fairly high degree of customer satisfaction. However, what more can be done to benefit both the client's & software administrator's needs? This is what we would like to determine through a panel discussion with software administrators from other institutions.

What educational software services are being offered by peer institutions? What challenges are they experiencing implementing those services? Are these challenges unique to that institution or do others have solutions that may work elsewhere?

If you are exploring software delivery methods, challenged by compliancy, struggling with managing software sales and inventory, let's get together. By sharing our knowledge and experience we may be able to help and provide answers which can be successfully implemented at all institutions.

Categories and Subject Descriptors

D.0 GENERAL

General Terms

Management, Measurement, Economics, Human Factors

Keywords

software site license, educational, software, sales, contract, customer service, electronic software delivery, centralizing, virtualization, staff, students, research, administration, faculty, inventory

1. INTRODUCTION

Addressing software needs on campus can be approached in many ways. What software services do you provide and what challenges do they present? Where does the money come from? What methods of software delivery are being utilized? What tools for software management and compliancy are being used? What software is being virtualized and centralized?

We provide some answers here. Hopefully, our experiences will give some confidence in the software services that you provide.

2. BACKGROUND

2.1 Pima Community College

Pima Community College serves nearly 80,000 students a year in southern Arizona, located in Tucson. There are six main campuses, two district offices and several sites in Pima County.

We manage all site and volume licensing; college-wide use software, some individual licensing and some campus-specific applications. Our clients are the employees and all the labs and conference rooms.

The district office that handles the software has two primary people managing the licenses. The academic licenses are negotiated for and distributed through Client Services.

We do some charge-back but also have a technology fee for academic purchases.

2.2 Bloomsburg University

Bloomsburg University of Pennsylvania is a public, four-year coeducational institution and a member of the Pennsylvania State System of Higher Education (PASSHE). Enrollment is approximately 9200 students and over 950 faculty and staff. My area is Technology Support Services and I negotiate and track licenses used in our faculty/staff/lab common desktop as well as specialized software used in academic labs and classrooms. Within the department my position, Software Administrator, is the only one that does this.

Since Bloomsburg University is one of 14 universities that make up the Pennsylvania State System of Higher Education (PASSHE) consortium, the university licenses software through three different sources. Through the PASSHE system we purchase Microsoft products, ArcGIS, Mathematica and our distant learning programs. The university purchases programs such as SPSS, SAS, Minitab and others that are used in multiple areas. Individual academic departments purchase programs specific to their areas. All academic software is paid for through either the Academic Enhancement or Technology fees. We only track software that is installed by our Technology Support Services area and not specialized software that is used by administrative areas (GasBoy, Planning and Development's AutoCad, etc.)

2.3 University of Alberta

The University of Alberta is located in the province's capital of Edmonton, Alberta, Canada and has an enrollment of 37,000 full and part time students and approximately 10,000 staff. The main North campus covers about 50 city blocks with more than 90 buildings on the edge of the North Saskatchewan River valley. Additional campuses include South Campus & Michener Park, Augustana, Campus Saint-Jean and Enterprise Square.

We negotiate, obtain and manage a wide variety of site licensed software, volume licenses, and specialty software that supports educational teaching, research and administrative use for faculty, staff and students.

The software is negotiated and distributed through Academic Information and Communication Technologies (AICT). Negotiating and managing contracts is handled through 2 full time Site License Administrators. Presently, our Products Sales area handles distribution and front line counter sales of software to our clients via 2 full-time and 2 part-time staff members. Last year, AICT Product Sales handled 7500 software sales transactions totaling approximately $850,000 in sales. By managing site license agreements and volume purchases the University saves time and money across campus and eliminates duplication of separate purchases.

University of Alberta students do not pay a technology fee. As such, we operate on a cost recovery model. Our full time positions are centrally funded whereas the part time positions are partially funded from software sales profits.

2.4 University of NC Greensboro

UNCG, the University of North Carolina at Greensboro, is a mid-sized state university with approximately 17,550 on-campus (80% residential) and 950 distance education students.

ITS (Information Technology Services) services a campus community of about 20,000. For full-time students living on campus, 2009-2010 basic costs (including tuition and fees, room and board, other student expenses), total approximately $14,504 for in-state students and $26,842 for out-of-state students.

Central ITS manages virtually all of the site licensing for software provided through our campus network. Individual departments buy workstation licenses as needed, and in some limited cases do cost-sharing, but software for the open access labs and on the campus network is managed by ITS.

ITS overall employs 142 people, my area, Client Services, employs 48.

The only people directly involved in license management is myself (Software Coordinator), the CSV office assistant who physically handles sales from our office, and the ITS budget office that pays the bills.

Academic licenses are negotiated and distributed by myself and to some extent my supervisor, the Assistant Vice Chancellor for Client Services. She tends to get involved when there is a crisis or a major enterprise-wide contract that is beyond the routine.

Technology fee money is used to purchase "academic software" that is used by students and faculty. Other state funds are used to purchase other types of software for administrative use. We have just started allowing the research departments and now administrative units to "buy into" our concurrent use licenses via a modified charge back model. Some cost recovery is done for software that we duplicate for home use or workstation installations.

3. ELECTRONIC SOFTWARE DELIVERY

3.1 Pima Community College

Electronic software delivery is done via Ghost and/or Altiris, user preference or training level usually dictates which method is used. Benefits of downloading include the ease and timeliness of distribution while duplicating CD/DVDs has run into issues when the burner fails but we don't know until several dozen copies have been burned!

Those with access to download and install software should have the Certified Software Manager (CSM) training and certification. We limit who has access to downloads and installation keys to those with the CSM certification.

Present issues encountered are that people forget the path to the software download location! Occasionally, the installation qualifiers need to be tweaked and tested to ensure it is properly loaded and pushed.

3.2 Bloomsburg University

All campus supported computers have a 'common desktop' software setup. This setup includes a specialized software category. Faculty and staff computers have a limited amount of software that belong in this category but there are over 200 programs that are used in various labs and classrooms The specialized software often changes from lab to lab each semester depending on where the class is scheduled. All software for the common desktop and those put on as specialized software are tracked by the Software Administrator. We do not track licenses purchased by individual faculty members for their own use.

3.3 University of Alberta

With over 400 titles of software that we carry, distribution can be demanding.

The majority of software distribution is handled via in house duplication of CD/DVD's. This method has two main benefits. It allows us to control the inventory we keep on the shelves and allows us the ability to make copies of software on demand. We have 2 burning towers capable of duplicating CD, DVD and Dual Layer DVD's. One, a Verity with 9 burners and the other is an Ajtech Pro Series with 11 burners. We have 2 Disc Printers with a

100 Disc Capacity, up to 4800 dpi quality printing. One is a Bravo Pro IX and the other is a Bravo Pro. These disc printers are also capable of duplicating but over the years we have decided that duplicating discs on the towers and then printing them on the Bravo is the most efficient way to complete the jobs.

As the popularity and demand of Electronic Software delivery grows we strive to deliver more of our software electronically. The method of electronic delivery varies depending upon the particular software's conditions of use.

With regards to free software products (i.e.: ChemDraw, F-Secure Anti-Virus) secure server downloads are made available to employees/students using their personal CCID (Campus Computing ID) to authenticate and receive access to the software.

When a financial transaction is involved (ie: Camtasia, DeepFreeze, Xwin) an email is sent to the client which contains a website address, download link and password to access the software.

With Microsoft employee work at home licenses we first verify that the client is indeed a University employee through an in house database system (BRUTUS). The employee is provided a website address and password to purchase the software from a third party provider for a nominal fee.

Convenience for the client is one of the biggest advantages of electronic software delivery methods. The client avoids waiting for media to be shipped in campus mail or travelling to the AICT Product Sales Desk. Logistically, the AICT Product Sales Desk is not centrally located and weather wise our winters are not always conducive to outdoor walks. As more computers are distributed without a CD/DVD reader in them the need for electronic methods of software delivery grows. From a distribution standpoint, it is efficient and less wasteful to keep multiple software versions up to date in an electronic format rather than destroying and copying new media.

That said, with electronic software delivery we sometimes find it challenging storing some of the larger versions of software on our servers. Another challenge issue is ensuring methods of delivery that allow only legally defined users to have access to the downloadable software.

To enforce compliancy we have every client read and sign a site license agreement form which stipulates conditions of use of software distributed by us before they can purchase software.

3.4 University NC Greensboro

We provide electronic software delivery only for use on campus machines via Active Directory

I am about to discuss working with e-Academy to move the sales we do from our office to ESD.

We are primarily using KeyServer and Active Directory/SCCM. We are just now migrating from Novell to AD, so we have not fully explored the software/license management functionality.

Have not yet done an audit, but that is my next goal.

It has become clear that we need to move to ESD both to free up staff time in an age of scarce resources (our administrative assistant is now doing her job plus one-half of another one as the position was eliminated)

ESD would also permit 24/7 software access which would improve client service.

I see no upside to duplication at this point as it is a waste of resources, especially with the inevitable "bad disks" that occasionally get produced.

Historically our biggest problems have been with Macs which can connect to the network and download software as long as the user authenticates. There is currently no way to prevent non-university owned machines from connecting. We are working to solve that.

PCs cannot connect to the network unless they are UNCG machines and have the UNCG image on them.

4. SOFTWARE ASSET MANAGEMENT AND TRACKING

4.1 Pima Community College

We primarily rely on Altiris for software asset management.

Compliancy is not an issue since all employees who have access to create packages and install software have earned the CSM

4.2 Bloomsburg University

Faculty and staff computers have a limited amount of software that belong in this last category of Specialized software but there are over 200 programs that are used in various labs and classrooms The software often changes from room to room each semester depending on where the class is scheduled. All programs are loaded locally on each desktop. Faculty and staff have administrative rights on their office computers but the student lab computers are locked down. All software for the common desktop and those put on as specialized software are tracked by the Software Administrator. We do not track licenses purchased by individual faculty members for their own use.

4.3 University of Alberta

Our existing system (APOSSL) is an in-house point of sales system. This system allows us to enter software licensing agreements with vendors, distribute and sell site licensed software to our clients. We do track and enter all software purchased. We can run reports from our database which shows both inventory and financial transactions detailing what has been purchased and sold.

The University of Alberta does not have a standardized asset Management tool.

Within our department, the AICT Labs group currently has about 1600 computers and presently does some metering.

We have both completed the CSM and ASM courses. We strive to ensure and adhere to compliancy across campus at all times.

Throughout our Product Sales Software website we specify for each software product the rules for distribution and use based on the legal contract. There are different rules for different products. Our sales staff will verbally explain the licensing rules to the clients at time of purchase.

4.4 University of NC Greensboro

KeyServer is our primary tool at this point. It's been working reasonably well, but since the vendor refuses to do site visits; it's been problematic as we got it up and running. Because of some initial inexperience with the app, and too many people with their hands in it, some of the early data is not reliable. That is being addressed.

We are presently metering software via KeyServer and various proprietary license managers like FlexLM and its variants. It has made a huge difference in convincing vendors to allow concurrent use, even for apps not specifically designated as CUL. It immediately cut our Adobe costs, for example, dramatically, as we moved from having to buy hundreds of workstation licenses to 100 CULs.

The current problem is that the way it works on our network, we control ALL instances of an app, including those workstation licenses that individual departments bought.

Somewhat, although the license managers go a long way in enforcing compliance. Individual piracy is another story. I have no doubt there are significant compliance problems across the campus for software that ITS does not control.

5. MANAGING SOFTWARE SALES AND INVENTORY

5.1 Pima Community College

Software purchases are tracked in two separate areas, Altiris and Track-It!. Track-It! is our work order management system. A copy of the purchase order is attached to software installation work orders to verify eligibility for use of the application. We also add that purchase order copy to the Altiris inventory management database. Our long range goal is to incorporate all of this information into Altiris. Another long range goal is to use Altiris to help us determine application usage and move apps where they are needed, determine if site or volume licensing is appropriate and remove obsolete applications.

5.2 Bloomsburg University

Technology Support Services does not sell any software or have any charge back fees.

5.3 University of Alberta

We currently use a home grown system which was built using SQL a number of years ago. We are quickly outgrowing this system and would like to find or develop a system that more adequately supports our needs and addresses existing issues such as:

- Implementing a fully functional software license inventory and combined license contract maintenance function. Our existing system does both of these tasks, but separately.
- Providing an improved product sales interface for orders and entering payment information.
- Streamlining frequents tasks, such as quickly and easily accessing existing licensing held by clients when they are standing in front of Product Sales staff (i.e. click one button to quickly see their license history purchase as opposed to running a report).

We are facing the challenge of finding a robust system to track our inventory and sales as well as one that gives the reports and statistics required. We send out thousands of renewal letters to clients and would like to see a system manage letters and emails directly without having to export data to Excel and then use Microsoft Word to complete the task. The system should also have a component that ties our point of sales system both into the inventory and our website for product information.

We would eventually like to incorporate e-commerce into our software website. We are currently working with a group of developers to examine these possibilities.

5.4 University of NC Greensboro

We track most software sales in Remedy. A few apps are tracked by spreadsheet, due to some legacy arrangements, which I am working to change, to move into our Remedy.

Our main issue is solving the problem with KeyServer wanting to control everything. Previously we were able to "key" some apps, and control only those, but the vendor no longer recommends that. In addition, automated updates will often "blow out" the keyed component which results in it no longer being keyed. Our network security also does not allow keyed apps as the altered executables are recognized by security software as viruses.

We are presently exploring E-Academy for ESD

6. CENTRALIZED SOFTWARE

6.1 Pima Community College

We have a volume license agreement with Microsoft for the operating systems, Office suite, Project, Visual Studio and Expressions that can be installed on all college-owned computers. We also have volume license for AutoDesk products, primarily used in classrooms. One of our other largest agreements is with Adobe for low-cost purchases for classrooms, offices and personal use at home. Our latest agreement with Symantec will allow home use of the EndPoint solution. The most obvious benefit is the cost savings followed closely with compliance, accurate product purchase, ensure compatibility and that the app meets the user's requirements. Standardization in application purchase/usage has a direct correlation to the ability to provide support to the end-user, too.

6.2 Bloomsburg University

Technology Support Services does not sell any software or have any charge back fees. Distribution of the Microsoft programs for home use is done through the University bookstore for a nominal fee. The only other software that we distribute is Mathematica for student's free personal use. This is a very small number of students, usually less than 10 students per semester, and that software cd is copied via a disk duplicator for distribution.

6.3 University of Alberta

The University of Alberta recently signed agreements with Microsoft for Windows and Enterprise CAL's and Citrix for XenDesktop Platinum. Benefits of these agreements include, ensured compliancy, predictable costs, up to date software, less license tracking, less administrative processing of payments.

6.4 University of NC Greensboro

What virtualization software are you currently using (WMWare, Citrix, Other)?

We are just beginning to do this. We are using AppV, and exploring Citrix. We are collaborating with NC State University on their Virtual Computing Lab initiative, where they host it through a home-grown application, and our campus users can log in. Concerns about remote access more than virtualization has made this a limited effort.

7. VIRTUALIZED SOFTWARE

7.1 Pima Community College

We tested Citrix as replacements for 50 desktop systems. There were many points of failure, so after many months of research, work and angst we abandoned Citrix and installed desktop computers. We have been most successful; however, in virtualizing our server environment using VMWare. There are many benefits to virtualization of the servers, including hardware cost savings, minimal time to setup a new server, and ease of support.

7.2 Bloomsburg University

Our Mathematics department has used HperV to virtualize SAS and some departmental software for their area. Though HyperV works, it has been cumbersome to implement. We have just recently purchased VMWare and are starting to experiment with the capabilities it has to offer. We hope to put all specialized software in a virtualized environment but I have not yet looked into licensing issues that we may have. I hope to have some of my own concerns addressed during this panel discussion.

7.3 University of Alberta

We are currently testing and using virtualization software on campus. For servers VMWare is being utilized and for desktops Citrix Zen Desktop Platinum. Testing is underway to virtualize software in the AICT Labs on 1600 desktops with the goal of 3000 desktops within the next three years.

The University of Alberta has migrated to Google for e-mail, calendaring and documents.

The main concerns are cost and commitment of this technology.

7.4 University of NC Greensboro

As part of our migration to AD, we are just beginning to determine what can and can't be virtualized.

In our VCL we offer ArcGIS Desktop, Atlas.ti, EndNote, MS Office, Stats, SAS, Matlab, NVivo, PC-TAS, Raptor, and Stata, along with some small, UNCG specific apps.

What are some of the benefits, implications or concerns?

i. Concerns: Inconsistent licensing rules but mostly due to remote access to virtualized apps
ii. Lack of familiarity with virtualization by vendors
iii. Licensing and contracts haven't kept up with technical innovations
iv. Technical limits on what can be virtualized

Benefits:

Greater flexibility in delivering apps to our labs that otherwise might conflict if they weren't delivered in:

i. Virtual "bubble" – no clashing dlls
ii. Potential of wider remote access

Utilizing Educational Lean to Enhance the Information Technology Project Intake Process

Robin Honken
Winona State University
Somsen Hall 208d
Winona, MN 55987
1-507-457-2215
rhonken@winona.edu

Kenneth Janz
Winona State University
Somsen Hall 111i
Winona, MN 55987
1-507-457-2299
kjanz@winona.edu

ABSTRACT

Winona State University utilized the Lean principles of process improvement (five high-level values principles to eliminate wasteful steps within a process) to enhance the project intake process for IT. Prior to 2009, Winona State's IT Department struggled with the successful completion of projects and decided to take a unique approach to resolving the issue. This approach allowed a core team of individuals to spend a focused amount of time documenting and discussing the current process, researching best practices, and brain storming ideas for a new and improved process. At the end of the four-day Kaizen event, a new process was proposed and presented to a larger group of stakeholders for feedback and approval. After multiple revisions to the initial proposal, the new process was implemented in August of 2009.

The process that now currently exists for IT project requests is documented on Winona State's website, http://www.winona.edu/it/itsprojects.asp. It allows for project owners and community members to make their requests online and includes automated communication back to them notifying them as to the status of their request. An IT project team reviews requests on a weekly basis, approves, denies or defers the requests, and assigns a project lead to communicate back with the requester. All approved, deferred and completed projects are tracked and displayed to campus via a project dashboard.

The new process centralizes the documentation of all project requests and their statuses. This allows for more thorough research of requests to ensure alignment with the Campus Technology Master Plan. It promotes better communication between the IT units and allows for realistic expectations to be set to the WSU community. The return on investment has been great as we've shown an increase in the number of significant IT projects completed, as well as an increase in customer and stakeholder satisfaction.

Categories and Subject Descriptors
K.6.1 [**Project and People Management**]: Management techniques.

General Terms
Management, Measurement, Documentation, Standardization.

Keywords
Project Management, Higher Education, Information Technology, Quality Improvement, Educational Lean, Kaizen event, Current State, Facilitator, Future State, Project Owner, Project Sponsor, Stakeholders, Starbursts, Continuous Improvement, Value Stream.

1. INTRODUCTION
Many information technology units within higher education struggle with conflicting priorities of administrative and academic units requests concerning project personnel, time, and energy. In addition, with the current economic environment, stress is being placed on higher education institutions to do more with less and organizations are being required to find ways to continuously improve services. While few would disagree that most business processes in higher education can be improved, how to go about this activity is a matter of much debate.

One method of collaborative process improvement finding its way into higher education is Educational Lean [1], [2], [3], [4]. Educational Lean focuses on processes by:

- Eliminating outdated practices,
- Leveraging collective knowledge,
- Finding the best way to provide services and education, and
- Redistributing resources [5].

With the need to improve processes and a method in which to examine institutional processes, the stage is set.

2. BACKGROUND

Winona State University (WSU) (mid-sized university located in southeast Minnesota of 9,000 students) utilized the Educational Lean principles of collaborative process improvement to enhance the project intake process for information technology services. Prior to 2009, Winona State's information technology services unit struggled with the successful completion of projects and decided to take a unique approach to resolving the issue.

Using Educational Lean as a method of process improvement provided a framework to allow a core team of individuals time to document and discuss the current process, research best practices, and brain storm ideas for a new and improved process. At the end of a four-day event, a new project intake process was proposed and presented to a larger group of stakeholders for feedback and approval. After multiple revisions to the initial proposal, the new process was implemented in August of 2009. To better understand the activities surrounding this process, this paper will provide a literature overview of lean, a review of the lean training activity, project management training, lean event and new process implementation.

3. LITERATURE REVIEW

3.1 Historical Foundations of Lean

The philosophy of lean has been around even prior to the 20th century. The idea is simple; applying lean principles will increase efficiencies by reducing wasteful activities, which in turn leads to increased value for all stakeholders [6]. Lean started in the area of manufacturing and has since moved to healthcare, government and education [7].

Although lean started in the manufacturing industry, specifically the automotive industry, it has made its way to many types of organizations, primarily because because lean is a way of thinking [11]. The Lean Enterprise Research Centre (LERC) was founded in 1994 by Daniel Jones, James Womack and Peter Hines. Today LERC is helping to adapt lean thinking to many organizaions, including educational organizations [10].

3.2 Lean Principles

"Lean thinking" follows five high-level principles in order to provide a framework for making change in any organization. These principles are:

- Determine what creates value from all stakeholder perspectives,
- Identify all current steps within a process or value stream,
- Continue with steps that create value,
- Discontinue steps that are wasteful, and
- Contine to evaluate and remove steps that are wasteful. [11]

3.3 Lean Model

The lean model reflects the ideas of transformational change and continuous improvement by planning, doing, studying, and acting [9]. Keeping in mind the lean principles listed above; there are multiple steps that should to be followed in order to create an environment of continuous improvement:

The Planning Phase

- Identify a process that needs to be improved and define a scope statement
- Identify all stakeholders involved with the process
- Organize a Kaizen event - Kaizen is the process of breaking down a process and putting back together after removing the wasteful activities. Kaizen events generally last from two to five days with the following participants:
    - Facilitator – An individual responsible for planning and executing the event.
    - Project owner – An individual who has a key role in the process needing improvement. He/she is responsible for ensuring the implementation of the new, improved process.
    - Project sponsor – An individual who oversees the process needing improvement. This individual typically does not participate in the event, but provides support to those participating and will work to overcome obstacles standing in the way of success.
    - Workgroup participants (subset of stakeholder group) – Those individuals selected to participate in the kaizen event.

The Doing Phase

- Identify stakeholder values,
- Map the current state of the process needing improvement through the use of a value stream map. A value stream map is a visual diagram of the steps associated with a process. This diagram is typically outline on paper with sticky notes, and later can be converted to an electronic flowchart, [9]
- Determine measures associated with current state. For example, how many steps are involved in the process, or how much time between steps. This will help determine where there may be waste,
- Research best practices and study current state,
- Facilitate a brainstorming session to identify ideal characteristics for future state,
- Map a future state, or ideal new process ensuring stakeholder values are met, and
- Create a future state implementation plan.

The Studying phase

- Organize a stakeholder meeting to receive feedback. This meeting should consist of anyone that has a stake in the outcome of the Kaizen event, and
- Evaluate feedback and adjust future state and implementation plan as needed.

The Acting Phase

- Implement, and
- Measure and continuously improve.

4. LEAN TRAINING

In May of 2009 several of members of the information technology services leadership team at Winona State University participated in five day training over the main constructs behind educational lean. During the training participants learned the principles and practices of educational lean including: identifying symptoms of non-value added activities, developing value stream maps and future state implementation plans, applying lean tools more appropriate for a particular process improvement, conducting effective root cause analyses, and facilitating Kaizen events.

This training provided the foundation for continuous collaborative process improvement within the information technology services unit far beyond that of the project management. The training provided an occasion for team building within the ITS leadership team it also provided an opportunity to build connections across campus. Since the lean training several members of the ITS leadership team have been asked to facilitate a number of non-ITS lean events across campus.

5. PROJECT MANAGEMENT TRAINING

Later that summer members of the information technology services team attended a three-day project management workshop presented by *Fissure*. This training focused on team building, soft skills, project plans, resource planning, status reports, and control charts. This training provided the core leadership team with a common vocabulary to discuss project management. With this training, the leadership team determined that the most important part of the project management process was the initial evaluation of the request, discussing how the request supports the university mission, and conversation about the best way to develop a solution for the WSU community. This in turn led to the lean event to help IT develop a project intake a process.

6. LEAN EVENT

As part of the Lean Facilitator Training, each participant needed to identify a process to improve and facilitate a kaizen event. The Information Technology (IT) members that attended the event agreed that the process of taking in, approving and completing projects was a huge issue. I agreed to work with another facilitator outside of IT to organize the event. Together we worked to refine a scope statement and came up with the following:

Improve and streamline the IT project life cycle starting with initial project request and ending with implementation of final product.

One thing that became clear through the training was that facilitating an event looking to improve a process within one's own department is challenging. It is very important that a facilitator remain a neutral party throughout, and this is much more difficult to do when one holds a stake in the outcome. As a result, I became the project owner for the IT project life cycle process to improve.

To prepare for the four-day kaizen event, members of the team were tasked with researching best practices from other institutions or companies related to taking in IT projects requests. I sat down with the facilitator to ensure she had a basic understanding of the current process and issues with the current process. We created a kaizen informational sheet sent to all team members with the following information: project scope, workgroup members, timeframe/location of the event, an agenda for each day, and specific information related to our process we were working to improve. In this case, it was important to know our departmental definition of a project in contrast to the definition of an operational task. It was also important to document some basic assumptions, which clarified the scope.

During the kaizen event, after introducing the event agenda, the facilitator presented the lean process improvement model to the group. This allowed them to obtain a better understanding about what they would be doing over the next four days. Then the group started documenting what constitutes value for each of the stakeholder groups. Some examples of value from the customer perspective were communication and project completion in the expected timeframe. From the IT staff perspective, some examples of value were having clear requirements before starting, and time to create a quality product.

Next, with large white poster paper and sticky notes, they started mapping out the current state and determining the starbursts, or larger pain points (see Figure 1). It became obvious to the group fairly quickly that the lack of any formal project intake process was the main reason there were issues. Because IT is broken up into four distinct units, each unit was taking in and managing project requests uniquely. This led to many issues. First, there was duplication of effort because multiple units may be working on the same project. Next, it was difficult to prioritize anything without any centralized list of projects, and this led to many projects going unfinished as new priorities surfaced. Finally, stakeholder satisfaction was low, while frustration high due to lack of communication and uncompleted projects.

Through the value stream mapping process, the work group came up with the following starbursts:

- IT project intake, evaluation and unit assignment process
- Unit workload management and prioritization process
- Project design, build and test process
- Implementation and ongoing support process

Figure 1.Photo of Value Stream Map Developed During Kaizen Event

The work group addressed the first starburst by documenting and evaluating the issues with the current process, looking back at values from each stakeholder perspective, and discussing symptoms of non-value with the current process. They also had researched some best practices at a couple of other institutions, as well as the company, Kwik Trip, a local convenience store chain based out of La Crosse, Wisconsin, to see if practices there could be adapted for Winona State.

These discussions led to a green light brainstorming session on what the group would like to see in an ideal project intake process for IT. The ideas focused on improving communication, setting realistic customer expectations, and transparency. The following ideas became part of the future state:

- One method of making project requests to IT, to alleviate any confusion, preferably an online method.
- Centralized database to store all project requests to which all units would have access
- Automated communication to customers, but not to replace all communication with customers.
- Document expectations to those making requests of IT, and have them acknowledge that they have read and understand them
- Require a departmental project sponsor approve the request before it is sent to IT in order to ensure communication happens within the department making the request
- Use of the governance process to provide guidance on larger project requests to ensure approved projects fit within the vision of the University
- Formalization of a recurring meeting where all IT Directors and Leads discuss new project requests and approved projects, but allow a mechanism for all IT staff to provide input on project requests
- A dashboard view accessible by the entire campus community to show the status of current projects

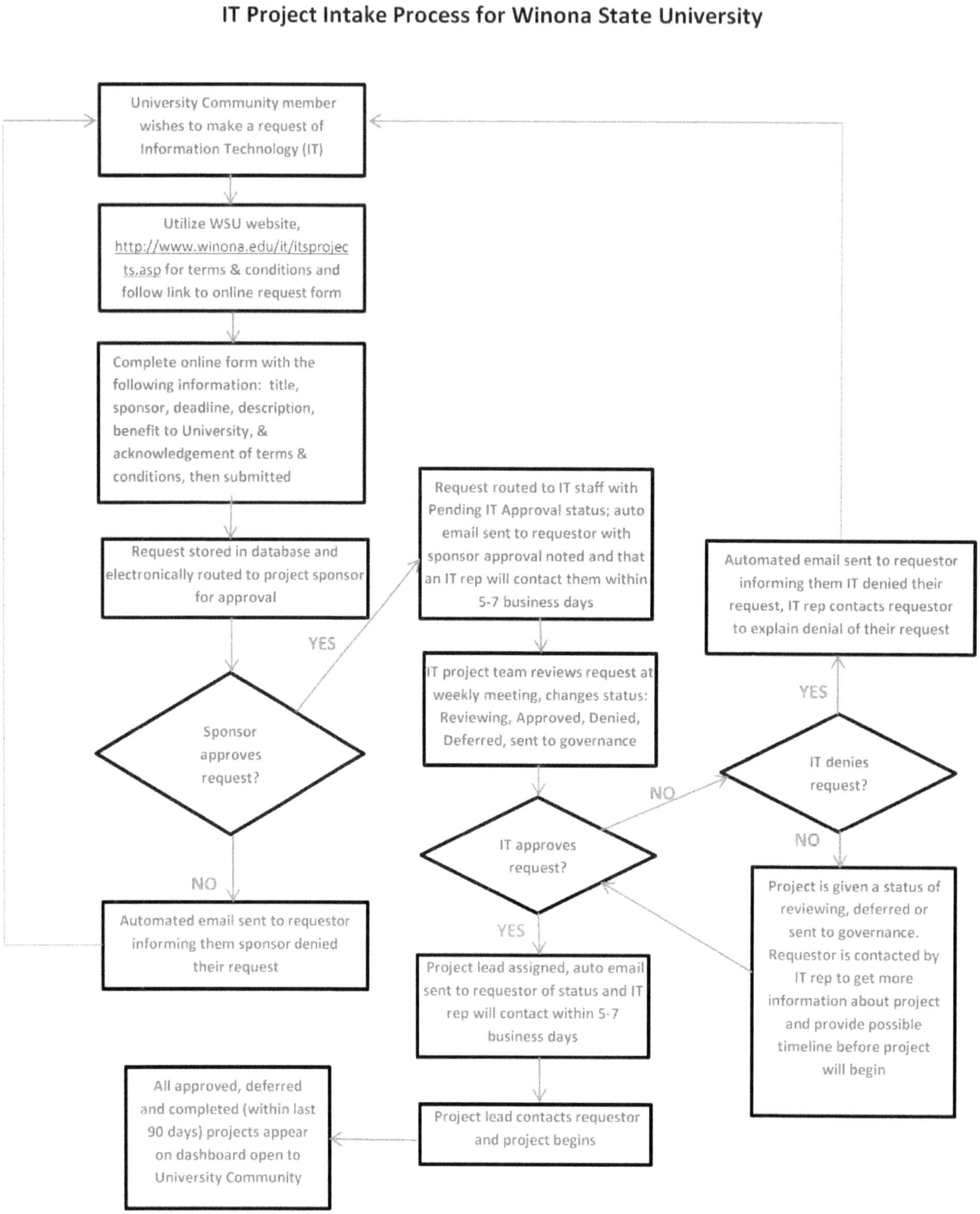

Figure 2. IT Project Intake Process.

7. NEW PROCESS IMPLEMENTATION

At the conclusion of the lean event, a task list was created with individual assignments and deadlines. One of the assignments for the facilitator was to set up a meeting with a larger stakeholder group. The intent of this meeting was to present the proposed new process, receive feedback from this larger group and ultimately receive support for implementation. At the conclusion of this meeting, the lean workgroup received feedback, much of which was able to be incorporated into the final state. There was a one-month window for everyone to complete their tasks, with rollout of the new process occurring at the beginning of fall semester 2009. The new process is shown above in the form of a flow chart (see Figure 2).

The implementation of a new IT project intake process was successful primarily because we followed the lean model, and we had great support from the project sponsor. The beauty of this model is it allows a work group dedicated time to evaluate the current process, issues with the current process and best practices. In addition, the lean model allows a group of stakeholders to be part of building the solution, and with feedback from a larger stakeholder group, this ensures support from the bottom on up.

8. CONCLUSION

In conclusion, Winona State University utilized the Lean principles of process improvement to enhance the project intake process for IT. Prior to 2009, Winona State's IT Department struggled with the successful completion of projects and decided to take a unique approach to resolving the issue. This approach allowed a core team of individuals to spend a focused amount of time documenting and discussing the current process, researching best practices, and brain storming ideas for a new and improved process. At the end of the four-day Kaizen event, a new process was proposed and presented to a larger group of stakeholders for feedback and approval. After multiple revisions to the initial proposal, the new process was implemented in August of 2009.

The process that now currently exists for IT project requests is documented on Winona State's website, http://www.winona.edu/it/itsprojects.asp. It allows for project owners and community members to make their requests online and includes automated communication back to them notifying them as to the status of their request. An IT project team reviews requests on a weekly basis, approves, denies or defers the requests, and assigns a project lead to communicate back with the requester. All approved, deferred and completed projects are tracked and displayed to campus via a project dashboard.

The new process centralizes the documentation of all project requests and their statuses. This allows for more thorough research of requests to ensure alignment with the Campus Technology Master Plan. It promotes better communication between the IT units and allows for realistic expectations to be set to the WSU community. The return on investment has been great as we've shown an increase in the number of significant IT projects completed, as well as an increase in customer and stakeholder satisfaction.

9. ACKNOWLEDGMENTS

The authors would like to thank Theresa Waterbury and Ann MacDonald for providing training and support to the Information Technology Services leadership team. The authors would also like to thank Maryellen Kanz for facilitating the kaizen event that successfully worked to improve the IT project intake process.

10. REFERENCES

[1] Hines, P. and Lethbridge, S. New development: Creating a lean university. *Public Money and Management,* (February, 2008), 53-56.

[2] Moore, M., Nash, M, and Henderson, K. 2007. Becoming a lean university. *Best Practices of Southern Association of College and University Business Officers (SACUBO) 2007.* DOI= http://www.sacubo.org/sacubo_resources/best_practices_files/2007_files/UnivofCentralOkla-LeanUniversity.pdf

[3] Popli, S. Ensuring customer delight: A quality approach to excellence in management education. *Quality in Higher Education,* 11, 1 (April, 2005), 17-24.

[4] Waterbury, T. Using the collaborative improvement model to improve a university hiring process. *International Journal of Productivity and Quality Management,* 5, 1 (2010), 75-87.

[5] Waterbury, T. and MacDonald, A. Applied educational lean facilitator certificate. *Educational Improvement and Leadership,* (2009), p 9. Winona State University.

[6] Tischler, L. Brining lean to the office. *Quality Progress,* (July 2006), 32-38.

[7] Emiliani, M. L. Improving business school courses by applying lean principles and practices. *Quality Assurance in Education,* 12, 4 (2004), 175-187.

[8] Emiliani, M. L. Using kaizen to improve graduate business school degree programs. *Quality Assurance in Education,* 13, 1 (2005), 37-52.

[9] Waterbury, T. and Holm, M. *Educational Lean for Higher Education. 2011.*

[10] Hines, P. and Lethbridge, S. New Development: Creating a Lean University. *Public Money & Management,* (February, *2008*), 53-56.

[11] What is Lean Thinking, (2007), http://www.leanenterprise.org.uk/what-is-lean-thinking/what-is-lean-thinking-and-key-lean-thinking-principles.html (accessed, June 1, 2011).

Leading from the Middle

Melisa Tanger-Brown
University of Rochester
Rush Rhees Library G-138
Rochester, NY 14627
1-585-275-9162
Lisa.brown@rochester.edu

ABSTRACT
As a manager, one is often stuck in the middle of the operational needs of one's unit and the ideals of the organization's leadership team. Dealing with day-to-day operational issues, while also supporting the strategies and mission of a larger organization, with no supporting framework, can often lead to gaps in policy and process. In early 2010 the managers in University Information Technology at the University of Rochester decided that we needed a new strategy to connect our individual units, stop working in silos, and work towards a better integrated team environment. In March, the entire management team from across University IT went on a retreat and talked about our issues. The result of that retreat was a focus on building a better team that could take on major cross-functional issues and work on presenting solutions for them. Shortly after the retreat goals for the coming year were created, and a steering committee was formed. This committee has been guiding the work of the management team and a number of initiatives that started this past year. Additionally, a number of smaller focus groups have formed to work on making our IT department function in a more cooperative and collaborative manner.

Categories and Subject Descriptors
K.6.1 [Management of Computing and Information Systems]: Project and People Management – *Management techniques, Strategic information systems planning.*

General Terms
Management, Measurement, Performance, Human Factors, Standardization.

Keywords
Management. Cooperative. Collaborative. Focus Groups. Retreat.

1. BACKGROUND
Learn, Discover, Heal, Create – And Make the World Ever Better.

The mission of the University of Rochester, along with its motto "Meliora" (meaning "Ever Better") provides those of us that work there with a clear understanding of how we fit in. Anytime we can provide more services or better services, we are enhancing the experience at the University. While individually, we all strive to make the University of better place, our IT organization was at odds with itself and looking for a way to make things right.

University of Rochester is one of the country's top-tier research universities which include a teaching hospital (Strong Memorial Hospital). We host more than 200 academic majors, more than 2,000 faculty and instructional staff and approximately 9,300 students. Learning at the University of Rochester is on a very personal scale with smaller classes, a low 9:1 student to teacher ratio and increased interactions with faculty.

Also included at the University are the Eastman School of Music and the Memorial Art Gallery.

The University of Rochester is also Rochester's largest employer with about 22,000 employees and envisions itself as a community that welcomes, encourages and supports individuals who desire to contribute to and benefit from the institution's missions of teaching, research, patient care, performance, and community service.

2. INTRODUCTION
In 1999, the University of Rochester named its first Chief Information Officer. This newly created position was established in order to direct strategic planning efforts and bring together the diverse operations of academic computing, administrative computing, networking and telecommunications. While this was step toward a unified organization, it took ten years, a change in CIO and a change in many top leadership positions (including president and provost) for the organization to realize that being one organization is more than just calling yourself by the same name.

In 2009, the Information Technology division continued to struggle to manage projects and work together to provide consistent and comprehensive services. The new CIO had just finished putting together a new leadership team and that group of individuals was beginning to lead the organization as a cohesive team. However, managers in the organization struggled to manage projects, manage staff and send a consistent message.

After months of struggling to work together, the management team took a step back and requested a retreat, without the directors, to reconnect and reevaluate. The result was a transformation in our ways of working.

SIGUCCS'11, November 12–17, 2011, San Diego, California, USA.

3. RETREAT

In March 2010, the management team from across the various IT units came together in a full day off-site meeting to talk about a vision for the future. The retreat was facilitated by an outside organization and forced us to look at what we could do for the organization as a team, rather than as individuals. This retreat was a rare opportunity for the members of the management team to voice their opinions and appreciate shared intentions. Never before had this group met and been able to freely discuss issues. Nor had this group ever verbalized what made them a "team".

The end result was a group that wanted to work harder together to make our organization better. The group left the retreat wanting to bring shared issues to our leadership team and wanting to provide cohesive guidance to our staff. Additionally, the team wanted to be empowered to make certain types of decisions for the organization, but realized that this would require a track record of offering good solutions and suggestions.

The team agreed that its purpose (as a whole) was to provide strategy, guidance, mentoring and problem-solving for the organization. Individually we needed to allocate our staff resources to projects; however as a team we needed to offer solutions to resource allocation problems. As individuals we needed to manage day-to-day activities; however as a team we needed to foster collaboration amongst our units and work across existing boundaries.

Another result of the retreat was a better appreciation for our peers. Seeing that we are all on the same page in a number of issues provided an eye-opening experience. Many left the retreat with the hopefulness that we would continue these dialogues and work toward a common goal.

4. GOALS, MISSION and STEERING COMMITTEE

One of the initial goals of the management team was to develop a collaborative and consistent management team through communications, relationships and common methodologies and practices. We also wanted to be involved in strategic planning with our leaders and wanted ownership of operational planning.

Our IT organization focuses on the following pyramid for strategic projects and operational activities: Solidifying Infrastructure, Developing Enabling Systems, and Supporting the Mission. Each IT activity falls into one of these three catagories.

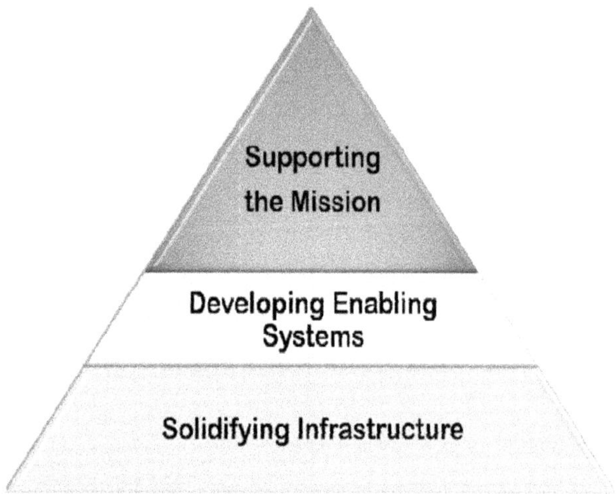

We decided that our management team should focus on the following activities: Resource Management, Project Management, Operations, Strategic Planning, Metrics & Measures, Finance, Benchmarking and Collaboration and Customer Relations.

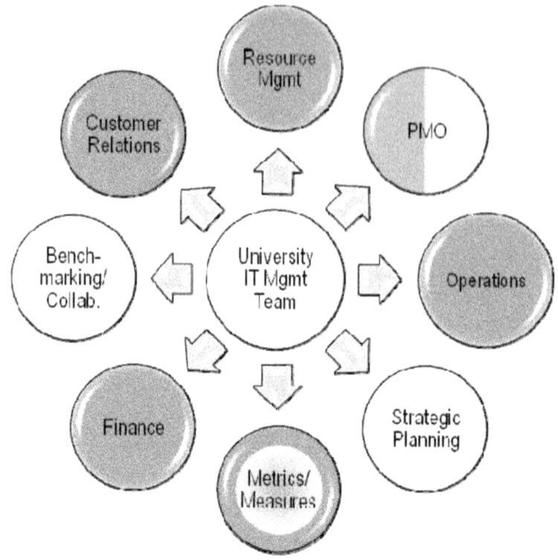

Additionally, we developed a mission statement:

Our mission is to function as a collaboration team to drive and deliver operational excellence across all facets of IT in support of the University mission.

Vocal and engaged members of the management team came together to form a steering committee and to move the goals and mission of the management team forward. This is an inclusive group that embraces new membership and looks to the whole team to provide input and substance to initiatives.

We also needed to set some goals for the coming year. The following is the initial list that was developed.

- Redefine the management team membership
- Review the management/leadership team meeting format
- Focus on measurements
- Review Change Management processes and develop efficiencies
- Share multi-year operational plans across units

One of the first things that the management team decided was that in order to function as a team, we needed to meet regularly. We scheduled a twice monthly meeting to vet ideas, work on various initiatives, and review metrics.

The steering committee also meets twice a month to move initiatives forward and help set goals for the coming months.

5. KEY EXPECTATIONS and RESPONSIBILITIES

Our next step was to define the key expectations of our team – what did leadership expect of us and what did our staff expect of us? This helped us determine next steps in the process of forming a team. We realized that although we each managed individual and distinct areas, the expectations were the same.

Our leadership team expects us to participate in strategic planning and carry out the strategic plan, foster employee morale, manage to the defined budget and manage issues and escalations.

Our staff expects us to act as a buffer to leadership and represent their best interests, prioritize tasks and set boundaries, clarify their roles in the organization's strategic vision, be fair, consistent and have an open door policy and to manage service level agreement, metrics and measurements that improve our efficiency and effectiveness.

We also defined our responsibilities – what areas did we want to take ownership for in our organization? Some obvious areas were day-to-day operations and areas dealing with staff (development, evaluation, training and recruitment). But we also wanted responsibility for building relationships with our customers and fostering ideas. We wanted to drive changes in the organization in all areas – technical, tactical, process and strategic. We wanted to be responsible for managing projects, setting priorities and delivering results.

Once we had all of these areas defined, it helped us begin to think more like a team and to determine how we could most effectively work together to make our organization function more efficiently.

6. FOCUS GROUPS

As the steering committee began to explore these different areas, it was clear that in order to make progress, we needed to form small groups and focus on specific areas.

6.1 Metrics

The steering committee began with a focus on metrics. Initial analysis showed that we needed to limit our initial investigation into a single area of measurement. So we asked the entire management team to vote on one of five areas: Service Availability, Operational Excellence, Customer Satisfaction, Project Management, and Finance. Operational Excellence was the top vote-getter, followed by Service Availability and Customer Satisfaction. The steering committee decided to dig deeper into the category of "Operational Excellence" to determine what metrics should be kept.

After review, the team came up with three areas: Operational Process Effectiveness (How well are our processes working?), Technology Effectiveness (How well are we utilizing our technology investments?) and Service Request Resolution (Are we closing requests with quality and in a timely manner?). Within each of these areas we have measures and targets to help determine how well things are working.

For Operational Process Effectiveness we review Root Cause Analysis measures and Change Management measures. Each of these areas already had some measurements in place so we just needed to bring the measurement together in a single location, set goals and review the measures periodically.

Within Technology Effectiveness, we looked at the use of Security Tools, Patch Management Tools, Renewal and Replacement programs and Networking Utilization. For each of these we wanted to verify that we were using the tools to the capacity intended and making use of the data provided from the tools.

Finally for Service Request Resolution, we reviewed metrics regarding requests coming through the Help Desk for resolution on first touch. Eventually we would like to track and review completion of all tickets, regardless of assignment.

After a number of meetings to define these metrics and their associated targets, we implemented a dashboard where data owners could enter their monthly measures. Each category is automatically measured against its target and designated as either Red (meaning that it falls outside the target expectation) or Green (meaning that it falls within the target expectation). If any one component in a category is Red then the entire category is considered Red and a Root Cause Analysis is done for that component to determine what caused the measure to be off-target. At one of the monthly meetings, we review the metrics and discuss root cause (if necessary).

6.2 Change Management

One area of operational excellence that stood out was Change Management. We thought that we had issues in our change processes, but our metrics review began to show us where the issues lay. A number of changes were running beyond their scheduled timeframes, or encountering issues during the change. Upon review of metrics, a focus group for Change Management was formed and a number of initiatives were begun to better manage changes.

During the Change Management process review, it was decided to let the staff – those that typically have to make the changes – have a say in the processes and procedures. The focus group provided team members from their areas to participate in a half-day retreat to discuss change and make suggestions for improvements in the process.

Out of this retreat, a technical advisory group was created that allows someone to talk through a technical issue with staff from various teams to determine if the change will have an adverse effect in some other area.

The staff also suggested that change requests have a "second set of eyes". This means that there is one person responsible for the change and a second staff member that knows enough about the change to review the process during the change.

We are also in the process of implementing a new change management process tool and this focus group, along with the staff group, is key in determining processes for implementation.

6.3 Standard Maintenance Windows

As we explored Change Management, a number of managers mentioned that infrastructure changes that affected the services that they manage were hard to coordinate and get approval for. One line of business manager mentioned that, in the past, she had been required to request four different downtime windows in a single week because of various changes to underlying technologies that her customer depended on. Because the various units didn't coordinate downtimes, this could happen frequently and make end users quite unhappy.

The first suggestion was for each area to come up with standard maintenance windows for services. However, with each area working in isolation, the end result was still the possibility of multiple downtimes for a business system within a single week.

A small focus group was created to discuss this issue. The group came back with a proposal to create a single weekly maintenance window for infrastructure and major system changes. It would be up to the Change Management team to oversee the usage of the window and manage the set of changes that could use the window. This idea was presented to various campus groups and met with great enthusiasm and is planned for implementation this summer.

6.4 Project Management

While not on our radar as a focus area immediately, project management has continually been an area of weakness in our organization. We take on too many projects and many are delayed. We have never had a good way to determine why projects are delayed or to prioritize projects. A small group of managers have begun to meet to help prioritize projects, allocate resources and determine new processes that will help advance projects and keep deliverables on track.

7. ONE YEAR LATER

We've made significant progress in one year. We have accomplished all of the initial goals set forth immediately after the retreat, as well as taken on some additional tasks.

We also have some "lessons learned" and new goals for next year.

The first set of "lessons" focuses on collaboration. Putting forth a unified front requires more meetings and more time to work through the activities than developing in isolation. This is time away from our respective teams. At the same time, it provides an avenue for early detection of issues and solutions to organization wide problems.

The second set of "lessons" centers around top-down communications. We have spent the past year focusing on issues and reporting up to leadership but have neglected to include our staff in these discussions. We need to include our staff in similar collaborative endeavors across the organization (similar to the Change Management process and Technical Advisory Group) and provide them with information about the value in our activities.

The third set of "lessons" is about small group collaboration. Focus groups are necessary to move initiatives forward. Initially we tried to focus on these different areas with the entire management team at our twice monthly meetings. The group was too large to accomplish anything. Instead smaller groups met more frequently and put together proposals to bring to the larger group. This allowed those with real energy to focus on the topic and still allowed everyone else to have a say in the processes.

Our next steps moving forward are to implement the Standard Maintenance Windows and enhancements to the Change Management process. We also plan to begin looking at Service Availability metrics and measures.

Additionally, in keeping with our "lessons learned", we need to take advantage of our staff and find ways for them to collaborate with others in the organization in order to better appreciate it. And we need to find ways to provide them with updates on what we are doing as a team and how our work betters the organization.

Lastly, we plan to have a 360 degree feedback plan to get input into how we are doing as a team.

8. ACKNOWLEDGEMENTS

Thank you to the wonderful members of the Management Team Steering Committee: Debora Beegen, Andrea Campbell, Alice Durie, Cynthia Hervey, Joseph Pasquarelli, Jason Pickup, Richard Pink, and Lisa Sprague. It has been a pleasure to work with you through this process and I am looking forward to continuing to work with you to make University IT a better organization.

CourseCast – A New Angle on Course Capture Technology

William C. Klein
Valparaiso University School of Law
656 S. Greenwich St.
Valparaiso, IN 46383
219.465.7928
william.klein@valpo.edu

ABSTRACT

To address the increasing need to deliver, improve upon the quality, and track usage of class review sessions, the Valparaiso University School of Law has invested resources in course capture software called CourseCast offered by Panopto Systems. The ability to provide a discounted service to educational institutions through Panopto's Socrates Program was a high selling point to our school. While the software was free, some minimal costs were incurred for non-proprietary hardware. CourseCast's ability to synchronize audio, video, and screen captures with PowerPoint was an option that was highly desired. Additional benefits beyond the original scope of the system included the ability to capture other events, such as lectures, class sessions, interviews, instructional sessions, and self/peer-review of teaching styles. Some risks, challenges, and rewards in both the technical and instructional aspects of the system were encountered during the implementation of this project. The evaluation of current uses and strategic planning for the future use of CourseCast at the Valparaiso University School of Law continues to be a high priority.

Categories and Subject Descriptors

K.3.1 [Computers And Education]: Computer uses in education—computer-assisted instruction (CAI)

General Terms

Lecture Capture, CourseCast, Silverlight, PowerPoint synchronization, audio/video capture

1. INTRODUCTION

At the Valparaiso University School of Law, professors requested that their review sessions be tape recorded, catalogued with the library, and made available to students at their convenience. In previous year, these recordings were made with VHS™ camcorders and tapes, but then VHS™ started to become an outdated format. Trying to find camcorders to record sessions became increasingly difficult. Students were less likely to have VHS™ players and the few that were housed in the School of Law were located in areas that were continually in use. Over time, the technology in this arena changed, yet the local process evolved more slowly as plain audio recordings were introduced. This format was easier to copy and make available to students, but we were still faced with the issue of having only limited numbers of copies to check out through the library. After experimenting with the audio recordings, we tried using digital recordings that were transferred to DVD™. The common issue with these processes continued: limited availability of the recordings. It was possible to duplicate recordings, but that took extra time and resources. Tapes and DVDs™ would have to be copied. If more than one or two people wanted to view the recordings at the same time, they might have to wait for the checked-out items to be returned. Making copies of a DVD™ took less time, but physical resources were required in the process, so only a few copies were made available when requested. The process to digitize recordings took more time than it did to actually record the review session. It took staff time to setup and teardown the recording process in each of these scenarios. We needed to find a way to reduce the following:

- Staff time in recording process
- Student time in finding, checking out, reviewing materials
- Turn around time for presenting materials
- Use of physical resources that took up space and monetary resources that could be put to better use

2. PANOPTO SOCRATES PROGRAM

In 2008, we started looking at different solutions and options to move from physical recordings to an online format. Some of the options we researched and considered were Camtasia, Jing, and Echo360. We heard about Panopto through a listserv called Teknoids that focuses on using technology in legal academia, non-profits, the judiciary, and law firms plus others with interests in this area. [1] The Socrates Program through Panopto [2] gave us a solution that we were searching for: the ability to capture lecture content and deliver the material to students in a timely fashion through a medium that was readily available and could be sustained throughout their career at the School of Law.

3. INCENTIVE / DRIVING FACTORS

The move from physical media to online media was a driving factor. Having copious amounts of VHS™ tapes and DVDs™ lying around was unsightly, had a limited shelf life, and only a limited amount were available. Moving online allowed multiple students to access the same recording at the same time; plus they were able to watch the videos off-site at whatever time they wished.

One of the additional benefits was the capability to synchronously capture a PowerPoint presentation, along with the audio and or video of the concurrent lecture. This unique ability was not available with the other programs during our initial search. This gave us the ability to hold classes in a delayed distribution model for a number of different scenarios such as summer courses, leave of absence, unforeseen circumstances, (medical/disease outbreaks, adverse weather conditions, and additional school closings).

Its ease of use granted us flexibility in terms of who could use the CourseCast system. As long as the CourseCast Recorder was downloaded onto the computer, it could be run from the desktop either in online mode or offline (to be uploaded later). Connecting a FireWire© (IEEE 1394) camera or using an internal webcam and microphone would be the next level of complexity. It has been easy to teach faculty, staff and students how to use the program and success stories from professors and staff will be shared later in this paper.

Due to the online nature of CourseCast, the ability to manage from essentially anywhere made the role of being an administrator easier. If something wasn't working with the system or a recording outside of regular work hours, a support staff person can login to solve the problem and keep the event moving.

Between the Fall 2010 and Spring 2011 semesters, over 590 hours of CourseCast content was accessed either through viewing or listening. We anticipate that these figures will continue to rise as we incorporate more classes and content into the CourseCast system.

4. ONE TOOL, MANY MISSIONS

For what are we using this product? The ability for CourseCast to be used for a variety of purposes was appealing. It was not going to be a one-task operation and here are just a few examples of the current usage:

4.1 Course Lecture Capture

The primary task for the CourseCast system has and will be capturing course lectures, review sessions and make-up classes.

4.2 Training Sessions

Our Career Planning Center has been using the CourseCast system to create videos showing students how to use the software products and websites that they support over the course of a student's career at Valpo Law. They have also provided CourseCasts of PowerPoint presentations with voice-overs of actual presentations that they have hosted. For students who were not able to attend these presentations, they can review them online. From our Career Planning Center office to Information Technology, the CourseCast system is used to show the end user how to use various software products with screen captures coupled with voice-overs.

4.3 Reference for Information Technology

The Valpo Law Information Technology group has used CourseCast to successfully record and deliver "how-to" videos to the students, faculty and Law Library.

4.4 Presentation Archive

As special presentations, lectures, and discussion panels have been hosted at the Law School; we have been able to record them for historical purposes and for those individuals who were not able to attend.

4.5 Self/Peer-Critique of Teaching Techniques

We have had at least one example of a professor who approached the Information Technology group about recording some of his lectures and classes so he could review his teaching technique. We are still in the process of determining if this would be a good way to allow other Professors to review courses, the teaching techniques of other professors and to make a general review of their own teaching technique.

4.6 Negotiation Practice

We were asked by the Advanced Dispute Resolutions' Professor to record student negotiation practice. The process was fairly simple: a room was reserved; the camera/computer placed in the room along with instructions, and a sign-up sheet was posted. The students were able to record their sessions without any major issues. The Professor and the students review the session at their discretion.

4.7 One-on-One Interviews with Students (audio)

One Legal Writing professor wanted to have individual conversations with his students as he reviewed their legal writing assignments with them. At first, the professor wanted to record their conversations with a handheld device, extract the electronic files, copy over to a computer, and send the files to the individual students. This was a complicated process that would have taken considerable time and effort on the part of the professor. Instead, we offered the use of Panopto's CourseCast system for this task. Since the Panopto system can handle recording from a variety of inputs, the professor was able to quickly make audio recordings of these interviews. CourseCast allowed the professor to create offline recordings that didn't require logging into the system. After the interview was done, the recording could be uploaded to the server. Due to the location of the professor's office and various issues surrounding his wireless connection, we found that the recordings didn't upload correctly all the time. Panopto allowed us to create offline recordings and then upload at the discretion of the professor.

5. WHAT DOESN'T WORK

5.1 Importing Video from External Sources

Importing video from external sources is an issue that continually challenged us. In some instances we are presented with recorded material from a student or professor that they want to upload to CourseCast. We initially had only one portable CourseCast setup that we would use for recording. We've since moved to having two portable setups that could be used at the same time. If someone from the Information Technology team was not able to setup a CourseCast, we would sometimes give a faculty member or student a camera to record with. From that point, it was up to them to record their event and then return the camera to us. We would then need to extract the recordings from the camera, convert them, splice them together depending on the length of the recording, and upload to the server. Of course, this meant multiple points of potential failure and we have experienced some at every step of the process.

By far, the majority of issues have occurred during the conversion and uploading of externally recorded files. The type of operating system we used changed the type of file that we could upload. The process of uploading an external video file started with converting the video to the correct format. Then, using the offline recording feature of CourseCast, we created a short "placeholder" video. Next, we would rename the converted external video to match that of the offline "placeholder" video. The offline video would be removed on the computer and the external video copied into that exact place in the file structure. After that, the video could be uploaded into the CourseCast system with manual cues that CourseCast offered. It often took considerable time to convert the external videos and post to the CourseCast system; a slight drawback to using this system

5.2 Not Instantaneous

Even after recording an event, it would take some time to upload and convert the file to be viewable through the CourseCast system. Typically, this would take 5-10 minutes after a lecture was finished. While this is not a huge issue for typical classes, presentations and lectures, it would not work for instances that required immediate playback such as reviews for trial skill courses.

5.3 First come/first serve

As of right now, we need to setup and tear down the CourseCast system every time we need to use the system, and there are 8-10 classrooms where the system could possibly be set up and used for a review session or a lecture. Until recently, we only had one CourseCast system, so if we needed to capture two lectures at the same time then we would loan out a separate camera that could be used to capture the other event and import the video later. We have since added a second CourseCast setup that is essentially the same equipment as the first system. We also need staff time to setup and tear down each time that a recording was requested.

6. EXPECTATIONS/PANDORA'S BOX

6.1 Will we really put this in all of our classrooms?

This is certainly a question that will need to be addressed sooner rather than later. It would be wonderful to have a camera and CourseCast setup in each classroom, but what levels of expectations would come along with this? Would we be required to record every single class, lecture, review session? Probably not, but it would be an intriguing question to try and answer. This is a Pandora's Box that once having released the software and hardware to record, removing the technology out of the hands of faculty and others using it would be quite difficult. Having the server space to record every event would not be that difficult to come up with. The software would be the easy part to install, but adding a digital video camera and proper audio to capture both the students and the professor would be challenging. A more realistic goal would be to have at least one classroom with multiple camera angles on the presenter and a separate hi-res camera to capture what is being written on a whiteboard.

6.2 Enhancing course materials

Most likely we would add to the multi-use function of the CourseCast system to allow Professors to enhance their course materials with existing review sessions and new lessons. We would also like to populate our Blackboard Course Management system with recordings from CourseCast and integrate them into their respective classes.

7. ACKNOWLEDGMENTS

I would like to thank John Obermann and Donna Patterson of the Valparaiso University School of Law for their support and advice during the writing process.

8. REFERENCES

[1] *http://www.teknoids.net/*

[2] *http://www.panopto.com/site/Company/News/PressReleases/aug08.aspx*

UMConnect One Year Later: Promoting Live@Edu Services

Kathy Garramone
The University of Montana
IT-Client Support Services
Missoula, MT 59812
406-243-5392
kathy.garramone@umontana.edu

ABSTRACT

In 2010, the University of Montana successfully switched student email service from a campus hosted system to Microsoft's Live@Edu services. For the most part, student email, called UMConnect, is robust and dependable. However, marketing some of its related features proved more difficult than we imagined.

Live@Edu offers three kinds of services for universities: communication, collaboration, and productivity. Communication services include student email mailboxes with 10 GB of storage space, a calendar for personal and educational use, and contacts. Collaboration opportunities are available through SkyDrive, 25 GB of online storage space allowing for individual use, file sharing, and working together with fellow students. Productivity tools through SkyDrive offers access to Microsoft Office Web Apps, online companions to Word, Excel, PowerPoint and OneNote.

During the first year of implementation, UM's primary focus was on Live@Edu communication services. Once we determined that students were successfully using these services, our focus expanded to include Sky Drive and Office Web Apps. Information about these services is now available in our student brochures, on student email web pages, display boards, bulletin boards, and is also included in demonstrations at student orientations, technical group meetings and workshops.

As we began marketing SkyDrive and Office Web Apps, we noticed two things: either students had no idea these services were available and they wanted to learn more, or they had negative impressions of them.

How did we address these very different student attitudes? We needed more information to determine the best way to continue marketing Live@Edu collaboration and productivity services. In this paper we look closely at these services, how they function, additional student input on the positives and negatives, and how we arrived at a marketing plan that successfully promotes Microsoft's Live@Edu SkyDrive and Office Web Apps at UM.

SIGUCCS'11, November 12–17, 2011, San Diego, California, USA.

Categories and Subject Descriptors

H.5.2 [Information Interfaces and Presentation (I.7)]: User Interfaces (D.2.2, H.1.2, I.3.6) – *training, help, and documentation.*

General Terms

Documentation, Performance, Assessment

Keywords

Student email system, cloud services, service evaluation

1. INTRODUCTION

The University of Montana, located in Missoula, Montana, has a student population of approximately 15,000 students. In 2010 UM outsourced student email from a campus-hosted service to Microsoft's Live@Edu services and labeled it UMConnect. UMConnect offers students email, contacts, and a calendar tool. In addition, Live@Edu services are available to students and include a 25 GB SkyDrive for online storage, Office Web Apps, instant messaging, video chat and more. Microsoft categorizes these services into three areas: email, collaboration and productivity.

Throughout the outsourcing process and beyond, our primary focus of this implementation was the email component of Live@Edu services. UM requires students to use official email for their University-related business. Therefore, it is critical that students understand how to access and use UMConnect to meet this requirement. IT-Client Support Services spent many hours creating documentation, flyers, brochures, and slides to help students achieve proficiency with UMConnect. Staff members attended orientations, meetings, and student fairs assisting students in whatever ways were necessary.

Once we approached the one year mark of UMConnect implementation, the service was functioning well and the number of email-related support requests decreased over time. As a result, beginning spring semester 2011, IT-Client Support Services was directed to focus on marketing other Live@Edu "cloud" services to students, specifically the collaboration services (SkyDrive) and productivity tools (Office Web Apps).

Also during this time, another campus initiative began. A cloud computing lab committee was formed and charged with identifying, evaluating, and recommending enhanced ways for student access of computer lab services. The committee is exploring options for needed software for courses, computers, internet access, printing and assistance with applications. Since Live@Edu services provide "cloud" or virtual opportunities for students, it is very fitting to include Live@Edu services as part of this initiative.

2. ABOUT LIVE@EDU SERVICES

In order to effectively promote Live@Edu collaboration services and productivity tools we spent time experimenting with and testing the various features of each.

Collaboration services are available with SkyDrive providing 25 GB of free online storage space, file sharing, and the ability to work together with others. SkyDrive can be accessed from any location with a computer or a mobile device with an internet connection using a web browser. Individual files can be uploaded to SkyDrive and the maximum upload size is 50 MB. SkyDrive can be used to back up files online, or share files with others. Also included is the ability to assign permissions and set folders and files in a public or private status, so that users share files with only those they select.

Students can collaborate with fellow students through their UMConnect email accounts to allow access to specific files and folders on their SkyDrive.

Office Web Apps are located on SkyDrive and include companion versions or light versions of Microsoft Word, Excel, PowerPoint and OneNote. Students do not need Office installed on their computers to use Office Web Apps. All that's necessary is a web browser with internet access.

Some features from full Office programs are not available with the companion versions. However, basic functions like text editing in Word, formula editing in Excel and co-authoring simultaneously in OneNote allow students to have flexibility with their educational course work that they might not otherwise have.

3. TESTING LIVE@EDU SERVICES

Student workers from our central IT support help desk, IT Central, assisted in testing both SkyDrive and Office Web Apps. In addition, we have a student test account that was also used by staff to test the various features. Students were asked to access their SkyDrive, create folders, allow sharing with others, and upload files and photos. With Outlook Web Apps, we asked students to test the various functions within each program, and using a spreadsheet, record their results.

Feedback indicated that SkyDrive is a very useful solution for online document storage and sharing. Students were able to easily create folders, both private and public, create file shares, as well as upload photos. The only issue noted was that the upload file size is only 50 MB and entire folders could not be uploaded. This is not a major problem, but could be an inconvenience and time-consuming task if a student has large or multiple files to upload.

Regarding Office Web Apps, there are technical functions not available within the programs, especially with Excel. At times the interfaces seemed slow and clunky. However, for basic document creation and sharing, these programs proved very useful. If a student had the full Office program on their desktops they could easily save the files to their SkyDrive and open them using the online companion version of that program, and continue working on those files.

Prior to the transition to UMConnect, student email was hosted internally on our Exchange environment, along with faculty and staff email. We had one Global Address Listing (GAL) for all UM. Students could locate their instructors in the GAL and vice versa. It was a very convenient feature. When we switched to UMConnect, this feature was no longer available as the systems are separate. This has two ramifications. First, there is not a shared GAL, and second, student and faculty collaboration possibilities using SkyDrive and Office Web apps occur outside UM's systems.

Regarding the GAL, students have an address directory in UMConnect. However, only student email addresses are available in this directory. On a positive note, if a student enters in an instructor address in the "TO" field, that address will become part of that particular students address book. The only downside is locating the email address in the first place. UM has an online directory that provides faculty, staff and student email addresses, so since the switch, we offer this as a solution to this issue. Unfortunately, the situation is the same for faculty when wanting to communicate with their students. If they do not know their students email addresses, they need to find them, and then enter the addresses in manually in the "To" field of a new email message. Microsoft Outlook has the ability to save email addresses entered in this field, so once entered, the addresses will populate. Microsoft and UM are discussing this issue and currently exploring a solution.

Regarding collaboration possibilities, Live@Edu is set-up such that services come with an email account. A campus-hosted Exchange environment is not setup through Live@Edu; therefore faculty members do not have Live@Edu accounts. In order to collaborate with their students, faculty need to create a Windows Live account which includes a Hot Mail email account and then access to SkyDrive and Office Web Apps is available. It is not possible to setup a Windows Live account using a campus email address. Collaboration occurs through Hot Mail email accounts. This does not prohibit collaboration possibilities. However, it is a confusing process to work through as well as challenging to communicate to campus. As with the GAL issue mentioned above, Microsoft and UM are discussing this problem and exploring a solution.

4. INITIAL MARKETING PLAN

Taking the results of our testing and issues discovered into consideration, during Spring Semester 2011 we begin a marketing campaign. We promoted SkyDrive and Office Web Apps as viable, convenient, and practical online solutions for today's students. We held off on promoting the services to faculty as we struggled with the issue of working outside of our campus email system.

In promoting the services to students we created a communication plan including the following: information in our new student brochure, flyers for table tops and bulletin boards, a Live@Edu specific bulletin board, training for student staff on how to inform and encourage students to use SkyDrive and Office Web Apps, additional questions and answers in our Ask Monte campus knowledge database system, and demonstrations of these services during Orientations and campus technology meetings.

About mid-semester we discovered that despite our efforts, we didn't think they were working. Informal inquiries indicated that many students were still unaware of these services. We took one step back and decided we needed a baseline assessment. We needed to find out: 1) What do students know about services beyond UMConnect; 2) How many students use these services; 3) What services do they use, and; 4) of the services they use, how satisfied are they with them?

5. ASSESSING STUDENT SATISFACTION

To obtain this feedback, we conducted a survey. We had already conducted a student satisfaction survey in 2010, several weeks after we initially outsourced student email to Live@Edu, and were pleased with the results. We surveyed all current UM students via email to determine their satisfaction level with UMConnect regarding the activation process, the transition process, the tools they use (email, SkyDrive, Office Web Apps), and satisfaction in general. 900 students responded to the survey. Overall satisfaction or neutral was 67%. Regarding use of the tools, 92% were using email, 8% were using SkyDrive, and 5% were using Office Web Apps.

This survey, also conducted via email to current UM students, inquired about student satisfaction with UMConnect tools and services, satisfaction with central IT's help desk support, the UMConnect activation process, what tools they use (email, SkyDrive, Office Web Apps), and if they use SkyDrive, how do they use it. We received 865 responses to the survey. One year later, 78% of respondents are either satisfied or neutral about UMConnect and 11% of students use SkyDrive. Of those 11 %, 9% use SkyDrive for online document storage, 1% share documents and photos, and 1% view Office docs on line. Approximately 1% has used one or more of Office Web Apps in the following order: Word, PowerPoint, Excel, and OneNote.

In addition to the survey's rate questions, two open-ended questions were asked: "What do you like best about UMConnect", and "What would you change about UMConnect?" We received 375 responses to the first question and 377 responses to the second. There are many students who are satisfied with UMConnect. Many students commented that before this survey, they were unaware about SkyDrive and Office Web Apps. When responding to making changes to UMConnect, some students voiced their dissatisfaction with Microsoft in general and suggested moving to a different vendor, such as Google.

6. THE CHALLENGES

One of the challenges with outsourcing student email to UMConnect has been campus attitudes about selecting a Microsoft product for the service. This decision was made based on a very detailed review of Microsoft's Live@Edu and Google mail. Both offer email and collaboration services, but we selected Microsoft for technical, legal, and accessibility reasons. Microsoft was compatible with the current IT infrastructure, the campus was familiar with Microsoft software, and implementation meant minimal interface programming. Microsoft's legal agreement is FERPA compliant and also ADA compliant. We informed campus of the reasons for selecting Microsoft over Google, but the attitude still exists and some campus members continue to express reluctance towards the Live@Edu system and services. It's important that we understand this attitude and prepare strategies for responding proactively and positively about Microsoft's Live@Edu services.

In conjunction with the UM student satisfaction survey, the cloud computing lab committee conducted a cloud computing survey to be used to assess access to software used for UM classes. Based on responses to both surveys, it's clear that students don't utilize Office Web App for their coursework. However, what we don't know is whether students don't utilize these online programs because they don't know they exist, or because they think these companion versions of Word, Excel, PowerPoint and OneNote are insufficient. We will need further analysis to answer this question.

7. THE MARKETING PLAN REVISED

During summer 2011, one specific activity was carried out to obtain additional feedback from students about Live@Edu services. A pilot study was conducted using students from a UM online summer course. The course entitled "Electronic Publishing on the WWW" is an introduction to browsers and the web and web site design using several multimedia programs. Student collaboration was necessary for several projects. In this study, students worked in groups of two collaboratively in SkyDrive on an online MS Word document. Once they completed this activity they were asked to respond to several questions about their experience with SkyDrive and the online version of MS Word.

Responses indicated that working collaboratively in SkyDrive on a Word document was easily accomplished. Most students had not worked collaborative prior to this experience, so we were pleased that they found the experience to be acceptable. The only issue students reported was the process involved in sharing the document with their instructor. Since UM faculty email service is campus-hosted, and the instructor did not have a Hot Mail email account, students had to download the document to their desktops and then forward them to their instructor. Once they realized what they needed to do, they were fine, but this issue could be problematic for faculty and student collaboration. Additional study is necessary.

As we prepared for Fall 2011, we updated our communication plan to include more visible marketing activities: a story on the UM home page, demonstrations through our IT short course training program, desktop images on IT and other campus computer lab monitors, training of other campus help desks, short "how to" videos on our website, and meeting presentations. During Fall 2011 IT hosted a campus Tech Fair, an opportunity for the UM campus community to come together to share and learn more about campus technology. During this event, several students promoted and demonstrated Live@Edu services. This activity was well received and provided more exposure to and feedback about Live@Edu services. Initially we focused on students. Our focus now expanded to faculty, for a two-way knowledge experience.

8. THE FUTURE

When this paper went to press, we were in the midst of our Live@Edu services marketing campaign. At that point, we had received many good comments from students who had not heard of these services, and were glad they are available to them.

Discussions with Microsoft will continue as changes are implemented to improve services. Microsoft recently announced that Live@Edu is transitioning to the Microsoft Office 365 platform. Office 365 will bring together many services and software into a cloud service; software and services such as

Office, SharePoint, Exchange, and Lync. This move won't change the UMConnect processes and services that are currently available, but GAL synchronization is expected to be available. There have also been discussions about outsourcing employee email to Microsoft. This would be fee-based, so no decision has been made about moving in this direction.

Finally, as the University of Montana moves forward with the cloud computing concept this next year, our hope is that our Live@Edu marketing efforts will pay off, and that students and faculty will be using SkyDrive and Office Web Apps as tools for work and collaboration.

Moodle Integration of an Automated Account Enabling System and a User Status Collection System

Hideo Masuda
Kyoto Institute of Technology
Matsugasaki, Sakyo, Kyoto
Kyoto, Japan
+81 75 724 7956
h-masuda@kit.ac.jp

Kazuyoshi Murata
Kyoto Institute of Technology
Matsugasaki, Sakyo, Kyoto
Kyoto, Japan
kmurata@kit.ac.jp

Yuki Shirakawa
Kyoto Institute of Technology
Matsugasaki, Sakyo, Kyoto
Kyoto, Japan
y-srkw11@dsm.cis.kit.ac.jp

Yu Shibuya
Kyoto Institute of Technology
Matsugasaki, Sakyo, Kyoto
Kyoto, Japan
shibuya@kit.ac.jp

Yasuaki Kuroe
Kyoto Institute of Technology
Matsugasaki, Sakyo, Kyoto
Kyoto, Japan
kuroe@kit.ac.jp

ABSTRACT
In this paper, we present a Moodle integrated system that combines an automated account enabling subsystem (AAES) and a user logon status collection subsystem in a computer lab (CULS).

The AAES lets each new user learn how to use our computer system and the terms of use. After that the user can enable various computer services such as on-demand printing, network outlet service, and remote access after passing our automated examination in Moodle.

The CULS shows information on users in the computer lab through our Moodle system. We have also implemented the capability of setting privacy levels for each role. For example, in the teacher role of a course, a user can get information about course-registered users, while the ordinary student role users can only get the number of free PCs available.

The Moodle system content is available in both Japanese and English.

Categories and Subject Descriptors
H.4.3 [**Information Systems Applications**]: Communications Applications.

General Terms
Design, Management, Experimentation.

Keywords
Identity Service, Self-Learning, Automated Service, Shibboleth, Moodle, Course Management System.

1. INTRODUCTION
At Kyoto Institute of Technology, the Center for Information Science (CIS) provides a variety of computer services for the members of our university. The authentication and authorization functions are important for safe use of computer services. We provide computer accounts (a username and password) to all university members, about 5000 accounts. It is very important for the integrity of the computer system that we manage and operate the accounts securely Some basic principles of safe account management include creating accounts only for valid members, generating a "good" password for initial use, and so on. Teaching users how to use the accounts is one of the most important things. This education should be done as soon as possible when user gets the account, but it is difficult to educate users with the insufficient staff in our center. Therefore we decided to use an e-Learning system for educating novice users. However, there was no guarantee that the users would make use of the e-Learning system for self-study. As the result, we thought that some mechanism to link the e-Learning system to the account management system would be better.

At the same time, we provide computer labs equipped with PCs for the university members. We have about 200 PCs for 4500 students so it would be a great service to gather and display the current status of each PC for the convenience of users. From the viewpoint of privacy, the details of the user state could have different levels. For example, a student might be only interested in the availability of machines, while teachers and administrators might want to know who is at what machine. Thus, the system can show different levels of information and detail of user status according to the role and privilege of the viewer. The roles include system administrator, teacher, and student.

In this paper, we show how we integrated both an automated account enabling subsystem (AAES) and a collecting user logon status subsystem (CULS) into Moodle to meet the needs of our university.

2. AIMS OF THE OUR SYSTEM

2.1 The Automated Account Enabling Subsystem

Needless to say, a user identification mechanism is very important for the safety of our computer services. Authentication and authorization are essential. Users authenticate by providing account information consisting of a username and password. We provide and maintain about 5000 accounts including about 300 faculty, about 150 staff, and about 4500 students. We find the most important part of managing the account system is educating users on how to manage their own account. Without education, users tend to keep the initial password, use a weak password, and even rent their own account to others. With such practices, the account system will become unreliable.

Moreover, it is also important to let users know which subsystems can be used by their account. In our university, we have an integrated authentication system. In order to efficiently create new accounts, we generate and register the new users' accounts right as we get the list of all newcomer users from each office section. An account comes with access to various subsystems. These subsystems might include for example: PC access in the computer labs, e-mail service, e-Learning service (Moodle system), on-demand printing service, network outlet service, and account management (password management). However, users do not have to use all services. The account Terms of Use from our university is often not read diligently. With only 3 staff in our division, it is very difficult to educate all users about their account efficiently. Hundreds of users get new accounts in April every year (April is a start in Japan at the semester). We provide the e-Learning content for users to study by alone. However, most students are not making use of our instructional materials.

As a result, we decided to develop an automated mechanism as follows; the user can use minimal services such as PC access in the computer labs and e-Learning right away, but access to other services require reading the terms of use and other important account management information and then pass quizzes on the content.

2.2 Collecting and Displaying User Logon Status in the Computer Lab

We provide the computer labs for the students at the university. To operate it efficiently, we have to collect and display the system status of each PC. PCs in the computer lab are operated by the network boot system and a service management agent program is running on each PC. This program collects each user's logon status and running application information on each PC.

For convenience to users, we want to provide the information display subsystem about whether PCs in the computer lab are available or in use. We have about 200 PCs, but all PCs are not in one place. Our university's facility has PCs distributed into 8 locations on the campus and each location has different hours. Therefore, the mechanism of the information display subsystem should be able to access the data from remote devices through the Internet. From the viewpoint of privacy, the details of the user state should have different levels. For example, the levels of system administrator, teacher, student enrolled in a course, and other students would all have different levels of data access. Thus the subsystem should be able to show the various levels of user status details according to the role of each viewer. For example, the teacher of a course can get the information of course-registered students during the lecture time slot, but ordinary students can only get the number of free PCs, and so on.

To create such a subsystem, the information already in our Moodle system can be used to distinguish the roles. All lectures in our university are registered in our Moodle system as courses, and the accounts of the teachers of each lecture are also registered as the teacher role for that specified course. We decided to develop the information display subsystem as module within Moodle.

3. BASIC DESIGN ISSUES

3.1 E-Learning System (Moodle)

Moodle is open source course management system, also known as a learning management system, or a virtual learning environment. Moodle is developed with a high modularity. In our university, we started to operate the Moodle system as e-Learning environment in 2007. We called it the "Moodle pilot system" [2]. All courses are made for the Moodle system based on data obtained from the Office of Educational Affairs beforehand. The students' list of each course is also provided from the Office of Educational Affairs after checking enrollment information.

We thought that our system could be achieved if the activity module on Moodle is made based on the course information and role information.

3.2 Authentication System (Syntheuniv/UMS)

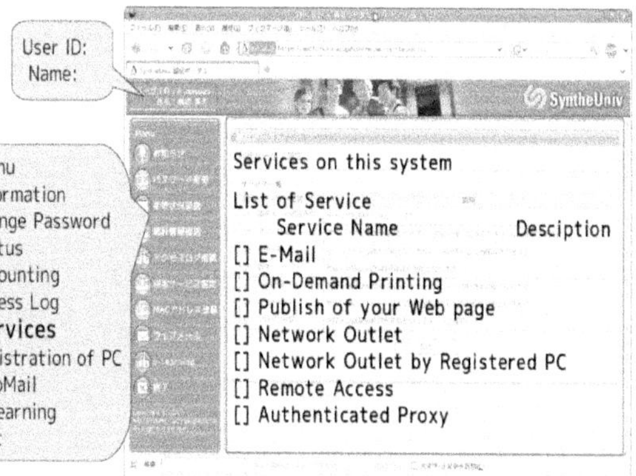

Figure 1: Example of User's Portal (Syntheuniv/UMS)

In our system [1], an integrated user management system is used called "Syntheuniv/UMS" provided by NEC System Technology who is the vender in Japan. Syntheuniv/UMS stores all information into PostgreSQL database, and can distribute the authentication information into LDAP, RADIUS, Windows Active Directory, and some other services with an arbitrary filter. The Web interface for own password changer, allows the viewing of login history. Thus this is the basis for electronic authentication and identification of all members of the university.

In addition, Syntheuniv/UMS has the account management portal function which users can select "enable" or "stay disabled" for each service (Figure 1). As a result, the user can enable only necessary services. From a security point of view, it is desirable that unnecessary services stay disabled. Moreover, we provide the Single Sign On system by Shibboleth with this system. The Shibboleth system is a standard based, open source software package for web single sign-on across or within organizational boundaries. It allows sites to make informed authorization decisions for individual access of protected online resources in a privacy-preserving manner. At this time, Shibbolized services are password changing, service-registration, a Web mail system, Moodle (e-Learning System), and authenticated network outlet.

3.3 Lab PC's Management System (SMA)

The PCs of our computer system (called System8 [1]) are operated by the network boot system called XenDesktop Provisioning Service provided Citrix Co, Ltd. Service Monitoring Agent (SMA) provided by NEC is also running on each PC for monitoring. SMA enables us to get a detailed status of PC including the health of the PC, a logon user name, a title of the activated window, and so on.

.

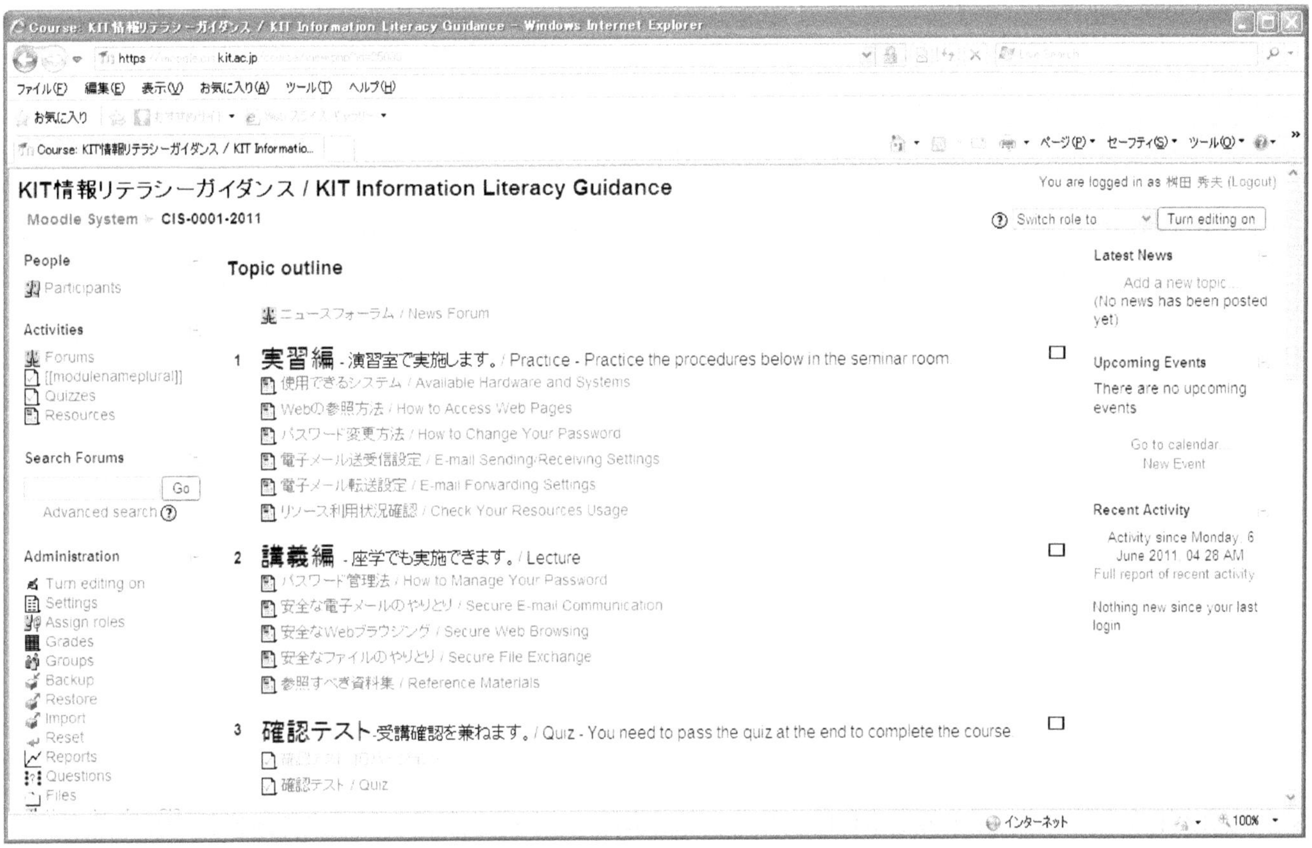

Figure 2: Example of KIT Information Literacy Guidance on Moodle

4. IMPLEMENTATION

4.1 AAES

For AAES, we created an online course for "KIT's guidance for Information Literacy" on Moodle (Figure 2).

This course includes 3 parts: Practice part, Lecture part, and Quiz part. In the practice part, we introduce our available subsystems in our Center, how to change the account password, how to setup an e-Mail client, how to forward e-Mail automatically into a private e-Mail address, and how to check resource usage. Because almost all subsystems have a Web GUI interface, we also provide information on how to access Web pages in a secure mode in the practice part.

In the lecture part, we introduce some aspects of security such as: using an account in our system, management of account passwords, secure e-Mail communication, secure Web browsing, secure file exchange, and reference materials.

In the quiz part there are 10 questions. The question type is "multiple choice" and feedback comments are shown immediately to user. Users can attempt the quiz unlimited times.

For the quiz, we developed a modified online quiz module on Moodle that links to the Syntheuniv/UMS (authentication system). Syntheuniv/UMS connects the Moodle database backend (we use PostgreSQL) with the SQL interface, and checks to see that new users pass the quiz periodically. Figure 2 is the display after this checking process is complete and the user passes the quiz and accesses our account management subsystem.

4.2 CULS

For CULS, we designed a framework of a Moodle module which links other data on a non-Moodle system. This enables Moodle to maintain the contents from the non-Moodle system via HTTP/CGI. Moodle has **$MOODLEROOT/admin/cron.php** for periodical tasks. We implemented this feature to retrieve an outside content.

Moreover, we created a capability set (Table 1) for this module to realize the suitable level of detail for the user status.

Figure 3 is an example of the CULS display.

Table 1: capability set for CULS module

Capability name	Description
Mod/uls: with-UserFullName	User can see a PC status with Full name
Mod/uls: with-UserID	User can see a PC status with User ID
Mod/uls:InUse	User can see whether PC is occupied or not
Mod/uls:IgnoreCours e	User can see all members regardless belonging this course

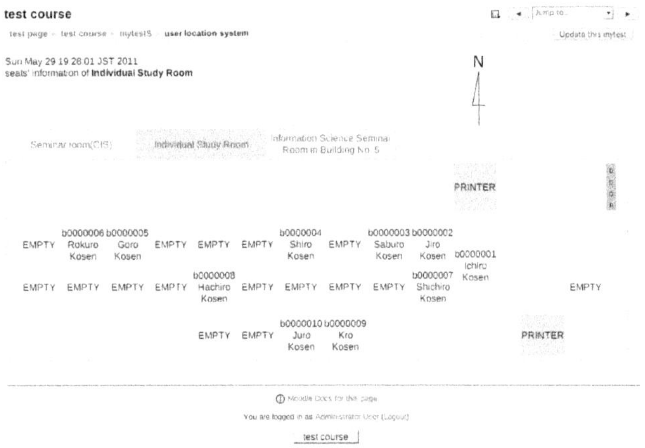

Figure 3: Example of CULS (Teacher's view)

5. LESSONS LEARNED

Implementing these subsystems has had several results.

First, the forgetting of passwords has decreased. Recovering passwords is one of the major tasks in the operation of the authentication service. In the previous system, users who forgot their password came to our office and said "I did not think that such an account was important". After this integration, few users say the same. We believe that AAES is a very nice mechanism for the computer center.

Second, it is now easy to see which terminals are free for student use in computer labs, and teachers can see which students are logging in during classes.

Third, Moodle use has increased to accommodate additional use of these modules.

Work still needs to be done.

There are complaints that the services available are not comprehensive. In our e-Learning course, account owners use the PCs and Moodle, and the password management subsystem, but other subsystems are not covered. It seems that our content needs updating and expansion. This is future work.

6. CONCLUSIONS

In this paper, we described systems integrated into Moodle including the automated account enabling subsystem (AAES), and the collecting user logon status subsystem for the computer labs (CULS). These tools help us reduce educational costs, increase services, and increase computer system security.

We continue to manage and operate these subsystems and try to get the operational know-how to apply refinements.

7. ACKNOWLEDGMENTS

The authors thank to International Affairs division of our university for helping translate the e-Learning content.

We also thank NEC System Technology, JAPAN.

8. RESOURCES

Citrix Systems, Inc.: Citrix Provisioning Server (PVS), http://support.citrix.com/products/provsvr/

Shibboleth, http://shibboleth.internet2.edu/

Moodle: open-source community-based tools for learning http://www.moodle.org/

9. REFERENCES

[1] H. Masuda, K. Murata, Y. Shibuya, K. Wakasugi and Y. Kuroe: "KIT's Campus Computer System by Virtual Machine Technology and Integrated Identity Service", ACM SIGUCCS 2010, pp.251-256 (2010).

[2] H.Masuda, K.Murata, S. Yasutome, Y. Shibuya and M. Nakanishi: "An Integrated Moodle System using VM Technology to Achieve High Availability and Lower TCO", ACM SIGUCCS 2008, pp.315-319 (2008).

Homework and Hangovers: The Joys of Empowering a Student Staff

Thom Mattauch
VCU helpIT Center Manager
901 Park Ave Room B-30
Richmond, VA 23284
804-827-0532
mattauchtj@vcu.edu

Hannah Pettit
VCU helpIT Center Supervisor
901 Park Ave Room B-30
Richmond, VA 23284
804-828-4727
pettith@vcu.edu

ABSTRACT

Living in the economic climate that exists today, many universities are looking at ways to cut cost while maintaining a high level of service. One method to cutting cost is to increase the staffing of students in support roles that in the past were held by full time employees. However, managing students can be a hassle. Not only are they prone to sudden schedule changes due to academic obligations (that need to be completed within 24 hours...), they have yet to be able to discern between a hangover and a legitimate illness. There exist many hurdles need to be overcome on a daily basis. When managing students, these hurdles include utilizing successful hiring techniques, scheduling around class and academic activities, motivating a student employee, dealing with the unexpected, helping the student employee develop a strong work ethic, walking the thin line of appropriate social media usage, along with many more issues. The VCU helpIT Center has attempted to tackle the issues that arise with student employment, and has maintained a high level of customer satisfaction while utilizing a primarily transient student staff. This presentation will focus on their successes, while highlighting the lessons they learned along the way.

Categories and Subject Descriptors

K.6.1 [**Management of Computing and Information Systems**]: Project and People Management — *staffing, training.*

General Terms

Management, Measurement, Documentation, Performance, Reliability, Experimentation

Keywords

Management, Hiring Techniques, Motivation, Empowerment, Staffing, Customer Satisfaction, Mentoring, Training

1. INTRODUCTION

Virginia Commonwealth University (known to the locals as VCU) sits in the heart of Richmond, Virginia, enrolling more than 32,000 students and employing close to 18,000 faculty and staff members. Since its establishment in 1968, VCU has expanded to include two downtown campuses in Richmond, as well as 6 satellite locations throughout the state of Virginia as well as Doha, Qatar. Offering 216 degree and certification programs through 13 separate schools and one college, VCU has been able to provide students with a full range of courses, from sculpture to microbiology, engineering to foreign language, business to philosophy, and many others.

The helpIT Center (Image 1) is the central computing support office for the VCU community. Supporting an estimated user base of over 120,000 people, the helpIT Center provides "over the phone" tech support in addition to two walk-up support locations on our main downtown campuses. It is currently staffed by eight full-time employees, as well as an additional 12-18 part-time students and hourly workers.

Image 1. Walk-up counter at the main office on the VCU Monroe Park Campus.

2. What Makes a Student Worker Unique?

The average student worker is a young adult, tackling their first degree, and almost always juggling work, school, internships, volunteering, and their active and sometimes wild social life. For many, they are experiencing independence for the first time, which for some poses the problem of balancing homework, classes, term papers and the ever-present desire to party all the time. These factors and many more all combine to make a very unique employee within a Help Desk environment.

2.1 Scheduling

School is the main priority for all student workers. It is placed on the front burner, while other things like jobs, internships, etc. are all lined up behind. Because of this, scheduling can be a pain. Not only does creating a "set" schedule become near to impossible, but it also changes with the dawn of a new semester. Unlike an average full-time employee (or even some non-student part-time workers), who put in their regular 8 hours a day, and who generally come in at the same time every shift, a student worker is constantly working around a class schedule. This causes their shifts to be varied from day-to-day. In addition to working around their scheduled class times, they are also working around deadlines for papers, examinations, etc. These all play a role in being able to provide the best support in one's Help Desk environment. When an organization is highly dependent on their student staff, adequate scheduling has to guarantee that enough coverage is provided during crucial times throughout the day. This entire process of scheduling is something that a manager must deal with multiple times of year with the changeover of each new semester.

2.2 Age and Work Experience

Most student workers fall between the age of18 and 25. For many, the student worker positions they have throughout college are the ones that they will list on their resumes (not their ice cream parlor job at 15). For some, it is their first job. Keeping all this in mind when working with student workers is important. The roles that they hold within your organization during their student academic years are the positions that are teaching them how to be a young professional. They are establishing a work ethic, acquiring useful skills that can apply to future jobs, as well as learning responsibility. For some, this learning experience is a breeze. They are able to come into a position, pick up the job, and run with it. For others, however, this is not always the case. Many student workers are in the process of gaining and establishing maturity during this time in life and unfortunately, this learning curve almost always affects their performance in the workplace. Many have not yet realized that a hangover is not a legitimate illness which justifies them to be out sick. Others have not quite taken advantage of the entire month they've had to complete a project, and wait until the last minute and thus have to call out of work to meet the deadline. This combination of maturity and experience is another daily struggle that oftentimes goes hand-in-hand with managing student workers.

3. Managing by Trial and Error

Like most things in life, sometimes finding the *best* way to do something is through trial and error. In the last few years, Management at the VCU helpIT Center has put an emphasis on trying out new techniques in order to create a highly productive support center for the University. Our main focus has been related to staffing, more specifically, testing new methods to fine-tune our staffing needs as a support center.

3.1 Recognizing "Critical Times"

In academia, the critical times throughout the year are generally the beginning and ends of semesters. At the helpIT Center, our most frantic time of year is a three-week period in August prior to the start of the Fall semester. During the semester, we take around 1,000 calls a week. During the August rush, our call volume rises to an average of 1,800 calls per week. Our main campus walk-up counter continually has a line out the door during this time period as well. As the numbers have increased throughout the years, a greater emphasis was placed on these time periods in order to ensure that we are giving the best customer service possible. Scheduling of student staff has been given a greaterpriority. The helpIT Center tries to create a set schedule that students will follow throughout a semester. These critical times, however, are scheduled separately from the rest of the semester. We've made these time periods "no time-off zones". Upon hiring, all new student staff are informed of these zones and agree to not schedule any major time-off requests during these weeks. This way, we are better able to ensure proper coverage of our office if we have all hands on deck. Many of our student workers work close to full-time hours during these weeks. By establishing these critical times as a priority from the beginning of a student worker's employment with our department, we are better able to provide the support we need during the Fall and Spring rushes.

3.2 Better Hiring Practices

A crucial part of acquiring a solid student worker staff is the hiring process. Being able to properly screen potential employees is very important. When a student worker position is advertised for the helpIT Center, we generally get up to 200 applicants per position (that number has increased dramatically in the last few years as a result of the current economic crisis). The first step of proper screening is to weed out the less qualified candidates. This can be extremely difficult, especially since many of the applicants don't have much work experience. Management first sifts through the applications and selects the candidates to be interviewed. We will then randomly select some of our student staff members to participate in the interviews with us. We follow many of the same guidelines and procedures in interviewing and hiring student workers as we do hiring full-time classified staff. By establishing this hiring practice with our student staff, it sets a very high standard for our student worker positions we have available. When a candidate participates in one of our interviews, they are not only able to get a glimpse into the professional environment in which they are applying, but also gain first-hand experience in interviewing (which they can use towards their future career searches). In addition to setting this standard, it also builds better morale with our existing student staff by showing that we value their input and include them in the hiring of new staff members.

3.3 Training

In the past, the hiring manager trained new student workers. They would shadow the hiring manager. After a week or two they would begin working either at the front counter or on the phones (once they've gained a base knowledge of the job). Issues arose with this method: the main problem being that the hiring manager had other duties that they needed to tend to and were unable to focus all of their attention on training new staff members. Additionally, with the high turnover rate of student workers, there was a constant stream of new student staff who needed proper training.

A new training process was implemented during the Summer months before the start of the Fall 2010 semester. The new training process began with the first wave of new hires that occurred in September after the semester had begun. On their first day of employment, new student staff participate in an orientation session with their main manager. They are introduced to the existing staff, given a walking tour of our departmental offices, and given an overview of the organization (Figure 1).

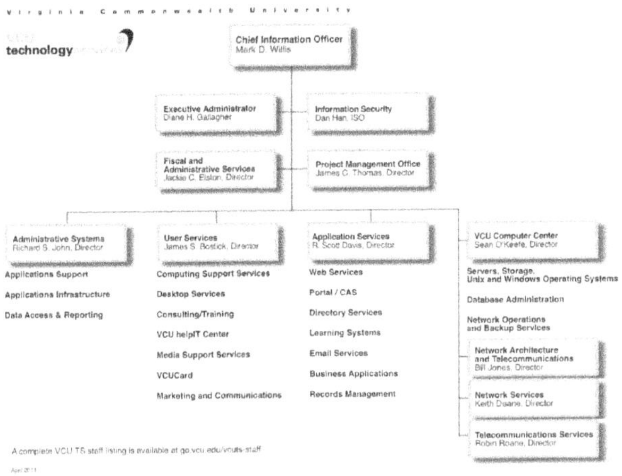

Figure 1. VCU Technology Services Organizational Structure

During this first day, they are also provided with a copy of our student worker manual, which specifically outlines the job requirements and duties, and other policies and procedures they are expected to follow. By providing them with this fundamental understanding of how our organization fits into the bigger? picture of VCU, they are able to envision our role within the University and gain a better understanding of the job requirements of a student worker position within our department. After this first day of training with their manager, they then go on to a week of shadowing other student workers at our front counter. They wear special nametags which indicate that they are in training, and the existing student staff provides the bulk of the training for new staff members. New student workers will also work individually with full-time staff members, learning specific features of the job which results in a more in-depth, one-on-one training session with their co-workers. This also gives them the ability to establish individual relationships with the full-time staff members so that they will feel more comfortable in going to them for assistance in solving problems in the future. After a week of shadowing and individualized training sessions, they then start to assist customers on their own (of course with another student staff member always nearby for assistance when they need it). We have found that this training process improves the morale of our existing staff (since both full and part time staff members are important participants in the training process), it creates a closer bond between new and existing staff members. Additionally, it produces better trained student workers who are able to quickly learn the intricacies of the job.

3.4 Documentation

Since the helpIT Center has continually expanded its services to the VCU community over the past few years, a need for documentation has grown as well. In the past, policies and support procedures were not widely documented, generally made up of scattered emails sent amongst the staff, and a few outdated procedures that were documented but not easily accessible to be used as a quick reference guide when assisting customers. The helpIT Center has tried to expand its documentation, and made an effort to continually update the materials as needed. The documentation is available to our staff both in paper form (a binder stored at our front counter), but also stored on our departmental shared drive and a Blackboard organization (similar to a course) that has been created solely for that purpose. This effort to document our procedures has resulted in increased sufficiency when supporting customers. It has also aided in the training of new staff, creating a more streamlined level of support.

4. A Manager's Responsibilities to Their Student Staff.

One of the most important roles of a manager is to basically "oversee" the growth and development of their workers. For managers of student workers, they also have the added responsibility of assisting the next generation of young professionals in a few important areas.

4.1 Developing a Work Ethic

For many student workers, their position within the organization is sometimes their first serious job. Previous to their employment with you, they may have had other jobs, but generally these former jobs do not always require the same skill set and demands as their new position. Due to this, managers are oftentimes tasked with the responsibility of assisting in the development of their student worker's own personal work ethic. For many student workers, the tools that they learn in their position within your organization are the tools that they will use in their future "real" jobs once they are out of school. At the helpIT Center, we try to inform our student staff from the beginning that their job with us is almost like an "extended interview". We let them know that the entirety of their time with us will be considered when the time comes for references and recommendations for future jobs. With this point in mind, the students understand from the start our expectations of them as employees. We try to constantly stress to our staff the importance of doing a good and thorough job and to take pride in the quality of their work. This emphasis on quality allows the students to better see that the service they provide on the job not only affects the customers, but also affects them personally. By teaching them to value and take pride in the level of service they provide, they are then able to take ownership of their work. Assisting student workers in this development of their work ethic is and should be one of the most important roles as a manager.

4.2 Motivation

Motivation, by far, is one of the hardest things when managing student workers. It seems that for many of them, by the time they fulfill their educational requirements, there is little to no desire left to properly fulfill their job requirements. For some student workers, their college job is solely to make enough money to get by. Not a lot of energy is put into the development of their job within your organization (unless, of course, it is directly aligned with their field of study). This is where it is the manager's role to step in and give them incentives to improve their job performance. Reiterating the importance of a strong work ethic, discussed in the before mentioned section, is of course important. But another successful way to do this is through motivation. Motivating student workers can be done in both positive and negative ways.

At the helpIT Center, we try to positively motivate our students by providing them incentives, such as small raises to reward good job performance. After a few months, if a new student worker is doing well, they will be rewarded with an increase in wages. In the current economic climate, with diminished budgets and funding, it is not always possible to justify a raise in wages for a student worker based solely upon good job performance. To work around this issue, the helpIT Center has created different student worker roles within our organization, with each role incorporating a different pay band. This way, if a student worker is excelling in their position, we give them a small amount of additional duties around the office in order to justify an increase in pay. This not only allows us to reward our staff through monetary measures, but also allows us to teach them a valuable lesson in the process. They understand from the start that any reward will only be earned with good performance and an increase in duties. When new student workers are hired they are informed of these pay bands, and thus have something to work for during their first few months with the organization. In addition to raises, we also have set goals that, once met, results in staff pizza parties. This hasn't always been the most successful of motivational techniques, but it does seem to increase performance on a smaller scale (since they are poor, starving college students after all).

On the other hand, there are ways to motivate student workers from a more constructive side. The helpIT Center clearly defines the consequences for poor job performance, and quickly takes action to address the situation once it occurs. At the helpIT Center, when a student worker's job performance is on the line, their manager meets with them and the issue at hand is discussed. The meeting is then documented in a follow-up email sent to the student worker outlining the discussion as well as the resolutions that have been agreed upon.

The student is then given a chance to improve their performance, with the understanding that if the issue continues to occur, more severe disciplinary actions will ensue. These actions can range from being taken off the schedule for a few shifts to termination. By addressing the issue first with the student, we've found that the issues don't tend to frequently repeat themselves. The student is given a chance to defend his/her actions, or at the very least, given an opportunity to discuss their job performance with their manager. Additionally, this puts the responsibility on the student to improve their performance.

5. Conclusion

With the increase in student staffing due to the current economic climate, it is always important to keep in mind the uniqueness of the student worker position. Since their main focus during their employment within the organization is the pursuit of their education, their job oftentimes come second on their list of priorities. Many workers also come to the organization with little to no previous work experience to draw from. These characteristics create a situation where a manager must take a proactive, hands-on approach to management. They not only have to ensure proper training and motivation of their student staff, but also play a large role in assisting in the development of a work ethic. In the end, they have the privilege of participating in the creation of successful, responsible, and charismatic young professionals entering the work force fresh out of college.

Bringing Students and Faculty Together Through Mobile Devices

Allison Czapracki
University of San Diego
5998 Alcalá Park
San Diego, CA 92109
(619) 260-7400
allison@sandiego.edu

Cyd Burrows
University of San Diego
5998 Alcalá Park
San Diego, CA 92109
(619) 260-7400
cburrows@sandiego.edu

ABSTRACT

The ubiquity of mobile devices such as the iPad and smartphones on the University of San Diego (USD) campus inspired the iTeam to identify a need to get faculty on the same wavelength as their students, who are leading mobile, digital lives. The team's goals included promoting awareness of mobile apps they support and teaching faculty how to meet students where they are -- constantly plugged in to mobile devices -- and to promote a more mobilely fluent campus.

Because digital natives tend to be fluent in the language of social media but often lack expertise in knowing how to efficiently use productivity and academic applications, the iTeam strove to expand students' technical skill sets through devices they were already familiar with, and engage students and faculty with the iTeam and its services. Through this workshop, they wanted to collaborate with faculty, teach them how to use mobile devices to reach their students, and connect them with the real skill sets of digital natives.

In response, the iTeam designed and delivered a mobile-device workshop for both faculty and students that promotes apps with the goals of encouraging academic collaboration, keeping learners connected to their coursework even outside of class, and helping students feel less detached and more immersed in their learning. Featured apps included: MySanDiego Mobile, Blackboard Mobile Learn, iClicker, eBook apps, and apps for note-taking such as Evernote.

In this session, the iTeam will discuss the workshop format, its impact on and future potential for USD students and faculty, and reactions to the workshop.

Categories and Subject Descriptors
J.3 [**Cellular Computing**]: General

General Terms
Measurement, Performance, Design, Human Factors, Standardization

Keywords
Technology workshops, mobile initiatives, apps, clickers, iPads, learning, faculty, collaboration

1. INTRODUCTION
Each academic year, the iTeam assesses the needs of asked two important questions, "What do students and faculty want that will benefit them in a higher-education setting that we don't currently offer or support?" and "How can we better meet the technology needs of USD faculty and students?" After assessing which technologies to focus on, the iTeam designs and delivers new technology workshops each academic year. Workshops are advertised on the iTeam's training calendar, through an e-mail blast at the beginning of the semester, and and via fliers in academic buildings.

With the release of iPads and a surge of new apps emerging (for all mobile devices), faculty began inquiring how they could use iPads and other mobile devices in the classroom. Some faculty were actively using clickers, and the iTeam receives several inquiries from new clicker users each semester.

USD licenses a mobile app, mySDmobile (http://my.sandiego.edu/mobile), created by TerriblyClever. It is currently available for the iPhone, iPod touch, and Blackberry devices. Other than that and an iPad project in the works for a few classes, no previous emphasis had formally been placed on mobile technologies at USD -- hence the need for a workshop to educate the USD community on how mobile technologies can improve the academic experience, in and out of the classroom.

2. BACKGROUND
This section provides context about the University of San Diego, Information Technology Services, the campus culture in regards to faculty and students using technology, and the iTeam's role in deploying and promoting technology at USD.

2.1 Overview of USD and Information Technology Services
The University of San Diego (USD) is a private, Roman Catholic university in San Diego, California, founded in 1949. Undergraduate and graduate student enrollment is approximately 8,200, and USD employs around 1,340 full- and part-time faculty. Most students own an iPad, iPhone, Android-based phone,

Blackberry or other type of smartphone. ITS (Information Technology Services) is a centralized-IT department that consists of three units: Network Services, Enterprise Administrative Systems and Services, and Academic Technology Services (ATS). ATS consists of seven units Computing Labs, Desktop Support Services, Instructional Support and Training, Instructional Media Services, Policy and Standards, Library Systems, and Web Services.

2.2 The iTeam and Technology Initiatives at USD

Instructional Support and Training (the iTeam) designs and delivers technology workshops year-round to the campus community, and one of its major responsibilities is to keep abreast of mobile trends in education and show faculty how to use mobile and other technologies to enhance their teaching and students' learning. Each spring, USD faculty and staff are invited to the annual faculty technology showcase, which the iTeam plans from start to finish. Its common goals are connecting faculty, encouraging them to share ideas and getting them excited about academic technologies. Faculty exemplars present to their peers the innovative things they are doing with technology in their teaching and learn about new classroom technologies from nearly 30 vendors. Approximately 200 faculty and staff (with the majority of participants faculty) attend each year, though attendance has reached 300 in past years.

In addition, the iTeam also puts on a yearly, two-full day Boot Camp the week before fall classes begin. It consists of posted drop-in hours where faculty can bring their materials and receive technology help, do short individual or small group trainings, and work with an iTeam member on any technology that they might have questions with. Boot Camp also includes break-out sessions, which will include the Mobile Devices Workshop this year. Faculty members are highly encouraged to bring all of their semester start-up needs during these times. Boot Camp is open to all faculty -- new and returning, full-time, part-time and adjuncts, and in past years attendance has been approximately 30 faculty members throughout the two days.

In the fall of 2011, the iTeam is launching an iPad project in which accepted faculty receive wi-fi enabled iPads for themselves and their classes to use for an academic semester. Faculty wishing to participate will submit a detailed proposal providing information such as: how the device is to be used in their course, what specific applications will be woven into the curriculum, and to what degree the use of the device is integrated into the course delivery methods. Projects will be selected based on clear, well-defined goals, and will need to demonstrate infusion of this technology into the curriculum. ITS has funding approval for two to three classes of up to 20 students each. Faculty and students will be required to participate in surveys and to comply with minimal research-related inquiries initiated by ITS. They will have to agree to the terms of the project and to USD's Policy on Responsible Use of University Computing Resources. Devices will be inventories and checked-in upon completion, and ITS hopes to offer an incentive offering students the option of purchasing their iPads at the end of the project for 50% of their original cost (pending approval).

2.3 Campus Culture

Historically, the campus culture has been that there is a divide between what technologies the students are using and what the faculty are using. Engaging USD's faculty to adopt and learn new technologies has never been an easy sell. The iTeam has had to show faculty how technology can make their teaching more effective in order for them to be interested, and has found that if they see a visible effect of technology making their lives easier, they will listen.

3. WORKSHOP FORMAT

This section outlines the discussion questions, format, and structure of the mobile devices workshop.

3.1 Registration and Recruitment

In hopes of getting the most diverse audience possible, students and faculty are allowed to register for the same workshop, which will be conducted twice during Boot Camp, and three times throughout the fall semester. Workshops are promoted via an e-mail blast, the Training Calendar on the ITS website, the iTeam blog, fliers, and faculty outreach sessions in academic buildings. Before the workshop, participants are encouraged to bring their own devices so they can share and explore new things learned.

3.2 Participant Discussion

The workshop begins with an icebreaker (such as "What mobile device do you have, and what app could you not live without?") and is followed by a dialogue to help students and faculty understand the different ways in which each group uses technology, both in their daily lives and in academe.

During the discussion, the instructor prompts participants with questions such as, "What are your three biggest frustrations or disappointments with mobile devices in your education or classroom?" and "What one mobile app or tool would make your academic life easier?" Students are asked, "What mobile apps or technologies would you like to see your professors using?" and professors answer the question, "What could your students do in or outside of class with technology to show increased engagement?"

3.3 Apps Showcased

The instructor showcases apps that are inherently academic in nature, or mySDmobile, Blackboard Mobile Learn, eBook apps such as Inkling, CourseSmart and Stanza, iClicker's web>clicker app for classroom response, and apps for note taking such as Evernote and Use Your Handwriting. Most of these apps are free, so faculty can download them from the App Store or Android Market. There is a charge for students to use the web>clicker, but faculty interested in using iClickers can pick up a kit with receiver from the iTeam at no charge. He or she demonstrates ways in which these apps are beneficial to learning, and allows students and faculty ample time for idea generation and testing the apps on their devices or devices (five iPads, two iPad 2s, an Android phone, and an iPod Touch) provided by the iTeam and owned by Information Technology Services.

3.4 Mobile App Recommendations and Privacy Warnings

Since this workshop is aimed at mobile fluency and education (versus a session that requires participants to use certain mobile technologies and applications in their teaching and learning), we will simply be providing participants with recommendations of applications for various disciplines and letting them know whether or not there is a charge for the download.

Participants will be informed of some of dangers regarding privacy and mobile computing, and will be warned that they should be cautious when navigating the web on any device -- whether a desktop computer or mobile phone. They will also receive a handout with data-security resources they can pursue on their own.

During the question-and-answer period following the demonstration, the instructor introduces discipline-specific apps (such as Brain and Nerves and 3D Brain for Biology, Molecules for Chemistry, and scientific calculator apps for Mathematics), depending on what disciplines were represented among participants in that workshop.

4. INITIAL REACTIONS, FEEDBACK AND LESSONS LEARNED

This mobile-device workshop will be fully deployed to the USD campus community in the fall of 2011, and findings from this workshop will be presented at SIGUCCS. In this section, we will discuss feedback and initial impressions from Student Technology Assistants (STAs) who previewed the workshop in the summer of 2011.

4.1 Initial Reactions

After perusing the workshop outline, one STA said: "As a student, it would be nice to know that my professors are keeping up to date with mobile technologies so they can deliver information to students the way the expect to get it." STAs liked that both Android and iOS platforms would be showcased.

Another STA said: "I like that the iTeam will be fostering an atmosphere where other students and I could make suggestions to professors in an open environment and potentially influence how they teach with technology."

4.2 Feedback

STAs also thought it might be fun to have a drawing in each workshop to give away one app ($5 or under) of the user's choice that was demonstrated or discussed in the workshop to a random participant, or participant who had a very insightful contribution to the discussion.

Another STA suggested that iTeam members could train them to teach future mobile-device workshops. Additionally, this session could be turned into a "Lunch and Learn" session, which typically draws in more participants than a typical workshop.

One STA suggested showcasing the iClicker web>clicker app first so that participants would get comfortable early on using the clickers, and could participate in on-the-fly polls during the workshop.

4.3 Lessons Learned

As the iTeam has been exploring mobile apps that can be used in academe, several lessons have been learned. Mobile devices can be compared to Swiss Army knives, but can't do it all and aren't yet substitutes for computers. For example, an iTeam member discovered that she was unable to make edits to a course in the university's learning management system using an iPad 2. Faculty and students will be told in the workshop not to get frustrated when mobile devices don't work exactly like their Macs or PCs.

Application sharing and discussing different tools is a great way for the iTeam to develop a knowledge base for future consultations with faculty looking to incorporate mobile technology with teaching and connect with their students.

Lastly, in developing this workshop, the iTeam realized how important it is to emphasize safe computing, security, and awareness to its workshop participants. Specifically, they'll caution that just because a technology is available doesn't mean it's 100% safe, and to always do at least a little research before openly storing or transmitting sensitive data to the cloud.

4.4 About the STA Program

Each semester, the iTeam employs up to 10 Student Technology Assistants (STAs) to work one-on-one with full-time faculty to design and develop projects that require significant technical skills, such as the editing and production of podcasts, 3-D modeling for the Naval Warfare Simulation Lab, and Second Life 3-D modeling and development.

5. ASSESSMENT, FOLLOW-UP, AND CONCLUSION

This section describes how the workshop will be assessed and refined for the future, and discusses how faculty can learn more about incorporating mobile technologies into their teaching.

5.1 Workshop Assessment

The iTeam will be assessing and refining this workshop after each iteration. Participants will receive 10-question Qualtrics surveys at the end of each session. These surveys assess the instructor's effectiveness, the dialog between students and faculty about, and to what extent students and faculty plan to use the mobile technologies they learned about in their academic or personal lives. Participants would be informed that the iTeam plans to take their feedback to a conference for discussion on mobile computing. The iTeam would also survey a random sampling of students to uncover expectations of their instructors using and embracing mobile technology.

5.2 Faculty Follow-Up

After the workshop, the iTeam will offer one-on-one consultations to any faculty member who wants to integrate one or more of these technologies into his or her teaching. In addition, the iTeam has a drop-in center where faculty can stop by between 8:30 a.m. and 5 p.m., Monday through Friday, to request academic technology assistance from iTeam members. Findings and ideas from this workshop, as well as a mini-mobile devices workshop, will also be presented at the faculty technology showcase in February.

6. ACKNOWLEDGMENTS

We would like to thank our team of Student Technology Assistants for assessing the workshop, and for the support of

Shahra Meshkaty, Senior Director of Academic Technology Services, in creating and deploying this project.

7. REFERENCES

[1] Burrows, Cyd, and Allison Czapracki. *Instructional Support and Training at the University of San Diego.* (24 March 2011). Retrieved 8 June 2011. http://usditeam.wordpress.com.

[2] mySDmobile website. Retrieved 8 June 2011. http://my.sandiego.edu/mobile/

[3] Student Technology Assistant Program. *Instructional Support and Training at the University of San Diego.* Retrieved 8 June 2011. http://usditeam.wordpress.com/sta/

Enriching Scholarship: Sustaining Effective Campus Collaborations

Laurie Sutch
University of Michigan
206 Hatcher Graduate Library
Ann Arbor, Michigan, 48109
011 734 647-7406
lasutch@umich.edu

ABSTRACT
For almost 15 years, the University of Michigan's Teaching and Technology Collaborative (TTC) has been working to help faculty and instructors learn and incorporate technology into their teaching and research. Our premiere event, *Enriching Scholarship*, is held each May before faculty leave for the summer. How does a group of volunteers from units all over campus organize and host an event like this not just once, but for 15 years? More importantly, how could **you** do it on your campus? The interactive session at the conference and this paper will walk you through our planning process, from identifying potential campus partners with similar goals to establishing a group focused on planning and funding a campus-wide event.

Categories and Subject Descriptors
K.3.1 **[Computers and Education]** Computer Uses in Education.

General Terms
Human Factors.

Keywords
Software skills, collaboration.

1. BUILDING A COLLABORATIVE
In the fall of 1997, several units from across the University of Michigan (U of M) Ann Arbor campus began meeting to share information about their services – what services each unit provided, how to avoid overlap, and ways to collaborate. U of M is very decentralized; at the time, there was little cross-unit, let alone cross-campus, collaboration. We found that almost all of us worked with faculty and we all provided instructional support. While most of us provided some type of training, we also felt that we were "hidden" resources on campus, and more people would use our services if they knew what type of physical, human, and technological resources were available and where to find them.

Feeling that we could make a larger and more effective impact together rather than individually, we began planning an event to increase campus awareness of our services and provide a professional development opportunity for the campus faculty and instructional staff. To express the unity of those involved, we named our group the Teaching and Technology Collaborative (TTC). The resulting event, *Enriching Scholarship*, is a week-long series of workshops, seminars, and demonstrations for faculty and instructional staff on integrating information, teaching, and technology, and has been held annually in May since 1998.

The rest of this paper will discuss U of M's campus partners in more detail and show how a group of volunteers collaborate to put on a successful campus-wide event year after year. It will also include suggestions on how to find partners on your campus, and how to create an event appropriate for your campus' needs.

2. MEMBERSHIP
As we looked around campus for potential partners, we not only considered units that supported the entire campus community, but those that serve large, but specific, populations. Current members of the TTC are:

- Center for Research on Learning and Teaching (CRLT)
- College of Literature, Science, and the Arts (LSA)
  - Instructional Support Services (ISS)
  - Language Resource Center
  - Science Learning Center
- ITS Education Services
- School of Medicine Learning Resource Center
- University Library
  - Digital Media Commons
  - Faculty Exploratory

Staff from member units commit to meeting regularly and to actively participating in the planning and coordination of Enriching Scholarship. TTC member units donate funds as well as in-kind services – staff member hours, facilities, photocopying, etc. During the 2010-2011 academic year, TTC members contributed an estimated 850 hours – over five months of FTE – not including time spent by certain individuals planning and teaching the sessions during the week of Enriching Scholarship.

In its first two years, the operation of the TTC and planning of Enriching Scholarship were unstructured and informal. As the organization and its annual program grew, we developed a mission statement and a set of criteria for membership that we share with potential new members. The mission statement and member criteria also helped to clarify and codify a common understanding of what our purpose was for both current and new members.

The mission of the Teaching and Technology Collaborative (TTC) is *"to assist faculty to navigate the complex campus technology landscape in order to enrich the quality of teaching and research at the University of Michigan. The TTC accomplishes this through sharing and disseminating information about the resources of member units, collaborating on events and projects, and focusing services on specific niches to avoid duplicating services. By working together in this successful cross-campus collaboration, we are able to do together what none of our units could do individually."*

In addition to creating a formal mission statement, we changed our leadership structure. The person who had initiated the conversations among the group had been informally chairing the group for two years, and was ready for a break. We instituted a one-year rotating chair, with a vice-chair position that was the incumbent chair, though there are still times when the same person serves as chair for two years in a row.

3. CREATING A CAMPUS-WIDE EVENT

In the late 1990s, the technology landscape was rapidly changing at the U of M. Faculty members were frustrated by their lack of time and knowledge, and while some units had technology support, others had none. At such a large institution, spread out on three campuses in Ann Arbor and one in both Dearborn and Flint, faculty members were confused about where they could go for different types of assistance.

As the TTC members started talking, we realized that creating a single event that we could all participate in would benefit both the units involved and the faculty.

Enriching Scholarship aims to:

- increase awareness of services provided by the TTC units
- provide instruction, information, and inspiration for faculty members on using technology in their work (teaching, researching, presenting)
- provide skills-based, hands-on workshops in a simple, goal-oriented manner, and at a time when faculty have time to participate
- show faculty how to take "next steps" in using the information and technology resources available to them

This week of hands-on sessions, discussions, and seminars happens just after winter semester, but before people leave for the summer, and provides an opportunity for faculty and instructional staff to focus on their technology needs as well as explore new possibilities. Over the last 14 years, the offerings have changed, but the intent of the week remains the same. Evaluation data for this program is consistently positive, with many participants reporting plans to incorporate their new skills or knowledge into their teaching.

3.1 The Impact of Enriching Scholarship

Since its inception in the spring of 1998, Enriching Scholarship has become an annual event, attended each year by several hundred faculty and staff members (as well as some students) from every school and college at the Ann Arbor campus as well as UM Flint and UM Dearborn. During the first year, we offered around 50 sessions; since then, we have averaged around 110 per year. Not only have we met our goal of creating a better understanding between the service units, we have shared workshop materials and have created a joint registration system to use throughout the year to cross-promote workshops and sessions. By dedicating a week to this event, we provide faculty with a time to focus on their skills and network with others who may or may not be in their discipline, while physically bringing them into our facilities.

Without a doubt, Enriching Scholarship continues to impact teaching on the U of M campus. Faculty are coming in to the TTC support units talking about projects that were inspired by the sessions that they attended during Enriching Scholarship. Faculty members are increasingly using more technology in their teaching and research, and Enriching Scholarship is one avenue many take to increase their knowledge and skill.

Faculty members view Enriching Scholarship not only as a way to learn new information, but also as an avenue to disseminate their experiences teaching with technology. In 2011, approximately 10% of Enriching Scholarship presenters or panelists were U of M faculty members or Graduate Student Instructors. The event is highly anticipated and people are excited to participate both as learners and presenters.

In recognition of this impact, the American Library Association honored the University of Michigan and the Enriching Scholarship program with the *Information Today Library of the Future Award* in 2010.

4. COMMITTEE STRUCTURE

Planning Enriching Scholarship takes a great deal of time and effort. Over the years, we have created the following committees to ensure the success of the program:

- Administrative (includes Chair, vice-chair, budget)
- Evaluation
- Instructor's Orientation
- Keynote
- Publicity
- Registration/Website
- Scheduling/Proofreading
- Showcase/Social Event

Committee members work together to provide physical resources such as facilities for sessions and money, as well as human resources, including hours spent on the planning committees and on instruction during the event. While some of the committees are fairly self-explanatory, a few bear a closer look.

4.1 Administrative

One of the primary roles of the **TTC Chair** is to be the head taskmaster: keeping the overall group on track and meeting deadlines, ensuring active participation from members, and submitting the funding request to the Provost's Office. Other roles include coordinating meetings (scheduling times and locations, setting agendas, facilitating the meeting itself), and representing the group to the larger campus community.

The **Vice Chair** steps into these roles as needed on behalf of the chair, thereby learning to become the leader the next year. In addition, the Vice Chair keeps track of the budget.

4.1.1 Funding

Since the beginning, the units involved in the TTC have contributed financially to the costs of Enriching Scholarship. As costs for brochure design, printing, hosting, speakers, and so on increased over the years, the units struggled to keep pace, particularly as unit budgets became tighter and tighter. In the summer of 2004, the group wrote a funding request letter to the Office of the Provost to augment unit contributions.

For five years, the added central support from the Provost's Office to the ongoing unit contributions allowed the TTC to continue providing Enriching Scholarship, develop a new registration system that is used by the units throughout the year, and invite national leaders in education and technology – such as Jane McGonigal, Mimi Ito, and Michael Wesch – as our keynote speakers. Evaluations from these keynote events demonstrate the interest and hunger U of M faculty and instructional staff members have for these ideas and innovations. While we did not receive funding for fiscal year 2010-2011, we are hopeful that we will receive this additional funding for 2011-2012.

4.2 Publicity

Not surprisingly, the way the TTC publicizes Enriching Scholarship has evolved over the years. For a long time, we mailed out a print brochure that included every session with all the details: title, date and time, location, description, level, and a list of similar sessions. As print and mailing costs increased, we decided to create a pamphlet that listed the bare minimum information: title, date and time, and location. We augmented that with a PDF of the "full" version that people could access via the website. This combination worked well, but as Enriching Scholarship grew, trying to fit so many sessions on a small amount of paper became increasingly difficult. For the last few years, we have sent out a postcard highlighting the keynote event, listing the types of sessions people will find, and referring them to the website for the details, where we still offer the "full" PDF.

Each year there is a new design for the website and brochure or postcard (see http://teachtech.umich.edu/espast.html and examples below). The postcard is mailed to the faculty on the Ann Arbor campus. Over the years we have used outside designers as well as "in house" (and therefore, in-kind) designers. This design is then incorporated into the keynote publicity as well.

Figure 1: Samples of Enriching Scholarship Publicity

In addition to the brochure (whether print or online), we send out various emails throughout the year. In the early fall, we email the previous year's participants, giving them the next Enriching Scholarship dates and encouraging them to participate in workshops sponsored by the TTC throughout the year. In late fall, we send a "Save the Date" email to all faculty and instructors at all campuses (Ann Arbor, Dearborn and Flint), and send another one in late January/early February. The final email goes out right before registration opens – the first Monday in April.

We also try to publicize the event in as many ways as possible: submitting to online campus event calendars, placing an ad in the faculty/staff newspaper, putting up posters in participating units and so on. As technology has changed, we have added other elements as well, such as a twitter feed that we are trying to maintain throughout the year.

4.2.1 Planning Timeline

Particularly with publicity, deadlines are important. After a few years of scheduling same types of things over and over, we created a planning calendar that we can reuse and adapt every year (see example below). If we are planning print materials, we work backwards from when we want them in the faculty mailboxes to determine when other goals (first draft, final draft, to printers, etc.) need to be met.

Enriching Scholarship Planning Calendar

October	December	January	February	March	April	May	June
First week: Units send anticipated donation amounts **Late Oct, Early Nov:** Initial "Hold the Date" e-mail to previous ES participants	**Mid month:** Subcommittees submit anticipated expenditures Discuss expenditures at ES Meeting Duplicate website for data entry	**First week:** Start entering workshop info (everything except blurbs required) into placeholder system – no cutsey titles, rather what it's really about **Early/mid Jan:** Reserve training rooms Prep website with new look **Second week:** "Hold the date" e-mail sent to all faculty	**First week:** All units have transferred donations to Library All workshops entered Schedule drafted AM Schedule discussed PM Draft of eval. instrument ready **Second week:** All details (except descriptions) of workshops finalized **Last week:**	**First week:** Text ready (ALL blurbs) for PDF **Second week:** Draft DONE for PDF (ready for proofing) ES posted on campus websites; campus info centers, etc. Evaluation instrument ready to go **Third week:** PDF finished and posted **Last day of March (Sunday eve?)** Registration info e-mail to faculty	**First Monday:** Registration opens/website goes live	**Week prior:** Instructor orientation **First full week M-F: ES 2007** Evaluation reminder emails sent	**By second week:** All receipts submitted

Figure 2: Example of a Planning Calendar

5. MAKING IT LAST

When we first decided to create Enriching Scholarship, none of us imagined we would be doing it 15 years later. In some ways it is easy to do this type of thing once – it is exciting and new, the energy is high, and people can make the effort *once*. Doing it year after year takes hard work and dedication. People are the most important resource we have to sustain this effort, but there are also tools that have helped as well.

5.1 The People

The team that organizes this event is extraordinary group of individuals with a passion for teaching and learning, volunteers who commit to this event above and beyond their normal duties, because they know it is important and valuable to the campus. Having at least one individual with the drive to push forward, to make sure deadlines are met, to look at the big picture – to be the leader – is paramount to success.

The Enriching Scholarship presenters play a key role as well. Around 60 staff members from TTC units volunteer to teach sessions based on what they do and see all year long, suggesting new sessions as technology changes and new pedagogical strategies are needed. The role of the participants cannot be overlooked either; Enriching Scholarship is a highly anticipated event, and some times participants ask the dates of the next year's, even before the current one is over.

5.2 Tools

5.2.1 Getting Organized

Originally, committee members kept digital and paper files on their own desks and computers. As we realized the event had taken on a life of its own, we knew we needed to get organized. We use CTools, our course management system based on Sakai, as our main tool. There is an email archive as well as resource folders. In addition to folders for each year of Enriching Scholarship and other purposes, we also have an "Annual Info" folder, which has research on potential keynote speakers, samples of publicity, email templates, proofing guidelines and more. Keeping this information in a central repository has been key as TTC members have changed and ensures we do not have to "reinvent the wheel" each year.

5.2.2 Registration System

The technological backbone of Enriching Scholarship is our registration system. We also use a version of the system throughout the year, and share the tool with the larger U of M community. Currently over 30 different units (including TTC members) from across campus use the system year-round to coordinate workshops and manage registrations, providing one stop shopping for users looking for workshops.

6. DOING IT ON YOUR CAMPUS

6.1 Finding Partners

The first step to establishing an event such as Enriching Scholarship on your campus is to find other stakeholders who might be interested in collaborating with you. Keep an open mind and look broadly as you seek potential partners from across campus. Think outside of your normal sphere and consider the library, academic units, media centers, human resource departments, language or specialized centers. Offer an open invitation to an informal meeting, and gather other suggestions from that meeting.

Start with information sharing about what each unit does, and talk about what type of collaborative event might benefit (and fit!) your campus community.

6.2 Creating an Event

You will want to think strategically about what type of event would work in your environment for your campus community. Consider the following questions:

- What is the main focus?
- Who is it for?
- How long should it be and when?
- How will it be funded? How will you get buy-in to get funding?

6.2.1 Establish Committees, Publicize the Event

Evaluate what types of committees and what leadership structure will work for you; a list of possible committees is above, but they have changed over the years. Be flexible enough to reorganize as needed. Don't be afraid to try different approaches if one avenue doesn't seem to be going where you want. It may help to have the same leaders for the first few years to give continuity to the process.

Find out where is best to advertise on your campus. Additionally, Have information available at all the unit locations and show cohesion and collaboration to those who attend the event. Create a look or name that people start to associate with the event as they start to look for it annually.

6.3 Sustaining an Annual Event

Establish goals and expectations for the group. Be especially flexible in the first few years, but articulating that common understanding is important from the beginning.

Every few years, review the goals and expectations and make sure they still fit the needs of the group.

Be sure to archive email messages sent to potential participants as well as final drafts of publicity items, budgets and so on. We use our course management system (based on Sakai) as a project space, but SharePoint or some other resource will work. This will allow you to share and retain information even after staff members move on to different roles.

7. BENEFITS OF COLLABORATION

After almost 15 years of close collaboration, the Teaching and Technology Collaborative and its Enriching Scholarship event continue to positively impact teaching, research and productivity at the University of Michigan. The use of technology by faculty, staff and graduate students continues to grow and evolve, and these constituencies all look to this event as a free, local avenue to support their professional development. The TTC and Enriching Scholarship illustrate how collaboration on a decentralized campus, between very different units, can effectively and efficiently stimulate and disseminate technological innovations in teaching and research without a top-down directive.

As we look towards the future, we are excited by the evolving needs of faculty. With the quick pace that technologies are now developed and brought to market, Enriching Scholarship offers a wonderful arena to introduce how the newer technologies that people are buzzing about can be effectively used in the classroom. At the same time, we are committed to providing a base level of instructional and technical support so that we are able to remain a valuable resource for those who are at the novice end of the spectrum, as well as those who are constantly pushing the borders of current practice.

By identifying potential partners and establishing goals for your group, you can build an event that is appropriate for your faculty and your campus. Since it is no one unit's responsibility, creating a committee and leadership structure that works is imperative. Developing marketing and budget plans and using backwards planning to create a timeline for your event are essential tools for success.

This type of partnership not only builds a better understanding between the service units, but also can create new, unexpected opportunities for collaboration throughout the year. Faculty members know where they can go for assistance and campus awareness of each unit involved is increased. A great deal of effort goes in to planning an event like this, but the benefits reaped by all involved are beyond measure.

Student Employees: Hire 'em, Mold 'em, Keep 'em

Dana Peiffer
User Services Support Specialist
University of Northern Iowa

Benjamin Arnold
Student Services Support Specialist
University of Northern Iowa

ABSTRACT

Hiring Student Employees

Making the transition from hiring any warm body to selecting from a pool of applicants.

Implementing Effective Training Methods

Designing a training program that properly prepares your student employee for your environment and also

addresses some differences in generational philosophies in the work place.

Maintaining Student Employees

Creating and providing a work environment that is productive for both and employee and customer and is also a pleasant place and rewarding place to work.

Without effective advertising/posting of open positions for student employees in our ITS departments we were constantly faced with the scenario of hiring any warm body due to a low number of applicants. Through our new process we are now seeing an increased number of applicants for available positions and also just to keep on file as new positions open up.

A few examples of how this was accomplished would be:

1) Strategic advertising (orientation, online job board)

2) Streamlining the online application process

3) Hiring students from one ITS division for another based on experience

4) Fast-tracking the training process for each position

Generational philosophies can also affect not only promptness to the job but the way your student employee handles both walk-in and phone-in customers. This can also be related to the "texting" syndrome where both dialogue and typing at the work place take on an abbreviated atmosphere.

Categories and Subject Descriptors

D.3.3 [**Hiring and Management of Student Staff**]: Posting openings, interviews, hiring, training, retention.

General Terms

Management, Documentation, Performance, Human Factors, Standardization.

SIGUCCS'11, November 12-17, 2011, San Diego, California, USA.

Keywords

Training, Coaching, Retention, Evaluation

1. INTRODUCTION

The University of Northern Iowa has just over 13,000 students, with a Faculty and Staff of 2,800 and is one of the three Regent Universities located in Iowa. Student Employees make up a large part of our support model for both our computer lab environment and also in the Computer Consulting Center (CCC). The Computer Labs employ approximately 60 students and the Computer Consulting Center employs 9-11 student employees. The process of finding prospective students for the Consulting Center has been by word of mouth and also from recommendations from current employees. For the most part this has worked out OK in the fact that we were adequately staffed; however, we found ourselves quite often hiring "warm" bodies and not having the opportunity of choosing from a pool of applicants. It was decided last year that this process really needed to be re-designed so to increase the number of applicants so that the end result would be to staff the Consulting Center with the best students for the job. At the same time we hoped to hire (CCC) students from the Computer Lab pool of students so that we were hiring students already experienced with the University environment and also having some Customer Service skills. In order for this to occur we also decided to do the Customer Service training for all new student employees for the (CCC) and Computer Labs at the same time. Our final goal for hiring (CCC) students was to contact the Lab manager prior to the beginning of each semester and indicate the number of openings we had.

The Lab manager would then send a message to all of his/her current student employees advising of the openings.

2. PROBLEM

The problem we faced was how to transition smoothly to this new process and at the same time maintain the same level of good customer service we currently provide. Training methods also had to be designed to best prepare the students for their jobs. Finally, we need to better understand as managers the ever changing thought process of students and apply that to the training program. The text should be in two 8.45 cm (3.33") columns with a .83 cm (.33") gutter.

3. SOLUTION

The following paper will attempt to explain in detail the steps in this program to:

1) Hire qualified student employees through new advertising strategies

2) Effectively train these new employees to meet the needs of the IT environment, which change often

3) Provide a work environment that is productive to both the customer and employee and is a pleasant work experience to maintain employee retention.

4. POSTING JOB OPENINGS

Placing ads pertaining to current job openings in strategic locations is key when trying to get the maximum number of applicants.

We chose to advertise in 3 different ways. We decided we would advertise in the online job board, advertise by word of mouth during the summer Freshman orientation sessions, and finally continue to take recommendations from our current student employees.

The online job posting proved quite beneficial as we had enough applicants to fill the vacancies we had for our upcoming Fall semester within two weeks. This occurred in late April, long before we had a chance to speak at the summer orientation.

We will still advertise during summer orientation, adding that there are no current openings, but any interested students should check the job board for updates. The same will be true for recommendations we received from our current student employees.

An online application form was created to ease the application process for interested students. By completing the form the applicant was able to specify areas of interest, strengths/weaknesses in various areas of technology, any customer service experience if any, and finally what area of ITS they were applying for. Currently the form has to be printed out and delivered to the ITS departmental secretary, who then forwards them to the appropriate area within ITS for further action. An online form is currently being designed that will guide the applicant through a series of relevant questions based on the area within ITS they wish to work in and also can be submitted online. The design of the form was also created with an ease of use approach. Several students were polled to find out what was or was not easy to read, understand, and use. Our goal was to create an online application that offered a pleasant experience for the future employee.

5. IMPLEMENTATION

To best prepare our new student employees for that first day on the job we put together a comprehensive one-week program.

5.1 Training

Training begins the Monday before classes start and covers all subjects related to the job that they have been hired for, with an emphasis on good Customer Service.

5.2 Customer Service

Good Customer Service is essential to anyone who deals with people as part of their daily routine. Day 1 and part of the day 2 of training is focused on Customer Service only. When we hire new students we make it very clear that the number one skill we are looking for is the ability to deal and work with people in a positive manner. We can teach them the technical pieces; however, good Customer Service skills experience are preferred because they are harder to teach.

5.3 Training Manual

Beginning the last half of day two we begin going through our Consulting Center training manual. The manual covers all aspects of the daily routine of our office beginning with duties specifically for those who open up in the morning and ending with our daily closing procedures. As we go through the manual we constantly pause to allow the trainees to practice what they have learned on computers specifically setup for training purposes. This training continues through the end of day 3 of training and also part of day 4.

5.4 Applying Knowledge

On the afternoon of day 4 the trainees are ready to shadow the current student employees who are staffing the front desk. For the remainder of the day they sit at the front desk, ask questions, assist with walk-in traffic, and actively participate in assisting customers under the guidance of permanent staff and student employees.

5.5 Pick up the phone!

Beginning on day 5 the trainee is now ready to answer the phone and begin what will be a successful career in Good Customer Service. They will use our standard initial greeting and set of questions with each phone call. After that they will be charged with learning the skills necessary to gain the confidence of the caller and to resolve their issue in a timely manner.

6. THE REWARD

Service tickets are created for each contact with our office regardless of the reason for the call. The ticket remains open until the problem is resolved. When the ticket if closed a survey link is automatically sent to the customer. The survey takes less than 5 minutes to complete and participation varies between 10 and 15%. (See Customer Service Survey)

The surveys also allow for comments. Whether positive or negative the comments are used as tools to improve our customer service skills (see examples below).

My contact today was wonderful. The consultant was friendly and helpful, and when he did not know the answer he was able to connect me with someone who did. My experience today was a vast improvement over previous encounters. Thank you for your efforts!

FY2011 - CCC Customer Surveys Year-To-Date

January 2011 through April 2011

Total Survey's YTD			
	Total Sent	2682	
	Responses	432	15.0%

	Totals	Per Cent
Did the Consultant provide her/his name?		
No	166	38.4%
Yes	266	61.6%
How did you contact the Computer Consulting Center		
Chat Session (www.meebo.com)	1	0.2%
Email (ITS-Consult@uni.edu)	16	3.7%
Phone (319-273-5555)	205	47.5%
Walk-in (ITTC rm 36)	210	48.6%
Problem resolved in a reasonable number of contacts		
One	290	67.1%
Two	121	28.0%
Three	16	3.7%
Four	3	0.7%
Five or More contacts	2	0.5%
Rate the consultant's ability to understand your problem		
Excellent	338	80.7%
Very Good	69	16.5%
Average	8	1.9%
Not Very Good	2	0.5%
Poor	2	0.5%
Rate the consultant's attitude		
Excellent	308	73.5%
Very Good	81	19.3%
Average	23	5.5%
Not Very Good	5	1.2%
Poor	2	0.5%
Rate the consultant's communication skills		
Excellent	292	69.7%
Very Good	96	22.9%
Average	27	6.4%
Not Very Good	1	0.2%
Poor	3	0.7%
Rate the consultant's cooperation		
Excellent	355	84.7%
Very Good	50	11.9%
Average	12	2.9%
Not very good	2	0.5%
Poor	0	0.0%
Rate the consultant's courtesy and professionalism		
Excellent	314	74.9%
Very Good	78	18.6%
Average	23	5.5%
Not Very Good	3	0.7%
Poor	1	0.2%
Rate the effectiveness of the contact (Graph)		
Excellent	298	71.1%
Very Good	100	23.9%
Average	16	3.8%
Not Very Good	4	1.0%
Poor	1	0.2%
Rate the wait time before you were in contact with a consultant		
Immediate	243	58.0%
Fairly quickly	131	31.3%
Average	30	7.2%
Long	10	2.4%
Too long	5	1.2%
Rate your overall satisfaction with THIS one contact (Graph)		
Excellent	315	75.2%
Very Good	75	17.9%
Average	26	6.2%
Not Very Good	1	0.2%
Poor	2	0.5%
Rate your overall satisfaction, during THIS academic year, with the Computer Consulting Center (Graph)		
Excellent	253	60.4%
Very Good	129	30.8%
Average	32	7.6%
Not Very Good	2	0.5%
Poor	3	0.7%
What is your University Status?		
Faculty	92	21.3%
Staff	60	13.9%
Student	280	64.8%
Would you like a follow-up contact		
No Thanks	408	97.4%
Yes, via email	11	2.6%

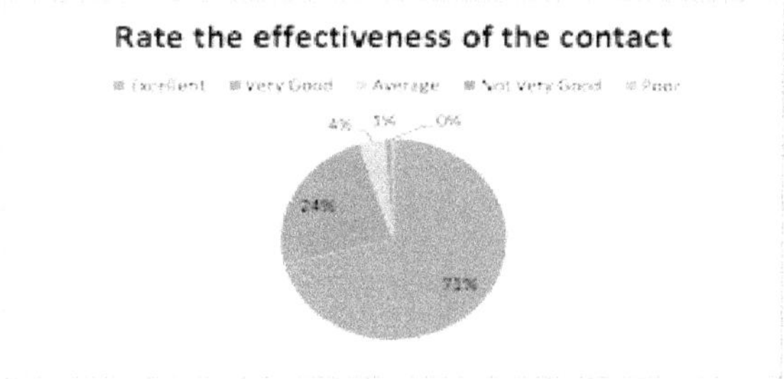

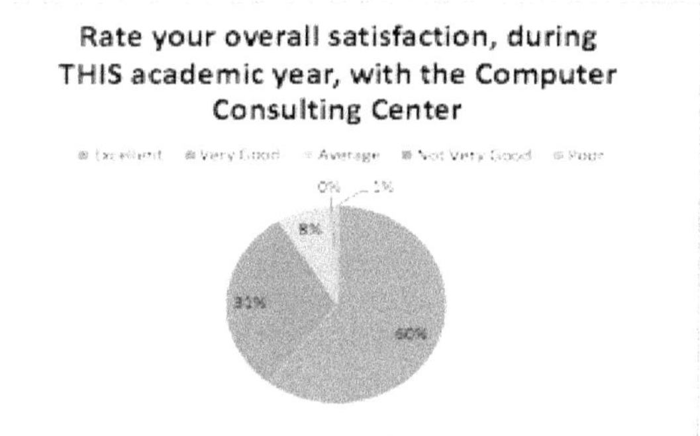

I gave conflicting answers because the first person I spoke with (Adam?) talked so fast and wanted to process me so quickly I don't think he understood what I did know about my ID and what I needed. If he could slow his rate of speech a bit and have a friendly not rushed tone in his voice it would go a long way toward excellent customer service. As soon as the second older person came on the line the customer service was fabulous. The tone was friendly, caring and acknowledged that I did know something that was helpful. I had my password promptly re-set and then was given value added information about how to know what my student ID was. So I had average to poor service at first & then EXCELLENT customer service. Thanks for asking.

I've noticed in this academic year, it is much easier to actually get a live person quickly, and that is very much appreciated! Everyone is always very helpful and knows exactly how to help with any problem I call them about. I'd say keep up the good work with having enough consultants on hand who are obviously being trained well.

My contact today was wonderful. The consultant was friendly and helpful, and when he did not know the answer he was able to connect me with someone who did. My experience today was a vast improvement over previous encounters. Thank you for your efforts!

We have noticed that the majority of the comments are positive indicating that customers felt compelled to take the time to leave a positive comment. We share these comments with our students so that they can see the influence they have with customers and how their hard work helps to maintain the positive image our office has.

7. RETENTION-KEEP THOSE STUDENTS!

The final goal for our office is to keep our student employees until they graduate. Unlike the case of a permanent employee where there is a dollar amount to consider that is invested in new employees, constantly training new student employees is a time investment. Also, the longer the student works in our office the more opportunities they have to fine tune their customer service skills. Unfortunately at our University the students have many opportunities to take part-time jobs elsewhere on campus and near our campus that pay more. The challenge this presents is what we can do as employers to keep our students.

7.1 Perks

What are the students allowed to do and not allowed to do while working at their stations? The amount of traffic our office sees can vary from a couple of calls/hr to calls in cue and a line of walk-in traffic. Our goal is to accommodate each customer in a timely fashion and yet maintain a pleasant and fun work environment for our students. Therefore we ask them to follow a few simple rules while working. They are allowed to work on homework during their shift as well as casual web surfing. They are also allowed to "chat" online. What we ask from the students in return for this is that when the phone rings, or a customer walks in that they immediately minimize all windows on their computer except for those necessary for them to assist the customer.

8. THE GENERATION GAP

Understanding the student perspective can at times be challenging as a supervisor. As digital natives, students are a valuable resource in the area of computers, internet usage, and the ability to explore, search, and research on the web. As a digital immigrant, I had to very quickly accept that my students were as valuable to me as the internet was in regards to information. At the same time part of the new training addressed a few areas that presented themselves as problem areas while on the job.

8.1 Promptness

The definition of showing up to work on time seems to vary significantly, especially between generations. We see quite often with our students that on time to them means "Close" to their assigned start time. When a customer calls or comes into our office they are expecting immediate assistance. As part of the training we stress that on time means that you are in the seat, logged into your computer, and ready to begin at your assigned start time. This area is addressed in the Customer Service part of the training.

8.2 Texting

Spelling and Grammar seem to be not quite as important in the lives of people who communicate largely by means of chat and IM. Unfortunately this becomes a problem when our students create service tickets. We therefore try to stress regularly that Spelling and Grammar are very important for two reasons. First, good grammar provides complete sentences, therefore providing a better explanation of the problem and resolution to all who may read the ticket. Second, regarding "Who may read the ticket," service tickets are available to a large number of people, specifically supervisors and directors, so good Spelling and Grammar reflect a more professional image for our office.

8.3 Responses

Finally, correct responses can affect the image of our office. This area probably requires the most attention on a regular basis because it isn't just students doing this. For this example I will use the terms "Incorrect" and "Correct" keeping in mind that this very well could just be my view and not the view of others.

Incorrect: No Problem

Correct: You're Welcome

Incorrect: Have a good one (Used by all ages)

Correct: Have a great or nice day

Incorrect: Hold on

Correct: Could you please hold?

9. PERFORMANCE EVALUATION (SUPERVISOR)

We also began student evaluations this year. The purpose of the evaluation is to provide the student employee with input and observations that will help the student improve on their customer service skills. Evaluations should always consist of positive feedback, never negative.

Examples of Negative:

1) You are doing this wrong

2) Your tone of voice is not friendly

Examples of Positive:

1) Here is a suggestion that might make that task easier

2) I've noticed a couple of areas that offer room for improvement, presenting the opportunity for you to excel.

3) Here are a couple of things that I have found work well.

9.1 Performance Evaluation (Self)

A self-assessment is always beneficial for the student. We try to encourage the students to offer suggestions to each other in an effort to provide consistent Customer Service to all customers.

One exercise I like them to use is to listen to each other but with their eyes closed. Without being able to see the student they have the opportunity to focus on the student's tone of voice. First impressions are formed at first sight, or in the case of a phone call tone of voice. If you remember, one of the comments referred to Adam and talked about his "rate of speech" and also "rushed tone."

10. Conclusion

Our goal with the new hiring/training/maintaining program was to be able to hire from a larger pool of candidates, streamline our training process so that new employees were ready for "Day 1", and finally to keep our well trained students for the duration of their stay at our University. A bonus that derived from this new approach was that we saw our Customer Service Ratings improve dramatically, specifically the comments that were submitted.

11. Acknowledgments

Tom Peterson, Director User Services
University of Northern Iowa

Jack Miller, Computer Consulting Center Manager
University of Northern Iowa

Benjamin Arnold, Student Services Coordinator/User Consultant
University of Northern Iowa

Jeffrey Copeland, Department Head & Professor
English Language & Literature
University of Northern Iowa

Karen McCritchie, Academic Technology Manager
Drake University

Visualizing User Activity In Open E-Learning Contexts: Challenges and Techniques for Operational Management

Owen G. McGrath
Educational Technology Services
University of California, Berkeley
omcgrath@berkeley.edu

ABSTRACT

This paper describes the practical application of four visualization techniques that have been developed to deal with high-volume, large time-scaled, and high-dimensional data sets that are characteristic of Internet-based user activity. Visualization techniques can be useful for monitoring and studying online user activity in settings where many thousands of users are involved in web-based educational endeavors. Simple numerical summaries of server requests and server performance trends cannot adequately answer the kinds of questions posed by those who desire to understand e-learner activity in web-based e-learning systems. Tracking and understanding remote users and their distant, round-the-clock activities present major technical and analytical challenges, especially in terms of the sheer scale and volume of the generated usage data. With web-based teaching and learning systems, four aspects of the usage tend to hinder analysis: high density, broad time scales, many variables, and veiled patterns. The paper looks at possible solutions in the application of four visualization techniques, using open source statistics software, in the contexts of key scenarios where such techniques can support operations management and decision making processes.

Categories and Subject Descriptors

K.6.1 [**Management of Computing and Information Systems**]: Project and People Management – *systems analysis and design.*

General Terms

Management, Human Factors.

Keywords

Web usage visualization, data mining, usage analytics.

1. INTRODUCTION

As more teaching and learning processes are moved online, there arise both needs and opportunities for tracking, analyzing, and improving the online institutional systems involved [1]. Before the advent of the Internet, the observation of computer-based learning activities was comparatively simple in scope and straightforward to carry out [2]. Users were physically near at hand in computer labs or special technology enhanced classrooms. With today's global access to open content via open source applications on the web, however, the volume and dimensionality of logged interactions quickly outstrip conventional statistical methods.

This paper surveys four plotting methods – hexbin, mice and elephant, parallel coordinate, and self-organizing maps – as they are applied in supporting usage analyses for two large web-based e-learning deployments: an online collaboration system and a digital video repository for coursecasting. As examples of systems that are increasingly popular in higher education, these cases point towards some of the practical benefits of applying usage visualization models in production environments used daily by tens of thousands of users. Applied here from freely-available implementations for the R statistics software [3], the four plotting techniques are demonstrated in usage analysis cases occurring in two typical higher education e-learning contexts: an enterprise-level open source collaboration environment and a large, open-content coursecasting system. In describing the issues and challenges that motivate usage visualization applications in these two e-learning systems, the paper also provides examples of how visualization techniques integrate into operational data mining processes.

2. BACKGROUND

2.1 General Internet Usage Research

Research into and modeling of Internet usage offers a story of debate and surprises. Important challenges to early assumptions about usage patterns and traffic models came from visualization efforts, which revealed disparities between empirical data and conventional models [4]. Recent approaches towards deriving accurate and comprehensive models of Internet traffic flow continue to rely heavily on advancements in visualization techniques in order to shed light on the unconventional queuing models and observed phenomena such as long tail distributions, long range dependency, and self-similarity [5,6]. Interestingly, many of these general Internet usage studies have also relied for empirical evidence on visualizations of user activity in and around servers and networks in academic environments, the setting of the cases in this paper. Especially relevant to the focus of this paper is the research into the visualizing characteristics of web user activity at the session level. The browsing and interaction patterns of identifiable user sessions have been noted as an important boundary, the space of protocol/human interactions in general Internet usage research [7].

2.2 E-Learner Usage Visualization

The nature of the data involved in Internet usage studies has always posed major challenges. In particular, four aspects of the data tend to hinder usage analysis: high density, broad time scales, many variables, and veiled patterns [8]. The multi-dimensionality and sheer volume of the captured data require new methods of sampling, transformation, discovery, and display in order to be presented and analyzed meaningfully [9].

Usage visualization in web-based e-learning systems in higher education settings has served as the basis for discovering categories and characteristics in student participation patterns. Looking within particular course sites, visualization tools embedded in e-learning systems allow instructors to examine participation patterns across hundreds of online sessions to reveal useful characteristic aspects of students' interactions with e-learning content, progress on assessments, and their participation in online discussions [10]. The visual representation of these analyses is mainly meant to help instructors with pedagogical design, such as whether subgroups of students share similar difficulties, or how the content and sequencing might be re-ordered [11].

3. VISUALIZATION CASE STUDIES

3.1 High Volume Usage Data

Many universities have opened up vast amounts of library, museum and e-learning content online over the past decade. Among the more popular open content assets made available are digital video and audio recordings of university-level course lectures. Coursecasting, the video and audio recording of lectures and events for live or on-demand playback, has become a significant IT service at many institutions of higher education. By making available on the Internet collections of full-length digitized recordings, college and university educational technology groups find themselves supporting large and varied distributed audiences – from local students to faraway e-learners. With both campus and world-wide audiences, it becomes very difficult to understand the usage activity of on-demand and live Internet video and audio services.

The sheer size of the usage data involved in such a service leads to an example of the first problem in visualizing high-volume usage: density. Traditional two-dimensional methods of viewing data tend to get overwhelmed by high density. Serious overplotting issues are caused by so many overlapping data points set in limited resolutions of display devices. For instance, a traditional scatter plot of coursecast server session duration counts (Figure 1) results in blotching and banding that are not particularly useful as a starting point for exploratory analysis.

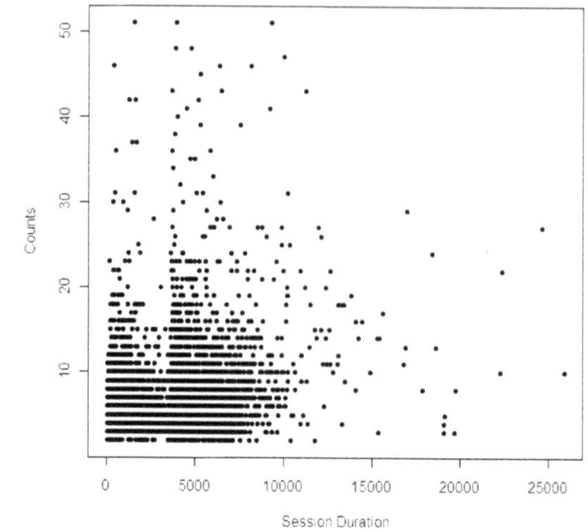

Figure 1. Coursecast session durations scatter plot.

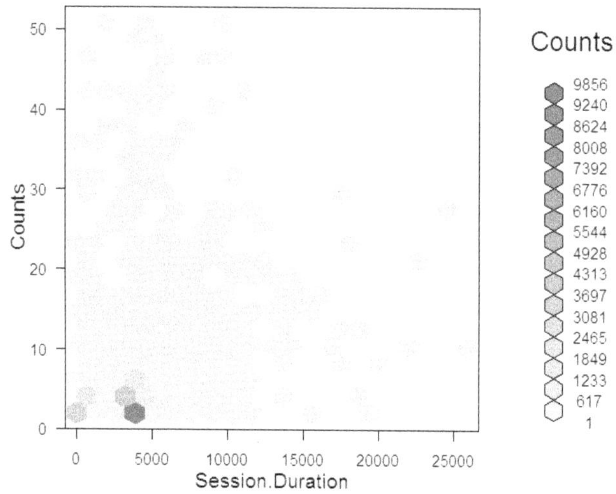

Figure 2. Coursecast session durations as hexbin plot.

An alternative for plotting in the case of high volume data is provided by the hexbin plot [12]. The hexbin plot gets around the overplotting issue by using a geometric binning technique in combination with shading and colors to draw out the different underlying densities. For the hexbin package implementation in R [13], the degree of shade and color depends on the underlying count of data points. The geometric bins themselves are hexagons, which were originally chosen in part because of they fit together predictably without leaving gaps [14]. In Figure 2, the hexbin plot of the session data reveals more of the underlying structure of the data, including a bi-modal distribution. The two modes, representing brief vs. hour-long sessions, point to two common user patterns of either browsing or playing the full-length video media, as revealed by further analysis.

3.2 Time Scaled Usage Data

Inquiry into e-learner behavior naturally turns towards looking at how users are interacting with each other and with content in e-learning settings within various intervals of time. A corollary to the high-density count problems solved above by hexbin plots often occurs when attempting to understand user behavior within or across time segments. Innovative techniques developed by researchers for visual analyses of time-scaled usage data have included Time Histograms and Time Bars, both of which offer ways of displaying distribution values in 2-dimensional graphical representations where time is one axis [15,16]. For visualizing e-learner user sessions along time dimensions, one particularly elegant and practical solution is the mice and elephant plot [17], which applies a random jittering factor to separate out different session flows on the y axis, with start and stop time traces demarcated by time intervals on the x axis.

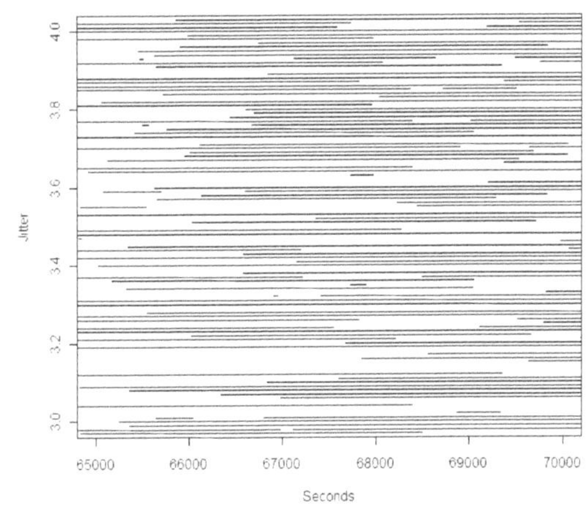

Figure 3. Mice and Elephant plots of Sakai user sessions.

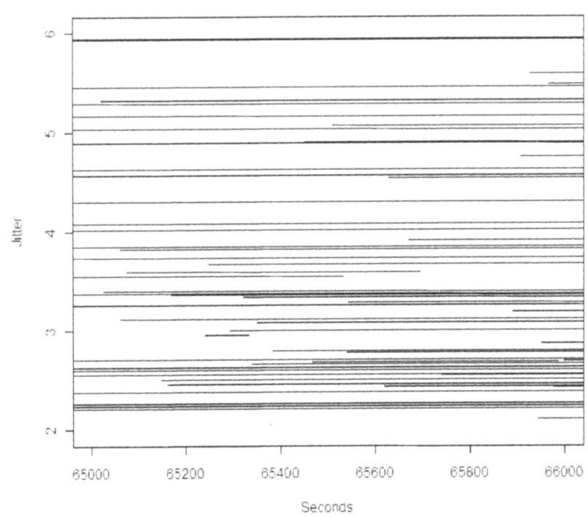

Figure 4. Mice and Elephant plots zoomed in.

For making sense of this user session activity within a particular time interval, Figure 1 shows some of the simple clarity of the mice and elephant plot visual analytic approach for visual analysis of online collaboration system usage. Using the ablineclip function in the plotrix package for R [18], the sessions are separated out along the y axis. The dashes and long stretches point towards a typical range of short (i.e., mice) and long (i.e. elephant) session flows. Sub-sampling of the data can provide for filtering, if needed. Panning and zooming in and out of a Mice and Elephant plot allows for exploration at different time scales (Figure 4). As a starting point towards understanding system usage and for considering next steps towards exploring activities, this pan and zoom technique can help in exploring behaviors of virtual visitors to the collaboration system across a wide range to time scales.

3.3 High Dimensional Usage Data

In addition to the density and time-scale issues, a third major obstacle to usage visualization arises from the data's multivariate nature. With so many variables captured and logged, choosing which variables to start looking at becomes a major question. In the case of the web-based collaboration system, for instance, one might be interested in looking across many events in online courses using data sets that record various user actions within many different tools (e.g., assignments, discussion, wiki). Traditional orthogonal axes plots in a plane tend to limit comparative visualization to three variables. Though a scatter plot matrix can provide summary variable-to-variable visualization of many paired variable combinations, an alternative technique exists for looking at relations across a large number of variables simultaneously in a single graph. With parallel coordinate plots [19], many axes can be arranged in parallel to each other as panels, with variable relations captured as a piece-wise linear path across the panel vertices.

Using parallel coordinate plots to explore multivariate usage data sets from the Sakai collaboration system activities can lead to the discovery of interesting co-relations.

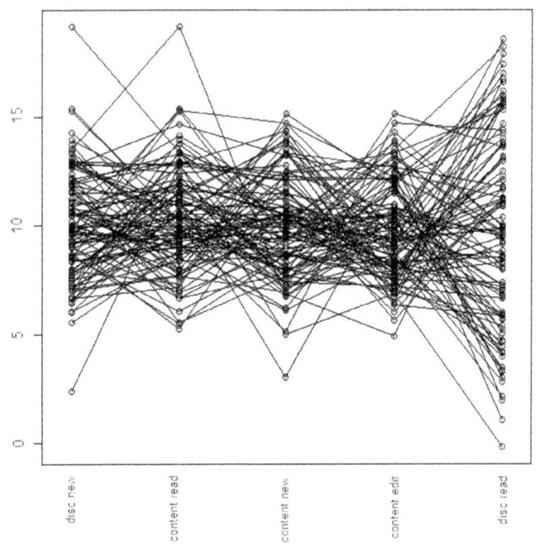

Figure 5. Parallel Coordinate Plots of Sakai user actions.

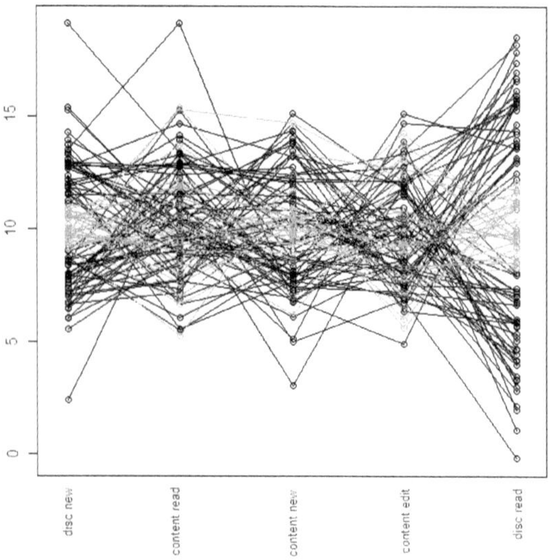

Figure 6. Parallel Coordinate Plot with highlighting.

In the case of Sakai usage data, the participants' activities, as revealed by event messages logged during each session, are displayed with different event types spread across the axes, plotted here using the paracoor function in the Denpro package for R [20]. While exploring different orderings of the axes, one might initially pick out tool activity events cases where the activity variables relate in ways that are unsurprising: content reads going together with content writes, login events going together with announcement reads. But further analysis reveals some less obvious co-occurrences: content read events often co-occurred with discussion forum posting events within sessions, as indicated by the many horizontal lines within the leftmost panel of Figure 5. One might also want to select subsets of sessions, such as activity sequences that seem to reveal an interesting relation. As an aid to doing so, basic parallel coordinate plots implementations provide functions for highlighting particular variables (Figure 6), while more sophisticated implementations also offer extensions for interactive brushing, smoothing, and overlays [21,22,23].

The discovery of relations using a parallel coordinate plot can become the starting point for more extensive data mining to identify association rules [24]. Association rules of student interaction with the learning management system might reveal aspects of the environment that need re-design in order to meet individual needs in the online user experience more effectively. Parallel coordinate plots as an exploratory method for revealing co-occurrence relations among and across item sets have also been used to make the results of e-learning data mining efforts more visible and communicable in instructional settings. The plots have been used in other settings to show instructors how learning activities and learner characteristics distinguish less successful students from their peers in terms of study habits, difficulty of the material, and student background [25].

3.4 Hidden Patterns in Usage Data

Visual exploration using parallel coordinate plots intimates the fourth and final usage visualization topic of this paper: automated discovery of patterns in data. Another commonly performed kind of data mining investigation is clustering analysis. In the area of clustering algorithms, data mining software usually offers a choice of algorithms that work particularly well with huge, multi-dimensional data sets. Often undertaken as part of an initial data mining exploration of e-learning data, the goal of clustering is a computational search for inherent groupings, i.e., what items in the data are alike [26]. Clustering analysis could make an even better first step in exploratory data mining if somehow combined with visualization techniques. However, a major difficulty encountered with most clustering algorithms is that their cluster results are not easy to visualize when more than two variables are involved [27].

One important exception is the 2-dimension self-organizing map (SOM) based on Kohonen networks [28]. A SOM clustering not only can reveal inherent patterns and similarities in large data sets but also provides a way of visualizing the results in the plane. Using a two-dimensional grid, a SOM reduces the high-dimensional variable input space into a flat output space where like clusters are arranged as neighbors. As implemented in the Kohonen package for R [29], shading, coloring, legend graphs, and u-matrix techniques extend the presentation capabilities of SOM towards an even fuller presentation of the results [30].

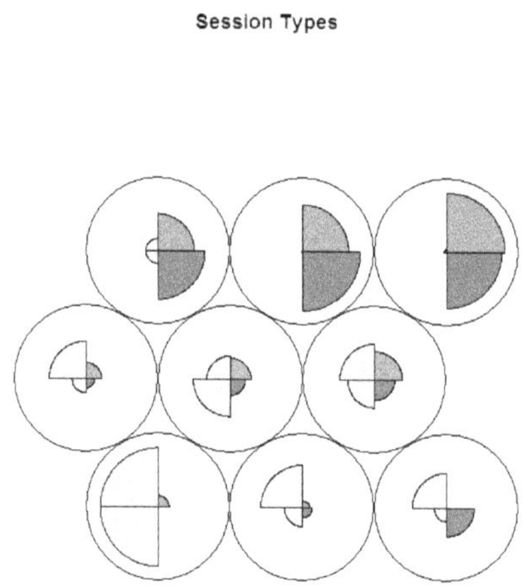

Figure 7. SOM plot of user session clusters.

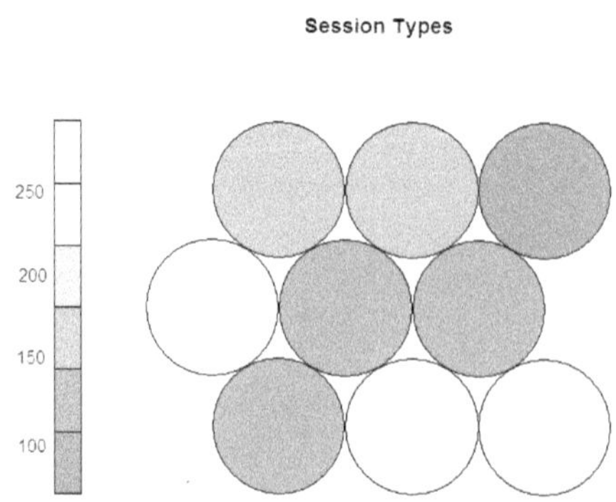

Figure 8. SOM plot showing cluster assignment counts.

In the context web usage analysis, a SOM can be used as a first step in looking for clusters of users while looking across many variables at once. Figure 7 shows a SOM plot with nine groupings, represented as circles, resulting from an input set with user session attributes displayed in segments plots with red for session duration, purple for number of actions, light blue for campus locale, and green for sessions occurring during the day. The neighborhood of the top row reveals clusterings of extended visits with higher action counts. On campus sessions during the day form another cluster neighborhood on the bottom row. These are marked by shorter duration and fewer actions. Viewing the count assignments for nine clusters in Figure 8, the biggest cluster at the bottom right suggest that, whether on or off campus, daytime sessions are fairly short with a moderate number of actions.

Though the example above should certainly not to be treated as an end-point in a usage analysis project, the SOM visualization results have been shown to offer fairly reliable clustering when compared to other algorithms for clustering [31]. Since the reliability of any clustering algorithm's results is never total, clustering's true usefulness comes into play mainly when followed up with repeated applications and even with other clustering algorithms for comparison's sake [32]. With the added benefit of a strong visualization component, the clusters offered up through SOM plots become a launch pad for collecting, analyzing, and inquiring further about how usage variables interrelate.

4. CONCLUSION

Intended as a brief tour of four practical visualization processes for e-learning usage analysis, this paper has demonstrated across the four contexts some of the major strengths these techniques offer. Given the problems posed by high-volume usage data, these visualization techniques offer crucial aid in exploring data sources commonly encountered in today's production e-learning systems. Data sources and methods are varied here. This is understandable given the range of contexts and systems involved, but the processes have much in common.

In visualizing user activity across many dimensions, trends and patterns can become discernable and better understood. The visualization processes, of course, still require careful follow-up and further empirical investigation. If verified, the results can lead towards a repeatable visualization process that leverages the potential and promise of data mining and visualization for e-learning systems. Singly or together visualization and data mining offer potential benefits for assisting those in higher education who are responsible for implementing and deploying on-line environments in support of teaching and learning.

As a complement to data mining, educational visualization techniques provide a toolkit for uncovering usage structure and access patterns within the enormous volume and variety of multivariate user data generated in such systems. For Internet-based services in higher education to keep up with the increasingly high standards that institutions place on them, the analytical tools and processes we employ will need ever greater power and flexibility. These cases involve fairly simple applications of visualization that only begin to tap the fuller potential usage visualization has shown in research systems. In all four cases, practical needs have been motivated by the ongoing need for understanding, supporting, and managing users and usage. And while exploratory in nature, the four cases described here offer convenient ways to integrate data visualization with operational management needs common in most universities and colleges e-learning environments.

5. REFERENCES

[1] Fielding, N G., Lee, R.M., Blank, G. (Eds.). (2008). The Handbook of Online Research Methods. London EC, Thousand Oaks CA, New Delhi, Singapore: Sage Publications.

[2] McGrath, O. G. 2007. Seeking activity: on the trail of users in open and community source frameworks. In *Proceedings of the 35th Annual ACM SIGUCCS Conference on User Services* (Orlando, Florida, USA, October 07 - 10, 2007). SIGUCCS '07. ACM, New York, NY, 234-239.

[3] The R Development Core Team. The R Manuals, 2009. [http://cran.r-project.org/manuals.html; accessed 15-May-2010].).

[4] Cleveland, W. S. 2002. Internet Traffic: Visualization, Discovery, and Very Large Displays. In Proceedings of the IEEE Symposium on information Visualization (infovis'02) (October 28 - 29, 2002). INFOVIS. IEEE Computer Society, Washington, DC, 3.

[5] Soule, A., Salamatia, K., Taft, N., Emilion, R., and Papagiannaki, K. 2004. Flow classification by histograms: or how to go on safari in the internet. SIGMETRICS Perform. Eval. Rev. 32, 1 (Jun. 2004), 49-60.

[6] Géczy, P., Izumi, N., Akaho, S. and Hasida, K. (2007) Long Tails and Analysis of Knowledge Worker Intranet Browsing Behavior, in Proceedings of BIS 2007, April 25-27, Poznan, Poland, 584-597.

[7] Park, C., Shen, H., Marron, J. S., Hernandez-Campos, F., and Veitch, D. 2006. Capturing the Elusive Poissonity in Web Traffic. In Proceedings of the 14th IEEE international Symposium on Modeling, Analysis, and Simulation (September 11 - 14, 2006). MASCOTS. IEEE Computer Society, Washington, DC, 189-196.

[8] Cadez, I., Heckerman, D., Meek, C., Smyth, P., and White, S. 2000. Visualization of navigation patterns on a Web site using model-based clustering. In Proceedings of the Sixth ACM SIGKDD international Conference on Knowledge Discovery and Data Mining (Boston, Massachusetts, United States, August 20 - 23, 2000). KDD '00. ACM, New York, NY, 280-284.

[9] Welser, H. T, Smith, M. A. Gleave, E., & Fisher., D. (2008). "Distilling digital traces: Computational social science approaches to studying the internet." In N. Fielding, R. L. Lee and G. Grant (Eds.), Handbook of online research methods. (pp 116-140). London: Sage Publications.

[10] Romero, C., et al. Mining and Visualizing Visited Trails in Web-Based Educational Systems. In Educational Data Mining 2008: 1st International Conference on Educational Data Mining. 2008.Montreal, Quebec, Canada.

[11] Mazza, R. and Dimitrova, V. 2005. Generation of Graphical Representations of Student Tracking Data in Course Management Systems. In Proceedings of the Ninth international Conference on information Visualisation (July

06 - 08, 2005). IV. IEEE Computer Society, Washington, DC, 253-258.

[12] Carr D, Lewin-Koh N, Maechler M. (2004). Available from http://cran.r-project.org/

[13] http://cran.r-project.org/web/packages/hexbin

[14] Carr, D. B. (1991) Looking at Large Data Sets Using Binned Data Plots, pp. 7–39 in Computing and Graphics in Statistics; Eds. A. Buja and P. Tukey, Springer-Verlag, New York.

[15] Kosarar., B., Hauser, H.: Timehistograms for large, time-dependent data. In Proceedings of the 2004 Eurographics/IEEE TVCG Symposium on Visualization(2004), pp. 45–54, 340.

[16] Matkovic, H. Hauser, R. Sainitzer, E. Gröller: "Process Visualization with Levels of Detail"; in: "IEEE Symposium on Information Visualization 2002", IEEE Computer Society Press, 2002, 67 - 70.

[17] Marron, J. S., Hernández-Campos, F. and Smith, F. D. (2002) Mice and Elephants Visualization of Internet Traffic, in COMPSTAT 2002 - Proceedings in Computational Statistics - 15th Symposium held in Berlin, eds. Härdle, W. and Rönz, B., Physika Verlag, Heidelberg.

[18] http://cran.r-project.org/web/packages/plotrix

[19] Q.A. Inselberg, "Parallel coordinates for multidimensional displays," in Spatial Information Technologies for Remote Sensing Today and Tomorrow, The Ninth William T. Pecora Memorial Remote Sensing Symposium, IEEE Computer Society Press, 1984, pp. 312--324.

[20] http://cran.r-project.org/web/packages/denpro

[21] Helwig Hauser , Florian Ledermann , Helmut Doleisch, Angular Brushing of Extended Parallel Coordinates, Proceedings of the IEEE Symposium on Information Visualization (InfoVis'02), p.127, October 28-29, 2002

[22] Klemz BR, Dunne PM. 2000. Exploratory analysis using parallel coordinate systems: data visualisation in N-dimensions. Marketing Letters 11(4): 323–333

[23] Theus,T and S. Urbanek. Interactive Graphics for Data Analysis. Computer Science and Data Analysis, 2009.

[24] Bruzzese, D. and Buono, P. 2004. Combining visual techniques for Association Rules exploration. In Proceedings of the Working Conference on Advanced Visual interfaces (Gallipoli, Italy, May 25 - 28, 2004). AVI '04. ACM, New York, NY, 381-384.

[25] Buket Dogan, A. Yilmaz Camurcu. (2010) Visual clustering of multidimensional educational data from an intelligent tutoring system, Journal of Computer Applications in Engineering Education, Wiley Publishing Company, Volume 18, Number 2, February 2009, pp. 375 - 382.

[26] Romero, C. and Ventura, S. 2007. Educational data mining: A survey from 1995 to 2005. Expert Syst. Appl. 33, 1 (Jul. 2007), 135-146. DOI= http://dx.doi.org/10.1016/j.eswa.2006.04.005

[27] Zdravko Markov , Daniel T. Larose, Data Mining the Web: Uncovering Patterns in Web Content, Structure, and Usage, Wiley-Interscience, 2007

[28] T. Kohonen, Self-organization and associative memory: 3rd edition, Springer-Verlag New York, Inc., New York, NY, 1989

[29] http://cran.r-project.org/web/packages/kohonen

[30] Merja Oja, Samuel Kaski, and Teuvo Kohonen (2003), Bibliography of Self-Organizing Map (SOM) Papers: 1998-2001 Addendum, Neural Computing Surveys, 3: 1-156.

[31] Waller NG, Kaiser HA, Illian JB, Manry M. A comparison of the classification capabilities of the 1-dimensional Kohone neural network with two partitioning and three hierarchical cluster analysis algorithms. Psychometrika 1998;63:5-22.

[32] Stenmark, D. 2008. Identifying clusters of user behavior in intranet search engine log files. J. Am. Soc. Inf. Sci. Technol. 59, 14 (Dec. 2008), 2232-2243.

Author Index

Adaikkalavan, Raman 83
Anand, Vijay 73
Anne, Kirk 79
Batzinger, Robert 83
Beppu, Yutoku 25
Brasier, Anne Elizabeth 25
Brouilette, Gordana 183
Burrows, Cyd 215
Camidge, Andy 79
Carpenter, Nathan 107, 143
Chaphalkar, Nik 1
Claffey Jr., George F. 161
Cooper, Michael 21
Czapracki, Allison 215
Dean, David 165
Dietiker, Kristen 49
Dogome, Kazuhide 25
Donald, Christopher 43
Dooling, Cynthia 183
Durant, Debbie 145
Feller, Dean 35
Fernandez, Javier 1
Fouser, Robert J. 25
Fox, Laurie 79
Freidank, Sara 1
Fujimura, Naomi 131
Fust, Chad 61
Garramone, Kathy 203
Graves, Loraine 7
Hakimzadeh, Hossein 83
Harper, Bryce 15
Herrick, Dan R. 65, 149
Hidaka, Masayasu 25
Higgins, Chris 171
Hirayama, Zen'ichi 131
Honken, Robin 189
Ito, Masakazu 25
Jannini, Nicholas 15
Janz, Kenneth 35, 189
Kerr, Susan M. 157
Kimmel-Smith, Stacey 95
Klein, William C. 199
Koan, R. Mark 87
Kuroe, Yasuaki 207
Laakso, Jace 129
Lewis, Stephen G. 95
Lyons, Kathy M. 11
Masuda, Hideo 207
Mattauch, Thom 45, 211
McGrath, Owen G. 229
McRitchie, Karen 123
Morris, Fred 171
Mukherjee, Amlan 1
Murata, Kazuyoshi 207
Murphy, Trevor 119
Nedachi, Munetomo 25
Nedachi, Yoko 25
Okamura, Toshihiko 25
Oruklu, Erdal 73
Oto, Noritaka 25
Peiffer, Dana 223
Perkins, Adam 135
Pettit, Hannah 45, 211
Regan, Harry J. 161
Rodriguez, Holmes 25
Rugg, Beth 53
Saniie, Jafar 73
Seto, Hiroyuki 25
Sharpe, Ryan T. 11
Shibuya, Yu 207
Shirakawa, Yuki 207
Siegfried, Bobby 31
Simpson, Nason 147
Stahler, Cheryl 183
Stawowy, Brian 1
Stewart, Cindy 183
Suenaga, Katsuyuki 25
Sutch, Laurie A. 153, 219
Suzuki, Yusei 25
Tagliamonte, Jean 61
Takenoshita, Akira 25
Tanger-Brown, Melisa 103, 195
Terada, Masaharu 25
Thomas, Shereese 135
Tucker, Ryan C. 107, 143
Tulloss, Janice 183
Tyndall, John B. 111
Wada, Tomohito 25
Wagner, Jason 141
West, Matthew 175
Yamada, Takeshi 25
Yamanaka, Yuichi 25
Yamanoue, Takashi 25
Yukawa, Koji 25
Zocher, Mark 7

www.ingramcontent.com/pod-product-compliance
Ingram Content Group UK Ltd.
Pitfield, Milton Keynes, MK11 3LW, UK
UKHW051509290926
15471UKWH00008B/1511

9 781450 313810